Biolinguistics
Exploring the Biology of Language

This book investigates the nature of human language and its importance for the study of the mind. In particular, it examines current work on the biology of language. Lyle Jenkins reviews the evidence that language is best characterized by a generative grammar of the kind introduced by Noam Chomsky in the 1950s and developed in various directions since that time. He then discusses research into the development of language which tries to capture both the underlying universality of human language, as well as the diversity found in individual languages (universal grammar). Finally, he discusses a variety of approaches to language design and the evolution of language.

An important theme is the integration of biolinguistics into the natural sciences – the 'unification problem'. Lyle also answers criticisms of the biolinguistics approach from a number of other perspectives, including evolutionary psychology, cognitive science, connectionism and ape language research, among others.

LYLE JENKINS is based at the Biolinguistics Institute, Cambridge, Massachusetts. He took his Ph.D. in linguistics at the Massachusetts Institute of Technology and has held lecturing posts at the Universities of Vienna, Salzburg, Paris VIII (Vincennes) and Hamburg. He has published a monograph, *The English Existential*, and a number of papers in various journals, including *Linguistics and Philosophy* and *Theoretical Linguistics*.

Biolinguistics

Exploring the Biology of Language

Lyle Jenkins

CAMBRIDGE
UNIVERSITY PRESS

P
132
.J46
2000

PUBLISHED BY THE PRESS SYNDICATE OF THE UNIVERSITY OF CAMBRIDGE
The Pitt Building, Trumpington Street, Cambridge, United Kingdom

CAMBRIDGE UNIVERSITY PRESS
The Edinburgh Building, Cambridge CB2 2RU, UK http://www.cup.cam.ac.uk
40 West 20th Street, New York, NY 10011–4211, USA http://www.cup.org
10 Stamford Road, Oakleigh, Melbourne 3166, Australia

© Cambridge University Press 2000

First published 2000

Printed in the United Kingdom at the University Press, Cambridge

Typeface Monotype Plantin 10/12pt.   *System* QuarkXPress® [SE]

A catalogue record for this book is available from the British Library

Library of Congress cataloguing in publication data

Jenkins, Lyle.
Biolinguistics: exploring the biology of language / Lyle Jenkins.
    p.   cm.
ISBN 0 521 65233 2 (hardback)
1. Biolinguistics.   2. Grammar, comparative and general.
I. Title.
P132.J46   1999
401–dc21   98–45694   CIP

ISBN 0 521 65233 2 hardback

Dedicated to My One and Only,
Lâle Berke-Jenkins

Contents

Preface

The last forty years have witnessed what has been called the "second cognitive revolution" (see Introduction). A central focus in the study of mind (the "cognitive sciences") is the study of language and its biological bases. Work on the biology of language, or *biolinguistics*, is directed at answering some traditional questions; viz., (1) What constitutes knowledge of language?, (2) How does knowledge of language develop in the individual?, and (3) How did knowledge of language evolve in the species?

There has been an explosion of knowledge about the first two questions from studies of languages and dialects that now number in the thousands. A small sampling includes: Basque, Bulgarian, Chinese, English, Dutch, Finnish, Flemish, French, German, Greek, Hindi, Hungarian, Icelandic, Irish, Italian, Japanese, Korean, Norwegian, Polish, Portuguese, Romanian, Russian, Spanish, Swedish, Turkish, Warlpiri, and Welsh. Evidence bearing on the answers to these questions is now available from numerous areas; e.g., syntax, semantics, morphology, phonology, articulatory and acoustic phonetics, language acquisition, language change, specific language impairment, language perception, sign-language, neurology of language, language-isolated children, creole language, split-brain studies, linguistic savants, and electrical activity of the brain, among others. The past year marks the thirtieth anniversary of Eric Lenneberg's *Biological Foundations of Language*, which surveyed the work in many of these areas and therefore provides a useful benchmark for the significant progress that has been made in recent years.

Although the three central problem areas for biolinguistics listed above have been investigated in parallel, most progress has been made in the first two areas: language and development of language. Now that the necessary groundwork has been laid, the study of the third area, evolution of language, is currently intensifying and questions about language design can be formulated more precisely and addressed. These include more general questions such as why language exhibits the particular modular design that it does, why we have the particular division of labor between genetic mechanisms and environmental factors that we find and what kind of factors played a role in the evolution of language. It also includes more specific questions such as why language has the particular computational operations that it has and how optimal these are from a design point of view.

Acknowledgements

I would like to express my great indebtedness to Noam Chomsky, first as his student and later as his colleague and friend. It was during my doctoral work at MIT in the 1960s that I first heard his exposition of what later came to be called the "argument from poverty of the stimulus," which forms the cornerstone for the argument that there is "one language (Human)," or that there is an initial state of the (cognitive component of the) language faculty, as described by the theory of universal grammar, which represents the genetic component of language. At the same time that we were learning to apply this mode of argumentation in the development of linguistic theories, we were also fortunate to hear Eric Lenneberg speak on his seminal work, *Biological Foundations of Language*, which was soon to be published. It was from this confluence of ideas from linguistics and biology that the central questions for a field of biolinguistics were born.

I would also like to acknowledge Allan Maxam's considerable influence on many of the ideas expressed in this book. He recognized the significance of the linguistic debate for biology very early on and has been as untiring an advocate from the field of biology as Chomsky has been from the field of linguistics in trying to take a few modest steps toward solving the puzzle of the "unification problem" posed for biolinguistics. I also remember with great fondness the many stimulating conversations on linguistics and a variety of other topics with my close friends and colleagues Richard Kayne, Cynthia Pyle, Ray Dougherty, Claudia Leacock, Steve Hammalian, Henk van Riemsdijk, and other colleagues of GLOW.

While teaching in the Department of Linguistics at the University of Vienna with Wolfgang Dressler and his colleagues, I also had the great fortune to meet a number of times with Konrad Lorenz and his colleagues, in particular Otto Koenig. They participated in some seminars that I had the pleasure of helping Gaberell Drachman to organize over the course of several summers in Salzburg, Austria, culminating in the LSA Summer Institute with the theme of Biology and Language. These seminars made us all aware of the similarity in the approach of linguists and ethologists to their subject matter. As Teuber has insightfully noted: ". . . it has become clear . . . that linguists are ethologists, working with man as their species for study, and ethologists linguists, working with nonverbalizing species" (Teuber, 1967:205). I also enjoyed and learned much from numerous meetings and conversations in the Viennese coffee-houses with my good friends and linguistics colleagues Hubert Haider, Alfred Nozsicska, and the others in our Vienna Syntax Circle, with Tasso Borbé in our short-lived Austrian Society for Linguistics and Biology, and with Tom Perry, John Colarusso, Robert Wall, and Larry Hutchison.

I am grateful to the American Council of Learned Societies for the opportunity to take time off to work on language and genetics and to Allan Maxam for the invitation to spend time as a Visiting Fellow at the Department of Biological Chemistry at Harvard University and as a Research Fellow at the Department of Viral Oncology at the Sidney Farber Cancer Institute (now the Dana-Farber Cancer Institute). In the lab of David Livingston and his colleagues I was able to do some experimental work with SV40, a monkey virus, and the workhorse of molecular biology that was later to play such a crucial role in unlocking the secrets of the oncogene. I also thank Ian Stewart for his comments on the ideas of symmetry-breaking and word order (in 1994) developed in chapter 5 and Murray Eden for his comments on an earlier version of that chapter (1995). I enjoyed many stimulating discussions at the International Workshop, "The Linguistics of Biology and the Biology of Language," hosted by Julio Collado-Vides and his colleagues in 1998 at CIFN-UNAM, Mexico. Finally, I am greatly indebted to Allan Maxam and Noam Chomsky for much valuable discussion of the issues in this book.

In the fall of 1980 the Harvard Medical School Biolinguistics Group was formed under the sponsorship of Allan Maxam's Laboratory of Molecular Biology to provide an interdisciplinary forum for researchers interested in the biological foundations of language. There were many stimulating lectures and discussions, including many memorable ones with Ethan Bier, not the least of which were many animated debates at the Windsor Bar across the street from the Dana-Farber. Many, but by no means all, of the interesting topics discussed by the HMS Biolinguistics Group are reflected throughout this book.

Many thanks also to my friends in Berlin for our friendship going back to my turbulent graduate school days when I made an unplanned detour for several years inside the prisons and labor camps of East Germany – Elisabeth, Brigitte, Ingo, Antje, and with special memories of Jack Strickland, who not only achieved his dream of sailing across the Atlantic with Brigitte on the *Tumbleweed*, but also lived more of life than most people ever do. And last, but not least, many thanks for the love and support of everybody in my extended clan, as represented by my mother on the East coast and my sister Lynne on the West coast.

We owe a special debt of appreciation to the editorial staff at Cambridge University Press – Judith Ayling, Alison Gilderdale, Katharina Brett, Natalie Davies, Nicole Webster, Brenda Burke, Camilla Erskine, Citi Potts, and Andrew Winnard – for shepherding this manuscript safely through its long voyage. Any errors remaining are due solely to our kittens, Ginger and Samantha, whose feline feet strolled tirelessly over the keyboard during the editing of this manuscript.

Introduction

A BRIEF CHRONOLOGY

Chomsky has posed what we consider to be the central questions for the study of language and biology (*biolinguistics*[1]):[2]

(1) What constitutes knowledge of language?
(2) How is this knowledge acquired?
(3) How is this knowledge put to use?
(4) What are the relevant brain mechanisms?
(5) How does this knowledge evolve (in the species)?

Chomsky asks "how can we integrate answers to these questions within the existing natural sciences, perhaps by modifying them?" (Chomsky, 1991a:6). This more general question is part of what he has referred to as the *unification problem*, a topic to which we return below (Chomsky, 1994a:37,80).

The discussion of the questions (1)–(5) above within the tradition of generative grammar began in the early 1950s: "At least in a rudimentary form, these questions were beginning to be the topic of lively discussion in the early 1950s, primarily among a few graduate students. In Cambridge, I would mention particularly Eric Lenneberg and Morris Halle, and also Yehoshua Bar-Hillel" (Chomsky, 1991a:6).

The period between the mid-1950s and the present is sometimes referred to as the "cognitive revolution." However, Chomsky has observed that contemporary work might be more properly viewed as a "renewal" of the "classical concerns" of the seventeenth and eighteenth centuries (Chomsky, 1997a). This earlier period of the study of mind, which includes as a central element the Cartesian theory of body and

---

[1] Our usage of the term "biolinguistics" derives from a report on an interdisciplinary meeting on language and biology, attended by Salvador Luria and Noam Chomsky, among others, that was held in 1974 under the sponsorship of the Royaumont Center for a Science of Man (Piattelli-Palmarini, 1974). The earliest use of the term "biolinguistics" with which I am familiar is from Clarence L. Meader and John H. Muyskens, *Handbook of Biolinguistics*, (1950, Toledo: H. C. Weller). It is also used by John Locke in more recent work (Locke, 1993).   [2] See, for example, Chomsky and Lasnik, 1993.

1

mind, might then be called the "first cognitive revolution" (Chomsky, 1994a:35). There are, in addition, many antecedents to modern-day studies of language and mind, both before and after this period. To reflect this fact, Chomsky often refers to the first question – what constitutes knowledge of language? – as *Humboldt's problem*, to the second question – how is knowledge of language acquired? – as a special case of *Plato's problem*, and to the third question – how is knowledge of language put to use? – as *Descartes' problem*, to highlight the fact that the modern study of these problems has a long and rich historical tradition.[3] In what follows we will be primarily focusing on a part of the "second cognitive revolution," the modern study of biolinguistics; i.e., on work going back to the early 1950s.

In the spring of 1955, the first version of *The Logical Structure of Linguistic Theory* was completed, duplicated, and circulated, although a version of the manuscript was not published until 20 years later (Chomsky, 1975a). In the introduction to that version, Chomsky notes:

LSLT [*The Logical Structure of Linguistic Theory*] is an attempt to develop a theory of transformational generative grammar. The "realist interpretation" of linguistic theory is assumed throughout, and it is argued that the competence attained by the normal speaker-hearer is represented by a transformational generative grammar, which determines the representation of each sentence on the levels of phrase structure and transformational structure (*inter alia*). These representations are then employed in the use and understanding of language, and provide the basis for the more general theory of language that will be concerned with meaning and reference, the conditions of appropriate use of language, how sentences are understood, performance in concrete social situations, and in general, the exercise of linguistic competence in thought and communication. The principles of this theory specify the schematism brought to bear by the child in language acquisition. They define the linguistic universals that constitute "the essence of language" (as distinct from accidental properties or properties determined by the exigencies of language use), and thus can be taken as one fundamental element in the characterization of the innate "language faculty." (Chomsky, 1975a:45)

Thus the basis for the study of biolinguistics, specifically for questions (1) knowledge of language (= competence), (2) acquisition of language, and (3) use of language, are laid out in LSLT. And once we have asked questions (1)–(3), questions (4) brain mechanisms, and (5) evolution, are automatically implied; see the discussion below of Lenneberg's work

---

[3] Chomsky has extensively documented the historical antecedents to modern discussions of language and mind (e.g., in the works of Plato, Descartes, Hume, Humboldt, and many others in the rationalist, empiricist, and romantic traditions). For some of this discussion, see *Cartesian Linguistics* (Chomsky, 1966). Much of this work was largely forgotten or ignored in the fields of structural linguistics and psychological behaviorism, to the detriment of studies on language.

along those lines. It is observed that the general theory in LSLT is "to be understood as a psychological theory that attempts to characterize the innate human 'language faculty.'" Here and below "psychological theory" and "biological theory" can be used interchangeably. As Chomsky put it during an interview in 1968, linguistics "is really a theoretical biology, if you like, a theoretical psychology" (Sklar, 1968:217). However, this seminal work, which set the stage for future work in biolinguistics, was promptly turned down for publication and only parts of it were published; e.g., some of the material was integrated into the much better known *Syntactic Structures*:

> After the revisions described were completed, I submitted parts of the manuscript to the Technology Press of MIT for consideration for potential publication. It was rejected, with the not unreasonable observation that an unknown author taking a rather unconventional approach should submit articles based on this material to professional journals before planning to publish such a comprehensive and detailed manuscript as a book. This was no easy matter, however. The one article I had submitted on this material to a linguistics journal had been rejected, virtually by return mail. I had lectured on some of this material at several universities, but as far as I could determine, there was little interest in these topics among professional linguists. (Chomsky, 1975a:3)

In the interview "The Birth of Generative Grammar," Chomsky talks about his "close friend Eric Lenneberg, who at that time was beginning his extremely interesting studies in the biology of language, working along rather similar lines" (Chomsky, 1979:133). This work was to culminate with Lenneberg's *Biological Foundations of Language* (Lenneberg, 1967), to which Chomsky contributed a chapter entitled "The Formal Nature of Language." Lenneberg anticipated many themes of the coming decades: genetics of language acquisition, genetics of language disorders (dyslexia, specific language disabilities), language of deaf children, "wolf children," critical period, twin studies, family pedigrees, aphasia[4] and language, evolution of language, etc.

What Chomsky realized early on was that linguistics could now suggest core internal properties of the language faculty, that in turn posed important questions for biology. These properties were discussed in various settings, as, e.g., the language acquisition device (LAD) and universal grammar (UG). It has taken quite a while for it to sink in that the syntactic computations of the language faculty are the biological evidence.[5]

---

[4] Aphasia is the loss of language due to brain disease or injury.
[5] A residue of the older attitude towards linguistics has been expressed most recently by the psychologist Steven Pinker, who dismisses Chomsky's arguments as "abstruse formalisms" (Pinker, 1994a:24). Like the scientists of Mendel's time, Pinker fails to comprehend that abstract computations are evidence on a par with any other kind of biological evidence.

Mendel was misunderstood for similar reasons; as the biologist George Beadle and author Muriel Beadle note, "There was no evidence for Mendel's hypothesis other than his computations and his wildly unconventional application of algebra to botany made it difficult for his listeners to understand that these computations *were* the evidence" (Beadle and Beadle, 1979:68).

Although the basic ideas of biolinguistics found a great deal of resistance in the academic fields of linguistics, philosophy, and in some areas of the cognitive sciences, by the early 1970s the results concerning the biological nature of generative grammar had been easily assimilated and well received by many geneticists and molecular biologists, who offered a number of speculations on biology and language with specific reference to generative grammar. For example, Monod stated that, given reasonable biological assumptions, it is not at all surprising that "the linguistic capacity revealed in the course of the brain's epigenetic development is today part of 'human nature', itself defined within the genome in the radically different language of the genetic code" (Monod, 1974:129).

Monod's colleague, Jacob also found this idea plausible: "According to modern linguistics, there is a basic grammar common to all languages; this uniformity would reflect a framework imposed by heredity on the organization of the brain . . . Many traits of human nature must be inserted in the framework established by the twenty-three pairs of chromosomes that make up the common inheritance of man" (Jacob, 1976:322).

And in his discussion of "modern linguistic analysis," Luria wrote: "To the biologist it makes eminent sense to think that, as for language structures, so also for logical structures, there exist in the brain network some patterns of connections that are genetically determined and have been selected by evolution as effective instruments for dealing with the events of life" (Luria, 1973:141).

The immunologist Niels Jerne commented as follows in his Nobel Prize address:[6]

It seems a miracle that young children easily learn the language of any environment into which they are born. The generative approach to grammar, pioneered by Chomsky, argues that this is only explicable if certain deep, universal features of this competence are innate characteristics of the human brain. Biologically speaking, this hypothesis of an inheritable capability to learn any language means that it must somehow be encoded in the DNA of our chromosomes. Should this hypothesis one day be verified, then linguistics would become a branch of biology. (Jerne, 1985:1059)

---

[6] See chapter 3 for a discussion of Jerne's ideas on selection and instruction.

Unification, whether in physics, linguistics, or any other science, has many cross-disciplinary connections. One such connection that Chomsky introduced into the linguistic discussion was work from the field of animal behavior or, as it was more commonly called in Europe, ethology. In a 1959 review of B. F. Skinner's *Verbal Behavior*, Chomsky introduces ideas and lines of arguments from genetics, (comparative) ethology, and biology in general, alongside a number of other kinds of arguments, in critiquing Skinner's "functional analysis" of verbal behavior, which was based on such behaviorist notions as stimulus, reinforcement, and deprivation (Chomsky, 1959).[7] Chomsky draws on the work of Lorenz, Tinbergen, Thorpe, Jaynes, and others. For example, he argues that learning, whether of bird song or human language, can be unrewarded; i.e., it need not proceed by means of "differential reinforcement":

Imprinting is the most striking evidence for the innate disposition of the animal to learn in a certain direction and to react appropriately to patterns and objects of certain restricted types, often only long after the original learning has taken place. It is, consequently, unrewarded learning, though the resulting patterns of behavior may be refined through reinforcement. Acquisition of the typical songs of song birds is, in some cases, a type of imprinting. Thorpe reports studies that show "that some characteristics of the normal song have been learned in the earliest youth, before the bird itself is able to produce any kind of full song." (Chomsky, 1964:561–62)

Chomsky concludes that any learning theory must account for the fact that children acquire grammars with "remarkable rapidity" and "to a large extent independently of intelligence," suggesting that "human beings are somehow specially designed to do this, with data-handling or 'hypothesis-formulating' ability" (p. 577), noting that these abilities are rooted in man's biological nature:

There is nothing essentially mysterious about this. Complex innate behavior patterns and innate "tendencies to learn in specific ways" have been carefully studied in lower organisms. Many psychologists have been inclined to believe that such biological structure will not have an important effect on acquisition of complex behavior in higher organisms, but I have not been able to find any serious justification for this attitude. (Chomsky, 1964:577, n. 48)

In the reprint of the review of Skinner, Chomsky annotates a footnote about Tinbergen and Schiller to drive home further the importance of biological analysis: "Lenneberg . . . presents a very interesting discussion of the part that biological structure may play in the acquisition of language, and the dangers in neglecting this possibility" (Chomsky, 1964:564).

---

[7] Citations are given from the version reprinted in 1964 (Chomsky, 1964).

As a further example, we can take Chomsky's discussion of the role of "primary linguistic data" in the process of language acquisition, where it can assume multiple roles; e.g., it can "determine to which of the possible languages . . . the language learner is being exposed" or it can simply "set the language-acquisition device into operation" (Chomsky, 1965:33). He remarks that "this distinction is quite familiar outside of the domain of language acquisition" in other areas of contemporary biology:

For example, Richard Held has shown in numerous experiments that under certain circumstances reafferent stimulation (that is, stimulation resulting from voluntary activity) is a prerequisite to the development of a concept of visual space, although it may not determine the character of this concept . . . or, to take one of innumerable examples from studies of animal learning, it has been observed . . . that depth perception in lambs is considerably facilitated by mother–neonate contact, although again there is no reason to suppose that the nature of the lamb's "theory of visual space" depends on this contact. (Chomsky, 1965:33–34)

Chomsky has introduced a number of intriguing proposals and ideas bearing on the evolutionary basis of human language into the linguistic discussion throughout the years, often in connection with particular linguistic models. For example, in a presentation of the background assumptions underlying what was later called the "standard theory," Chomsky makes remarks about "principles of neural organization" and "physical law," which have been echoed in much of his later work (see chapter 5):

However, there is surely no reason today for taking seriously a position that attributes a complex human achievement [language or other kinds of knowledge] entirely to months (or at most years) of experience, rather than to millions of years of evolution or to principles of neural organization that may be even more deeply grounded in physical law. (Chomsky, 1965:59)

At around the same time (1966), Chomsky noted the striking conceptual resemblance between the idea that universal grammatical principles determine "the class of possible languages" and Goethe's theory of Urform, as exemplified, e.g., by the Urpflanze:

Thus, the Urform is a kind of generative principle that determines the class of physically possible organisms; and, in elaborating this notion, Goethe tried to formulate principles of coherence and unity which characterize this class and which can be identified as a constant and unvarying factor beneath all the superficial modifications determined by variation in environmental conditions. (Chomsky, 1966:24)

The idea of the Urpflanze has resurfaced in interesting ways in work in developmental biology. We will explore the idea there that similar kinds of generative principles may be involved in the mental domain; i.e., in the development and evolution of human language. Thus the Urform idea ties in in interesting ways with other threads of Chomsky's ideas on evolution of language.

The question of "language design" has also been one of the central areas of interest in modern generative grammar. For example, in 1977, Chomsky and Lasnik proposed a (perceptual) filter to account for the contrast between the grammatical "That he left is surprising" and the ungrammatical "*He left is surprising" and concluded:

The first question to ask is whether the filter (20) is a true universal (that is, a principle of UG), or whether it is specific to the language under analysis. Suppose that [filter] (20) belongs to UG. Then it need not be learned, just as universal phonetics need not be learned; it is part of the genetically-determined language faculty. The functional explanation then holds, if at all, at the level of evolution of the species. (Chomsky and Lasnik, 1977:436–37)

We will return to this question in chapter 5.

Chomsky noted that although one must abstract away from genetic variation in universal grammar in the initial stages of study, he also emphasized the potential relevance of studies of genetic variation of the language faculty; see chapter 4 for further discussion.

At the same time, it would come as no surprise to discover that there is some genetic variation [of the language faculty], and if this could be discovered, it might lead to new and possibly revealing ways to study the intrinsic nature of the language faculty. It has occasionally been observed, for example, that unusually late onset of language use seems to run in families, and one might find other aspects of language use or structure that are subject to a degree of variability – a discovery that might be significant for therapy as well as for research into language. (Chomsky, 1978:312)[8]

Around 1978, Chomsky noted that the logic behind what later came to be known as the "principles-and-parameters" approach to language acquisition was "rather similar" to the problem of biological speciation, as discussed by the molecular biologist François Jacob. Jacob had written that

it was not biochemical innovation that caused diversification of organisms . . . What accounts for the difference between a butterfly and a lion, a chicken and a fly, or a worm and a whale is not their chemical components, but varying distributions of these components . . . specialization and diversification called only for different utilization of the same structural information . . . It is thanks to complex regulatory circuits, which either unleash or restrain the various biochemical activities of the organism, that the genetic program is implemented. [In related organisms, mammals for example], the diversification and specialization . . . are the result of mutations which altered the organism's regulatory circuits more than its

---

[8] Slightly amended version reprinted in Otero, 1988:233–50.

chemical structures. The minor modification of redistributing the structures in time and space is enough to profoundly change the shape, performance, and behavior of the final product. (Jacob, 1978; cited from Chomsky, 1980c:67)

Chomsky noted that the principles-and-parameters model of language acquisition had some of the same properties: "In a system that is sufficiently intricate in structure, small changes at particular points can lead to substantial differences in outcome. In the case of growth of organs, mental organs in our case, small changes in parameters left open in the general schematism can lead to what appear to be very different systems" (Chomsky, 1980c:67).

Jacob's remarks represent a concrete picture of the idea of Goethe's Urform, as Chomsky put it (see above), the "generative principle that determines the class of physically possible organisms." Thus one can envision that the ontogenetic principles-and-parameters model might someday find its place in a phylogenetic principles-and-parameters theory of language evolution. This theory of evolution would provide an "explanatory" account of the "descriptive" theory of language acquisition, in much the same way that an account of language acquisition provides an explanatory account for the properties of language.[9] We will return in chapter 5 to related ideas in developmental and evolutionary biology.

The program encompassed by these concerns came to be known in some circles as "biolinguistics." Under the sponsorship of The Royaumont Center for a Science of Man (with funding from the Volkswagen Foundation), and organized by Piattelli-Palmarini, an interdisciplinary meeting on language and biology was held at Endicott House, Dedham, Massachusetts in May 1974.[10] This meeting was part of a pilot project of the Royaumont Center entitled "Animal Communication and Human Communication" and was set up to explore among other topics "relations between brain structure and language, first recommended as a subject for enquiry by Salvador E. Luria and Noam Chomsky." Luria, Chomsky and participants from the fields of biology, neurophysiology, ethology, linguistics, psychology, psycholinguistics, philosophy, social psychology, biophysics, and mathematics met to discuss the possibilities of collaboration on a variety of proposed topics:

If certain areas of the brain, found to be highly correlated with specific language functions, are destroyed, is the ability to carry out the other language functions hampered? Can the region of lesion be circumvented? If so, what are the consequences to cortical or cerebral functioning (i.e. if a left hemispheral lesion occurs

[9] See Chomsky for a discussion of the technical notions of descriptive adequacy and explanatory adequacy (Chomsky, 1965).
[10] See Piattelli-Palmarini, 1974.

in the Temporal Gyrus (phonetic discrimination), the Superior Temporal Gyrus (phonetic production and semantic configurations), Supramarginal Gyrus and Angular Gyrus (syntactic and semantic configurations), etc.? What feedback effects are observed in adjacent cortical areas?

Do certain linguistic functions seem to be dominant with respect to one another? With respect to non-linguistic functions and vice-versa? If they are impeded by lesion, do they reroute to another area of the cortex which then suppresses its normal correlative function? Suppression? Mutual facilitation? In phonological production and reception? Semantic orientation? Syntactic composition and decomposition?

Why does syntax appear to obey structure-dependent rules of organization (computation) rather than intrinsically simpler structure-independent orderings?

The above topics and others concerning the biological foundations of language which are proposed for further investigation are referred to in the report on the meeting by the term "biolinguistics." [11]

After the Dedham meeting the Royaumont Center developed a project entitled "Communication and Cognition," under the sponsorship of Luria and Chomsky with the assistance of Jean-Pierre Changeux, Jacques Mehler, Klaus Scherer, Antoine Danchin, and Jean Petitot.[12] The last stage of this project was a conference on "Ontogenetic and Phylogenetic Models of Cognitive Development" at Royaumont Abbey near Paris in October 1975.[13] This conference was attended by many biologists, including Jean-Pierre Changeux, François Jacob, Jacques Monod, and others. Also subsequent to the Dedham meeting an MIT Work Group in the Biology of Language was formed during the period from July 1975 to August 1976, with the support of grants from the Alfred P. Sloan Foundation and from MIT on the basis of a proposal submitted by Noam Chomsky, Susan Carey-Block, and Salvador E. Luria (Walker, 1978).

In 1976 Konrad Lorenz and his colleagues traveled to Salzburg to participate with linguists in a symposium on language and biology at the Salzburg Summer School of Linguistics. In addition, Lorenz's colleague Otto Koenig hosted a series of meetings on sign (semiotics) and language with the Department of Linguistics of the University of Vienna at the Wilhelminenberg research station. And, finally, the Linguistics Society of America Summer Institute in 1979 in Salzburg was devoted to the topic of "Linguistics and Biology."

The influences of ethology on the study of language in the 1950s

---

[11] This report makes reference to "the study group on biolinguistics already active at M.I.T" (p. com.2).

[12] *Activities Report from February 18, 1975 (date of the last meeting of the Board of Directors) to November, 1976*, Part II, Centre Royaumont Pour une Science de l'Homme, Paris.

[13] Piattelli-Palmarini has thoroughly documented the conference and also presented a retrospective on the conference nearly twenty years later (Piattelli-Palmarini, 1980; Piattelli-Palmarini, 1994).

discussed above now came full circle. Lorenz introduced arguments from linguistics into the field of human ethology (Eibl-Eibesfeldt, 1970):

A strong support for human ethology has come from the unexpected area of linguistic studies; Noam Chomsky and his school have demonstrated that the structure of logical thought – which is identical to that of syntactic language – is anchored in a genetic program. The child does not learn to talk; the child learns only the vocabulary of the particular language of the cultural tradition into which it happens to be born.[14] (Lorenz, 1981:11)

In 1980 The Harvard Medical School Biolinguistics Group was formed under the sponsorship of Allan Maxam's Laboratory of Molecular Biology to provide an interdisciplinary forum for researchers interested in the biological foundations of language. Over the years topics ranged over theoretical linguistics, molecular biology, learning disorders, neurobiology of animal communication, neurolinguistics, brain lateralization, neural plasticity and critical periods, aphasia, dyslexia, vision, dreams, computational linguistics, pre-linguistic speech perception in infants, chromosomal language disability, and evolution of language.[15]

At around this time a set of experiments was designed to explore the language areas of the brain at the molecular level. Norman Geschwind and Albert Galaburda were to carry out the neurological part of the collaboration. The experiments were to be conducted at Allan Maxam's Laboratory for Molecular Biology at the Harvard Medical School. Noam Chomsky agreed to write the introduction to the proposal, but pointed out to me that time wouldn't permit him to actually be in the laboratory doing the experiments (not that he had been expected to). It was, on paper at least, the first cross-disciplinary collaboration between neurologists with an interest in the language areas, molecular biologists, and linguists. An attempt was made to get funding from the field of linguistics, but the proposal was neither written nor submitted, since no one would agree to even look at it.[16] Norman's subsequent tragically premature death was a further blow to the project.

By the first half of the 1980s, the "appropriate" subject material had swung full circle. There were now new buzzwords in academia and indus-

---

[14] This is a more elegant way of saying that the locus of cross-linguistic variation is in the lexicon, in terms of one variant of the principles-and-parameters model (discussed in chapter 3).

[15] For discussion of the application of linguistic and computational techniques to molecular biology, see Collado-Vides, Magasanik, and Smith, 1996.

[16] In the late 1980s, the peer review panel of a prominent federal scientific agency turned down a modest request for funding for biolinguistics in part on the grounds that it had not been shown that the relationship between linguistics and biology was more than an "analogy."

try – "AI" (artificial intelligence) and "cognitive science" – not the kind of cognitive sciences that Chomsky had argued for at Dedham and Royaumont, but, for example, theories of language based on ad hoc computer programs and unstructured "neural nets."[17] Chomsky's vision of biolinguistics had once again become the minority position. When I asked Samuel-Jay Keyser, at that time Chairman of MIT's Department of Linguistics and Philosophy, whether renaming everything "cognitive science" had actually led to any concrete collaboration between linguists and neuroscientists, he replied that "we do dry brain science, and they do wet brain science." Once again, the euphoria of the early 1980s was reminiscent of the early days of generative grammar, which Chomsky had described as follows:[18]

At the same time electronic computers were just beginning to make their impact. The mathematical theory of communication, cybernetics, sound spectrography, psychophysics, and experimental psychology were in a period of rapid development and much exuberance. Their contributions lent an aura of science and mathematics to the study of language and aroused much enthusiasm, in particular, among those who were attracted by the ideas then current concerning the unity of science. A technology of machine translation, automatic abstracting, and information retrieval was put forward as a practical prospect. It was confidently expected by many that automatic speech recognition would soon be feasible as well. It was widely believed that B. F. Skinner's William James lectures of 1947 offered an account of some of the most complex products of human

---

[17] Much work on psycholinguistics claimed to have shown that linguistics did not meet the criterion of "psychological reality" (see chapters 1 and 2). And work on philosophy of language and mind appeared to be frozen in time and dominated by Quine and his followers, as much as it had been 15 years before, when I was a graduate student. As Yogi Berra said, "it was déjà vu all over again." As always, there were notable exceptions.

[18] Some of the infatuation with unstructured neural nets appears to have since abated. In A Conversation, Why Connectionism?, Elman et al. have the following exchange (Elman et al., 1996:47)

B: I don't believe my ears! Connectionist nets are simply reactive, they just respond to statistical regularities in the environment.

A: No, that may have been true of the earliest models, but the more complex ones develop internal representations that go well beyond surface regularities to capture abstract structural relationships.

Also, AI became a bad word in the computer software industry, because many of the highly touted software products failed to materialize or were canceled. This is reminiscent of the cancellation of most of the machine translation projects in the 1960s by both the Americans and the Russians, after being greatly heralded in the 1950s. In 1964 I was a member of Victor Yngve's Machine Translation Lab at MIT as a first-year graduate student. I vividly remember being busy at work on my class project of programming a partial translation of German to English with Yngve's COMIT language on punch cards for the IBM time-sharing system, when it was rudely announced that MIT was dissolving the whole lab.

intelligence in terms of the science of behavior, grounding this study in a system of intelligible concepts and principles verified in animal psychology. (Chomsky, 1975a:39–40)

Another effort to keep biolinguistics going during the early eighties was the idea for the formation of a journal on biology and language.[19] Although Chomsky and some other linguists immediately supported it, what took us by surprise was the number of biologists who enthusiastically greeted it and offered to serve on the editorial board of the journal including, among others, Sydney Brenner, Jean-Pierre Changeux, Norman Geschwind, David Hubel, François Jacob, Niels Jerne, Konrad Lorenz, Victor McKusick, Peter Marler, Linus Pauling, Massimo Piattelli-Palmarini, Gunther Stent, and Lionel Tiger. However, the $40,000 in seed money for the first year was an astronomical sum for us, and proved to be the one insurmountable obstacle for our journal. The HMS Biolinguistics Group was only able to survive because the Laboratory of Molecular Biology arranged for us to use the computers for our newsletter (*Bioling*) and provided us with a meeting room at the HMS Countway Library. None of our guest speakers received a fee so that our total budget was exhausted buying beer for the speakers at the Windsor Bar across the street after their talks.

At this stage of inquiry, we have only partial and fragmentary answers to the questions (1)–(5).[20] In chapter 1, "The unification problem," we consider foundational issues, such as what the appropriate domain of inquiry is for the study of biology of language, issues of methodology, linguistics as a natural science, and formalization in linguistics.

In chapter 2, "Knowledge and use of language," we will see that a central part of the answer to question (1) is taken to be an (I-)language, where the notion of I-language is discussed further in chapter 2 (see also Chomsky and Lasnik, 1993:507). We consider the issues of idealization that arise in this study, including modularity and the notion of "psychological reality."

The answer to question (3) involves a number of elements, among them, parsing (Berwick, Abney, and Tenny, 1992), speech acts, pragmatics, etc. We consider also limits to cognitive capacity. Some of the issues concerning use of language are considered in chapters 1 and 2.

---

[19] Steve Hammalian, Allan Maxam, and I were involved in various incarnations of this project.

[20] This book will have time to go into only a few of the avenues of research exploring these questions and may devote more space to issues that we are particularly interested in, but this is not because other topics that could have been covered are less important. We will provide extensive references to these other areas so that the reader can pursue topics of interest in greater detail.

And an important part of the answer to question (2) is a universal grammar, or more precisely, the specification of principles of an epigenetically[21] given UG by parameter-setting (Chomsky and Lasnik, 1993; Roeper and Williams, 1987; Wexler and Manzini, 1987). This is taken up in chapter 3, "Acquisition (growth) of language." We also discuss the Argument from Poverty of the Stimulus, the device used by the generative grammarian to study principles of UG.

In chapter 4, "Mechanisms of language" and in chapter 5, "Evolution of language," we turn to the final questions posed for the unification problem for biolinguistics. Chomsky and Lasnik note that problems (4)–(5)[22] "appear to be beyond serious inquiry for the time being, along with many similar questions about cognition generally" (Chomsky and Lasnik, 1993:509). However, in spite of the difficulty in studying these questions, Chomsky and his colleagues in linguistics and in many related fields, including neurology, speech pathology, clinical genetics, and endocrinology have been intrigued by these topics and numerous areas of investigation have been opened up to answer these questions.

Chomsky himself has been interested in these questions since the earliest days of generative grammar, has encouraged the further study of these topics, and has also opened up many lines of thought on language, development, and evolution. These include such topics as language as a genetic/epigenetic system, functional explanation in evolution, language learning as selection (versus instruction), parametric variation, language as a by-product, language as an emergent system, evolution of language in a physical space of possibilities, implications of abstract properties of the language faculty – as a system based on digital computation with recursive enumeration, nonredundancy, modularity, least effort principles, symmetry – and limits to cognitive capacity. All of these have implications for the biology of language at the level of physical mechanisms, ontogeny (development in the individual), and phylogeny (evolutionary history).

---

[21] More exactly, UG is the "theory of the initial state" (Chomsky and Lasnik, 1993:507). As noted by Chomsky and Lasnik, "we may proceed to ask as well how environmental factors and maturational processes interact with the initial state described by UG" (p. 509). In our terms biolinguistics also subsumes the approach to language that has been variously termed "innatist, nativist," etc. However, we do not use these terms since all approaches to language have an innate component. Again, since any theory of language will have a genetic (as well as an epigenetic) aspect we do not employ the term "Genetic Hypothesis" (Jackendoff, 1994:30). However, Jackendoff uses "Genetic Hypothesis" in the sense that "the ability to learn language is rooted in our biology," which is quite in accord with the present discussion. UG has origins in the "Cartesian linguistics" of the Port-Royal theory of grammar (Chomsky, 1966).

[22] The exact wording they use for (4) (their [2e]) is "How are these properties realized in mechanisms of the brain?" and for (5) (their [2d]) is "How did these properties of the mind/brain evolve in the species?"

We will return to many of these topics in chapters 4 and 5 and else-where.[23]

In chapter 4, we will suggest that slight genetic variation may possibly seed linguistic variation. In chapter 5, we will offer the speculation that the physical basis for some of the word order variation in the world's languages may be the pattern-forming process of symmetry-breaking.

---

[23] We will not try to give a systematic historical account below of Chomsky's views on language and biology, evolution, etc. Rather we will provide a sketch of some of the ideas and possible lines of investigation of these issues that he has proposed over the years, often in conjunction with specific frameworks of linguistic theory, such as the principles-and-parameters model, the minimalist program, etc.

1   The unification problem

Chomsky has commented as follows on the futility of attempting "the study of everything":[1]

In this connection, it is perhaps worthwhile to recall some further truisms; in rational inquiry, in the natural sciences or elsewhere, there is no such subject as "the study of everything." Thus it is no part of physics to determine exactly how a particular body moves under the influence of every particle or force in the universe, with possible human intervention, and so on. This is not a topic. Rather, in rational inquiry we idealize to selected domains in such a way (we hope) as to permit us to discover crucial features of the world. (Chomsky, 1992:102)

The physicist David Ruelle, one of the founders of the field of nonlinear dynamics and chaos theory, writes in a similar vein: "Typically, if you are a physicist, you will not try to understand everything at the same time. Rather, you will look at different *pieces of reality* one by one. You will *idealize* a given piece of reality, and try to describe it by a mathematical theory" (Ruelle, 1991:11).

In biolinguistics, one such "piece of reality" that one might seek to describe is the relations and interpretations that hold between full phrases like *Jones* and "silent subjects," as in this example described by Chomsky:

To illustrate in a slightly more subtle case, consider the sentence "Jones was too angry to run the meeting." Who is understood to be running the meeting? There are two interpretations: The "silent subject" of "run" can be taken to be Jones, so that the meaning is that Jones wouldn't run the meeting because of his anger; in this case we say that the silent subject is "controlled" by *Jones*. Or it can be taken to be unspecified in reference, so that the meaning is that (say) we couldn't run the meeting because of Jones's anger (compare "the crowd was too angry to run the meeting"). Suppose that we replace "the meeting" by a question phrase, so we now have: "which meeting was Jones too angry to run?" Now the ambiguity is resolved; Jones refused to run the meeting (compare "which meeting was the crowd too angry to run," interpreted counter-intuitively to mean that the crowd was supposed to run the meeting, unlike "which meeting was the crowd too angry for us to run?" – which has no "silent subject" that requires interpretation). (Chomsky, 1994a:24)

---

[1] He notes that "the study of everything" he is rejecting here has nothing to do with "the theory of everything" (TOE) that the physicists are seeking (Chomsky, 1992:128).

For the physicist the "piece of reality" might be the boiling and freezing of water, as in the following example from Ruelle:

One puzzling natural phenomenon is the boiling of water, and the freezing of water is no less mysterious. If we take a liter of water and lower the temperature, it is not unreasonable that it should become more and more viscous. We may guess that at low enough temperature it will be so viscous, so stiff, as to appear quite solid. This guess about the solidification of water is wrong. As we cool water we see that at a certain temperature it changes to ice in a completely abrupt manner. Similarly, if we heat water it will boil at a certain temperature, i.e., it will undergo a discontinuous change from liquid to water vapor. The freezing and boiling of water are familiar examples of *phase transitions*. (Ruelle, 1991:122–23)

The first thing that has to be understood about both the example involving the English language data and the example involving the freezing and boiling of water is that there are problems here that need explanation at all! As Chomsky notes about the English example cited (and others he discusses along with these),

The reasons are well-understood in such cases as these. The crucial point is that all of this is known without experience and involves computational processes and principles that are quite inaccessible to consciousness, applying to a wide range of phenomena in typologically diverse languages. Even the relevant phenomena had escaped attention until recently, probably because the facts are known "intuitively," as part of our nature, without experience. Serious inquiry begins when we are willing to be surprised by simple phenomena of nature, such as the fact that an apple falls from a tree, or a phrase means what it does. If we are satisfied with the "explanation" that things fall to their natural place or that our knowledge of form and meaning results from experience or perhaps natural selection, then we can be sure that the very phenomena will remain hidden from view, let alone any understanding of what lies behind them. (p. 25)

The same considerations apply for the freezing and boiling of water, as Ruelle emphasizes, "These phenomena are in fact so familiar that we may miss the fact that they are very strange indeed, and require an explanation. Perhaps one could say that a physicist is a person who does *not* consider it obvious that water should freeze or boil when its temperature is lowered or raised" (p. 123). In many cases the "piece of reality" we have chosen to investigate will turn out to be too complex to analyze as it stands:

So, here is a problem for theoretical physicists: prove that as you raise or lower the temperature of water you have phase transitions to water vapor or to ice. Now, that's a tall order! We are far from having such a proof. In fact, there is not a single type of atom or molecule for which we can mathematically prove that it should crystallize at low temperature. These problems are just too hard for us. (p. 123–24)

In such cases it will be necessary to try to idealize it in various ways:

If you are a physicist, you won't find it unusual to be confronted with a problem much too difficult for you to solve . . . There are ways out, of course, but they require that your relation to reality be altered in one way or the other. Either you consider a mathematical problem analogous to the one you cannot handle, but easier, and forget about close contact with physical reality. Or you stick with physical reality but idealize it differently (often at the cost of forgetting about mathematical rigor or logical consistency). Both approaches have been used to try to understand phase transitions, and both approaches have been very fruitful. On the one hand it is possible to study systems "on a lattice" where the atoms instead of moving freely can be present only at some discrete sites. For such systems one has good mathematical proofs that certain phase transitions occur. Or one can inject new ideas into the idealization of reality, like Wilson's ideas of *scaling*, and obtain a rich harvest of new results. Still, the situation is not quite satisfactory. We should like a general conceptual understanding of why there are phase transitions, and this, for the moment, escapes us. (p. 124)

These examples suggest that, as we approach the study of the mind/brain, we should not let the intuitive familiarity of the linguistic data lull us into thinking that the problems will become any less hard: "Scientists know how hard it is to understand simple phenomena like the boiling or freezing of water, and they are not too astonished to find that many questions related to the human mind (or the functioning of the brain) are for the time being beyond our understanding" (Ruelle, 1991:11).

In a review of work on the visual system, David Hubel comments on the surprisingly long time it has taken to verify a hypothesis about brain cells that, although of great interest and importance, still makes up only a tiny corner of what Ruelle terms the "many questions related to . . . the functioning of the brain . . . [that are] beyond our understanding":

Thirty-five years ago Wiesel and I would have been incredulous had anyone suggested that only now would our scheme for explaining simple cells be vindicated or disproved. At this rate we may expect to have a verdict on a similar proposal we made for complex cells by 2031. (Hubel, 1996:197)

Apart from the unfeasibility of the "study of everything" Chomsky has also distinguished problems, which "appear to be within the reach of approaches and concepts that are moderately well understood," from mysteries, that "remain as obscure to us today as when they were originally formulated" (Chomsky, 1975b:137). Short recounts the experience of the molecular biologist Lubert Stryer:

Lubert Stryer (Stanford Medical School) told of a conversation in 1969 with Henri Peyre, then professor of French at Yale. Unimpressed by Stryer's account of how he intended to determine the molecular basis of vertebrate vision, Peyre remarked that the truly interesting question was the molecular basis of remorse. (Short, 1994:583)

However, "truly interesting" does not necessarily translate into "easily amenable to scientific investigation." It is not obvious whether the study of a topic like remorse falls into the "problem" or "mystery" category. One can at least imagine approaches to the problem, like studying serial killers with controls to try to define a behavioral phenotype, and then look for polymorphisms (variations) or mutants.[2] But given the state of both molecular biology and psychology in 1969 (and probably now), Stryer was probably wiser to attack the unification problem for vertebrate vision rather than that for remorse.

Some may be disappointed to see the grand questions like, "what is the relationship between language and thought?" reformulated as a series of less romantic questions like, "what are the constraints on the distribution of pronouns, Case-marked noun phrases, etc., in English?" There have been similar misgivings in biology about general questions like: what is life?, as P. B. and J. S. Medawar have pointed out (Medawar and Medawar, 1978:7). And, they note, Keats denounced Newton "for destroying all the beauty of the rainbow by reducing it to its prismatic colours . . ." (p. 166). Although the question concerning the logical form of the reciprocal pronoun *each other* and "silent subjects" may seem less romantic than broader questions concerning language and thought at first glance, in the long run, we hope to be able to piece together a more satisfactory answer to the latter question by breaking the problem down into smaller, more tractable problems. Jacob has elegantly stated this as follows:

Science proceeds differently. It operates by detailed experimentation with nature and thus appears less ambitious, at least at first glance. It does not aim at reaching at once a complete and definitive explanation of the whole universe, its beginning, and its present form. Instead, it looks for partial and provisional answers about those phenomena that can be isolated and well defined. Actually, the beginning of modern science can be dated from the time when such general questions as, "How was the universe created? What is matter made of? What is the essence of life?" were replaced by such limited questions as "How does a stone fall? How does water flow in a tube? How does blood circulate in vessels?" This substitution had an amazing result. While asking general questions led to limited answers, asking limited questions turned out to provide more and more general answers. (Jacob, 1977:1161–62)

THE ROLE OF TECHNICAL TERMS IN UNIFICATION

Chomsky has devoted many essays to elucidating and teasing apart the uses of such terms and expressions as "language," "the English language,"

---

[2] A polymorphism is the presence in a population of two or more relatively common alleles of a gene.

"know English," "the word X refers to Y," etc., as they occur in the literature of linguistics, philosophy of mind, and the cognitive sciences. When we embed a term like "language" into a theory, it becomes a technical term and takes on the meaning assigned to it within that theory. It need not have any more connection to the commonsense use of the word than the sub-atomic particle "quark" has to the "quark" of James Joyce. We could spell "language" backwards, but for convenience we retain the original word for the theory, just as words like "mass" and "energy" are retained in physics. What linguists do is to define the term "I-language" to denote the biological object under study, but to continue to use the term "language" (instead of "I-language") where the context leaves no possibility of confusion. Similarly, in exactly the same way, we use the term "biolinguistics" for roughly the study of the five questions posed in the Introduction, but where the context is clear, we often use the shorter form "linguistics."

This kind of analysis has been a crucial step in the unification process in every natural science, and is always carried out, either implicitly or explicitly. For example, Max Planck dedicates a long essay, "The Unity of the Physical Universe," to the topic of unification and technical terms in his area of expertise, thermodynamics. He is concerned with exorcising the anthropomorphic element in the usage of the pivotal term *entropy*. Planck notes that many physical concepts and whole branches of physics arose out of human needs and from the sense perceptions. For example, the concept of *force* "without doubt referred to human force, corresponding to the use of men or beasts to work the first and oldest machines – the lever, the pulley, and the screw." Heat was characterized by the sense of warmth, etc. Energy involved the idea of "useful work" and attempts to build a "perpetual motion machine." Progress in physics was finally made by "emancipating" physics from its anthropomorphous nature: "we may say briefly that the feature of the whole development of theoretical physics, up to the present, is the unification of its systems which has been obtained by a certain elimination of the anthropomorphous elements, particularly the specific sense-perceptions" (Planck, 1993:4).

Much of the rest of the essay involves the "emancipation" of the Second Law of Thermodynamics from such notions as "human ability," "human agency," "ability to carry out certain experiments," "limits to human knowledge," etc. He considers a number of alternative definitions of this law in terms of irreversible processes and, finally, entropy. He argues that the statistical formulation of Boltzmann is the best one – "anthropomorphism is eliminated." But we pay a price for this "step towards unification"; viz., in using statistical methods, we are "denied the complete answer to all questions relating to details of operations in physics"; e.g., about individual elements. Once again, physics isn't the "study of everything," in Chomsky's terms. And just as Newton destroyed Keats' rainbow, Planck admits "that the picture of the future appears colourless and drab when compared with the glorious colouring of the original picture, tinted with the manifold needs of human life, and to which all the senses contributed their part." But what we gain in turn is the "*unity* of the picture."

Planck goes on to make the following prescient observations:

> As fundamental in mechanics we need principally the conceptions of space, time, and motion, and it may be denoted by matter or condition. The same fundamentals are equally necessary to electro-dynamics. A slightly more generalized view of mechanics might thus allow it to include electro-dynamics, and, in fact, there are many indications that these two divisions, which are already encroaching upon one another, will be joined in one single general scheme of dynamics.

In a short time Einstein was to embark on this project, by scrutinizing the classical (technical and commonsense) notions of space and time in much the same way that the founders of thermodynamics had scrutinized the technical and commonsense notions of energy and work.[3]

"REALITY" IN LINGUISTICS AND NATURAL SCIENCE

Weinberg provides a useful characterization of "real" for natural science:[4] "Wave functions are real for the same reason that quarks and symmetries are – because it is useful to include them in our theories" (Weinberg, 1992:79). This should be an adequate rule-of-thumb for any study of the natural world, including biolinguistics, the study of the biological object (I-)language, and we assume it here. But often linguists are held to a higher standard by philosophers, cognitive scientists, and even by many other linguists. After having presented evidence and arguments for some linguistic concept or principle to show that it is "useful to include them in our theories," linguists are then asked to jump through some more philosophical hoops, to show that the concept or principle has the alleged property of "psychological reality," "neurological reality," or even "mental reality." We discuss an example of this in a review of Chomsky's *Rules and Representations* by Colin McGinn (McGinn, 1981).

McGinn lists several "Chomskian theses" (p. 288), of which the following two are considered here:

---

[3] The date of Planck's essay is not provided, but it appears to predate Einstein's work on special relativity.
[4] Weinberg is actually speaking through the figure of "Scrooge" in a discussion with "Tiny Tim" about the meaning of quantum mechanics, including the interpretation of the EPR paradox (see below). Weinberg notes: "I have some sympathy with both sides in this debate, though rather more with the realist Scrooge than with the positivist Tiny Tim."

(i) a grammar characterizes an internal structure of representations and computational principles
(ii) this structure belongs to the *mind* of the speaker

McGinn accepts thesis (i), but, after presenting some discussion, concludes about thesis (ii): "So I do not think that Chomsky has yet demonstrated his right to the claim that generative grammars have properly *mental* reality" (p. 290).

However, Chomsky has not claimed that generative grammars have any "mental reality" at all, above and beyond the reality that any scientific model of the universe has:

The grammar of a language . . . has a claim to that "higher degree of reality" that the physicist ascribes to his mathematical models of the universe. At an appropriate level of abstraction, we hope to find deep explanatory principles underlying the generation of sentences by grammars. The discovery of such principles, and that alone, will justify the idealizations adopted and indicate that we have captured an important element of the real structure of the organism. (Chomsky, 1980c:223)

Chomsky explicitly states that he uses "mental" in much the same way as "chemical," "optical," or "electrical," are used:

Take the term "mind," or as a preliminary, "mental." Consider how we use such terms as "chemical," "optical," or "electrical." Certain phenomena, events, processes, and states are called "chemical" (etc.), but no metaphysical divide is suggested by that usage. These are just various aspects of the world that we select as a focus of attention for the purposes of inquiry and exposition. I will understand the term "mental" in much the same way, with something like its traditional coverage, but without metaphysical import and with no suggestion that it would make any sense to try to identify the true criterion or mark of the mental. (Chomsky, 1994b:181)

"Mind" is meant to be understood in a similar fashion: "By 'mind,' I mean the mental aspects of the world, with no concern for defining the notion more closely and no expectation that we will find some interesting kind of unity or boundaries, any more than elsewhere; no one cares to sharpen the boundaries of 'the chemical.'"

But if "mental" and "mind" are understood in this way, then the thesis McGinn is attributing to Chomsky comes down to something like: I-language, or more generally, the language faculty, is a component of mind/brain. Stated this generally, there is no point in elevating it to a "Chomskian thesis." It could just as well be called a "Cartesian thesis," for example. In fact, the notion that the language faculty is a component of the mind/brain is not a particularly controversial thesis and is tacitly assumed in much work on language. When Damasio et al. did PET (positron emission tomography) scans on subjects to try to determine where lexical categories or semantic concepts related to persons, animals, tools, etc., were stored, they didn't waste brain scans on the kidney or the big toe, to rule out the possibility of the language faculty being there, nor did they justify leaving out these controls, since, rightly or wrongly, their audience assumes this on the basis of a lot of other evidence (Damasio et al., 1996); for commentary, see Caramazza, 1996.

So McGinn presumably has a much different kind of thesis in mind – and he even uses italics with the word *mental*. But now we are dealing with a technical term, *mental*, and we are stuck until McGinn tells us what it means. Just as we would be stuck in physics if we weren't told what technical terms like "work," "energy," or "entropy" meant. Note that we aren't helped out by the fact that McGinn's *mental* is spelled the same way that Chomsky spells "mental." It could just as well be spelled MENTAL or mEntAl, or with totally different symbols, to emphasize that it is a technical term. In order to evaluate the thesis, two things are needed: (1) some characterization of "*mental*" and "*mental* reality" and (2) we need to be told why we should care about it; i.e., how it is useful for or, alternatively, why it causes problems for, biolinguistic theory.

Later on we will show that Einstein, in arguing for the idea of "objective reality," carried out exactly the two steps just discussed. He (and his colleagues, Podolsky and Rosen) provided the following:
(1) a characterization of "objective reality"
(2) a problem that they thought it caused for quantum mechanics

The characterization given was in terms of assigning exact values to properties, like position and momentum, of particles (like electrons). The problem proposed was in the form of a thought experiment that resulted in a purported dilemma for quantum mechanics, the so-called EPR (Einstein–Podolsky–Rosen) paradox. Einstein felt that this thought experiment showed that the theory of quantum mechanics was "incomplete." Later on, after Einstein's death, when the EPR experiment could be performed, it was shown that the reasonable definition of "objective reality" given by EPR was ruled out by the experiment, the results of which were exactly predicted by quantum mechanics.

Einstein and his colleagues worked hard to characterize the technical notion of "objective reality" and to show why they thought it led to an impasse for the current theory of physics. We are nowhere near this situation for the analogous notion of "mental reality." First of all we don't even know the meaning of the technical term *mental*, as it is intended by McGinn. Until we know the meaning of this term, we can't evaluate the thesis that language has "mental reality." Nor can we know whether it helps (or counts against) biolinguistic theory. Chomsky notes that technical terms have both of the following properties – you can't have intuitions about them and you can't do thought experiments with them – you need to be told what they mean.[5] It is up to McGinn to tell us what "mental reality" is and it is up to McGinn, or whoever else wants to, to defend the thesis that language has this mysterious property. But the work has to be done by somebody, just as Einstein and colleagues did the work in physics to argue for "objective reality."[6] In any case, this (non-)thesis is not Chomsky's to defend.

McGinn gives us a few hints about what he has in mind. He holds that thesis (ii); viz., that (linguistic) "structure belongs to the mind of the speaker" raises "some difficult issues, to which Chomsky does not seem sufficiently sensitive." One problem, he claims, is that thesis (ii) is not entailed by thesis (i), the thesis that grammar is an internal structure, or else "far too much would be mental – computers, retinae, and digestive systems." McGinn concludes: "What is wanted is some criterion for when a system of representation and computation is genuinely part of the mind" (1981:290).

But recall that thesis (ii) is not Chomsky's thesis to begin with. So if anyone tries to derive thesis (ii) from thesis (i) and ends up not being able to distinguish linguistics from the digestive system, it is their problem to come up with a criterion that can. As for Chomsky, as noted earlier, he makes "no suggestion that it would make any sense to try to identify the true criterion or mark of the mental." Moreover, McGinn goes on to claim that a "philosophical (or indeed common-sense) account of the boundaries of the mind needs to respect distinctions insignificant to the cognitive psychologist" (p. 290). As we have already noted, we don't have

---

[5] That is to say, you can't do a thought experiment to determine what the term means. That must be told to us. In the case of the EPR paradox, of course, you *can* do a thought experiment because EPR have told us what "objective reality" is.
[6] As the physicist Wolfgang Pauli might have said of the thesis on "mental reality," "it is not even wrong" (Zee, 1986:35). In this connection, it is interesting to note Pauli's opinions on Einstein's proposal about "objective reality" (see further discussion below):

As O. Stern said recently, one should no more rack one's brain about the problem of whether something one cannot know anything about exists all the same, than about the ancient question of how many angels are able to sit on the point of a needle. But it seems to me that Einstein's questions are ultimately always of this kind. (from the *Born–Einstein Letters*, cited in Mermin, 1990:81)

It appears that Pauli is saying of objective reality here too that "it is not even wrong." However, this was before John Bell presented his analysis of the EPR paradox, in which he showed it was possible to decide experimentally the question of Einstein's "objective reality" one way or the other:

Bell thereby demonstrated that, Pauli to the contrary notwithstanding, there were circumstances under which one *could* settle the question of whether "something one cannot know anything about exists all the same," and that if quantum mechanics was quantitatively correct in its predictions, the answer was, contrary to Einstein's conviction, that it does not. (Mermin, 1990:124)

a philosophical account of the boundaries of the mind, since we haven't been told the meaning of the technical term *mind*, and hence have no way to know what the boundaries of it is. And even if we are told, there is no more reason for the meaning of the technical term *mind* to reflect commonsense intuitions than there is for thermodynamic theory to make the technical term *entropy* reflect commonsense intuitions about work and energy, as Planck pointed out.

Furthermore, the question immediately arises of why one would need a "philosophical account of the boundaries of the mind" or a "criterion for when X is genuinely part of the mind" any more than one needs a philosophical account of the boundaries of the "mechanical" or the "optical." Especially given the fact that one of the great successes of unification in physics took place by ignoring the boundaries between the "mechanical" and the "optical." Sir William Rowan Hamilton once puzzled over a curious asymmetry between the mechanical and the optical:

If one compares Newtonian dynamics with classical optics, it appears that the dynamics describes only half a picture as compared to the optics; whereas the latter appeared in two different forms, the Newtonian corpuscular form and the Huygens wave form, the latter [*sic*] had no wave aspect at all. To one like Hamilton, who passionately believed in the unity of nature, this was a flaw in Newtonian physics that had to be eliminated, and he took the first step in this direction by extending the action concept to include the propagation of light. (Motz and Weaver, 1989:112)

That is, Hamilton noticed a curious gap:

	particles	waves
optics	geometrical optics	physical optics
mechanics	Newtonian theory	??
dynamics		

To unite mechanics with optics Hamilton took Fermat's principle of least time from optics and generalized it to a principle of least action. Hamilton's rationale is that he "passionately believed in the unity of nature." But he could have also dismissed the entire matter by claiming that the strange gap was the result of some unknown "criterion" that established the "boundary" between "mechanical reality" and "optical reality." Instead he chose to ignore any putative boundary between the mechanical and the optical and achieved an important unification of two domains thought to be separate from one another. Looking back at the table above, we notice the implication that one might expect physical entities in the mechanical domain to exhibit both particle-like and wave-like behavior. This was subsequently theoretically predicted to be the case by Louis de Broglie in 1923 and demonstrated by Davisson and Germer, who discovered electron diffraction. It was one of the great insights of Erwin Schrödinger to then simply take over the ready-made formalisms of Hamilton just discussed to formulate his famous "wave" equation in quantum mechanics, one case of which is given here (in the "Hamiltonian" form) (Lines, 1994:268):

$$H\phi = E\phi$$

Nor are such unification problems of solely historical interest. In a current survey of string theory, the physicist Edward Witten writes of the "bad news" for string theory:

Perhaps what is most glaringly unsatisfactory is this: crudely speaking there is wave-particle duality in physics, but in reality everything comes from the description by waves, which are then quantized to give particles. Thus a massless classical particle follows a lightlike geodesic (a sort of shortest path in curved spacetime), while the wave description of such particles involves the Einstein, Maxwell or Yang–Mills equations, which are certainly much closer to the fundamental concepts of physics. Unfortunately, in string theory so far, one has generalized only the less fundamental point of view. (Witten, 1996:26)

Witten depicts the situation in the following (modified) diagram:

The "magic square" of string theory (Witten, 1996:28)

	particles	waves
ordinary physics	classical particle (world-line)	$\int \sqrt{g} R d^4 x$ (Einstein–Hilbert action)
string theory	string (world-tube)	??

In other words, just as Hamilton set out to generalize the corpuscular aspect of Newtonian particles to a wave description, one of the tasks that Witten sees for string theory is to generalize to the more "fundamental point of view" of waves (p. 28). We have another typical unification problem, with no talk of a "criterion" for the physical or the "philosophical boundaries" of the world of strings.

Concluding, we also see no reason for biolinguistics to postulate a "psychological," "neurological," or "mental" reality, or find a criterion for, or delineate the boundaries of these "realities." There exists a voluminous philosophical literature (Quine, Putnam, Davidson, etc.), much of it critical towards the biolinguistic approach to language, since it does not admit the existence of these alleged "realities." Chomsky has reviewed much of this literature, concluding that it represents a deep-seated "methodological dualism": "the view that we must abandon scientific rationality when we study humans 'above the neck' (metaphorically speaking), becoming mystics in this unique domain, imposing arbitrary stipulations and a priori demands of a sort that would never be contemplated in the sciences, or in other ways departing from normal canons of inquiry" (Chomsky, 1994b:182).

EVIDENCE IN BIOLINGUISTICS

Since unification often involves linking "seemingly diverse objects" (Davis and Hersh, 1981:198) (and below), any and all evidence is a candidate for a theory of biolinguistics. Whether this evidence for our theory is compelling or noncompelling will depend on the depth of explanation that does or does not result. Chomsky has been insistent on these points:

Approaching the topic as in the sciences, we will look for all sorts of evidence. For example, evidence from Japanese will be used (and commonly is) for the study of English; quite rationally, on the well-supported empirical assumption that the languages are modifications of the same initial state. Similarly, evidence can be found from studies of language acquisition and perception, aphasia, sign language, electrical activity of the brain, and who knows what else. (Chomsky, 1994b:205)

Let's give another example. When linguists study English phonetics,[7] let's say the distinction between the r and l sounds, they will also draw on evidence from other languages such as Japanese. It has been noted that although adult Japanese speakers do not recognize the distinction between r and l, it can be shown that Japanese infants make the relevant distinction before a certain age. The idea here is that this distinction is available in universal phonetics in all the languages of the world, but that if the distinction is not utilized in the sound system of a particular language, as in Japanese, the distinction atrophies during the course of language development. Again, this is by no means an outlandish idea, if a system of universal phonetics is given by the genetically determined initial state. If we are interested in studying that initial state, that "grows" into English, we will use data obtained from other languages, including Japanese.

Turning to syntax,[8] Bobaljik reviews evidence that certain syntactic distinctions observed in English adult speakers are made by children in languages where the distinction is not found in the speech of adult speak-

---

[7] Phonetics is part of the study of the sound aspect of language, closely related to the articulatory and perceptual properties of speech.

[8] Syntax is the study of sentence structure, the organization of words and phrases into sentences.

ers (Swedish) (Bobaljik, 1995:330). Thus English speakers make syntactic distinctions between main verbs (*eat*, etc.) on the one hand, and modals (*will, can*, etc.) as well as auxiliaries like *have* and *be* on the other; e.g., *Can John come?* versus **Came John?* (Chomsky, 1957; Jenkins, 1972).

Bobaljik cites work by Håkansson suggesting that Swedish children make the distinction during a certain stage of language learning, after which it is lost (Håkansson, 1989). Thus we have a syntactic parallel to the phonetic *r–l* example just discussed. Moreover, Bobaljik reviews work by Hackl on German-speaking aphasics, in which the subjects exhibit a distinction between main verbs and modal verbs/auxiliaries, even though the distinction is lacking in the speech of adult German speakers (Hackl, 1995). What is being suggested is that this syntactic distinction is part of UG and can be indirectly observed in languages where the distinction is not overtly made in adult speech (and hence is not available to the language learner). Again, assuming we are interested in the initial state of the language faculty, it is quite legitimate to draw on evidence from Swedish, from language acquisition, from aphasia, or, as Chomsky says, from "who knows what else."

However, the literature of philosophy of mind and cognitive science is full of pronouncements about the privileged status of one kind of evidence over another. For example, paralleling the "psychological reality," that we discussed and rejected earlier, we learn that there is "psychological evidence" apart from, and superior to, purely "linguistic evidence." McGinn makes claims in this vein: "What seems to me true is that grammar can legitimately be taken as a psychological theory of competence, but it requires empirical underpinning from considerations external to simply characterizing (however, illuminatingly) grammaticality for the language in question" (McGinn, 1981:289).

The giveaway that we are dealing with stipulation here is the phrase "however, illuminatingly." It wouldn't be sufficient to McGinn if our grammatical theory provided all kinds of interesting grammatical explanations of the behavior of children learning language, of aphasics, of the deaf, of people with learning disorders, of language change and typology, etc. That would only be illuminating "linguistic evidence," but not "psychological evidence." We haven't gotten our evidence by "psychological methods," whatever those might be – say, by strapping electrodes to somebody's head. Nor are we told whether this other kind of evidence has to be illuminating, good, bad, or indifferent.

Biolinguistics, like Mendelian genetics, posits abstract epi(genetic) properties of the internal mechanisms of organisms. Mendelian genetics says that there are abstract "factors" and abstract principles like

Segregation and Independent Assortment that explain observed facts of inheritance. Biolinguistics says that there are abstract linguistic principles encoded in the genome that guide the growth of I-languages, permitting some parametric variation during epigenesis. Again, observed facts about knowledge, acquisition, and use of language are explained along with some facts in areas like language change and typology. It makes no more sense to say that (bio)linguistics is not "psychologically real" than it does to say that Mendelian genetics is not "physiologically real."

McGinn notes that one *could* choose not to study psychology (hence biology) at all: "it seems that a linguist could set himself the goal of devising a grammar capable of generating all and only the grammatical strings of some language and not commit himself on the matter of psychology" (McGinn, 1981:289). Similarly, a lepidopterist could set himself the goal of classifying all the different patterns of spots on butterfly wings and "not commit himself on the matter of biology." Or the linguist could collect short stories that contain only words without the letter R. In fact, the description just given by McGinn might even be taken to be reminiscent of the study of "Platonist linguistics" (Chomsky, 1986).

Let us take another case from the cognitive sciences. In an interview with the *Journal of Cognitive Neuroscience*, the cognitive psychologist Steven Pinker is asked (by Michael Gazzaniga):

MG: ...Before going into details, how does your MIT view differ from other MIT views?

SP: Obviously, some of the key ideas in the book come from Chomsky – that there is an innate neural system dedicated to language; that his system uses a discrete combinatorial code, or grammar, to map between sound and meaning; that this code manipulates data structures that are dedicated to language and not reducible to perception, articulation, or concepts. But there are also some differences in style and substance. Chomsky's arguments for the innateness of language are based on technical analyses of word and sentence structure, together with some perfunctory remarks on universality and acquisition. I think converging evidence is crucial, and try to summarize the facts on children's development, cross-linguistic surveys, genetic language disorders, and so on.

In that sense the book is more in the tradition of George Miller and Eric Lenneberg than Chomsky... (Pinker, 1997a; originally printed in Pinker, 1994b:92)

Here Pinker introduces the idea of "converging evidence," things like "children's development, cross-linguistic surveys, genetic language disorders, and so on." This is contrasted with Chomsky's "technical analyses of word and sentence structure, together with some perfunctory remarks on universality and acquisition." Although Chomsky has developed his ideas on "universality and acquisition" in a voluminous output over the last forty years, for Pinker these amount to "perfunctory remarks," since they don't meet his criterion of "converging evidence," a very odd notion that we will now examine more closely. From Pinker's viewpoint, whatever the latter evidence is, it is not "converging evidence" and puts Chomsky in a different "tradition" from Pinker, Miller, and Lenneberg.

The issues under discussion have been framed in the wrong way here. It is totally irrelevant in the larger biolinguistics picture, whether Professor X's views at MIT do or don't overlap with Professor W, Y, and Z's views – what ultimately matters is what the nature of the biological object language is. And as for deciding what evidence we use to discover this nature there is only one tradition worth belonging to – the tradition of rational scientific inquiry. Chomsky calls this "methodological naturalism," which "investigates mental aspects of the world as we do any others, seeking to construct intelligible explanatory theories, with the hope of eventual integration with the 'core' natural sciences" (Chomsky, 1994b:182). This is to be contrasted with the "methodological dualism," discussed earlier, "the view that we must abandon scientific rationality when we study humans 'above the neck' (metaphorically speaking)."

Skinner's and Quine's views, for example, would fall into the tradition of methodological dualism, as would the view that insists that evidence be "psychologically real," for the reasons given earlier. The views expressed above by Pinker on "converging evidence" place him in this tradition as well (see also chapter 5). For Pinker, the reams of evidence put forth "on universality and acquisition" over the past forty years, most recently as the principles-and-parameters theory are not "converging evidence," but are, at best, "perfunctory remarks." However, what is "converging evidence" from one point of view may be "diverging evidence" from another point of view – evidence does not come labeled as "convergent" or "divergent." What could account for the peculiar idea that the study of principles and parameters in UG is not "converging evidence" for Pinker, as "children's development?" is.

Part of the explanation might be the implicit assumption that the generative grammarian is not doing experiments, whereas the developmental psychologist is. For example, Chomsky proposed that one might attribute to an inborn UG the knowledge that adult English speakers have that the sentence "is the man who is hungry tall," is acceptable, while the sentence "*is the man who hungry is tall" is not.[9] Now compare Pinker's discussion of this:

---

[9] These example sentences and Chomsky's account of them (one case of "the argument from poverty of the stimulus") are discussed in more detail in chapter 3.

Chomsky's claim was tested in an experiment with three-, four-, and five-year-olds at a daycare center by the psycholinguists Stephen Crain and Mineharu Nakayama. One of the experimenters controlled a doll of Jabba the Hutt, of Star Wars fame. The other coaxed the child to ask a set of questions, by saying, for example, "Ask Jabba if the boy is unhappy is watching Mickey Mouse." Jabba would inspect a picture and answer yes or no, but it was really the child who was being tested, not Jabba. The children cheerfully provided the appropriate questions, and, as Chomsky would have predicted, not a single one of them came up with an ungrammatical string like Is the boy who unhappy is watching Mickey Mouse? (Pinker, 1994b:42)

The tacit assumption here by Pinker seems to be that Chomsky is making an unsupported "claim," not verified by experiment whereas the psycholinguists have taken this claim and verified it by "experiment."

But generative grammarians had already performed years of experiments to provide (tentative) verification; viz., by introspection and querying other speakers on this kind of grammatical construction and countless others, in English and across many different languages. As Chomsky notes in an interview with Kim-Renaud:

KIM-RENAUD: *What kind of evidence is used? You don't really do actual experiments?*
CHOMSKY: You actually do. For example, if I ask you as a speaker of English whether "Who do you believe John's claim that Bill saw?" is a sentence, that's an experiment. Now it happens that most of the relevant evidence for the study of psychological reality – that is, truth – of linguistic theories now comes from experiments of this kind. It would be very nice to have experimental evidence of other types, from a laboratory of neurophysiology or whatever. We don't have much of it. If it would ever come along, it'd be delightful. (Chomsky, 1988b:268–69)

So why does Pinker think that Chomsky is merely making a claim, whereas the psycholinguists are performing a (psycholinguistic) experiment? Would it satisfy Pinker if Chomsky were waving a Jabba the Hutt puppet in front of the linguistics students?:

One of the most fascinating syndromes recently came to light when the parents of a retarded girl with chatterbox syndrome in San Diego read an article about Chomsky's theories in a popular science magazine and called him at MIT, suggesting that their daughter might be of interest to him. Chomsky is a paper-and-pencil theoretician who wouldn't know Jabba the Hutt from the Cookie Monster, so he suggested that the parents bring their child to the laboratory of the psycholinguist Ursula Bellugi in La Jolla. (Pinker, 1994b:52)

The "paper-and-pencil theoretician" is performing experiments on language, as much as Pinker is with Jabba the Hutt.[10]
Another part of the explanation might be that Pinker can't bring

---

[10] These kinds of experiments are well known in other areas of the cognitive sciences, where vision research has a distinguished tradition (psychophysics) which includes "paper-and-pencil theoreticians" working with visual illusions.

himself to accept arguments based on one kind of evidence, "abstract computations" (in the case of language, syntactic computations): "Though I happen to agree with many of his [Chomsky's] arguments, I think that a conclusion about the mind is convincing only if many kinds of evidence converge on it" (Pinker, 1994b:24).

Suppose, contrary to fact, that no converging evidence at all of the kind Pinker detailed in his book – on sign language, aphasia, language disorders, etc. – had turned up yet. Would one be justified in accepting Chomsky's arguments that the "basic design of language is innate," to use Pinker's words? Not according to Pinker, since "a conclusion about the mind is convincing only if many kinds of evidence converge on it," not if all you have is Chomsky's argument from poverty of the stimulus. We think that one would be justified – that the results from the application solely of the argument from poverty of the stimulus are strong enough to support the conclusion that the "basic design of language is innate."

Or suppose that some of this evidence was "diverging evidence"; i.e., appeared to be at odds with the conclusion that language design is innate. Again, if the abstract arguments for innateness are strong, one could well opt to follow Eddington's rule: "it is also a good rule not to put overmuch confidence in the observational results that are put forward *until they have been confirmed by theory*" (Eddington, 1935:211).

But if we ignore Pinker's "converging evidence," and even perhaps some "diverging evidence," haven't we abandoned the canons of rational scientific inquiry (methodological naturalism)? Not necessarily, as the following example illustrates:

Einstein's indifference to attempts to confirm or disprove his theories has become legendary. The first to put the special theory of relativity to the test was the German physicist Walter Kaufmann, who attempted to detect changes in the mass of fast-moving electrons. Kaufmann regarded his results as a categorical disproof of the theory, but Einstein was not discouraged. Remarkably, he was equally indifferent to experimental confirmation of his work. Ilse Rosenthal-Schneider, one of his students in Berlin, tells how Einstein once interrupted a discussion of relativity to hand her a telegram that had been lying on the windowsill. It contained Sir Arthur Eddington's report that the bending of starlight predicted by the general theory of relativity had indeed been observed during the 1919 eclipse. Surprised by Einstein's indifference, she asked him how he would have reacted had Eddington's expedition not borne out his theory. "Then," said Einstein, "I would have been sorry for the dear Lord – the theory is correct." (Sorensen, 1991:262)

Many similar illustrations can be found throughout the history of science.[11]

---

[11] Note that we are not saying that theories of language have the explanatory depth of the theory of general relativity or the like. What is being discussed is whether the argument from poverty of the stimulus supports a specific conclusion about the mind; viz., that the "basic design of language is innate."

Conversely, both Miller and Lenneberg are clearly in the tradition of methodological naturalism; i.e., rational scientific inquiry. Miller was one of the early pioneers, perhaps the earliest, to introduce linguistic considerations into psychology; e.g., cf. his collaborations with Chomsky (Chomsky and Miller, 1963; Miller and Chomsky, 1963). Moreover, Miller regards this early work as an "anticipation of a view that I think Noam is now calling methodological naturalism, to which I would like to subscribe in so far as I understand it" (Chomsky, 1994a:69); see also Miller, 1991. As for Lenneberg, we have already noted that he was one of the first biologists to present linguistic evidence alongside other kinds biological evidence (discussed in an appendix to Lenneberg, 1967 by Chomsky, called "The formal nature of language").

In any case, what biolinguistics does do (as spelled out in the citation above from Chomsky) is drop all restrictions on evidence, whether to "grammaticality" or to "psychologically real" evidence, "converging evidence," "DNA evidence," or to any other kind of evidence:

An empirical observation does not come with a notice "I am for X," written on its sleeve, where X is chemistry, linguistics, or whatever. No one asks whether the study of a complex molecule belongs to chemistry or biology, and no one should ask whether the study of linguistic expressions and their properties belongs to linguistics, psychology, or the brain sciences. (Chomsky, 1995a:33)

REALITY OF WAVE FUNCTIONS – "SPOOKY ACTION AT A DISTANCE"

We have accepted as a working hypothesis the formulation of Weinberg: "Wave functions are real for the same reason that quarks and symmetries are – because it is useful to include them in our theories." We wish now to motivate and hopefully to illuminate this idea with a brief discussion of each of the theoretical entities that Weinberg mentions – wave functions, quarks, and symmetries. We begin with wave functions.

Chomsky describes the origins of modern science and the outcome of the attempts to solve the Cartesian case of the unification problem, the so-called "mind–body problem":

Just as the mechanical philosophy appeared to be triumphant, it was demolished by Newton, who reintroduced a kind of "occult" cause and quality, much to the dismay of leading scientists of the day, and Newton himself. The Cartesian theory of mind (such as it was) was unaffected by his discoveries, but the theory of body was demonstrated to be untenable. To put it differently, Newton eliminated the problem of "the ghost in the machine" by exorcising the machine; the ghost was unaffected. (Chomsky, 1994b:189)

Newton had demolished "body," leaving us with no coherent notion of the "physical" world:

The mind–body problem disappeared, and can be resurrected, if at all, only by producing a new notion of body (material, physical, etc.) to replace the one that was abandoned; hardly a reasonable enterprise, it would seem. Lacking that, the phrase "material" ("physical," etc.) world simply offers a loose way of referring to what we more or less understand and hope to unify in some way. Ibid.

What we will do here is briefly set out one such contemporary attempt to resurrect such a physical reality; viz., Albert Einstein's failed arguments for an "objective reality."

What had bothered Newton and his contemporaries was the problem of action at a distance by an "occult" force; viz., gravity. It was hard for them to accept the idea that, as Chomsky puts it, "the moon moves when you move your hand." This notion of action at a distance was shown to be incompatible with Einstein's relativity theory.[12] Einstein and some of his contemporaries were also deeply disturbed by another kind of action at a distance problem, seemingly also occult in nature, which Einstein himself referred to as "spukhafte Fernwirkungen" ("spooky action at a distance"; phrase from Einstein–Born correspondence). Here the problem is that "the moon is . . . not there when nobody looks": "We often discussed his notions on objective reality. I recall that during one walk Einstein suddenly stopped, turned to me and asked whether I really believed that the moon exists only when I look at it" (Mermin, 1990:81, citing A. Pais).

In a set of interesting essays, the solid state physicist David Mermin discusses Einstein's unsuccessful attempts to reconstruct what he called "objective reality" (Mermin, 1990). Mermin argues that Einstein was less concerned about the statistical issue ("God doesn't play dice") than he was about the implications of quantum theory, in particular the Heisenberg uncertainty relations, in undermining "objective reality," where objects could be assigned properties, independent of measurement (while agreeing that there were limits to what could be measured on a quantum scale). Einstein, Podolsky, and Rosen showed that one of the implications from quantum theory was that the measurement of position or momentum of an object at one point A could have an effect on the position or momentum of another object at another point B, where there was no connection between points A and B. In order to avoid these unpleasant "spooky actions at a distance," EPR concluded that these objects must have had position or momenta all along, independent of measurement.

Mermin illustrates the dilemma with a particle source which, when you push a button on it, sends out two particles toward two independent detectors (unconnected in any way). Each detector has a green and a red

---

[12] Einstein provides an accessible account of how various notions of action at a distance in classical physics gradually came to be supplanted in modern formulations of field theories (Einstein, 1996).

light, one of which flashes, depending on whether a switch on the detector is in position 1, 2, or 3:

green   green
1 2 3 ←——— particle source ———→ 1 2 3
red   red

A typical run might be 23GR. Here we have (randomly) set the switch on the left-hand detector to 2 and the switch on the right-hand detector to 3 and the lights have flashed green (on the left) and red (on the right). Over millions of runs, we note the following patterns: GG, GR, RG, and RR occur equally often; i.e., the lights flash the same color half the time. But whenever the switches have the same settings (11, 22, 33), the left and right lights flash the same color all the time, even if you throw the switches after the particles have been emitted! How can this be if there is no connection between the two detectors? (I have greatly compressed Mermin's much more lucid presentation.)

Mermin shows the only possible answer would be if each particle contained an instruction set, say GRG, which means flash green if the switch is set to 1, flash red if it is set to 2, and flash green if it is set to 3. The point of all this is the same as the one EPR were making – we must be able to assign objects (at least some) properties independent of measurement – and so we save objective reality.

But now we have a problem with the other observation made above – the lights flash the same color (GG, RR) half the time over long runs. What instruction set(s) will give us this 50 percent result? There are nine switch settings for both detectors: 11, 12, 23, etc. The instruction GRG will cause the same lights to flash the same in five of the cases: 11, 22, 33, 13, and 31. Hence the lights will flash the same five ninths (55.5 percent) of the time, instead of the predicted 50 percent. The other instructions also yield 55.5 percent, except for GGG and RRR, which yield 100 percent. This result is known as Bell's Theorem. The conclusion is that there can't be instruction sets in the sense of EPR, and we are left with "spooky actions at a distance" as our only explanation. The actual experiment (using properties like spin and polarization) was finally able to be carried out by Aspect and collaborators in the early 1980s, disproving objective reality and leaving us with "spukhafte Fernwirkungen."

Mermin (1990) presents an interesting cross-section of the attitudes toward all this:

POPPER: The general antirationalist atmosphere which has become a major menace of our time, and which to combat is the duty of every thinker who cares for the traditions of our civilization, has led to a most serious deterioration of the standards of scientific discussion. (p. 196)

BOHR: If you do not get *schwindlig* [dizzy] sometimes when you think about these things then you have not really understood it. (p. 114)

FEYNMAN: Okay I still get nervous with it...you know how it always is, every new idea, it takes a generation or two until it becomes obvious that there's no real problem. (p. 175)

As for Mermin himself, he has a different view about these matters:

If I were forced to sum up in one sentence what the Copenhagen interpretation says to me, it would be "Shut up and calculate!" But I won't shut up. I would rather celebrate the strangeness of quantum theory than deny it, because I believe it still has interesting things to teach us about how we think – about how certain powerful but flawed mental tools we took for granted continue to infect our thinking in subtly hidden ways. (p. 199)

Mermin refocuses the question about quantum reality to ask what it can tell us about "how we think." He is, I believe, suggesting that the problem may be a problem of the biology of language and mind. We return to Mermin's interesting proposal in the next section.

One can try to resurrect "physical reality" (or "body") in some other form. But one can't present a general argument against all conceivable attempts to do so. But that is not important for our present purposes. We are only interested in showing that many scientists are content to do science *without* any such notion of objective reality. As Weinberg says (through Tiny Tim), "wave functions are real . . . because it is useful to include them in our theories."

LIMITS TO COGNITIVE CAPACITY[13]

Chomsky has made a rough distinction between "problems" and "mysteries" (Chomsky, 1975b:137). Problems are issues that at least seem amenable to study with approaches currently available to us. Examples from the study of mind might be the five questions (1)–(5) posed on p. 1. For example, much progress is being made in the study of the structure and acquisition of language (questions [1] and [2]); these are then "problems." Much less is known about physical mechanisms and evolution of language (questions [4] and [5]); but again, there are a number of approaches that show promise of eventually shedding light on these areas as well. Hence, parts of these areas also pose "problems" for us.

---

[13] As Chomsky remarks, there is a positive aspect to "limits" on cognitive capacity:

Note, incidentally, how misleading it would be to speak simply of "limitations" in human science-forming capacity. Limits no doubt exist, but they derive from the same source as our ability to construct rich cognitive systems on the basis of limited evidence in the first place. Were it not for the factors that limit scientific knowledge, we could have no such knowledge in any domain. (Chomsky, 1975b:25–26)

Let us turn to use of language (question [3]). Here some areas under active study, e.g., parsing problems, appear to be susceptible to inquiry (Berwick, Abney, and Tenny, 1992). However, Chomsky notes that other aspects of language use, what he terms "causation of behavior"; i.e., how and why humans "make choices and behave as they do," and the "creative aspect of language use" (Chomsky, 1975b:138) are as mysterious to us today as they were to the Cartesians, who also studied them. He has suggested that some of these topics might be outside the range of our cognitive capacities: "There is, surely, no evolutionary pressure that leads humans to have minds capable of discovering significant explanatory theories in specific fields of inquiry. Thinking of humans as biological organisms in the natural world, it is only a lucky accident if their cognitive capacity happens to be well matched to scientific truth in some area" (Chomsky, 1975b:25).

The reference to "evolutionary pressure" is to an idea of the philosopher Peirce (for discussion of Peirce's ideas, see Chomsky, 1968:90; Chomsky, 1975b:155):

Some have argued that this is not blind luck but rather a product of Darwinian evolution. The outstanding American philosopher Charles Sanders Peirce, who presented an account of science construction in terms similar to those just outlined, argued in this vein. His point was that through ordinary processes of natural selection our mental capacities evolved so as to be able to deal with the problems that arise in the world of experience. (Chomsky, 1988a:158)

Chomsky rejects this argument on the basis that "the experience that shaped the course of evolution offers no hint of the problems to be faced in the sciences" and could not have been a factor in evolution: "But this argument [Peirce's] is not compelling. It is possible to imagine that chimpanzees have an innate fear of snakes because those who lacked this genetically determined property did not survive to reproduce, but one can hardly argue that humans have the capacity to discover quantum theory for similar reasons" (p. 158).

So it is a lucky accident if there is a (partial) "convergence of our ideas and the truth about the world": "Notice that it is just blind luck if the human science-forming capacity, a particular component of the human biological endowment, happens to yield a result that conforms more or less to the truth about the world" (pp. 157–58).

Eugene Wigner, who was one of the pioneers in the use of group theory and symmetry considerations in quantum mechanics, reached similar conclusions about the role of mathematics in the natural sciences in an influential essay, "The Unreasonable Effectiveness of Mathematics in the Natural Sciences" (Wigner, 1979). One of his main points is that "the enormous usefulness of mathematics in the natural sciences is something bordering on the mysterious and that there is no rational explanation for it" (p. 223). He uses the analogy of a man trying to figure out which key in a bunch of keys opens a door:

mathematical concepts turn up in entirely unexpected connections. Moreover, they often permit an unexpectedly close and accurate description of the phenomena in these connections . . . We are in a position similar to that of a man who was provided with a bunch of keys and who, having to open several doors in succession, always hit on the right key on the first or second trial. (Wigner, 1979:223)

Concerning mathematical concepts Wigner notes that it is "hard to believe that our reasoning power was brought, by Darwin's process of natural selection, to the perfection which it seems to possess" (p. 224).[14] He gives a number of examples[15] to illustrate that "the mathematical formulation of the physicist's often crude experience leads in an uncanny number of cases to an amazingly accurate description of a large class of phenomena" (p. 230). These laws of nature are not a "necessity of thought"; instead Wigner speaks of the miracle of "the human mind's capacity to divine them" (p. 229).

Wigner examines the consequences of this for the unification problem:

The question which presents itself is whether the different regularities, that is, the various laws of nature which will be discovered, will fuse into a single consistent unit, or at least asymptotically approach such a fusion. Alternatively, it is possible that there always will be some laws of nature which have nothing in common with each other . . . it is even possible that some of the laws of nature will be in conflict with each other in their implications, but each convincing enough in its own domain so that we may not be willing to abandon any of them. (Wigner, 1979:234)

He gives an example of inconsistent theories of nature – quantum theory and the theory of relativity: "All physicists believe that a union of the two theories is inherently possible and that we shall find it. Nevertheless, it is possible also to imagine that no union of the two theories can be found. This example illustrates the two possibilities, of union and of conflict, mentioned before, both of which are conceivable" (pp. 234–35). Wigner observes that a similar conflict might arise in the science of mind:

A much more difficult and confusing situation would arise if we could, some day, establish a theory of the phenomena of consciousness, or of biology, which would

---

[14] Wigner also notes, without pursuing the topic here, that "it is useful, in epistemological discussions, to abandon the idealization that the level of human intelligence has a singular position on an absolute scale. In some cases it may even be useful to consider the attainment which is possible at the level of the intelligence of some other species" (p. 235, n. 11).

[15] The examples he gives are (1) the law of gravitation, (2) quantum mechanical calculation of energy levels of helium and heavier atoms, (3) the theory of the Lamb shift in quantum electrodynamics.

be as coherent and convincing as our present theories of the inanimate world. Mendel's laws of inheritance and the subsequent work on genes may well form the beginning of such a theory as far as biology is concerned. Furthermore, it is quite possible that an abstract argument can be found which shows that there is a conflict between such a theory and the accepted principles of physics. The argument could be of such abstract nature that it might not be possible to resolve the conflict, in favor of one or of the other theory, by an experiment. (p. 236)

The reason that "such a situation is conceivable is that, fundamentally, we do not know why our theories work so well."

Alongside of the language faculty and interacting with it in the most intimate way is the faculty of mind that constructs what we might call "commonsense understanding," a system of beliefs, expectations, and knowledge concerning the nature and behavior of objects, their place in a system of "natural kinds," the organization of these categories, and the properties that determine the categorization of objects and the analysis of events. (Chomsky, 1975b:35)

Interestingly enough, Mermin concludes that the problem seems pretty much settled as far as physicists are concerned and puts the problem back into the court of the mind sciences, including biolinguistics: "My current version of the answer, not very well developed, is that it has something to do with certain deterministic presuppositions that are built into our thought and language at some deep and not very accessible level, that have somehow infected even the way we think about probability distributions" (Mermin, 1990:202).

This recalls similar remarks by Chomsky concerning the dualistic picture, which has also "infected" the study of language and mind:

one would want to ask why such ideas appear so compelling. The answer could be that our commonsense picture of the world is profoundly dualistic, ineradicably, just as we can't help seeing the setting of the sun, or sharing Newton's belief in the "mechanical philosophy" that he undermined, or watching the wave that "flees the place of its creation," as Leonardo put it, independently of what we may know in some other corner of our minds. (1995a: 57)

Summing up, we observe that the theory of quantum mechanics makes spectacularly accurate physical predictions. The theory of quantum electrodynamics is able to predict correctly the magnetic moment of the electron to the ninth decimal place (Weinberg, 1974:53).[16] Discussing more recent refinements to these results, Weinberg remarks that "the numerical agreement between theory and experiment here is perhaps the most impressive in all science" (Weinberg, 1992:115).

Quantum mechanics also has the property of what Weinberg calls

[16] The predicted value of the magnetic moment of the electron (in natural units) is 1.0011596553. The observed value is 1.0011596577, an uncertainty in both figures of ±.0000000030 (Weinberg, 1974:53).

(logical) "rigidity," in that "it has so far not been possible to find a logically consistent theory that is close to quantum mechanics, other than quantum mechanics itself" (1992:86). As a result, quantum mechanics has remained essentially unchanged for over a half-century. It makes experimental predictions (discussed above) that fly in the face of Einstein's "objective reality"; it logically implies "spooky action at a distance." Not only does the moon move when you move your hand, but it's not there when nobody's looking.

This suggests that we may be looking at a limit in our cognitive capacities ("deterministic presuppositions that are built into our thought"), that although evolution may have wired us up with assumptions about "objective reality," it did not wire us to comprehend the quantum world. As it is, it was a "lucky accident" that our science-forming faculty stumbled onto the mathematics of quantum mechanics (what Wigner called the "unreasonable effectiveness of mathematics"). Although the problem might, of course, fall into the "mystery" category, one could try to investigate Mermin's proposal in the manner of I-language – explore probability intuitions using puzzles like the flashing lights experiment given above, look for arguments from poverty of stimulus for a universal schema leading to "objective reality, etc."

Wigner has also considered the unification problem from the perspective of a physicist in his essay, "Physics and the Explanation of Life," and again comes to conclusions which are strikingly similar to Chomsky's. The question he is specifically considering is how "man shall acquire deeper insights into mental processes, into the character of our consciousness" (Wigner, 1987:687). He warns that this may only be "a hope" because of built-in limits to man's cognitive capacity; in particular, "the intellectual capabilities of man may have their limits just as the capabilities of other animals have."

He considers two alternative approaches to account for the phenomena of life, mind, and consciousness. The first approach assumes that the laws of physics for inanimate matter are also valid for living matter. Wigner asks whether this logically possible assumption need mean that "the whole science of the mind will become applied physics?" No, he answers, for:

What we are interested in is not only, and not principally, the motion of the molecules in a brain but, to use Descartes' terminology, the sensations which are experienced by the soul which is linked to that brain, whether pain or pleasure, stimulation or anxiety, whether it thinks of love or prime numbers. In order to obtain an answer to these questions, the physical characterization of the state of the brain would have to be translated into psychological–emotional terms. (p. 682)

Wigner presents an analogy from electromagnetic field theory (p. 682) in which an equation involving the magnetic field H (where H plays the role of a physical variable) has to be translated into an equation involving the electric field E (where E plays the role of a psychological variable), since the first equation is not very useful without the translation into the second equation. In his view, "the present laws of physics are at least incomplete without a translation into terms of mental phenomena" (p. 687). From this point of view, it need not be the case that "the mind and the consciousness are only unimportant derived concepts which need not enter the theory at all. It may even be possible to give them the privileged status" (p. 684).

The opposite assumption to the first approach just discussed is that "the laws of physics will have to be modified drastically if they are to account for the phenomena of life. Actually, I believe that this second assumption is the correct one" (p. 684).

He reviews some examples from the history of physics showing how unification ("unifying power of science") has typically worked. What has usually been the case is that one theory can be seen as a "limiting case" of another – gravitational theory as a limiting case of macroscopic physics, macroscopic physics as a limiting case of microscopic physics (where quantum effects are ignored). Similarly, microscopic physics "describes only situations in which life and consciousness play no active role." Summing up, "The view given here considers inanimate matter as a limiting case in which the phenomena of life and consciousness play as little a role as the nongravitational forces play in planetary motion, as fluctuations play in macroscopic physics" (p. 688).

Also parallel to the above developments is the fact that "all extensions of physics to new sets of phenomena were accompanied by drastic changes in the theory" (p. 686). He cites as examples, Newton's theory, Maxwell's theory of fields, and quantum mechanics. Wigner's discussion recalls Chomsky's distinction between "reduction" and "expansion": "Sometimes unification will be reductive, as when much of biology was incorporated within known biochemistry; sometimes it may require radical modification of the more 'fundamental' discipline, as when physics was 'expanded' in the new quantum theory, enabling it to account for properties that had been discovered and explained by chemists" (Chomsky, 1994a:44).

REALITY OF QUARKS

Glashow notes that when Gell-Mann, the co-inventor of the quark, proposed the quark in his paper "A Schematic Model of Baryons and

Mesons," he stopped short of calling them physical particles, writing "It is fun to speculate about the way quarks would behave if they were physical particles . . . instead of purely mathematical entities" (Glashow, 1988:188).

Gell-Mann has recently tried to set the record straight on this topic. Although he admits to having used the term "mathematical" quark along with the term "real" quark, this was not because he did not believe in the existence of quarks:

When I proposed the existence of quarks, I believed from the beginning that they were permanently confined in some way. I referred to such quarks as "mathematical," explaining carefully what I meant by the term, and contrasted them with what I called "real quarks," which would be capable of emerging so that they could be detected singly. The reason for the choice of language is that I didn't want to face arguments with philosophically inclined critics demanding to know how I could call quarks "real" if they were always hidden. The terminology proved unfortunate, however. Numerous authors, ignoring my explanation of the terms "mathematical" and "real," as well as the fact that the situation I was describing is the one now generally accepted as correct, have claimed that I didn't really believe the quarks were there! Once such a misunderstanding becomes established in popular literature, it tends to perpetuate itself, because the various writers often simply copy one another. (Gell-Mann, 1994:182)

In short, Gell-Mann's view was (and is) that quarks are real and that they exist, but that they cannot be directly observed in isolation, as, e.g., protons can (due to the property of quark confinement). The "philosophically inclined critics" he is referring to might not be willing to call such entities "real" if they cannot be directly observed. Thus the great mass of currently available theoretical arguments and experimental evidence for the existence of quarks provides a nice argument against a strong form of positivism which would try to exclude such entities; see Weinberg for additional discussion of positivism in physics (Weinberg, 1992).

The physicist Abraham Pais, who has chronicled the history of modern physics, writes

"The reaction of the theoretical physics community to the [quark] model was generally not benign . . . The idea that hadrons were made of elementary particles with fractional quantum numbers did seem a bit rich."[17] A question not asked since the days when the reality of atoms was at issue now returned: is this a mnemonic device or is this physics? (Pais, 1986:558)

George Zweig, who independently proposed the quark model, writes of the resistance to these ideas ("vehemence" in Fritzsch's words)

Getting the CERN report published in the form that I wanted was so difficult that I finally gave up trying. When the physics department of a leading university was

---

[17] The quote is from Zweig (1980:439).

considering an appointment for me, their senior theorist, one of the most respected spokesmen for all of theoretical physics, blocked the appointment at a faculty meeting by passionately arguing that the model was the work of a "charlatan." (Fritzsch, 1983:75)

In the case of quarks, it was nearly a decade before the idea was generally accepted.

Chomsky notes that Quine considers physics to be "theories of quarks and the like," and that he holds that "the world is as natural science says it is, insofar as natural science is right" (Chomsky, 1994b:196). Chomsky observes that "that is not informative until we are told what 'natural science' is."

A further problem for Quine is that his thesis is not informative until he lets us know what the criterion is for deciding when natural science is right, and how that differs for deciding when linguistics is right. Let's take Quine's example of quarks. We can replace Quine's characterization of physics as "theories of quarks and the like" with "theories of X and the like, where X are purely mathematical entities with weird properties like fractional electric charge and that in principle can't be isolated (quark confinement) and with the further property that you can get branded as a charlatan for proposing the very idea." We have argued that in physics, as in linguistics, abstract concepts and principles are embedded in explanatory theories and stand or fall on the basis of available evidence. Outside of this evidence, there is no substantive content to the question of the "physical reality" of constructs in physics or to the "psychological reality" of constructs in linguistics.

REALITY OF SYMMETRY – DUALITY

How far removed are we from the contact mechanics of Descartes, from the commonsense notions of objects moving around and striking each other, like billiard balls? Taking a look at a report by Mukerjee, we find a new symmetry called "duality" is "redefining what physicists consider a fundamental particle – or string" (Mukerjee, 1996).[18] Edward Witten of the Institute for Advanced Study in Princeton, N. J. "believes duality not only will lead to a TOE [theory of everything] but also may illuminate why the universe is the way it is. 'I think we are heading for an explanation of quantum mechanics,' he asserts." Mukerjee gives a simple example of duality

[18] Conference reports such as this often provide some rare insights into what scientists are thinking about foundational issues, in this case unification issues. Such insights have usually been totally excised from refereed journal reports, not to mention textbooks.

Broadly, two theories are said to be dual if they are apparently dissimilar but make the same physical predictions. For example, if all the electrical and magnetic quantities in Maxwell's equations for electromagnetism are interchanged, one nominally obtains a different theory. But if in addition to electrical charges, the world is presumed to contain magnetic charges (such as the isolated north pole of a bar magnet), the two theories become exactly the same – or dual. (Mukerjee, 1996:89)

Since the 1960s, we've been told that the world contains irreducibly fundamental elements called quarks. In addition, it was later proposed that other (composite) elements called monopoles can be built up from quarks. Then came along the idea that "instead of quarks being elementary and monopoles composite" (p. 90), the field theories that describe these elements might be dual. Then quarks could be thought of as being composite elements built up from monopoles, which now assume the role of the fundamental building-blocks: "Either the quark or the monopole approach to the theory should give the same physical results" (p. 90). Finally, it was argued that the concept of duality could help merge together various alternative string theories, based on the idea that all particles in the universe, such as quarks, could be thought of as vibrations of tiny strings.

Let us return to the question of how far removed this is from Descartes' contact mechanics and from the commonsense notions of "folk physics." "String mathematics," we are told, "is so complex that it has left behind the vast majority of physicists and mathematicians" (Mukerjee, 1996:89). As Leonard Susskind (age 55) puts it: "It's a good sign there is a generation in the process of giving up. [This] means the field is moving in directions that older people can't follow" (Mukerjee, 1996:93). According to Mukerjee, Sheldon Glashow who, with Steven Weinberg, developed electroweak theory, a cornerstone of the so-called Standard Theory, now in all the physics textbooks, "was entirely unaware that something had changed" (Mukerjee, 1996:93).

If the theory of duality does not derive transparently from common sense, then presumably what converted the physics community over to it was reams of empirical data. Wrong again.

Most theorists were skeptical [about duality]. Even if duality did exist, it was thought impossible to establish: the mathematics of QCD [quantum chromodynamics] is extremely hard, and it would be necessary to calculate two sets of predictions for comparison. "In physics it's very rare that you can calculate something exactly," remarks Nathan Seiberg of Rutgers University. In February 1994, however, Ashoke Sen of the Tata Institute in Bombay, India, showed that on occasion predictions of duality could be precisely tested – and were correct.

The calculation converted the string community. "Witten went from telling everyone this was a waste of time to telling them this was the most important thing to work on," Harvey chuckles. Witten, often referred to as "the Pope" by detractors of string theory, has initiated many trends in particle physics during the past two decades. (Mukerjee, 1996:90)

Moreover, we learn, "of course, the validity of all this work hinges on the assumption that supersymmetry exists." But confirmation of this may have to wait: "Theorists pray that when the Large Hadron Collider at CERN starts operating in 2005, supersymmetry, at least, will be discovered" (p. 93).

It is probably clear by now that we are as remote as you can get from the commonsense ideas of "folk physics." The string community was converted over not by overwhelming experimental data, but by a single calculation, largely on grounds of depth of explanation:

There is an immediate, startling benefit. QCD is difficult to calculate with because quarks interact, or "couple," strongly. But monopoles interact weakly, and calculations with these are easy. Duality would allow theorists to deal with monopoles – and automatically know all the answers to QCD. "It's some kind of magical trick," Harvey says. "We don't understand yet why it should work." (Mukerjee, 1996:90)

We now pose the question "What is physical reality?" along the lines of the oft-raised question in the cognitive sciences "What is psychological reality?" The short answer is that for now it depends on the validity of Sen's calculation, the "magical trick" worked out by Seiberg and Witten, and whether or not it is found that supersymmetry exists in the year 2005. Moreover, assuming you have done all your string mathematical homework, your view of physical reality may be in for some rapid sea changes, depending on how often you log in to Los Alamos:

An explosion of activity followed [a conference on duality in March 1995] and has continued unabated. Every day scientists log on to the electronic preprint library at Los Alamos National Laboratory to find some 10 new papers in the field. "It's the first thing you do every morning," remarks Anna Ceresole of the Polytechnic of Turin. "Like reading the newspaper." (Mukerjee, 1996:91)

If Descartes were to come back today to restudy the "mind–body" problem, in particular, the "body" part, he would need to be plugged into the Internet.

Consider once more the following kinds of "reality" that we have discussed:

(1) reality (in sense of Weinberg) – the reality of wave functions, quarks, and symmetries
(2) physical reality
　　(a) "body" (Descartes)
　　(b) "objective reality" (Einstein)

(3) psychological reality
(4) neurological reality
(5) mental reality

At least the first kind of reality (1) – "X are real . . . because it is useful to include them in our theories" – is subscribed to by anyone doing work in the natural sciences. We have illustrated this with citations from Weinberg, Ruelle, and Chomsky, although many other similar views could be cited. There have been serious attempts throughout history to give arguments for an additional reality, "physical reality" (2). Two examples have been mentioned – the Cartesian interpretation of "body" in terms of contact mechanics (2a) and Einstein's attempt to resurrect a physical reality, called "objective reality," within the modern framework of quantum physics (2b). Both of these careful attempts were refuted on both experimental and theoretical grounds. As for the last three kinds of reality, "psychological reality" (3), "neurological reality" (4), and "mental reality" (5), although they have often been appealed to throughout the literature on cognitive science and philosophy of language and mind, we have argued that no coherent formulation or justification has as yet been put forth for these levels, as a level separate from (1); i.e., the ordinary scientific practice of attempting to construct explanatory theories.

THE ROLE OF MATHEMATICS IN UNIFICATION

Davis and Hersh, writing about mathematics, characterize unification as follows: "Unification, the establishment of a relationship between seemingly diverse objects, is at once one of the great motivating forces and one of the great sources of aesthetic satisfaction in mathematics" (Davis and Hersh, 1981:198). Thus there is often no way of knowing ahead of time what domains can or cannot be unified, since the relationship sought is between "seemingly diverse objects." Davis and Hersh note that this is "beautifully illustrated by the formula of Euler which unifies the trigonometric functions with the "power" or "exponential" functions:

$$e^{ix} = \cos x + i \sin x, \text{ where } i = \sqrt{-1}$$

Thus, the "exponential emerges as trigonometry in disguise" (p. 199), and vice versa.[19]

Occasionally, progress in unification proceeds in interesting ways when mathematical understanding and physical understanding get out of

---

[19] Davis and Hersh note that when one inserts π in place of x in Euler's formula, one obtains an equation "which links the five most important constants in the whole of analysis: $0, 1, e, \pi$, and i" (p. 199).

synch. Often, physical intuition comes in advance of mathematical under-standing, as the development of Fourier analysis clearly shows. But some-times mathematical understanding seems to progress more rapidly than does the comprehension of the underlying physical concepts; Witten has noted that this appears to be the current situation in string theory.

Davis and Hersh give the following example of an application of "Fourier's theorem": "To give a performance of Verdi's opera *Aida*, one could do without brass and woodwinds, strings and percussion, baritones and sopranos; all that is needed is a complete collection of tuning forks, and an accurate method for controlling their loudness" (Davis and Hersh, 1981:255). This theorem says that complex periodic functions, like those corresponding to musical sounds, can be decomposed into simpler periodic functions, as in

$$y = 7 \text{ sine } 200\pi t + 0.3 \text{ sine } 400\pi t + 0.4 \text{ sine } 600\pi t + \ldots$$

Such an expansion is known as a "Fourier series" and the coefficients 7, 0.3, 0.4, etc., which are adjusted to fit the individual sounds, are called "Fourier coefficients."

Fourier developed his theory for heat conduction, which involves equa-tions similar to those involved in sound vibration. In fact, "Fourier analy-sis" rapidly became a staple of engineering and applied physics for a variety of topics ranging from vibrating strings to solid state physics.

Hence one might find it surprising to learn that "Fourier was right, even though he neither stated nor proved a correct theorem about Fourier series" (p. 263).[20] When Fourier set out to calculate what we now call "Fourier coefficients," he did not know that Euler had already provided an elegant one-line argument to deduce the correct formula. Instead, Fourier "went through an incredible computation, that could serve as a classic example of physical insight leading to the right answer in spite of flagrantly wrong reasoning":

He started out by expanding each sine function in a power series (Taylor series), and then rearranging terms, so that the "arbitrary" function f is now represented by a power series. This already is objectionable, for the functions Fourier had in mind certainly have no such expansion in general. Nevertheless, Fourier pro-ceeded to find the coefficients in this nonexistent power-series expansion. In doing so he used two flagrantly inconsistent assumptions, and arrived at an answer involving division by a divergent infinite product (i.e., an arbitrarily large number). The only sensible interpretation one could give to this formula for the power series expansion was that all the coefficients vanish – i.e., the "arbitrary" function is identically zero. (Davis and Hersh, 1981:262)

[20] Davis and Hersh base their observations on an in-depth analysis of Fourier's writings by Langer, 1947.

As Langer noted, "Fourier had no intention whatsoever of drawing that conclusion, and hence proceeded undismayed with the analysis of his formula." He then made the conceptual leap that "every temperature distribution – or if you will, every graph, no matter how many separate pieces it consists of – is representable by a series of sines and cosines." Lines notes the reaction to this "startling pronouncement" to the French Academy in 1807:

The lack of rigor in its discussion of the infinite limit was the point of contention, and the eminent trio of French mathematical moguls of the day, Laplace, Lagrange, and Legendre, all focused on this weakness and expressed their reservations in no uncertain terms in a written report stating that "the manner in which the author arrives at his equations leaves something to be desired in the realms of both generality and rigor." (Lines, 1994:64)

Langer concludes that: "It was, no doubt, partially because of his very disregard for rigor that he was able to take conceptual steps which were inherently impossible to men of more critical genius."

It required many years and the efforts of many prominent mathematicians to provide the mathematical basis for Fourier analysis. Before it was over such mathematicians as Dirichlet, Cauchy, Hilbert, and Schwartz had gotten involved. It was Fourier series that provided the point of departure for Cantor's abstract theory of sets. However, the physicist Lines notes the theoretical problems with the foundations of Fourier analysis had little practical effect on its continued application: "It is interesting to note that the lack of rigor of Fourier's theorem during the nineteenth century, and the countless attacks upon it from the standpoint of pure mathematics, in no way prevented it being put to good use during this period by applied mathematicians and physicists" (Lines, 1994:65). Lines notes that this resulted from the different kinds of goals of pure mathematicians and applied scientists:

Once again, this is an interesting contrast of the approaches of the different disciplines. Pure mathematicians, armed with the weapon of sharp and rigid proof, tend to have little use for any alleged theorem until it can successfully withstand the severest criticism of the day. Scientists, on the other hand, are interested primarily in the interpretation of experiment, and are fully aware that absolute accuracy is never attainable in their field. For them, therefore, any mathematical "tool" that appears to assist in experimental interpretation is happily employed, and is discarded only if found to be wanting at the level of the experimental precision available. (Lines, 1994:65)

Neither Davis and Hersh, nor Langer, nor Lines are recommending shoddy mathematics as the best way to do science. What they are saying is that sometimes physical insight can and must take precedence over mathematical rigor. Exact formalization then takes a back seat to physical intuition. Heisenberg has called this "dirty mathematics": "Heisenberg later confessed that throughout his career he had used 'rather dirty mathematics,' but said that this forced him 'always to think of the experimental situation . . . [and] somehow you get closer to reality than by looking for the rigorous methods'" (Crease and Mann, 1987:428; citing Heisenberg).

Heisenberg (along with Born and Jordan) had developed the "matrix mechanics" formulation of quantum mechanics. Just as Fourier had rediscovered Euler's method for calculating Fourier coefficients, so too had Heisenberg rediscovered the mathematical theory of matrices, which Cayley had formulated many years earlier. Moreover, some "dirty mathematics" was involved: "Heisenberg, Born, and Jordan had developed their methods for a simple, two-dimensional model, then substituted three-dimensional terms in the equations, an erroneous procedure that Schrödinger, at least, had spotted" (Crease and Mann, 1987:428). However, Heisenberg and Schrödinger sharply disagreed on which approach afforded the best physical intuition of "reality": "When Schrödinger's wave equation appeared, Heisenberg reacted in a fury; he must have envisioned all his work being consigned to oblivion. He berated Born for deserting matrices and told Pauli that the wave business was so much 'crap.'"(Crease and Mann, 1987:57). Schrödinger, for his part, found the impossibility of picturing matrices to be "disgusting, even repugnant." However, the matrix method was found to be formally identical to the "wave mechanics" approach of Schrödinger.

Formalization in linguistics

Pullum has decried what he sees as the demise of "formal linguistics" since around 1979 (Pullum, 1989; reprinted in Pullum, 1991). However, he is referring to "formal linguistics" in a particular technical sense, not in the sense of biolinguistics, as we are developing it here; viz., as the attempt to study the five fundamental questions about language regarded as a biological object. As Chomsky notes, Pullum's project is "dubious if Pullum's remark is intended to suggest that there should be some 'pure' study of language isolated from discoveries about acquisition, use, and physical mechanisms" (1990:145). As for the formalization of biolinguistics (I-linguistics), Chomsky makes the following observation:

Even in mathematics, the concept of formalization in our sense was not developed until a century ago, when it became important for advancing research and understanding. I know of no reason to suppose that linguistics is so much more advanced than 19th century mathematics or contemporary molecular biology that pursuit of Pullum's injunction would be helpful, but if that can be shown, fine. For the present, there is lively interchange and exciting progress without any sign, to my knowledge, of problems related to the level of formality of ongoing work. (Chomsky, 1990:146)

The mathematician Keith Devlin has proposed the term "soft mathematics" to describe the kind of formalization that is employed in some of the sciences of mind and behavior, including linguistics. In fact, he gives the example of the linguistic formalisms used to describe phrases such as noun phrases, verb phrases, adjective phrases, prepositional phrases, etc. (Devlin, 1996a).[21] He notes that mathematics can be used not only to prove theorems, but also to gain insight into a new domain (see also Devlin, 1997): "In short, we use the process of formalization as an analytic technique. The aim is not to produce a formal theory . . . *The purpose of formalization is insight, not a formal theory*" (Devlin, 1996b).

Devlin regards "soft mathematics" as a legitimate alternative to "hard mathematics" for doing science, but he also seems to be claiming that it is a permanent state of affairs for the study of mind:

Like Plato and Aristotle before him, Descartes believed that his method, the method of science and mathematics, could be applied to the inner world of the mind as well as to the outer world of the physical universe. Four hundred years later, after decades of failures in artificial intelligence and mathematical linguistics, it would finally be realized that, in this belief, Descartes had been wrong. (Devlin, 1996b)

However, it should be noted that there has been no demonstration that Descartes' "method of science and mathematics" does not apply to the "inner world of the mind," certainly not in artificial intelligence or mathematical linguistics. "Decades of failures" do not constitute a demonstration. An alternative viewpoint might be as follows.

In the early stages of the study of any scientific discipline, whether physics or the study of mind, we try whatever works, whether that is "soft mathematics" in Devlin's sense, to gain new insight, unrigorous mathematics à la Fourier, "dirty mathematics" in Heisenberg's sense, or "hard mathematics." We know that physics moved through all of these stages, in one area or another throughout its history. We also know that unification proceeded slowly in some areas, more rapidly in others and sometimes piecemeal.

There is no reason to expect the situation to be any different for the study of mind, including biolinguistics. In the area of acoustics, a subdiscipline of biolinguistics, the "hard" mathematical machinery of Fourier

---

[21] The example he uses is "X-bar theory," which has been eliminated in the form in which he discusses it from some current linguistic theories. However, his point carries over for other formal devices used in theoretical linguistics.

analysis, is available and routinely used. In other areas, "soft mathematics" may come to be replaced by "hard mathematics." Even in areas where this happens, the "soft" abstract notation may continue to be of use. For example, Mendel's "laws," crystallographic notation, etc., continue to be useful, even after we have obtained a deeper understanding of their physical meaning. The same may well turn out to be true of linguistic notations, or other notations, developed in the study of the mind.

It may also be the case that, as unification proceeds, mathematical machinery will get carried over from one area to another; see the discussion of phyllotaxis[22] and the Fibonacci numbers in chapter 5. There it is noted how "hard mathematics" used to study "soft lattices subjected to strong deformation" might turn out to be applicable to the study of botanics.[23] In still other areas of the study of mind, including language, the development of new kinds of mathematics may be necessary, e.g., Stewart's "morphomatics":

> But that is how mathematics grew in the first place. When Newton wanted to understand planetary motion, there was no calculus, so he created it. Chaos theory didn't exist until mathematicians and scientists got interested in that kind of question. Morphomatics doesn't exist today; but I believe that some of its bits and pieces do – dynamical systems, chaos, symmetry breaking, fractals, cellular automata, to name but a few. (Stewart, 1995c:150)

On the other hand, for some areas there may be no understanding or unification at all. Certain areas may well remain shrouded in mystery, either because we're not smart enough to understand them, or because they represent problems beyond our cognitive capacity (i.e., "mysteries," not "problems," in Chomsky's sense).

Unification and methodological dualism

Earlier we noted that the study of language and other cognitive faculties has been hampered by what Chomsky has termed "'methodological dualism,' the view that we must abandon scientific rationality when we study humans 'above the neck' (metaphorically speaking);" i.e., the insistence that the mind cannot, in principle, be studied with the same methods and in the same manner as the growth of physical systems such

---

[22] Phyllotaxis includes the study of such topics as the principles governing the arrangement of leaves on a stem.

[23] This case illustrates why "decades" of failure in artificial intelligence and mathematical linguistics can't tell us anything about Descartes' vision that the "method of science and mathematics" can be applied to the study of mind. Unification can arise from quite unexpected and unpredictable sources.

as the immune system. Anyone from outside the field of biolinguistics cannot fail to be struck by the fact that the idea of a genetic endowment for language has been met with extreme resistance over the last forty years. There are probably a number of reasons for this, but an important (and understandable) one is that these ideas often go counter to commonsense ideas that people have about the nature of mind, just as the ideas of Galileo, and later Einstein, went against commonsense ideas that people have about the nature of the physical world, about space and of time.

This has had a very pernicious effect not only on linguistics, but also on other fields that investigate language, such as psychology and philosophy. We consider some examples below taken from the book *The Third Culture*, not to single it out (many other examples could be cited), but because it is illustrative of the irrational reaction that the study of the biological basis of mind seems to evoke, occasionally spilling over into ad hominem argument. In reading this it is useful to bear in mind the following comments by Chomsky:

Debates are an utterly irrational institution, which should not exist in a reasonable world. In a debate, the assumption is that each participant has a position, and must keep to this position whatever eventuates in the interchange. In a debate, it is an institutional impossibility (i.e., if it happened, it would no longer be a debate) for one person to say to the other: that is a good argument, I will have to change my views accordingly. But the latter option is the essence of any interchange among rational people. So calling it a debate is wrong to start with and contributes to ways of thinking and behaving that should be abandoned. (Piattelli-Palmarini, 1994:323)

THE THIRD CULTURE: A CASE STUDY

Steven Pinker has written that Chomsky "is currently among the ten most-cited writers in all of the humanities (beating out Hegel and Cicero and trailing only Marx, Lenin, Shakespeare, the Bible, Aristotle, Plato, and Freud) and the only living member of the top ten" (Pinker, 1994a:23). What also comes with the territory is that he gets to be one of most-misrepresented writers as well. At least this has been the case with Chomsky's views on the biological basis of language.

Let's have a look at a recent book, *The Third Culture*, which presents the views of scientists primarily from biology, physics, artificial intelligence, and the cognitive sciences; e.g., Gould, Dawkins, Gell-Mann, Penrose, Minsky, Schank, Dennett, Pinker, and many others (Brockman, 1995). And not any ordinary scientists, according to John Brockman, editor of this book, but "third-culture" scientists, "communicating directly with the general public."[24] Brockman has found that the public has "great intellectual hunger," and wants to "make the effort to educate themselves." So he has assembled a team of "third-culture thinkers" whose virtue is that they "tend to avoid the middleman and endeavor to express their deepest thoughts in a manner accessible to the intelligent reading public" (p. 18).

Flipping to the index, we find that five of our third-culture intellectuals reference Chomsky, who we recall, is "one of the most-cited authors in all of the humanities." They are Minsky, Schank, Dennett, Hillis, and Pinker. Remembering that we are here to sate our intellectual hunger and learn about the "deepest thoughts" of the third culture, we turn to Marvin Minsky, Toshiba Professor of Media Arts and Sciences at MIT and co-founder of MIT's Artificial Intelligence Laboratory, and laureate of the Japan Prize, that nation's highest distinction in science and technology. Minsky informs us that Schank, Director of the Institute for the Learning Sciences, at Northwestern University, "has been opposed and almost persecuted by the language theorist Noam Chomsky" (pp. 177–78). Wanting to "educate ourselves" further, we read on and find that it was "quite hard to persuade our colleagues [including Chomsky, presumably] to consider these kinds of theories [Schank's theory of conceptual dependency]." In this theory, Schank's technical representation of the example "Jack threatened to choke Mary unless she would give him her book" is "Jack transfers into Mary's mind the conceptualization that if she doesn't transfer the possession of the book to him, he'll cut off her windpipe, so that she won't get enough air to live" (p. 178). Minsky notes that "sometimes, it seems that the only way to get their [their colleagues'] attention is by shocking them . . . I once asked Roger why so many of his examples were so bloodthirsty. He replied, 'Ah, but notice how clearly you remember them.'"

Schank presents an account of a hypothetical argument with Chomsky: "Here's an example of an argument I might have had with him in the late sixties. The sentence 'John likes books' means that John likes to read. 'Oh no,' Chomsky might say, 'John has a relationship of liking with respect to books, but he might not like to read'" (Brockman, 1995:175). This argument is supposed to reveal to us Chomsky's "intolerant attitude" and "intellectual dirty tricks" and to show us how "Chomsky stopped people from working on meaning." Actually, Schank tells us, it wasn't Chomsky

---

[24] A reference to C. P. Snow's *The Two Cultures*, in which literary intellectuals and scientists were to merge into a new "third culture." Brockman's third culture, on the other hand, consists of scientists communicating directly to the public: "Throughout history, intellectual life has been marked by the fact that only a small number of people have done the serious thinking for everybody else. What we are witnessing is a passing of the torch from one group of thinkers, the traditional literary intellectuals, to a new group, the intellectuals of the emerging third culture" (Brockman, 1995:19).

that represented a problem for Schank, for Chomsky was "always an easy target." It was the "cadre of religious academic zealots behind him who would listen to no one else."

However, consider again Schank's example sentence, "John likes books." It is apparent that John, the rare book dealer, might very well like books, but not like to read them. This is a fact about the meaning of this English sentence that was true in "the late sixties" and it is still true "in the late nineties," and hence must be accounted for in any theory of meaning. Since it was difficult for Schank to persuade his colleagues with "technical representations," or even bloodthirsty examples, apparently he has decided to have a shot at vilifying his colleagues in public. After all, as editor Brockman notes: "Here they are communicating their thoughts to the public and to one another" (p. 20).

As we have seen, Minsky is no slouch himself in this department, but apparently feels he can learn a few tricks from his third-culture colleague, Murray Gell-Mann:

What is there to say? He (i.e., Gell-Mann) is wonderful. He's right up there with Feynman as one of the great thinkers. He knows a lot about many things, including artificial intelligence. But I think his major contribution is inventing new kinds of insults. For instance, if somebody says something that isn't exactly perfect – Murray has developed one of the best inventories of put-downs that exists. I hear he's getting mellower. That would be a terrible loss for civilization. A collection of anecdotes about his remarks about other people would be priceless. (p. 332)

We next turn to another of the third-culture computer scientists for further enlightenment, W. Daniel Hillis, Cofounder and Chief Scientist of Thinking Machines Corporation and holder of thirty-four U.S. Patents. But alas, "Growing up in the Minsky School, I was always taught to be wary of linguists, because Minsky had a very strong reaction against the Chomsky School. I would characterize that school as studying language without studying the fact that people are talking about anything" (p. 238).

But wait, there's hope! Rapidly losing our intellectual appetite at the feet of the third-culture intellectuals, we thumb through the pages of *The Third Culture* to Daniel C. Dennett, Director of the Center for Cognitive Studies and Distinguished Arts and Sciences Professor at Tufts University. Finally, we find an explanation for the "resistance to the Chomskyan view" (we've guessed by now that there may be some):

One of the motivations for resistance to the Chomskyan view was that it seemed to be invoking magic at a crucial point. At least, the behaviorists – who viewed language as something learned by a general-purpose learning mechanism – were clear that they wanted a no-nonsense, no-miracle theory of how each human being comes to have language. It's not a gift from God, it's something that has to develop, has to be designed, has to emerge from an elaborate process of R and D, as you might say. Chomsky seemed to be saying, No, it isn't learned, it's innate in the individual, just a God-given language organ. That, if you stop there, is just anathema to anybody of scientific temperament. It can't be that way. Pinker has driven that point home to people. (p. 238)

and "He [Pinker] saw the light . . . The light he saw was evolution" (p. 237). For forty years Chomsky had seemed to Dennett to be 'invoking magic' and saying that language is a gift of God. Then Pinker[25] came along in 1990 to exorcise the God-given language organ. Dennett has gone on to popularize this theme as the "Chomsky contra Darwin" debate in a book called *Darwin's Dangerous Idea*, nominated for the National Book Award.

So now this takes us to the last of the five third-culture thinkers we are surveying, Steven Pinker, Director of the McDonnell-Pew Center for Cognitive Neuroscience at MIT, the author of the best-selling *The Language Instinct*. In a commentary on Roger Penrose, Pinker states: "It's not uncommon among some kinds of scientist to be skeptical of Darwin and natural selection" (pp. 248–49).

Who are these scientists skeptical of Darwin and natural selection? Some physicists and mathematicians and Noam Chomsky, we learn. Why are they skeptical of Darwin and natural selection? Because natural selection seems a "repugnant kind of explanation . . . too kludgey . . . too ugly and weak." In an essay "Language is a Human Instinct," Pinker makes further suggestions about what Chomsky allegedly thinks about evolution (see also the discussion below).

So much for being one of the "ten most-cited writers." Of course, remember that what we are supposed to be witnessing, in Brockman's words, is "a passing of the torch from one group of thinkers, the traditional literary intellectuals, to a new group, the intellectuals of the emerging third culture," who are to do the "serious thinking for everybody else" (p. 19).

In this book, we attempt to set the record straight on what Chomsky and other linguists have actually proposed on the topic of language and biology. We explore and expand on many of these themes throughout the remainder of the book, with the aim of presenting a coherent view of the field of biolinguistics that has emerged over the last forty years and is still evolving. We believe that that work stands on its own merits and provides the most adequate answer to the extreme "third culture" misrepresentations.

As the science of biolinguistics matures, we hope that slogans like the "Third Culture," "Darwin's Dangerous Idea," and the "Chomsky contra

---

[25] With Paul Bloom (Pinker and Bloom, 1990).

Darwin" debate will fall at the wayside. Although Chomsky was not speaking of the "Chomsky contra Darwin" debate at the time, his comments on the irrationality of debates that we cited earlier are appropriate in this case as well.

Contrast this with the following ultra-Darwinian view of argumentation within academia presented by Pinker (attributed in part to references he provides):

The goal of argumentation is to make a case so forceful (note the metaphor) that skeptics are *coerced* into believing it – they are powerless to deny it while still claiming to be rational. In principle, it is the ideas themselves that are, as we say, compelling, but their champions are not always averse to helping the ideas along with tactics of verbal dominance, among them intimidation ("Clearly . . ."), threat ("It would be unscientific to . . ."), authority ("As Popper showed . . ."), insult ("This work lacks the necessary rigor for . . ."), and belittling ("Few people today seriously believe that . . ."). (Pinker, 1997b:498)

Pinker wants to make the point that "the stinging question, the devastating riposte, the moralistic outrage, the withering invective, the indignant rebuttal, and means of enforcement in manuscript reviews and grant panels" are the academics' substitute for "brandishing a switchblade" in a pool hall, and that natural selection has built us to be that way. However, we would maintain that this ultra-Darwinist model does not describe any of the argumentation that has led to real scientific ideas or breakthroughs. At best it describes argumentation in dubious science. Let us imagine that a scientist were to submit a paper on elementary particles along the lines of "clearly the proton is constituted of jelly beans" (intimidation), "it would be unscientific to suppose that quarks have fractional charges" (threat), and "Gell-Mann's work on quarks lacks the necessary rigor for . . ." (insult). These tactics are quickly weeded out once science is beyond the primitive stages. For example, it is not clear how Pinker would classify Einstein into his ultra-Darwinian schema: "Academics are known by their fellows as 'the sort who can be pushed around' and 'the sort who won't take any shit,' as people whose word means action or people who are full of hot air, as guys whose work you can criticize with impunity or guys you don't want to mess with" (Pinker, 1997b:498).

Moreover, phrases such as "Darwin's biology," not to mention "Darwin's Dangerous Idea," should be discarded as quickly as possible in favor of the kind of "cooperative enterprise," that Chomsky describes as follows:

Though the point is obvious enough, it may nevertheless be worth saying that to the extent that a subject is significant and worth pursuing, it is not personalized; and I think that the questions we are addressing are significant and worth pursuing. The topic "X's biology" – or economics, or psychology, or whatever – select X as one likes, could only have a useful sense in a primitive stage of some inquiry, a stage that one would hope would be quickly surpassed as the subject becomes a cooperative enterprise, with "X's linguistics," in our case, changing every time a journal appears, or a graduate student enters the office with some ideas to be thrashed out, or a classroom discussion leads to new understanding and fresh problems. (Chomsky, 1991a:3)

As is perhaps inevitable in a still-developing science, many of the views of biolinguists have become oversimplified through popularization or otherwise misunderstood or misrepresented. Going back to the original sources, we will set out these views as a base line for the discussion and consider the validity of objections to these ideas and note alternative lines of investigation. Since Chomsky is typically singled out as the representative arch-villain in work on the biology of language by evolutionary psychologists, ultra-Darwinists, and others, we find it necessary to present citations of his positions on various issues in the area of biology and language in an effort to set the record straight. This is not done from the point of view of setting up an authority figure for the field. For this would not be in the spirit of Chomsky's own approach to the subject, as was just noted. The contributions to the growing field of biolinguistics stem from many researchers from a wide variety of fields far beyond linguistics. We have provided numerous references on biology and language from a number of sources, some supportive, some critical, some orthogonal to the lines of research explored in this book. We hope they will serve as a starting point for the reader to continue down the many interesting paths that we did not have time to pursue.

2 Knowledge and use of language

THE FIVE FUNDAMENTAL QUESTIONS OF BIOLINGUISTICS

As already noted, since the earliest days of generative grammar five questions have been the focus of intensive research (see p. 1). Chomsky has often referred to question (1) as "Plato's problem," question (2) as "Humboldt's problem," and problem (3) "Descartes' problem," to give some indication of the rich tradition, at times forgotten, of these classic questions (Chomsky, 1991a). In addition, Descartes' problem may be a special case of the problem of explaining how it is that the human science-forming capacity sometimes yields a "partial convergence" with "our ideas and the truth about the world" (Chomsky, 1988a:158).

As Chomsky has noted, the answer to question (1), What constitutes knowledge of language? is of central importance to the study of the biology of language. This is because, to answer each of the questions (2)–(5), we have to have some idea of what the system of "knowledge" is. For example, to answer intelligently question (2), How is this knowledge acquired?, we need to know something about what knowledge the adult learner has acquired. If the computations of linguistic theory are properties of the language faculty, as will be argued, then these properties have to be accounted for somehow in a theory of language acquisition.

The same point can be made, with regard to physical mechanisms; i.e., question (4), What are the relevant brain mechanisms? To study mechanisms, you need to understand something about the computational properties of the system realized. As Chomsky says:

Now physics could not have developed the structure of the atom and the molecule if nineteenth-century chemistry hadn't provided the abstract theories. That's what told the physicists what they should look for. They had to look for things which had the very complicated properties described in the abstract theories. And the brain sciences are in the same state today. They have to ask the linguist or the psychologist what are the abstract structures that humans possess for which we have to search for the physical basis. (Chomsky, 1988a:186)

In the case of syntax, we are, of course, dealing with abstract properties of the language faculty, not directly with, say, brain circuits, but this does not affect the logic of Chomsky's point. When Mendel discovered the abstract computational laws of segregation and independent assortment, this was a contribution to the understanding of inheritance and evolutionary mechanisms, even though the physical substratum for Mendel's factors, the chromosome, was yet to be discovered. Even after the chromosome was discovered, the physical basis for Mendel's "factors," the gene, was not yet understood. For that reason much work on genetics and evolution continued to depend heavily on Mendel's (rediscovered) computational laws (Jenkins, 1979). This point also holds with regard to evolution; i.e., question (5), How does this knowledge evolve (in the species)? To study the evolution of a biological system, you need to understand something about the properties of the system that has evolved. Whatever you can find out about the abstract properties of this system is a first step on the way to understanding evolutionary mechanisms (see chapter 5). Similar remarks apply to question (3), use. Hence question (1) is logically prior to questions (4)–(5).

Modularity

We have already alluded to the "computations" of the "language faculty." So let's back up and spell out a few assumptions about the answer to question (1) in more detail. In order to study question (1), several working hypotheses have been adopted. One is the assumption of *modularity* of mind: "I am tentatively assuming the mind to be modular in structure, a system of interacting subsystems that have their own special properties" (Chomsky, 1980c:89).

A first assumption then is that there is a *language faculty*, one component of the mind/brain: "The basic concern is to determine and characterize the linguistic capacities of particular individuals. We are concerned, then, with states of the language faculty, which we understand to be some array of cognitive traits and capacities, a particular component of the human mind/brain" (Chomsky and Lasnik, 1993:506).

Chomsky has proposed thinking of the language faculty as a "mental organ," analogous to a physical organ like the heart or the visual system. Another way of putting this is to say that the brain is not a homogenous organ, but consists of subcomponents, or modules, each specialized for different purposes – vision, the number faculty, the language faculty, etc. This is because, when one studies the intrinsic properties of the language faculty, one finds principles operating that appear to be unique to that system. Moreover, when one examines the different subsystems of the language faculty (syntax, morphology,[1] phonology,[2] semantics,[3] the lexicon,[4] etc.), one finds further distinguishing properties. This picture suggests that when the brain is injured or has some disease or genetic disorder, one might find cases where one or another of these submodules is selectively impaired. For example, one might find cases where syntax is affected, but other kinds of cognition are spared (or vice versa) (Curtiss, 1981;Yamada, 1990). Or, where language production is affected, but not comprehension, and so on. And this is exactly what is found, although the effects are not always clear-cut, since the injury can have multiple effects. We introduce the idea of modularity by presenting a series of cameos, sometimes in the words of the persons affected, to provide a feel for the range of ways that the "language organ" can be affected. We will return to the theoretical issues involved below.

The language organ

Brother John (aphasia due to epileptic seizure) The first case shows how language functions can be affected by epileptic seizure (more often stroke or injury) while leaving other functions more or less intact, a condition known as *aphasia*, the loss of language due to brain disease or injury.

Brother John was a 50-year-old man who worked as an editor of letters for his religious order. He had suffered from epileptic seizures for 25 years . . . The important fact about Brother John's spells was that they selectively shut down language processing, while he remained conscious and able to remember what he was experiencing . . . During a long spell Brother John would reliably pass through a series of stages which successively resembled most of the various clinical subtypes of aphasia. He would initially manifest the symptoms of global aphasia, and after about half an hour his symptoms gradually changed, going through a period of jargonaphasia until he began to look more like a case of Wernicke's aphasia, characterized by anomias and paraphasias. As his recovery progressed, his symptoms gradually changed again, and he looked more like a conduction aphasic, while in the final few hours he was left mostly with amnestic symptoms . . . The extent to which he retained the ability to cope with practical challenges was quite remarkable. One episode, while he was traveling in Switzerland, was particularly striking. He found himself at the peak of one of his seizures as he arrived at his destination, a town he had never seen before. He took his baggage and managed to disembark. Although he could not read or speak, he managed to find a hotel and show his medic-alert bracelet to the concierge, only to be sent away. He then found another hotel, received a more sympathetic reception, communicated by

---

[1] Morphology includes the study of the internal structure of words.
[2] Phonology comprises part of the study of the sound aspect of language.
[3] Semantics is the study of the meaning aspect of language.
[4] The lexicon is the (mental) dictionary. It can be thought of as the collection of phonetic, semantic, and formal features for the lexical items (roughly, words) of a language.

mime, and was given a room. He was able to execute various procedures which formed a framework for linguistic operations; for example, he was able to point out to the desk clerk where in his passport to find the information required to fill out his registration slip, while not being able to read it himself. Finding himself too hungry and miserable to sleep, he went to the hotel restaurant. He could not read the menu, but he pointed to a line which he thought might be the hors d'oeuvres and randomly chose an item, hoping he would like it. In fact, it was a dish he detested, but he ate it, returned to his room, and slept for the remainder of his paroxysmal attack. When he awoke, he went to the hotel desk and explained the episode in detail. (Donald, 1991:83)

As Donald notes, a variety of functions were spared: coherent thought; recognition of music, voices, and faces; the uses of objects and places; spatial orientation; mechanical intelligence (he could tune a radio and operate an elevator); episodic memory, gestural ability, appropriate social behavior, etc. Moreover, his written production was largely spared. This case then illustrates a dissociation between language and other cognitive faculties.

Lyova Saletsky (loss of knowledge from bullet wound) The next case involves Lyova Saletsky, a soldier who suffered a fractured skull and brain damage from a bullet wound during the battle of Smolensk. The damage was primarily "in the posterior left hemisphere in the intersections of the occipital, temporal, and parietal cortex" (Kolb and Whishaw, 1980). Luria followed Saletsky over twenty-six years as he learned to read and write again (Luria, 1972). During this time Saletsky kept a diary, from which the following is taken:

I remember nothing, absolutely nothing! Just separate bits of information that I sense have to do with one field or another. But that's all! I have no real knowledge of any subject. My past has just been wiped out!

Before my injury I understood everything people said and had no trouble learning any of the sciences. Afterwards I forgot everything I learned about science. All my education was gone.

I know that I went to elementary school, graduated with honors from the middle school, completed three years of courses at the Tula Polytechnic Institute, did advanced work in chemistry, and, before the war, finished all these requirements ahead of time. I remember that I was on the western front, was wounded in the head in 1943 when we tried to break through the Germans' defense in Smolensk, and that I've never been able to put my life together again. But I can't remember what I did or studied, the sciences I learned, subjects I took. I've forgotten everything. Although I studied German for six years, I can't remember a word of it, can't even recognize a single letter. I also remember that I studied English for three straight years at the institute. But I don't know a word of that either now. I've forgotten these languages so completely I might just as well never have learned them. Words like *trigonometry, solid geometry, chemistry, algebra*, etc., come to mind, but I have no idea what they mean.

All I remember from my years in the secondary school are some words (like signboards, names of subjects): *physics, chemistry, astronomy, trigonometry, German, English, agriculture, music,* etc., which don't mean anything to me now. I just sense that somehow they're familiar.

When I hear words like *verb, pronoun, adverb,* they also seem familiar, although I can't understand them. Naturally, I knew these words before I was wounded, even though I can't understand them now. For example, I'll hear a word like *stop!* I know this word has to do with grammar – that it's a verb. But that's all I know. A minute later, I'm likely even to forget the word *verb* – it just disappears. I still can't remember or understand grammar or geometry because my memory's gone, part of my brain removed. (Luria, 1972:140–42)

In this case Saletsky has recovered many of his verbal skills, but large chunks of his "encyclopedic knowledge" appear to be inaccessible, if not destroyed.

Dissociation of color names from colors (color anomia) Damasio and Damasio have studied cases where a very specific ability is impaired; viz., the ability to match up color names like *red, green, blue* with the colors themselves (Damasio and Damasio, 1992). What is particularly interesting is that it can be shown that the color names themselves, as well as color recognition, are still perfectly intact in the patient:[5]

Other patients, who sustain damage in the temporal segment of the left lingual gyrus, suffer from a peculiar defect called color anomia, which affects neither color concepts nor the utterance of color words. These patients continue to *experience* color normally: they can match different hues, correctly rank hues of different saturation and easily put the correct colored paint chip next to objects in a black-and-white photograph. But their ability to put names to color is dismally impaired. Given the limited set of color names available to those of us who are not interior decorators, it is surprising to see patients use the word "blue" or "red" when shown green or yellow and yet be capable of neatly placing a green chip next to a picture of grass or a yellow chip next to a picture of a banana. The defect goes both ways: given a color name, the patient will point to the wrong color.

At the same time, however, all the wrong color names the patient uses are beautifully formed, phonologically speaking, and the patient has no other language impairment. The color-concept system is intact, and so is the word-form implementation system. The problem seems to reside with the neural system that mediates between the two.

M. D. (names of fruits and vegetables) A case of anomia, or difficulty with naming objects, that may shed some light on the organization of the lexicon, is the case of M. D. (Hart, Berndt, and Caramazza, 1985). M. D. suffered a stroke with damage to the left frontal lobe and basal ganglia. Although he was perfectly able to recall such words as

---

[5] See Davidoff, 1991, for a survey of modularity in color cognition.

abacus, protractor, sphinx, trellis, and *yoke,* he was at a total loss when trying to recall the names of fruits or vegetables (*apples, oranges,* etc.). Boxer aptly subtitled her column on this case as: "Does the Brain Have a Produce Section?" M. D. was also unable to identify the fruits and vegetables by sense of touch (Boxer, 1985). However, when given the names of the fruits and vegetables he could correctly classify them. It is as if the names play the role of "pointers" (or "key indices"), in the computer sense, without which the semantic information cannot be accessed (Marshall, 1985). What is also noteworthy is the great degree of specificity of semantic categorization in the case of M. D. (for other kinds of category-specific impairments, see McCarthy and Warrington, 1990).

      Dissociation of linguistic and emotional prosody (aprosodia) Additional evidence for modularity in the neural mechanisms underlying speech comes from the study of "aprosodias," or affective speech disorders. Ross argues that the classical left-hemisphere aphasias, such as Broca's and Wernicke's aphasias, are mirrored in the right-hemisphere by aprosodias, which involve the emotional elements of speech (Ross, 1981). Thus, corresponding to motor (Broca's) aphasia, which is (roughly) a deficit in speech production, we find "motor aprosodia" associated with damage to the homologous right-hemispheric region. In these cases the patient is unable to convey emotion appropriately (happiness, sadness, anger, etc.) by using linguistic utterances or spontaneous gestures; the voice of one patient described was flat, monotone, and emotionless even when talking about the recent shooting death of his son (p. 562). At the same time these patients can comprehend the emotional content of sentences and gestures made by the physician perfectly well. This is parallel to the case of a Broca's aphasic who can comprehend the propositional content of linguistic utterances, but is unable to produce fluently such utterances.

      Corresponding to sensory (Wernicke's) aphasia, a deficit in speech comprehension, "sensory aprosodia" is found, again associated with damage to the homologous right-hemispheric region. However, in these patients prosody and spontaneous gesturing are normal (although perhaps semantically mismatched); but they show poor comprehension of these affective elements (p. 565). This corresponds to the case of the Wernicke's aphasic who is unable to correctly comprehend utterances although he or she may produce syntactically fluent structures (though again often with inappropriate semantic content).

      Ross provides further clinical evidence that a number of additional kinds of left-hemisphere aphasias are mirrored by aprosodias in the homologous areas in the right hemisphere.[6] An interesting question for biolinguistic theory is what happens in the case of aprosodic patients who speak tone languages such as Chinese. The study of linguistic tone, part of the field of linguistics known as phonology, has revealed principles of organization which appear to have a significant genetic component (Goldsmith, 1995). Is linguistic tone affected any differently from emotional tone contours in aprosodic patients? Hughes, Chan, and Su studied eleven Chinese patients with aprosodia (with deficits in the expression and comprehension of such emotional states as sadness, happiness, anger, surprise, and neutral emotional content) and examined linguistic tone in these patients and in seven controls (Hughes, Chan, and Su, 1983). Only five of the patients showed a mild deficit in detecting semantic tonal variation in Chinese; the authors conclude, "all of our subjects, even those who had considerable difficulty comprehending affective prosody, performed reasonably well in identifying the tones in Mandarin that indicated different meanings for the same phoneme . . . Aprosodia from right-hemisphere lesions is apparently independent of propositional linguistic structure" (Hughes, Chan, and Su, 1983:736).

The picture that thus emerges is again a modular one, with propositional language lateralized in the one hemisphere (usually the left) and affective language in the opposite hemisphere (usually the right), with a striking correlation between the submodules in either hemisphere mediating comprehension, production, gestures, etc.[7]

Chromosome aberrations Occasionally there are reports of chromosome disorders where some aspect of language appears to be differentially affected. Bitoun et al. report the case of a five-year-old girl

---

[6] The "Broca-type" aprosodia was first described in Ross and Mesulam, 1979, and the "Wernicke-type" aprosodia in Heilman, Scholes, and Watson, 1975, and Tucker, Watson, and Heilman, 1977. In addition, Ross has clinically identified aprosodias corresponding to global aphasia, transcortical motor aphasia, transcortical sensory aphasia, mixed transcortical aphasia and global aphasia without alexia. In the latter syndrome, which Ross names "motor aprosodia with pure prosodic deafness," only emotional gestures are spared so that if the patient sees the examiner he has minimal difficulties with prosodic comprehension, but poor comprehension when the examiner stands behind him and speaks. Aprosodic homologues for conduction aphasia and anomic aphasia had not been observed at the time of the report.

Interesting additional support for these ideas comes from blood flow studies by Larsen, Skinhøj, and Lassen (1978), who noted that during automatic speech, blood flow increased not only in the speech areas in the left hemisphere, but also in the homologous regions on the right, an observation consistent with the data above, but which was puzzling at the time, since language was considered to be primarily a left-sided brain function. For additional discussion of these issues, see Heilman and Satz, 1983.

[7] For a recent review of these issues, see Ross, 1993.

with type I Incontinentia pigmenti, an X-linked dominant disorder, lethal in males. Although this syndrome includes skin pigmentation, tooth, eye, central nervous system and skeletal anomalies, it is also typically associated with language problems: "Language investigation showed a language dysphasia with age appropriate development in all mental functions except for verbal language where a specific severe expressive language dysfunction (she only said two words) was noted with near normal language comprehension and normal cognitive functions" (Bitoun et al., 1992). One of the interesting things about this case, and others like it, is that it is associated with an apparently balanced translocation between some autosome (in this case, chromosome 5) and the X chromosome; i.e., the two chromosomes have presumably recombined in such a way as to interrupt some important gene function(s) at the breakpoint. The known location of the breakpoint provides a backdoor for the geneticist to zero in on this region and study its connection with the language problems as well as with the skin pigmentation problems. We return to this case and others in chapter 4.

Modularity of language and mind

In linguistics the view of the brain as a *tabula rasa* for language has been superseded by the view that the brain consists of highly specialized language areas and/or circuits. This view is implicit in the work of the founders of the modern era of language neurology – Broca and Wernicke – and is argued for quite persuasively in recent times by Geschwind and others (Geschwind, 1974). The idea is also central to the work of Chomsky and modern generative grammarians; viz., the view that language is an "organ" like the heart, or more precisely, that the diffuse concept of language can be replaced with the more precise concept of "I-language" with its various subcomponents of syntax, phonology, and logical form, with some neural realization. Marshall has termed this view of linguistics "the new organology" (Marshall, 1980:23).

Geschwind notes the potential pitfall for the neurologist that arises when one attempts to localize higher functions such as language by studying syndromes that result from damage to the brain, where different disorders can result from what appear to be the same lesion (or when different lesions produce similar disorders) (Geschwind, 1974). He observes that geneticists were confronted with essentially the same problem when trying to "localize" physical characteristics (such as height, eye-color, etc.) on chromosomes after the latter had been discovered:

The "localizationist" approach to genetics has many of the same potential problems as a localizationist approach to the higher functions. Where is the gene for
philoprogenitiveness, and does it control the size of a cortical region subserving
this characteristic? Clearly it is not reasonable to expect that every nameable
feature will have a chromosomal or a cortical localization. Yet this does not mean
that certain other aspects of behavior could not be shown to depend critically on a
specific gene or a specific site in the nervous system. (Geschwind, 1974:431)

Note that modularity may be found at each biological level of description;
e.g., at the level of the modules of cognitive function (language, face recognition, etc.) such as Chomsky discusses or at the level of anatomical
structures of the brain, or even at the level of organization of cell structure
in individual neurons (compare the discussion of organelles below).
However, in general there need not be any simple mapping from the set of
modules at one level to the set of modules at some other level. Hence, as
Geschwind notes, we cannot expect every nameable feature; e.g., each
theoretical linguistic construct, to correspond in some obvious way to a
particular cortical location or gene. The same kinds of considerations
hold with regard to postulation of a "syntax center." Hence, although it is
theoretically possible that there is a well-defined cortical (or other) region
of the brain corresponding to the theoretical linguist's "syntactic component," it is just as possible in theory that such a component corresponds
to the intersection of several such regions, or even to no anatomically
well-defined region, but rather results from the complex interaction of
diverse neural circuits.[8] The second possibility is explicitly noted in the
study by Rothi, McFarling, and Heilman, who conclude that "it remains
possible that many peri-Sylvian areas are critical (i.e., Broca's area, foot of
sensorimotor cortex, insula, supramarginal gyrus, and perhaps
Wernicke's area) for the comprehension of syntax" (Rothi, McFarling,
and Heilman, 1982:275).[9]

We have no neurology of UG to draw from, but we can perhaps illustrate the point about modularity of neural structures with a few examples
from research on the neurology of the processing of linguistic commands.
Consider the act of smiling (or laughing) on linguistic command:

---

[8] Exactly the same qualification must be kept in mind in the case of the use of the term "language organ," which need not be exclusively identified with any particular localized area
(e.g., Broca's area, Wernicke's area, etc.), but must be understood to include neural language circuitry with a possibly quite complex topological distribution. The same is also
true in the case of such organs as the well-defined human heart which is only a subpart of
a complex circulatory network of arteries and vessels which themselves interact with still
other systems.

[9] However, the authors themselves favor a hypothesis that accords a more central role to the
supramarginal gyrus in the comprehension of syntax.

smile(laugh)! Is the neurological process for carrying out this action identical to the one which produces spontaneous smiling at a joke or even some nonverbal situation? In other words, is the algorithm for smiling homogeneous? Or are there separate processes for smiling in the brain, one for smiling on linguistic command and another for pragmatic or situational contexts? In this case, there turns out to be some evidence for the nonhomogeneous (or modular) solution.

Geschwind cites neurological research which strongly suggests that the process for smiling on linguistic command is separate from the algorithm for smiling at a joke or in response to a nonverbal situation (Geschwind, 1983b:125–27). He notes that most people have great difficulty in producing a natural smile (even more so with a laugh) upon linguistic command. This is so because the language area does not contain any program for executing smiles which would enable the motor cortex to control the facial muscles in the appropriate way and with the correct timing to produce a smile. Hence the smile we produce is usually an artificial one, like any attempt to execute a poorly learned motor skill would be. On the other hand, a joke or humorous situation stimulates a part of the limbic area of the brain which in turn triggers an innate algorithm for smiling in another subcortical area of the brain so that an appropriate smile is produced. It appears, however, that this algorithm cannot be directly accessed from the language areas.

Experimental demonstration of this phenomenon comes from neurological patients. Patients with a stroke paralyzing half of their faces often cannot produce a smile on the paralyzed side upon linguistic command, but are able to do so in response to a joke, since, in the latter case, the smile is under control of the subcortical algorithm. Still other patients exhibit the reverse situation; they can produce full smiles upon linguistic command, but smile with only one half of their face when amused. In this case, the motor cortex is undamaged, but the subcortical area with the innate smiling program has unilateral damage.

The preceding discussion of the neurological mechanisms of smiling is only one example of many kinds of linguistic modularity one finds in the brain. It has been known since the late nineteenth century that mechanisms for speech comprehension (*Wernicke's area*) are cortically distinct from those for speech production (*Broca's area*). Studies by Imura and others suggest that the cortical location of Japanese syllabic orthography (*Kana*) may be distinct from the cortical location of Japanese ideographic orthography (*Kanji*) (Geschwind, 1972). Ojemann has reported electrical stimulation studies of a bilingual speaker in English and Greek in which the site for the naming of pictures of objects in English was differentially affected by stimulation from the site for naming in Greek

(Ojemann, 1983). Dennis and Whitaker found that Sturge–Weber children that had had their left hemispheres removed due to a congenital malformation had difficulty using certain complex grammatical constructions at the age of ten, indicating that the right hemisphere is less suited than the left hemisphere for certain grammatical tasks (Dennis and Whitaker, 1976). See discussion in Calvin and Ojemann, 1994:189.

Poizner, Klima, and Bellugi (1987) provide important insight into questions of modularity of language in their investigations of sign-language. The question has arisen as to whether sign-language (e.g., American Sign Language, used by the deaf in the US) has as its primary substrate the left hemisphere (the dominant hemisphere for spoken language) or the right hemisphere (the dominant hemisphere for visuospatial relations such as mapping) or both. They investigated six signers with brain damage, three with damage to the left hemisphere and three with damage to the right hemisphere. They found impairment to signing in the patients with left hemisphere damage, but not in the cases with right hemisphere damage (although the latter had deficits in visuospatial relations). Hence even though sign-language heavily depends on visual gestures and 3–D spatial organization of signs, the fact that the underlying function of the signing system is language determines its physical substrate: "Taken together these data suggest that the left cerebral hemisphere in humans may have an innate predisposition for the central components of language, independent of language modality" (Poizner, Klima, and Bellugi, 1987:212).

We observe that the study of linguistics does not necessarily tell us anything about these surprising kinds of neuroanatomical modularity. Nothing in UG or pragmatics tells us that Broca's area is usually above and in front of the left ear and Wernicke's area is above and behind the left ear. Nor can it predict where on the cortex Japanese *Kanji* or Dutch as a second language will end up. Or that the left hemisphere is the primary home for both spoken and signed language. Studies of aphasics, electrical stimulation mapping, imaging, etc. are appropriate ways to investigate anatomic modularity, whereas poverty of stimulus (see chapter 3) provides a probe to study questions of modularity of grammar (a modularity which may ultimately be more evident in the organization of neural circuits rather than in gross anatomy). Hence UG and neuropsychology provide complementary tools to shed light on the organization of the brain.

Others, however, seem to regard UG and neuropsychology as alternative, perhaps even mutually exclusive, approaches to the study of language. Zaidel recasts what he calls the "fundamental" question in this regard from "What is the description of a theoretical device that generates all and only the sentences of a language" to "What neural process under-lies language processing in the brain?" or the even narrower question of what neural events lead from verbal perception to pointing (Zaidel, 1980:292). As just noted, however, these are complementary, not alterna-tive, pursuits. Personal interest, the amount of time available for research, hunches about what might be fruitful lines of investigation, etc. dictate whether one does poverty of stimulus experiments on Japanese syntax, or split-brain experiments or some other experiment. But the long-range task of biolinguistics is to pursue, interpret, and reconcile the findings of both UG and neuropsychology. Zaidel states that "adapting the Cartesian argument from the poverty of the stimulus, Chomsky has sought to dem-onstrate the innateness of linguistic knowledge by analogy to physical growth" (p. 293), but that the analogy is only partly correct.

In the first place an analogy never demonstrates anything; it provides at most a plausibility argument. It is the argument from poverty of the stim-ulus which demonstrates the innateness of linguistic knowledge, as noted earlier. As for the correctness of the analogy to physical growth, Zaidel notes there "seems to be no analogy in the growth of the human body to cross-linguistic differences." However, as we discuss in chapter 3, cross-linguistic variation finds a reasonable analogy in the variation of organs; i.e., variation is clearly present in all bodily organs; e.g., in the brain, in the immune system, in the liver, etc. Thus it is at least a reasonable possibility that the fixation of parameters which give rise to the cross-linguistic differences correspond to the environmental specification of yet unknown genetically given neural mechanisms of development.

Zaidel also argues that the fact that second languages may have different neurological substrates than first languages (and perhaps even first languages among themselves) "perturb[s] the strong concept of a biologically determined universal grammar in the sense that different lan-guages may be represented by biologically (cortically) distinct mecha-nisms" (p. 293). However, we are unfamiliar with any study on UG which insists on this "strong concept." Rather as we noted, UG is consistent with all the examples of neuroanatomical modularity given above. Poverty of stimulus studies do not suffice to specify the neural organiza-tion of language; this is a task for neuropsychology, aphasiology, and many other disciplines.

Nor does UG rely on what Zaidel calls "a strong version of a neuro-psychological criterion for linguistic universality" which "posits that two linguistic structures are the same if and only if they are neuroanatomically identical" (p. 291). For example, evidence reviewed by Geschwind indi-cates that such imperative structures as *look up*, *close your eyes*, and *bow* appear to be subserved by neuroanatomical structures which are distinct from those underlying such similar structures as *make a fist*, *salute*, and *kick*. This can be seen in apraxic patients who can perform axial movements involving the trunk of the body (*bow*, etc.) but not movements involving the individual limbs (*kick*, *make a fist*, etc.) (Geschwind, 1975). It turns out that the execution of each class of commands is to a large extent under the control of separate neuroanatomical systems; movements of the individual limbs are under the control of the pyramidal system, whereas the axial movements are under the control of the nonpyramidal system. As Geschwind notes, there do not appear to be any linguistic grounds on which to base such a distinction. That is, in linguistic competence, the rules for imperative (command) structures do not reflect the performance distinction axial/non-axial in the way that phonetic rules for high and low vowels sometimes reflect the physical organization of the articulatory tract. The imperative structures "close your eyes" and "make a fist" are (linguistically) the same in the relevant respects (imperative structures), even if the corresponding instructions to execute the commands are handled differently by the performance systems (which dispatch them along different neuroanatomical pathways). Examples like this show that Zaidel's "strong version ... for linguistic universality" must be weakened. So again, we find a case where UG is consistent with, although neutral to, the choice of a particular modular picture of neuroanatomical organization

Language

In order to answer question (1), "What constitutes knowledge of language?," it is first necessary to say what is meant by "language." It makes sense to regard the mind/brain as a set of interacting modules, including the language faculty, the number faculty, the visual system, etc., as was suggested by the case studies in the earlier discussion of modularity. Some of the evidence for distinguishing a language faculty comes from studies of the dissociation of language abilities from other abilities, but perhaps primarily from the demonstration of the intrinsic properties in the language faculty (the principles-and-parameters model, discussed in chapter 3). We also set aside the study of such issues as free will and causation of behavior (Descartes' problem).

We next identify a cognitive system in the language faculty, abstracting away from performance systems; viz., C–I, the conceptual–intentional component, and A–P, the articulatory–perceptual component. The cognitive system passes through a series of intermediate states $(S_0 \ldots S_i \ldots S_n)$. We can distinguish an initial state, S_0, from a final state, S_n, by the study of a wide range of judgments, including the argument from poverty of the stimulus (see chapter 3). We can identify the intermediate states, S_i, by acquisition studies in children, using similar kinds of evidence. Abstracting away from gross pathology as well as individual variation, the theory of the initial state is represented by the principles-and- parameters model of UG. During acquisition the parameters in UG are set, resulting in a system called "I-language," or simply "language," in the final state of the adult. I-language is not identical to the final state, S_n, but abstracts away from factors such as heterogeneity (multiple dialects, speech registers, etc.) as well as historical factors:

Two fundamental problems, then, are to determine, for each individual (say, Jones) the properties of the steady state that Jones's language faculty attains, and the properties of the initial state that is a common human endowment. We distinguish between Jones's *competence* (knowledge and understanding) and his *performance* (what he does with that knowledge and understanding). The steady state constitutes Jones's mature linguistic competence. (Chomsky and Lasnik, 1993:507)

"Psychological reality"

A subject of continued discussion is the "psychological reality" of linguistic constructs; i.e., are phonological segments, traces, syntactic representations, etc. real? Similar discussions have arisen in every science. Biologists asked whether Mendel's laws were "real" or whether they were only arcane algebraic computations (Jenkins, 1979). Physicists have always worried about whether atoms, neutrinos, quarks, etc. were "real" or not, right up to present times.[10] Lavenda reminds us that only eighty years ago not even the physical reality of the atom had won universal acceptance: "The German physicist Wilhelm Ostwald still regarded atoms as merely "a hypothetical conception that affords a very convenient picture" of matter. Ernst Mach maintained that all theoretical entities, including atoms and molecules, must be treated as convenient fictions" (Lavenda, 1985:77).

Einstein, on the other hand, took a "realist" view of the atom and came up with an atomic theory of Brownian motion and an equation which made it possible to measure the mass of the atom for the first time, which Perrin calculated, "the final blow to those who remained skeptical about the atomic theory." The neutrino was also thought by many to be a "convenient fiction," only an imaginary bookkeeping device to make energy conservation come out right. But physicists came to accept it as they were gradually able to explain a wider range of data (about pions, etc.), even

---

[10] See the discussion on the "reality of quarks" in chapter 1.

before there was any direct experimental confirmation of the particle itself.

A closely related question is that of the "psychological reality" of theories of (universal) grammar (Chomsky, 1976). Here psychological reality is understood as something like having the properties of real-time processing mechanisms. Since theories of (universal) grammar are formal systems describing structures which abstract away from real-time processes,[11] it has been claimed that they are somehow not "psychologically real." However, the standard assumption in linguistics has always been that the theory of the language faculty must be embedded in a real-time theory of speech synthesis, perception, parsing, and the like in accordance with the modularity viewpoint; for various proposals, see Berwick, Abney, and Tenny, 1992; Berwick and Weinberg, 1983; Berwick and Weinberg, 1984.

The situation is quite similar in molecular biology, as is seen by considering the study of proteins. One may study either their structure; i.e., determine the sequence of amino acids that make up their linear sequence. Or one may study their kinetics; i.e., the real-time chemical processes (reaction rate, etc.) that they enter into in a biologically active cell. Note that the experimental determination of the structure and that of the kinetics of proteins are largely independent of one another; i.e., we can determine protein sequence without reference to kinetics, and conversely. Furthermore, just looking at the sequence of a protein won't reveal its real-time kinetics. This depends on its three-dimensional configuration in a particular medium (its normal cellular or artificial test tube environment). Conversely, knowing the kinetic behavior of a protein won't allow one to deduce its sequence; the latter must be determined by other chemical sequencing methods. Nonetheless the kinetic behavior of a protein is intimately connected with its sequence. For example, the biological activity of insulin crucially depends on the placement of its two disulfide bonds which in turn both depend on the location of the amino acid cysteine at a particular place in the protein sequence.

---

[11] The fact that linguistic theory assumes a significant abstraction from the data should be no objection in itself. Even in extremely successful physical theories a high degree of abstraction is usually, if not always, present. For example, Dyson has noted that mathematical group theory, which has led to some of the best-known success stories in high-energy physics, such as the famous "eightfold way," the theory which correctly predicted the existence of the omega-minus baryon (independently formulated by Gell-Mann and Ne'eman), explains the facts relating to "abstract symmetry alone," but not the "messier facts of life, the numerical values of particle lifetimes and interaction strengths – the great bulk of quantitative experimental data that is now waiting for explanation" (Dyson, 1964:146). This case of abstraction from data is another situation in which one could apply Chomsky's rule of thumb that one need not impose more strict methodological requirements on linguistics than would be imposed in the more successful physical sciences.

Hence, knowing the sequence of a protein is analogous to knowing the grammatical structure(s) of a sentence, while understanding protein kinetics is analogous to understanding real-time mechanisms. Now let us ask: if we can determine the structure of proteins, but have not yet learned how to study their kinetics, is our theory about proteins "physiologically real?" The answer seems to be that our theory is perfectly real as far as it goes, but that the behavior of proteins depend on other theories as well; viz., as we now know in retrospect, it depends on theories of protein folding and 3–D configurations in ionic media.

Another similar kind of criticism has been made against such linguistic idealizations as the "ideal speaker-listener" in a "homogeneous speech-community" (Chomsky, 1980c:24–26).[12] For example, Lieberman remarks:

> The trend of modern molecular biology in recent years has been to stress the genetic variations that make up natural populations. Human linguistic ability, insofar as it is based on innate information, must be subject to the same variation as other genetically transmitted biological traits. Thus there cannot be any speaker or hearer in a population who has the grammar of Chomsky's ideal speaker-hearer. (Lieberman, 1984:14)

Lieberman concludes that there can't be an ideal speaker-hearer in any real population because grammar, like any other biological trait, is subject to genetic variation and hence will vary throughout a given population. Note that the actual *existence* of the ideal speaker-hearer in the real world is not really at issue here any more than the actual existence of an "ideal gas" ever was for physicists. The important question is whether such abstractions are useful for understanding grammar on the one hand or gases on the other. As nicely put by Eigen and Winkler, such an idealiza-tion "applies to language in the same way that thermodynamics does to the weather" (Eigen and Winkler, 1983:269).

An instructive example in this regard is the move from classical Mendelian genetics to population genetics, where use is made of idealiza-tions such as "Mendelian population." Note that "Mendelian popula-tion" itself is an abstraction, just like "homogeneous speech community." It is assumed that such a population is randomly breeding and is static; i.e., not undergoing evolution (Goodenough, 1978:750). Although real populations may, and in general will, deviate from this ideal, one can, nevertheless, derive useful generalizations about gene frequencies in pop-

---

[12] The full quotation originally from Chomsky, 1965 with the terms in question follows:

> Linguistic theory is concerned primarily with an ideal speaker-listener, in a completely homogeneous speech-community, who knows its language perfectly and is unaffected by such grammatically irrelevant conditions as memory limitations, distractions, shifts of attention and interest, and errors (random or characteristic) in applying his knowledge of the language in actual performance. (p. 3)

ulations such as the Hardy–Weinberg Theorem.[13] Population geneticists were able to show that one could explain things about populations without losing any insights gained from classical Mendelian theory. Although the latter theory was concerned with individuals rather than populations, it wasn't necessary to throw out the baby with the bath water in order to talk about populations. The laws of one level were compatible with those of the next. Moreover, the mathematical models for population genetics can and have been modified to take the effects of evolution into account. Analogously, corresponding to the levels of classical and population genetics, we can distinguish between two levels (among others) in the study of language: (1) "classical" linguistics and (2) the linguistics of social discourse. At the first level we have the principles of UG and, at the next level up, the sociolinguistic level, we would expect to find other, perhaps quite different, laws (of social interaction, discourse, etc.) holding.

Lieberman goes so far as to say that "there *cannot be* any speaker or hearer in a population who has the grammar of Chomsky's ideal speaker-hearer" [emphasis ours]. When discussing genes, geneticists often use the term "wild-type" to refer to the normal unmutated gene allele which is often found in nature. However, it may well be the case that no existing organism has all and only the set of what geneticists would term the "wild-type" genes. There is considerable heterogeneity among individuals in the wild population. However, no geneticist would maintain that "there *cannot be* any individual in a population who has all the wild-type genes"; i.e., it is not biologically impossible for an organism to have all the normal, unmutated gene variants, it is just statistically rare or nonexistent in practice. Similarly, a real gas might exhibit behavior closely approximating an ideal gas under (perhaps rare) special conditions.

Lieberman is actually raising two independent questions in the citation above. The first question, which we have been discussing, concerns the ideal speaker-hearer, and is about variation across a given speech community (e.g., an English-speaking community); i.e., it is about the "final state" of the speakers. The second question is whether there is genetic variation across the species in linguistic ability (e.g., UG). This question pertains to the "initial state" of the speaker. The two questions are in part independent since even if we assume that all the members of the speech

---

[13] The Hardy–Weinberg Theorem, also sometimes called the Hardy–Weinberg Law or Hardy–Weinberg Equilibrium, states that in a freely interbreeding population, equally divided as to sex, where we have (in the simplest case) only a gene A (with frequency p) and an allele a (with frequency q = 1–p), the frequencies of the gene combinations AA, Aa and aa are given by

$$p^2 : 2pq : q^2$$

(Medawar and Medawar, 1978: 46)

community have the same set of genes (e.g., they are all identical clones), and hence have the same UG, we might still observe considerable variation in their final state due to variations in environmental input (order of presentation of data, frequency effects, random fluctuations, etc.). As to the question of variation in UG across the species, we note that we might find some variation, subject to the empirical constraint that humans can apparently learn other languages quite well (at least to a first approximation), if they make the switch to another speech community at an early enough age. See chapter 4 for further discussion of such linguistic variation. This would also be completely consistent with Lieberman's observation that "human linguistic ability . . . must be subject to the same variation as other genetically transmitted biological traits" (1984:14).

Lieberman at the same time recognizes that such variation is not without limit:

Some biological properties of language may indeed be present in almost all "normal" human beings, but we can determine what these central properties are only if we study the total range of variation in linguistic behavior. Greenberg's [1963] studies of linguistic universals are therefore convincing since they are derived from the study of actual variations between different languages. Jakobson's [1940] discussion of the hierarchy of phonological universals again was convincing because it attempted to account for variations in linguistic behavior. The details of Jakobson's theory probably are not correct, but the basic premises are in accord with the principles of modern biology. (Lieberman, 1984:14)

Lieberman's insistence that one must study "the total range of variation" of a trait to determine its "central properties" excludes from study almost all of biology. Geneticists can study "the relationship of genotype to phenotype across an environmental range" or "norm of reaction" (Griffiths et al., 1993:17). For example, they may ask how eye-size varies with temperature in both wild-type flies and mutants. However, it is impractical to collect data for anything close to the "total range of variation"; i.e., the effects of all relevant environmental variables for all variations of the genotype, even leaving aside the question of "random developmental noise" (p. 15). Griffiths et al. note that human genetics faces additional ethical hurdles:

To carry out such a [norm of reaction] experiment, we must be able to obtain or produce many fertilized eggs with identical genotypes. For example, to test a human genotype in 10 environments, we would have to obtain genetically identical sibs and raise each individual in a different milieu. Obviously, that is possible neither biologically nor socially. At the present time, we do not know the norm of reaction of any human genotype for any character in any set of environments. Nor is it clear how we can ever acquire such information without the unacceptable manipulation of human individuals. (p. 13)

Of course, in practice, biologists are still able to learn about the "central properties" of traits in organisms, by studying the wild-type trait along with whatever information on variation is available for the trait under investigation.

Presumably the "basic premises" of the theory Lieberman (1984) is criticizing, "the transformational, generative school of linguistics" (p. viii), are not "in accord with the principles of modern biology" because such "studies of linguistic universals" are not based on the "study of actual variations between different languages" (p. 14). Despite what Lieberman's bibliography (which extends to 1982) would lead one to believe, there has been much work on variation across languages in the generative principles-and-parameters framework that we have been presupposing. Moreover, a number of principled arguments in favor of a principles-and-parameters-type approach to UG over Greenberg's taxonomic studies of surface word order have been presented (Coopmans, 1984; Lightfoot, 1991). Moreover, there have also been interesting attempts to incorporate "the hierarchy of phonological markedness" in the Jakobsonian sense that Lieberman talks about into generative studies of phonology and language acquisition; see Berwick, 1982, and Kean, 1974, on the "Kean hierarchy."

Continuing to assume the standard idealizations of grammars as mental objects, we note that there is some suggestive neurological evidence bearing on the issue of the dissociation of grammar from communicative and social situations. Huber observes that German-speaking aphasics often use personal pronoun forms like *du* ("you") reserved for intimate situations rather than the polite forms like *Sie* ("you") appropriate to formal situations (e.g., as in the doctor–patient relationship) (Huber, 1978). However, these patients do not switch from formal to intimate nonverbal behavior. He also notes that global aphasics are able to converse strikingly well even without lexical output by using symbolic gestures, mimic, and emotional and performative intonation contours carried by neologistic utterances such as /dadada . . ./, /titu. . . titu . . ./ and /piteli . . . piteli . . ./ (Stachowiak et al., 1977). Moreover, patients with severe global and Wernicke's aphasia who are unable to distinguish lexical content can recognize the performative function of intonation contours; i.e., they can distinguish commands, questions, and declaratives (Boller and Green, 1972; Green and Boller, 1974). Such evidence may suggest that different neurological mechanisms underlie the nonverbal strategies used to converse in communicative and social situations and hence provide some support for the view of modularity in this domain as well.

3   Acquisition (growth) of language

ACQUISITION

Principles-and-parameters model

Chomsky has proposed a "principles-and-parameters" model of language acquisition, which represents the first steps towards an account of the genetic basis of grammar (Chomsky, 1981, 1986, 1988a, 1993).[1] The principles refer to conditions specified by the linguist's theory of universal grammar and are assumed to be part of man's biological endowment, a *Bauplan* for human language.[2] The parameters are variables left open in the statement of the principles which account for the diversity found in human languages. The goal of the biolinguist interested in question (2) (p. 1), How is knowledge of language acquired?, is to come up with the formulation of genetic principles of UG narrowly enough constrained to account for the child's ability to learn structural properties of grammar of great subtlety from impoverished linguistic data, and at the same time, find parameters which can account for the manifest variation among, say, Germanic or Romance languages, or between these and non-Indo-European languages. As Chomsky remarks

These subsystems are not genetically preprogrammed down to the last detail. If they were, there would be only one human language. But heredity does set rather narrow limits on the possible ways that the rules governing each subsystem's function can vary. Languages like English and Italian, for example, differ in their choice of genetically permitted variations that exist as options in the universal grammar. You can think of these options as a kind of linguistic menu containing mutually exclusive grammatical possibilities.

[1] We use the principles-and-parameters model for discussion here and below for concreteness and because there are a number of in-depth studies now available based on this approach to language acquisition. But our comments on issues involving the biological basis of language acquisition are by no means restricted to this approach. Any approach to language acquisition has to deal with both the universality of language as well as its diversity, so our comments extend to any model dealing with language acquisition.

[2] *Bauplan* is a German term for the body plan of an organism. It is used here for the fundamental design of human languages, as specified by the theory of UG.

For example, languages like Italian have chosen the "null subject" option from the universal-grammar menu: In Italian you can say *left* when you mean "He left" or "She left." English and French have passed up this option and chosen instead the rule that requires explicit mention of the subject. (Chomsky, 1983:411)[3]

Part of the study of language acquisition is to determine what the set of parameters are that are found on the "universal-grammar menu." Another candidate is word-order:

In English the most important element in every major grammatical category comes first in its phrase. In simple sentences, for example, we say *John hit Bill*, not *John Bill hit*. With adjectives we say *proud of John* not *John of proud*; with nouns we say *habit of drinking wine*, not *drinking wine of habit*; and with prepositions we say *to John*, not *John to*. Because heads of grammatical categories always come first, English is what is called a head-initial language.

Japanese is a head-final language. In Japanese you say *John Bill hit*. And instead of prepositions, there are postpositions that follow nouns: *John to*, rather than *to John*. So here's another parameter the child's got to learn from experience: Is the language head-initial or head-final? (Chomsky, 1983:411)

Hence, a particular (I-)language,[4] such as English, is determined by a collection of parametric choices:

The grammar of English is the collection of choices – head-initial rather than head-final, and null subject forbidden, for example – that define one of a limited number of genetically permitted selections from the universal-grammar menu of grammatical options. And of course there are all the lexical facts. You just have to learn your language's vocabulary. The universal grammar doesn't tell you that *tree* means "tree" in English.

But once you've learned the vocabulary items and fixed the grammatical parameters for English, the whole system is in place. And the general principles genetically programmed into the language organ just churn away to yield all the particular facts about English grammar. (Chomsky, 1983:412)

Finally, it is important to note that the choice of one parameter may have an effect on the operation of parameters that are fixed later; i.e., "a slight change in just one of the universal grammar's parameters can have enormous repercussions throughout the language. It can produce an entirely different language."

The study of principles and parameters in language is much like that undertaken by the developmental biologist, who seeks to find the mechanisms of gene control or other cellular mechanisms in an effort to explain the differentiation of the zygote (fertilized egg) into its final state. As Chomsky has noted, "The gene-control problem is conceptually similar

---

[3] This is from a reprinted version of the original *Omni* interview by John Gliedman (Gliedman, 1983).

[4] Recall that "grammar" refers to the linguist's theory of I-language, while "universal grammar" refers to the linguist's theory of the initial state.

to the problem of accounting for language growth. In fact, language development really ought to be called *language growth*, because the language organ grows like any other body organ" (Chomsky, 1983:407). By "gene-control problem," Chomsky is referring to "the ways that genes regulate embryological development." Although the study of the language growth problem is in its early stages and is in part based on the study of abstract formal properties, as was Mendelian genetics initially, the ultimate aim is an explication of the mechanisms underlying language.

As we have already noted, human language is not entirely genetically pre-programmed. As Hubel puts it: "This is not to say that other regions of cortex are necessarily wired without benefit of experience. Most neurologists would guess that the circuits responsible for language are mainly cortical – and no one would contend that we are born knowing the details of our native tongues" (Hubel, 1988:216–17). As we saw, in English, the verb precedes the object (*John saw Mary*), whereas, in Japanese, the verb follows the object. This property is a candidate for being a language-specific "parameter."

Languages like English, which have movement rules, such as question formation, typically move whole phrases, not just words. Such a property is a candidate for being a universal "principle":

[this entire phrase] is permuted with the verb → is [this entire phrase] permuted with the verb?

Chomsky coined the name "structure-dependence" for this particular principle. Note that languages don't appear to form questions by "structure-independent" operations that permute odd and even words, return the mirror image of the string, etc.

Furthermore, it is arguable that the principle of "structure-dependence" is not learnable by such notions as "analogy" and "generalization." For one might expect the child to generalize from such pairs as "the man is hungry → is the man hungry" to "the man who is hungry is tall → *is the man who hungry is tall."[5] But such false generalizations are not reported among the errors that language learners make (nor are the corresponding corrections by the speech community). Since the data necessary to generalize to the correct question forms is absent from the input, this mode of argument has been termed the "argument from poverty of the stimulus" (see next section).

The basic idea then is that there is a universal *Bauplan* for language, described by the theory of UG, which specifies the set of principles that

5 * means ungrammatical here.

largely determine the growth of language. These principles may vary according to the parameters discussed above, depending on the particular language being learned. Another way to think about it is that there is actually only one language in a biological sense, sometimes called "Human," and that English, Hindi, Japanese, etc. are instantiations of Human, depending on which parameters have been fixed by environmental input. As Chomsky has put it:

the major task is to determine what are the principles and parameters that constitute the initial state of the language faculty and thus determine the set of possible human languages. Apart from lexicon, this is a finite set, surprisingly; in fact, a one-membered set if parameters are in fact reducible to lexical properties. Notice that this conclusion, if true, would help explain the surprising fact that there is more than one possible human language; namely, it would follow that in an interesting sense, there is only one such language. (Chomsky, 1991b:26)

The view that there is only one language, Human, apart from minor variation, is diametrically opposed to the view advanced in structural linguistics, that "languages could differ from each other without limit and in unpredictable ways," as Martin Joos put it (Chomsky, 1986; Joos, 1957).

The fact that the language organ permits a limited range of variation is thus no more surprising than the fact that the heart, the circulatory system, the visual system, or any other system of the body (or mind/brain), exhibits similar variation, corresponding to different courses of experience, within the limits imposed by the genetic endowment. It is a task for the biolinguist to determine the mechanisms that fix the parametric options in the developing microcircuits of the nervous system.

For a detailed justification of the principles-and-parameters framework in linguistics, we refer the reader to Chomsky and Lasnik (Chomsky and Lasnik, 1993; also included in Chomsky, 1995b); much of the early in-depth work from this point of view was done in the Romance languages (Kayne, 1984; Rizzi, 1982) and in Germanic (Riemsdijk, 1978; Haider, 1985a, 1985b, 1985c).

The argument from poverty of the stimulus

Earlier we alluded to the "argument from poverty of the stimulus." In a linguistic context the argument from poverty of the stimulus[6] is used when one assigns some property of grammar P to UG, as part of the genotype, just in case there is no evidence for property P available to the language learner from the data he or she is exposed to (Chomsky, 1980c:66).

---

[6] For more discussion of the meaning of the expression "the argument from poverty of the stimulus," see Chomsky, 1980c (34–38, 40, 41, 44, 68–69); Caplan and Chomsky, 1980 (99–100).

An example of this kind of argumentation is given in Chomsky, 1975b, where P = structure-dependence of rules (also see above). For other examples from linguistics, see Chomsky, 1980c (160–63). In fact, virtually all work on UG within the kind of generative grammar framework under discussion (Chomsky, 1995b), makes implicit use of the argument from poverty of the stimulus, even though this is not always, even rarely, explicitly pointed out in the technical literature.

Lightfoot poses the dilemma presented by the argument from poverty of the stimulus as follows: "The main question is how children acquire so much more than they experience" (Lightfoot, 1982:21). However, the answer that Lightfoot offers; viz., that language learners have help from their genes is an idea which is anathema to some. Butterworth considers this idea on a par with Erich von Däniken's idea (Däniken, 1970:chapter 7) that the great pyramids were built by a "mysterious helper" (Butterworth, 1983).[7] Butterworth believes that children learn language like the ancient Egyptians actually built the pyramids, using "considerable intelligence" and after making "many unsuccessful attempts," and also with "systematic help from their parents." He considers the root of the fallacy of the biological approach to result from "grossly underestimating the intelligence and ingenuity of those involved" (p. 187). However, the point of the argument from poverty of the stimulus is that if it is the case that during their lifetimes neither the child nor its parents have ever been exposed to or ever uttered the crucial sentences (negative evidence) needed to deduce some grammatical property (e.g., properties of structure-dependence, Subjacency,[8] distribution of empty categories, and the like [Chomsky, 1981]), then no amount of intelligence or ingenuity on the child's part, nor corrections and tutoring on the parents' will yield these properties. In such cases then, it is reasonable to hypothesize that the child must acquire these properties on the basis of internalized principles; e.g., from their genetic program for language. Note that one would expect that children would be worse at learning language systems based on principles not found in natural language, even if they utilized their "considerable intelligence" to solve the system as an intellectual puzzle. The evidence seems to go in this direction; see the case of Christopher described below. As for "systematic help" from parents, as Bishop notes, later in this chapter, there are cultures in which it is custo-

---

[7] If Butterworth had been raised together with a cat that received the same "systematic help" from his parents that he did and that ate all the same foods as well, then presumably Butterworth, but not the cat, would have acquired English. This means that more than linguistic and nutritional input is involved and that Butterworth got some help from a "mysterious helper"; i.e., his genome, that his cat didn't get.

[8] Subjacency is a constraint which prohibits the movement of phrases in certain syntactic configurations.

mary for the parents not speak to the children "until they have something to say," leaving it up to the children to pick up whatever unsystematic language they can. It may be true, as Butterworth claims, that "serious research on child language development has almost completely ignored this 'biological approach,'" but that may also be to the detriment of such studies. For work that takes the biological approach to language acquisition seriously and develops it in interesting ways, see, e.g., Berwick and Weinberg, 1984; Bloom, 1994; O'Grady, 1997; Radford, 1990; Wexler and Manzini, 1987, and much other work.

Bickerton also argues in favor of a biological approach to the study of language acquisition in the case of creole languages on other grounds, his "bioprogram" hypothesis (Bickerton, 1984:15–16, 25–28; 1990). He maintains that the bioprogram hypothesis is preferable to the theory of the "orthodox generativist" (p. 26). However, it is simply false to claim, as Bickerton does in this context, that generativists have "stubbornly refused to consider situations in which there was simply not enough (or the right kind of) data to give satisfactory results" (pp. 25–26). In actual fact, this situation is paradigmatic in generative discussion and even has its own terminology, as we have seen; viz., the argument from poverty of the stimulus or "Plato's problem."

Moreover, Bickerton incorrectly claims that "the possibility that there may be features in the innate language capacity that do not necessarily surface in all human languages . . . has simply never been considered by generativists" (p. 26, n. 3). Actually, no "generativist" (or anybody else, who has looked closely at more than their native language) has ever drawn the absurd conclusion that all language features surface in all human languages. That languages exhibit diversity in their features was a truism to the Cartesian Port-Royal school in the 1700s (e.g., Du Marsais, etc.), the descriptive grammarians (e.g., Jespersen, etc.), the structural linguists (e.g., Jakobson, etc.), and to every modern-day generative grammarian, in whose theories the centuries-old assumption that there is parametric variation across languages was taken over and elaborated in a number of interesting ways; see Roberts, for a recent presentation (Roberts, 1996).

Chomsky has noted that the argument from poverty of the stimulus might be considered a variant of classical arguments in the theory of knowledge, such as Socrates' elicitation of knowledge from the slave boy or Descartes' arguments for the innate idea of a triangle (Caplan and Chomsky, 1980:99–100; Chomsky, 1980c:34–38). Hence the problem that the argument from poverty of the stimulus was devised to illuminate is also referred to as "Plato's problem" (Chomsky, 1986). The notion "poverty of stimulus" is to be distinguished from the notion "degeneracy of stimulus," where the stimulus is degenerate if "the data-base for language acquisition contains expressions that are not well-formed" (Chomsky, 1980b:42).

Chomsky proposed that one might test hypotheses about such properties of language as structure-dependence by comparing how subjects learn real languages as compared to how they learn artificial symbolic systems lacking certain properties of UG:

One might seek other ways of testing particular hypotheses about a language-acquisition device. A theory that attributes possession of certain linguistic universals to a language-acquisition system, as a property to be realized under appropriate external conditions, implies that only certain kinds of symbolic systems can be acquired and used as languages by this device. Others should be beyond its language-acquisition capacity . . . In principle, one might try to determine whether invented systems that fail these conditions do pose inordinately difficult problems for language learning, and do fall beyond the domain for which the language-acquisition system is designed. (Chomsky, 1965:55)

For example, applying this idea to the property of structure-dependence, it would be the case that "one who proposes this theory [of structure-dependence] would have to predict that although a language might form interrogatives, for example, by interchanging the order of certain categories (as in English), it could not form interrogatives by reflection, or interchange of odd and even words, or insertion of a marker in the middle of the sentence" (p. 56).

Chomsky notes that one would not expect a system violating the principle of structure-dependence to be unlearnable, but that the system would be acquired in a qualitatively different way, using other faculties of the mind:

Notice that when we maintain that a system is not learnable by a language-acquisition device that mirrors human capacities, we do not imply that this system cannot be mastered by a human in some other way, if treated as a puzzle or intellectual exercise of some sort. The language-acquisition device is only one component of the total system of intellectual structures that can be applied to problem solving and concept formation; in other words, the *faculté de langage* is only one of the faculties of the mind. What one would expect, however, is that there should be a qualitative difference in the way in which an organism with a functional language-acquisition system will approach and deal with systems that are language-like and others that are not. (p. 56)

Support for these ideas can be found in the fascinating study by Smith and Tsimpli of Christopher, a linguistic savant, who can "read, write and communicate in any of fifteen to twenty languages," but who is institutionalized because "He is unable to look after himself; he has difficulty in finding his way around; he has poor hand–eye co-ordination, turning many everyday tasks such as shaving or doing up buttons into a burdensome chore" (Smith and Tsimpli, 1995:1).

Smith and Tsimpli present data from a variety of tests that, generally speaking, present a psychological profile of "a relatively low performance IQ with an average or above average verbal IQ."

Smith and Tsimpli document Christopher's remarkable speed at and facility for picking up new languages: "In March, 1992 shortly before he was due to appear on Dutch television, it was suggested that he might spend a couple of days improving his rather rudimentary Dutch with the aid of a grammar and dictionary. He did so to such good effect that he was able to converse in Dutch – with facility if not total fluency – both before and during the programme" (p. 18).

Smith and Tsimpli presented both Christopher and a control group of linguistics undergraduates an invented language Epun to test the hypothesis that a system which violated such linguistic universals as structure-dependence in various ways would be learned, if at all, in a qualitatively different way. The idea was that Epun might possibly be mastered by the control group of undergraduates who could treat the system as an intellectual puzzle, to be solved with the help of other cognitive faculties. On the other hand, Christopher should have greater difficulty with this task, since he was primarily dependent on his language faculty. The authors report that "although the data are rather complex, we think that these predictions are largely borne out" (Smith and Tsimpli, 1995:154).

Both Christopher and the control group could handle structure-dependent operations, as expected. However, neither Christopher nor the control group could handle the structure-independent operations. So the authors looked at structure-dependent operations which were "empirically unattested" and "theoretically implausible." These proved to be within the capabilities of the control group, but beyond Christopher, at least in the early stages: "Impossible structure-dependent operations, however, did separate Christopher from the controls in the manner anticipated, and accordingly lend support to the hypothesis being tested" (p. 154).

Growth versus learning

Chomsky pointed out several decades ago that the acquisition of cognitive structures and functions is more appropriately described as "growth" than as "learning": "My own suspicion is that a central part of what we call "learning" is actually better understood as the growth of cognitive structures along an internally directed course under the triggering and partial shaping effect of the environment" (Chomsky, 1980c:33).

For the particular case of the acquisition of language (question [2] [p. 1]), a great deal of evidence had accumulated by this time that pointed to this conclusion: "As for development, language grows in the child through mere exposure to an unorganized linguistic environment, without training or even any particular language-specific care" (Chomsky, 1980c:240).

Thus language "grows in the mind" (p. 134).The child no more "learns language," than he or she "learns to have arms rather than wings" (p. 236).The growth of the mental organ of language is regarded like the biological development of any other organs, such as the eye or the sexual organs.The study of language therefore becomes a subpart of the study of developmental biology.

Learning as selection (versus instruction)

In a well known essay the immunologist Niels Jerne developed the distinction between instructive and selective theories of biology that is applicable to discussions of the learning of language (Jerne, 1967). As Chomsky notes

He [Jerne] distinguishes between instructive and selective theories in biology, where an instructive theory holds that a signal from the outside imparts its character to the system that receives it, and a selective theory holds that change of the system takes place when some already present character is identified and amplified by the intruding stimulus. He argues that "Looking back into the history of biology, it appears that wherever a phenomenon resembles learning, an instructive theory was first proposed to account for the underlying mechanisms. In every case, this was later replaced by a selective theory." (Chomsky, 1980c:136–37)

Jerne gives examples from a number of areas, including the replacement of the instructive theory of the immune system by the selective theory. Jerne goes on to suggest that one should be willing to entertain the possibility that learning in the central nervous system might also proceed by selective mechanisms, even though on the surface it might appear to be instructive in nature. The many arguments based on poverty of stimulus argue for a rich innate biological endowment for language. The "already present character" alluded to above corresponds to the (universal) principles of language. The datum which fixes or "selects" the appropriate variant of the principle corresponds to the "stimulus." Chomsky has noted that these considerations apply to word meaning as well as to syntax, on grounds of poverty of stimulus: "However surprising the conclusion may be that nature has provided us with an innate stock of concepts, and that the child's task is to discover their labels, the empirical facts appear to leave open few other possibilities" (Chomsky, 1992:116).

Piattelli-Palmarini provides extensive discussion of the principles-and-parameters model as a selectional model of language acquisition, as opposed to an instructional model, against which he provides counter-arguments (Piattelli-Palmarini, 1989).

It is important to keep in mind that discovering that the principles-and-parameters model of language learning is selectional in nature, by no means obligates one to transfer the entire molecular machinery from the immune system (or any other part of biology) into linguistics. Cziko ascribes absurd views to Piattelli-Palmarini and Fodor about language genes being in mice and early primitive life forms (Cziko, 1995). The absurdity is of Cziko's own invention since he (1) assumes that the molecular machinery of the immune system carries over directly to language and then (2) gets the basic facts about the immune system wrong. We return to these issues in chapter 5.

Bates and Elman ascribe a different kind of absurdity to Chomsky and his colleagues, based on another confusion about selection versus instruction. At the end of the discussion of Jerne above, Chomsky remarks that "it is possible that the notion 'learning' may go the way of the rising and setting of the sun." He is clearly saying that language learning may well be selective, rather than instructive, in character. Bates and Elman assert on the pages of *Science* that "Noam Chomsky, the founder of generative linguistics, has argued for 40 years that language is unlearnable" and announce that now psycholinguists "have proven that babies can learn," an obvious fact which was never in doubt in the first place (Bates and Elman, 1996). However, we will return to this "proof" later in this chapter with regard to some other confusions; i.e., on the issue of innateness.

It is perhaps worth noting that the confusions about concepts like "selective," "innate," and "growth" of language have arisen only in parts of the cognitive sciences, not in biology proper. For example, as was noted in the Introduction, Jerne, who pioneered ideas on selection in the immune system, understood these issues and stated them clearly in his Nobel Prize address, where he used "innate" in the uncontroversial sense that is familiar in the biological sciences.

The language "instinct"

In the opening pages of *The Mind's Past*, Gazzaniga remarks: "Nonetheless, Chomsky's new view of language as a biologically based universal feature of our brain has taken hold. Steven Pinker, a colleague of Chomsky at MIT, has extended it by successfully arguing that language is an instinct – just like any other adaptation" (Gazzaniga, 1998:7). In the very next sentence, Gazzaniga tells us what this means: "Syntax is not learned by Skinnerian associative systems; rather, we can communicate through language because all members of our species have an innate capacity to manipulate symbols in a temporal code that maps sounds onto meaning."

Gazzaniga's formulation is bound to be confusing to new students of language as well as people outside the field. Pinker's use of "instinct" to describe the acquisition of human language does not "extend" the "view of language as a biologically based universal feature of our brain" – the views are one and the same. In fact, Pinker says so himself. Noting that the use of the term "instinct" to describe language goes back at least as far as Darwin, Pinker states: "In this century, the most famous argument that language is like an instinct comes from Noam Chomsky, the linguist who first unmasked the intricacy of the system and perhaps the person most responsible for the modern revolution in language and cognitive science" (Pinker, 1994a:21).

Similarly, as Gallistel has noted, the term "instinct to learn" (or "innately guided learning"; [Gould and Marler, 1987]) encompasses the same view: "However, as Gould and Marler have argued, these computationally complex specialized learning mechanisms [in animals] may be thought of as instincts to learn. When they make this argument, they link up with Chomsky's argument about the foundations of language learning" (Gallistel, 1997:88). The use of such terminology as the language "instinct," or the "instinct to learn" language, or the "genetic or biological endowment" for language are all informal ways to describe the subject of study for biolinguistics, not competing theories. The goal of everyone, putting aside terminology, is to determine the properties of language, its development and evolution. There are, of course, methodological and empirical differences in approaches to particular aspects of the study of the biology of language; i.e., the study of the language instinct. For example, Pinker makes a distinction between linguistic evidence and "converging evidence," a distinction that we argued earlier is invalid. He (and Bloom) also maintains that properties of language must be adaptations and are explicable solely by design by natural selection. We will present arguments later (chapter 5) that their particular formulation of the issues is unsound.

Biolinguistics versus the connectionist approach

As has been made quite clear in this book the biolinguistic (I-linguistic) approach involves the study of questions concerning (1) language, (2) language development, and (3) language evolution. It is explicitly considered to be the study of the *biology* of language. The connectionist approach is a radically different approach, as is explained in the book *Rethinking Innateness*. The authors ask "how seriously one should take biological constraints?" They consider this issue to lie at the "heart of this book." The answer given is:

First, we wish to make clear that we think that the connectionist paradigm is interesting in its own right, and that there are valid reasons to study connectionist models regardless of whatever biological plausibility they might or might not have. There are many routes to intelligent behavior. We see no reason to focus exclusively on organically-based intelligence and neglect (for example) silicon-based intelligence. Artificial intelligence may help us better understand natural intelligence. But even if it doesn't, artificial systems are fascinating on their own terms. (Elman et al., 1996:104)

We can see that connectionism has much different fish to fry than does biolinguistics. It is concerned with intelligent behavior in general; i.e., Intelligence with a capital "I." This includes organically based intelligence (human language, basket weaving, nest-building, etc.) as well as silicon-based intelligence (chess-playing computers, computers that recognize speech, etc.). Thus connectionists are interested in general-purpose learning algorithms that work across domains and across organisms, whether based on DNA or on silicon. But even if the models turn out to have no "biological plausibility" whatever, they could still be a resounding success for connectionists, for "artificial systems are fascinating on their own terms." As for biology, it is enough for connectionists if the models are "informed by the biology and at least roughly consistent with it."

The biolinguist, on the other hand, is not interested in Intelligence with a capital "I," for that is not a question either of biology or empirical science. It is a question of definition. Consider an old-fashioned soft drinks machine that dispenses coins. Does it have Intelligence? Could we say that the machine is more Intelligent than a human in coin-dispensing? I would imagine that if you did performance tests on a machine over a period of time you could show that the machine performs faster and more accurately and efficiently than most sales clerks. So we could say that the machine is more Intelligent than a human in the area of coin-dispensing or even that it "thinks" better, by definition. Could we make the machine still more Intelligent? In recent years we have seen the appearance of machines that can scan dollar bills and display the information in an LED. A company could now extend the metaphor and say in their marketing brochures that the new machines are more Intelligent than the old machines.

Suppose that we now upgrade the machine again with the latest in neural net technology so that it not only dispenses change, but can make a billion moves a second in chess and beat the world chess champion. By definition, our machine exhibits more Intelligent behavior. Now we upgrade the neural net in the machine one more time so that it can now parse syllables of human speech. We could even set up a competition between Baby Blue, the neural net-powered machine, against the babies at the Department of Brain and Cognitive Sciences at the University of Rochester and might be able to show that the neural net is fifty times as fast as the babies, and as a bonus, can at the same time flawlessly pick up all the song dialects of the swamp sparrow as well as the cricket.

Is the machine more Intelligent? There is no reason that our flexible definition of "organically based" and "silicon-based" Intelligence can't comfortably cover these cases as well. In this example we have, of course, long ago given up on any "biological plausibility." But are these neural net machines "fascinating on their own terms," which is a critical requirement for connectionists? To judge by the hysteria generated during the Deep Blue–Kasparov match, with desperate chess fans beseeching Kasparov to "humiliate Big Blue," IBM's latest chess-playing computer, we would imagine that a connectionist drinks machine able to outcompute young infants would be an instant media sensation. For the connectionist, it is only necessary that "connectionist models resemble biological systems," as our neural net machine does, where the meaning of "resemble" is left up to our imaginations.

Biologists are not interested in Intelligence with a capital "I." They are interested in questions like the ones we are considering in this book: (1) what constitutes knowledge of human language?, (2) how does human language develop (in the individual)?, (3) how does human language evolve (in the species)? If an algorithm that parses speech is proposed for humans, but operates fifty times faster than infants are capable of and simultaneously parses the songs of swamp sparrows and crickets, it is inadequate as a biological model of human language, no matter how "fascinating" it might be for the construction of silicon robots. Similarly, biologists are interested in how a particular wing in a particular bird developed, not in whether you can build a jumbo jet that can outfly a sparrow, however "fascinating" such a proposal might be to connectionists for the study of Flight with a capital "F."

A number of lines of converging evidence have been put forward that distinguish between the view that a general-purpose neural net mechanism underlies language and the view that there are language-specific mechanisms. For example, Gopnik has presented evidence from families with genetic disorders which appear to differentially affect the formation of regular (*walk–walked*) and irregular verb forms (*sing–sang*), where the regular forms are impaired. We review Gopnik's cases and Williams syndrome in chapter 4. Finally, Marslen-Wilson and Tyler show in priming experiments that there is double dissociation in agrammatic aphasics with respect to the ability to process regular and irregular forms (Marslen-Wilson and Tyler, 1997). They conclude:

The specific challenge this poses for single-mechanism connectionist accounts is to show how a neural network, exposed to the same training input as a child learning English, can learn to partition its representations of regular and irregular morphology in such a way that (1) its end state is functionally separable into apparently combinatorial and non-combinatorial operations, and (2) these two aspects of its function are doubly dissociable by different types of damage to the network. (Marslen-Wilson and Tyler, 1997:593)

In commentary on this article, Pinker goes on to make the unsubstantiated claim that the results of Marslen-Wilson and Tyler exclude not only connectionist accounts, but also symbolic or rule-based approaches of the type explored by Chomsky and Halle (1964) and many other linguists. However, the latter approaches always have some formal distinction between regular and irregular verb forms expressed somewhere in the syntax, the morphology, the phonology, and/or the lexicon. It has always been an open question, and one that any biolinguist is forced to entertain, that this distinction is subserved by multiple neural mechanisms. Pinker seems to believe that since "rules" are used to described both regular and irregular verb forms, one is automatically committed to the belief that the two verb classes must be realized in a single neural mechanism. But if one proposes that the grammar contains semantic rules, syntax rules, and phonological rules, this does not commit one to a single neural mechanism for "rules." A priori, there might be one, six, or twenty mechanisms. This must be discovered, not deduced from the terminology used, or otherwise stipulated. The results from genetic disorders, imaging, and priming, supports symbolic or rule-based approaches, as well as any other approach that formally distinguishes regular from irregular verb forms.

Below we will examine a few of the common misconceptions about the biology of language that have emerged in recent years. It is unusual to find nearly all the gross errors of interpretation being made in one place, as in the case with the recently published book *Rethinking Innateness* (Elman et al., 1996) and the related analysis, "Learning Rediscovered" (Bates and Elman, 1996). These provide many convenient examples, although the misconceptions and misrepresentations found there are by no means all original. We are speaking of such claims as "Noam Chomsky, the founder of generative linguistics, has argued for 40 years that language is unlearnable," and that John Maynard Smith and his colleagues believe in (and spawned) the "Grammar Gene Rumor," the belief in *the* "gene for grammar." The preceding two claims are related to "the twelve arguments

about innate representations," alleged to be held by Chomsky and colleagues. Before we turn to the innateness issue, let us take up the claim
that "language is unlearnable," apparently thought to be widely believed
within the biolinguistics (I-linguistics) tradition.

Learning "redefined"[9]

Saffran, Aslin, and Newport present a proposal about the way infants
segment words (Saffran, Aslin, and Newport, 1996), in which it is argued
that eight–month-old infants are able to use statistical information. In a
commentary on that proposal, entitled "Learning Rediscovered", by
Bates and Elman, it is asserted that Saffran, Aslin, and Newport "have
proven that babies can learn" and that "Noam Chomsky, the founder of
generative linguistics, has argued for 40 years that language is unlearnable" (Bates and Elman, 1996).

That "babies can learn" is not a proof, but a long-known and widely
accepted empirical observation. Saffran, Aslin, and Newport conclude
from their experiments that their "results raise the intriguing possibility
that infants possess experience-dependent mechanisms that may be powerful enough to support not only word segmentation but also the acquisition of other aspects of language." This is not just an intriguing possibility;
it is an empirical fact, demonstrated in a variety of ways. For example, if a
child born in America to English-speaking parents is sent after birth to
Japan to be raised by a Japanese family, that child will learn to speak
Japanese, not English. Secondly, if a child is raised without being exposed
to any human language, then that child will not come to speak one. Both
of these (often noted) observations clearly demonstrate that infants
possess "experience-dependent mechanisms" for learning language and
show why every reasonable theory of language acquisition, or language
learning, if one prefers the term, including Chomsky's and his colleagues', proceeds from the assumption that human language is not like
cricket song (the example given by Saffran, Aslin, and Newport), but is
experience-dependent, as is vision, and many other faculties of the mind.
These theories then go on to ask what kinds of internal structures are
sufficient to give us the variety of possible languages, given the language
data available from experience.

---

[9] The first part of this section contains arguments presented by Jenkins and Maxam in the
Letters section entitled "Acquiring Language" in *Science*, in reply to Bates and Elman's
perspective on Saffran, Aslin, and Newport (Jenkins and Maxam, 1997; Bates and
Elman, 1996; Saffran, Aslin, and Newport, 1996). See also further discussion in the same
Letters section by D. Pesetsky, K. Wexler, V. Fromkin, S. Pinker, R. Clark, L. Gleitman, A.
Kroch, as well as by Elman and Bates.

Not that infants learn, but rather how they learn, has been the subject of intense investigation for the last forty years in work on universal and comparative grammar, language acquisition and perception, sign-language, language-isolated children, creole language, family and twin studies of agrammatism,[10] expressive and receptive aphasias, split brains, linguistic savants, and electrical activity of the brain. All of this work converges on the conclusion that human language, like any other biological system, results from an interplay of genetic and environmental factors. The assertion that Chomsky claims that "language is unlearnable" is a blatant misrepresentation of his work, apparent to the linguistics community, but perhaps not to the general reader.

Chomsky has proposed that a central task for biology of language is to develop "the learning theory for humans in the domain language," and has put forward a variety of proposals about this learning theory over the past forty years. He went on to propose that one try to discover learning theories for other cognitive domains for humans (or for other organisms, with their own special cognitive capacities), suggesting facial recognition, determining the personality of other people, the ability to "recognize a melody under transposition," spatial intuition, etc. as possibilities (Chomsky, 1975b:21).

Compare now Bates and Elman: "he [Chomsky] and his followers have generalized this belief [that language is unlearnable] to other cognitive domains, denying the existence of learning as a meaningful scientific construct" (1996:1849). The quote that Bates and Elman provide about "learning" going the way of "rising and setting of sun" is taken out of context (see discussion above). It was proposed that the notion "growth" might better describe the biological process of acquiring language than "learning." Thus one might speak of babies growing language (in the mind), and drop the notion "learning" with its behaviorist connotations. But if we do this, then the "proof" claimed by Bates and Elman now reduces to the idea that "babies can grow languages" (long known) and the assertion that Chomsky claims that "language is ungrowable" (a misrepresentation).

Most researchers on the biology of language feel that the central issues are not the word games that some academics seek to play with definitions of learning (or innateness), but rather the many interesting questions about how to tease apart the genetic and environmental factors that interact to give us the knowledge, acquisition, use, neurological basis, and evolution of human language. Although Saffran, Aslin, and Newport

---

[10] Agrammatism is a disorder of speech or language, often inherited, affecting grammar. See chapter 4.

do try to raise some substantive issues about these matters, the points they make are obscured by the exaggerated claims made by Bates and Elman.

If the work done by Saffran, Aslin, and Newport holds up, it will provide yet another confirmation of the argument from poverty of the stimulus used so often in biolinguistics and which we discussed earlier in this chapter. As the authors point out themselves, there are no consistent acoustic cues available for word boundaries: "The infants' performance in these studies is particularly impressive given the impoverished nature of the familiarization speech stream, which contained no pauses, intonational patterns, or any other cues that, in normal speech, probabilistically supplement the sequential statistics inherent in the structure of words" (Saffran, Aslin, and Newport, 1996:1928). "Impoverished" is as in "poverty of the stimulus."[11] And, since the infants are not yet producing speech, there is also no caretaker feedback or correction involved. However, there is little doubt as to the essential correctness of the poverty of stimulus argument in the area of language perception anyway, as an impressive body of evidence for it has accumulated over the past forty years; see Jusczyk and Mehler and Dupoux for a review and many references there (Jusczyk, 1997; Mehler and Dupoux, 1994).

Note that Saffran, Aslin, and Newport are confronted with the same questions as the theories of language acquisition that they appear to be criticizing. For example, the authors claim that "eight–month-old infants are capable of extracting serial-order information after only two min of listening experience." Why serial-order, as opposed to processing the sequence backwards, or every odd or prime syllable? Why a statistical algorithm that takes two minutes instead of a less efficient algorithm that might take three hours? These are typical poverty-of-stimulus questions the answers to which will certainly involve genetics at some level. Similarly, we can go on to ask what parts of the brain this algorithm involves (localization). What is the developmental program that leads to this algorithm being expressed where it is (and, e.g., not in the visual area) at eight months; i.e., the typical questions that all theories of language acquisition are faced with.

Furthermore, the authors' distinction between "experience-independent" mechanisms and "experience-dependent" mechanisms cannot be taken too seriously. Biological theories of language do not slice the world into language mechanisms that are experience-dependent and those that

---

[11] Note that the authors are themselves applying the argument from poverty of the stimulus, even though they want to distinguish their experience-dependent mechanisms from experience-independent mechanisms, which, as they note, routinely rely on this argument.

are experience-independent, as do Saffran, Aslin, and Newport. All linguistic theories (e.g., the principles-and-parameters approach, categorial perception, etc.) are experience-dependent, contrary to what the authors seem to think. Put simply, there is no human language that develops independently of experiential input, as bat echolocation is said to do. Conversely, no language learning takes place independently of a genetic program; as Lorenz put it, in general "There does not exist a single case of teleonomic learning which does not proceed along the lines prescribed by a program containing phylogenetically acquired and genetically coded information" (Lorenz, 1981:261). Dissection of complex developmental systems has usually revealed an intricate interplay between genetic and external factors, and from what little is known about it, there is no reason to believe the situation will turn out to be different for the biology of human language.

What this new work would give us though is some idea of when the genetic machinery for word segmentation goes on line. Thus the authors' results would imply that the genetic machinery supporting word segmentation must already be in place at the age of eight months "The results demonstrate that infants *possess* powerful mechanisms suited to learning the types of structures exemplified in linguistic systems" (Saffran, Aslin, and Newport, 1996:1927, emphasis added). This may, of course, have similar implications for other genetic structure as well; infants would also have to "possess" already the necessary machinery to support memory storage.

Moreover, it is not clear that the authors' claim that the word segmentation algorithm is "innately biased" rather than based on "innate knowledge" means anything: "In particular, some aspects of early development may turn out to be best characterized as resulting from innately biased statistical learning mechanisms rather than innate knowledge" (p. 1928). The term "innately biased" has a special meaning in the literature on speech perception. As Jusczyk puts it: "Recall that the definition of innately guided learning that Gould and Marler provide is that organisms are preprogrammed to learn particular kinds of things and to learn them in particular ways" (1997:198). Jusczyk goes on to elaborate what these "particular ways" are: "what may be central to the process is a bias, or interest, to attend selectively to signals of a certain form" (p. 76). According to Jusczyk, a "classic" example of this process is bird song.

This bias is what Konrad Lorenz called "a biologically relevant situation." He and Tinbergen also anticipated misunderstandings about "innately biased" versus "innate knowledge" of the kind illustrated in the Saffran, Aslin, and Newport article. He decided to drop the term "innate scheme," which might suggest that "an image of the whole situation or object was innate," in favor of the expression "innate releasing mechanism":

At first I called this selective afferent mechanism the *angeborene Schema* – the innate scheme – because the organism seemed to have some sort of simplified, sketchy information about what the biologically relevant situation was like. Later, Tinbergen and I relinquished this term because its connotations suggested that something like an outline or an image of the whole situation or object was innate. In discussing the methods of dual quantification, I was forced to anticipate the important fact that it is by no means an image of the whole object or situation which is innately "known" to the animal, but a number of independently effective, very simple stimulus configurations whose releasing functions, obeying the law of heterogeneous summation, add up to a qualitatively unitary effect. For this reason Tinbergen and I [1938] abandoned the term *Schema* and decided to call the neural organization here under discussion the *innate releasing mechanism* (IRM) – in German, *angeborener Auslösemechanismus* (AAM). (Lorenz, 1981:153–54)

By the time of the early years of generative grammar and the Chomsky–Skinner discussions, a rich literature on these issues and distinctions existed in the literature of ethology. As we saw in the Introduction, Chomsky drew on this literature and these discussions; e.g., of "imprinting," to argue against behaviorist theories of learning in the 1950s. It was understood then and now that the key question is what the "biologically relevant situation" is in the language-learning environment, as the genetic program unfolds, and not whether one speaks of "innate knowledge" or "innately guided learning."

Finally, we also note that the fact that the algorithm being proposed is based on probabilistic properties does not serve to distinguish it from ideas on the nature of learning within the biolinguistics (I-linguistics) tradition. As Chomsky noted many years back:

Note that there is no question being raised here as to the legitimacy of a probabilistic study of language, just as the legitimacy of the study of meaning was in no way brought into question when we pointed out [. . .] that projection cannot be defined in semantic terms. Whether or not the statistical study of language can contribute to grammar, it surely can be justified on quite independent grounds. These three approaches to language (grammatical, semantic, statistical) are independently important. In particular, none of them requires for its justification that it lead to solutions for problems which arise from pursuing one of the other approaches. (Chomsky, 1975a:148)

In fact, Chomsky proposed at that time that work by Zellig Harris described in the paper "From Phoneme to Morpheme" (Harris, 1955), might be more effectively applied to ascertain word boundaries rather than morpheme boundaries. Chomsky had been a student of Zellig Harris and was thoroughly familiar with these kinds of structuralist "discovery procedures," having invested a number of years himself trying to get them to work, before turning to the "realist interpretation of linguistic theory" (I-linguistics, biolinguistics):

By 1953, I had abandoned any hope of formulating taxonomic "discovery procedures" and turned my attention entirely to the problems of generative grammar, in theory and in application. It was at that point that I began writing LSLT, bringing together and extending the work I had begun on various aspects of generative grammar, but now with conviction as well as enthusiasm.[12] (Chomsky, 1975a:33)

The focus then shifted from how the linguist can construct a grammar using restrictive taxonomic "discovery procedures," and towards how language is acquired by the child, who "is presented with unanalyzed data." "It is thus suggested that the language learner (analogously, the linguist) approaches the problem of language acquisition (grammar construction) with a schematism that determines in advance the general properties of human language and the general properties of the grammars that may be constructed to account for linguistic phenomena" (Chomsky, 1975a:12). Part of this schematism would necessarily involve a method for extracting words from the "unanalyzed data." "Our general theory seems to require that there be a method for determining words from the corpus almost to uniqueness [. . .], and the most important problem on this level is to develop such a method" (Chomsky, 1975a:165). This statement poses for biolinguistics a problem which has sometimes been called the "segmentation problem" (with variant formulations for phonemic segments, syllabic segments, etc.). Chomsky proposed that a distributional procedure like Harris' would be a reasonable candidate, if not the only candidate, particularly in light of the fact that there appeared to be no language-independent characterization of "word" available in terms of stress, juncture, etc. However, it was suggested that the method be applied to determine word boundaries rather than morpheme boundaries.

The most reasonable suggestion that I know of is Harris's in "From phoneme to morpheme." Investigation of his data seems to indicate that word boundaries can be placed much more effectively than morpheme boundaries by this method. (Chomsky, 1975a:165)

Thus investigation of Harris's results ("From phoneme to morpheme") on isolation of tentative segments in terms of independence seems to show that word boundaries are much more clearly indicated than morpheme boundaries, and that it might be possible to determine words directly from the phonemic record. The prospects for morphemes seem much more doubtful. (Chomsky, 1975a:153)

Hayes and Clark performed experiments on adult speakers to look for evidence of a "clustering mechanism" which allowed them "to detect the

---

[12] LSLT = *The Logical Structure of Linguistic Theory* (Chomsky, 1975a).

recurrent patterns that constitute words, even without the aid of pauses or of meanings" (Hayes and Clark, 1970). They had in mind a procedure of the kind proposed by Harris.

Harris [1955] has proposed just such a procedure for use by linguists in discovering the words of an unfamiliar language. His procedure is best described by working through one of his examples. He considered the utterance "He's clever," and its phonemic representation /hiysklever/[*sic*.]. He then turned to informants in the language (as the source of his correlational information) to determine how many different phonemes can follow /h/. He found that there were 9 different phonemes that could act as successors to /h/. In the same way, Harris found that 14 phonemes could follow /hi/, 29 could follow /hiy/, 29 could follow /hiyz/, 11 could follow /hiyzk/, 7 could follow /hiyzkl/, and so on. High successor counts correspond to little constraint from the context and hence to low correlations among phonemes. Harris interpreted high successor counts as indicating that a segment boundary had been crossed. Hence, he located these boundaries just before the peaks in the successor count, as in the sample utterance /hiy.z.klever/, where the periods indicate boundaries. (Hayes and Clark, 1970:223)

They too, as is Chomsky, are interested in such procedures not as discovery procedures, but as hypotheses about language acquisition. They are interested in the clustering mechanism as part of the biologically endowed nature of the language learner.[13] Although they performed the experiments on adults, because of the technical difficulty of performing the experiments with children, they explicitly note that their goal is in establishing the "plausibility of the mechanism in children's acquisition of language," and recommend that the experiments be repeated with children "of about a year old." To make sure no acoustic cues (like pauses and stress) are present they use artificial speech in the experiments. They conclude:

These two experiments demonstrate that humans do, in fact, have a clustering mechanism able to segment artificial speech. It is a mechanism which (a) can segment completely unutterable sounds, (b) works on "speech" that has no semantic and no significant syntactic structure, and (c) requires relatively little time – about three-quarters of an hour in our experiments – to come to at least some parsing of the speech. It seems to us that these are important properties of a mechanism that would be useful to a child first trying to sort out the sounds he hears around him. (Hayes and Clark, 1970:230)

"Redefining" innateness

To show that Noam Chomsky (and his "followers") have argued (and labored under the delusion) for forty years that "language is unlearn-

---

[13] They speculate that the clustering mechanism may be part of a more general cognitive mechanism, involving vision, but give no further evidence.

able," Elman et al. present arguments about innate representations, attributed to Chomsky and followers with "special reference to language" in a volume entitled *Rethinking Innateness*, which again might better be called "Redefining Innateness." Chomsky assumes his traditional role as arch-villain, this time as the "strong nativist" (p. 117) or even "radical nativist," fueled by "rising public interest in genes for complex outcomes from cancer to divorce." Among these are the "Grammar Gene Rumor" (p. 41) that localization and innateness are "the same thing."

In order to reach this conclusion, it is necessary for the authors to perform some sleight-of-hand with the terms "innate" and "learned." That is, the authors seem to me to be using the terms "innate" and "learned" in unorthodox interpretations, precisely in order to caricature the reasonable position that learning involves a complex interaction between genetics and experience.

Chomsky himself has tried to avoid using the term "innate," precisely because of the kind of confusion the term inevitably seems to generate in philosophical and cognitive science circles: "No-one defends the [innateness] hypothesis, including those to whom it is attributed (me, in particular). The reason is that there is no such hypothesis." However, the term "innate" is used in much the same way as it is and has been understood in contemporary biology and neurology; e.g., by Salvador Luria (1973): "To the biologist it makes eminent sense to think that, as for language structures, so also for logical structures there exist in the brain network some patterns of connections that are genetically determined" (p. 141). In using "genetically determined," to discuss the language structures, Luria is not denying a component of learning: "Thus the language that each individual develops is partly learned and partly an expression of the structure of his own brain" (p. 140). Luria is certainly not using "genetically determined" in the sense of "innate" as given in Elman et al.: "Here, the term innate refers to changes that arise as a result of interactions that occur within the organism itself during ontogeny. That is, interactions between the genes and their molecular and cellular environments *without recourse to information from outside the organism*. We adopt this working definition of the term in this book" (1996:22; emphasis ours).

No biologist (or linguist) would claim that human language is "innate" in Elman et al.'s terms; i.e. "without recourse to information outside the organism." Compare Hubel, cited earlier, on this matter: "This is not to say that other regions of cortex are necessarily wired without benefit of experience. Most neurologists would guess that the circuits responsible for language are mainly cortical – and no one would contend that we are born knowing the details of our native tongues" (Hubel, 1988:216–17). Similar views about human language can be found expressed throughout the biological literature. In fact, Elman's characterization of "innate" is a regression from the classic notion of Descartes, where it was understood that innate ideas are dispositional; i.e., are typically influenced by "information outside the organism" (Chomsky, 1965:48–49).

When Chomsky stated that "learning" would go the way of the rising and setting of the sun, he was simply making the point that the common-sense notion of "learning" (e.g., as "motherese") or the "learning" of radical behaviorism can be shown insufficient to account for central properties of language. These "learning" approaches incorrectly ignored internal properties of the learner, in part provided by (epi)genetics. He suggested that the term "growth" (in the biological sense) would more accurately describe the acquisition of language than does "learning" in the above sense. Of course, by tinkering with the definitions of "learned" and "innate," we can derive nearly any conclusion we want.

"Grammar Gene Rumor"

Elman et al. rail out against the "Grammar Gene Rumor" (p. 41), the belief in "single genes for complex outcomes." But a careful reading of Elman et al. reveals that the only such rumor is the one that they themselves originate in their own writings: "To evaluate the actual data in some detail, it is necessary to trace *the* "gene for grammar" back to its original sources, and follow the relevant literature up to the present day" (p. 373, emphasis ours). Here Elman et al. use the phrase "the 'gene for grammar'," but in the sources they cite, the phrase "a defective gene" (Sutherland, 1993) and "a single dominant gene" (Szathmáry and Maynard Smith, 1995) are used. In effect, they have put words into the mouth of Szathmáry and Sutherland and Maynard Smith and have included a lesson on elementary genetics to purge them of their erroneous belief in "single genes for complex outcomes": "Things would be much simpler that way! But the evidence to date provides little support for this view [the "Grammar Gene Rumor"]. Alas, a complex cascade of interactions among genes is required to determine outcomes as simple as eye color in fruitflies or body types in earth worms" (Elman et al., 1996:41).

Going back to the original sources (Gopnik, 1990; Gopnik and Crago, 1991), Elman et al. cite another alleged case of the "Grammar Gene Rumor": "It is not unreasonable to entertain an interim hypothesis that a single dominant gene controls for those mechanisms that result in a child's ability to construct the paradigms that constitute morphology" (p. 47). Again, we are talking about "a" gene, not "the" gene for anything. Note that this way of talking about genes is no different than the one one runs across in reading about the developmental genetics of fruit fly behavior. In fact, in the same issue of *Science* as the Bates and Elman critique we find "Humans are far from being the only animals with complicated sex lives. Take the fruit fly *Drosophila melanogaster*, in which males stalk the females and woo them with song before mating with them. Yet in the fly, at least, most of this complex repertory turns out to be controlled by a single gene" (Roush, 1996:1836). The author goes on to elaborate results that appear to indicate that a fruit fly gene *fruitless* (*fru*) may be a "high-level regulatory gene that somehow equips specific centers in the brain to coordinate male courtship behavior." Moreover, "males with severe mutations in *fru* lose the will to follow other flies, play courtship songs on their wings, or attempt copulation, indicating that the gene somehow orchestrates these behaviors. Further supporting that idea, Taylor showed that *fru* is expressed primarily in nine small clusters of nerve cells, including several previously mapped by Hall as 'courtship centers'" (p. 1836). Here we have a case of "single genes for complex outcomes," which is not the same as saying that it is "the" gene for anything. It is hypothesized to be a regulatory gene and hence could regulate the expression of many other genes.[14]

A connectionist "alternative" to biolinguistics

Seidenberg criticizes what he calls the "Standard Theory" of linguistics and suggests an "alternative theoretical framework" based on probabilistic constraints. By "Standard Theory," Seidenberg means biolinguistics (= I-linguistics) (Seidenberg, 1997). In fact, he specifically lists the five basic questions about language under discussion in this book: (1) knowledge, (2) acquisition, (3) use, (4) brain representation, and (5) evolution. But is Seidenberg really presenting us with an alternative? We can put aside (4) and (5) since he does not address these questions.

As for (1), knowledge, he objects to what he calls the "Competence Hypothesis" (his term) and "competence grammar" on the grounds that they are "idealizations" that are "abstract" and only "remotely related to the child's experience."[15] Yet when he discusses his neural net "alternative," he implicitly adopts the "Competence Hypothesis" himself. In discussing sentences like "I loaded the bricks onto the truck" versus "I loaded the truck with bricks," he says "speakers of a language eventually come to know both the meanings of verbs and a complex set of conditions

---

[14] A reader noted that one must keep in mind that a gene often exists in alternate forms, or alleles. A different allele can result in a phenotype different than the one that results from the allele usually found in the population under study. We will discuss the question of genetic variation in language in more detail in chapter 4.

[15] Seidenberg also repeats the unfounded claim made by Bates and Elman that "language therefore gives the appearance of being unlearnable" (p. 1601). We have already dealt with this misrepresentation of the "Standard Theory" above.

governing their occurrence in sentences" (Seidenberg, 1997:1601–2) and then goes on to discuss a neural net program (based on work by J. Allen) which learns these "meanings of verbs" and "complex set of conditions." But this is exactly what is meant by "knowledge of language" or "competence"; viz. that a speaker or, for Seidenberg, the neural net that models the person, comes to know the meaning of verbs like "load" and the "verbs and complex set of conditions governing their occurrence in sentences."

As for the charge that the "Standard Theory"; i.e., biolinguistics, involves idealizations, note that neural nets (quite properly) do so too. In fact, Francis Crick has taken neural-net theoreticians to task for radically idealizing away from properties of the brain, warning that their theories might go the way of "phlogiston" as Roberts points out:

The obvious problem with back-prop, says Crick, is that feedback messages would have to go down the axon the wrong way. And it implies the existence of a "teacher," which in the brain would presumably be another set of neurons. "Such a set of neurons, if they exist, should have novel properties and would be worth looking for, but there is no sign of back-prop advocates clamoring at the doors of neuroscientists, begging them to search for such neurons," says Crick, getting to the crux of his criticism. (Roberts, 1989:481)

D. Rumelhart replies that "this approach allows me to study aspects of the mind that can't be touched from the neuroscientist's approach" – leaving little doubt that neural nets allow radical idealization of the neuroscientist's "neuron."[16]

Nor are neural nets free from idealization of language behavior either. For example, neural-net work on language also assumes something like the "ideal speaker-hearer in a homogenous speech community." As only one example, it is now well established that any real population of language speakers exhibits genetic variation; subparts of the population exhibit Specific Language Disorders of various types – see chapter 4. To my knowledge, work on neural nets abstracts away from this kind of genetic variation, and to the same degree that the "Standard Theory" does.

Turning now to questions (2), acquisition, and (3), use, Seidenberg appears to be claiming that the incorporation of "probabilistic constraints" somehow represents an alternative to the "Standard Theory." Yet in a footnote he quotes Chomsky from 1957: "Given the grammar of a language, one can study the use of the language statistically in various ways; and the development of probabilistic models for the use of language

---

[16] In fact, Crick says that "almost my only contribution to their efforts [i.e., his co-authors, of the work *Parallel Distributed Processing* (Rumelhart et al.)] was to insist that they stop using the word *neurons* for the units of their networks" (Crick, 1995:186).

(as distinct from the syntactic structure of language) can be quite reward-ing" (Chomsky, 1957:17). That is to say, explicit provision for probabilis-tic models in the "Standard Theory" (biolinguistics), was made quite early on. And as we saw earlier, Chomsky had even proposed that some-thing very close to what Saffran, Aslin, and Newport established experi-mentally must be the case (Saffran, Aslin, and Newport, 1996).

It is not clear whether Seidenberg means to claim that probabilistic constraints will turn out to be the whole story for language use and acqui-sition. Certainly nothing of the kind has been established. As Seidenberg notes, "little of the work to date has addressed the kinds of phenomena that have been the focus of linguistic theorizing over the past several decades" and "vast areas of language have yet to be addressed at all" (1997:1601–2). The position of Chomsky and probably most biolinguists would be that how much of a role probabilistic constraints play in acquisi-tion and use is a matter to be discovered, not stipulated in advance.

Seidenberg concludes as follows:

Moreover, the claim that humans are born with innate knowledge of grammar does not rest solely on issues concerning acquisition; other phenomena such as universal aspects of language structure, creolization, and dissociations between language and other aspects of cognition are thought to converge on the same con-clusion. As with the poverty-of-the-stimulus argument, it will be necessary to reexamine these claims in light of the alternative theoretical framework before drawing definitive conclusions. (1997:1602–3)

We need to clarify what is meant by the thesis that "humans are born with innate knowledge of grammar." The linguist's theory of "grammar" is surely not intended here. However, it is certainly also not the case that "humans are born with innate knowledge of a language," i.e., are born knowing English or Japanese. So let's try spelling out the assumption more precisely as "humans are born with innate properties that play a role in acquiring knowledge of language." This assumption is surely shared by both the "Standard Theory" and neural-net theory (or any theory of lan-guage for that matter); i.e., the language-learning device must make some assumptions (have some internal structure), whether about properties of the initial state described by UG, probabilistic constraints, or both.

What Seidenberg presumably means to question here then is the "modularity thesis," that there is an innate component specific to the lan-guage faculty. But the modularity thesis is independent of the poverty-of-the-stimulus argument. The latter only establishes that there is some built-in (innate) internal structure, and depending on the data being ana-lyzed, allows one to put forth specific hypotheses about the constraints. Whether these constraints are specific to language, or carry over to other domains, say vision, is a separate question, the "modularity" question.

However, the only way we can decide whether a particular proposal about UG is domain-specific, or domain-independent, e.g., reduces to probabilistic constraints on chess-playing or whatever, is to compare the two proposals. But this is apparently not possible for Seidenberg. For, as he noted above, "vast areas of language have yet to be addressed at all" in Seidenberg's framework.

In conclusion, Seidenberg has not established an "alternative theoretical framework" to the "Standard Theory" (biolinguistics). What we are left with is the following: the use of probabilistic constraints, already an option in the "Standard Theory," is being explored using neural nets in several areas of language (plural formation, verb-argument structures of the "load the truck with bricks" type). The status of the issues of competence (vs. performance), idealization, poverty-of-the-stimulus argument and modularity remains exactly the same as before.

Language as an "emergent" phenomenon

We have been exploring the "unification" of biolinguistics with the rest of the natural sciences. In this section we will discuss the issues of "emergence" and "reductionism" that are often raised in this context. In a well-known essay, *More Is Different*, the physicist Philip Anderson has argued against what he calls the "constructionist" hypothesis in the sciences. Horgan calls this essay a "rallying cry for antireductionist approaches to science" (Horgan, 1994:34). But it is important to note that Anderson is not arguing against what he himself calls the "reductionist hypothesis"; viz., that "the workings of our minds and bodies, and of all the animate or inanimate matter of which we have any detailed knowledge, are assumed to be controlled by the same set of fundamental laws." In fact, he says quite clearly that "we must all start with reductionism, which I fully accept." Anderson is arguing instead against a "corollary of reductionism," which is that you can start from those fundamental laws and "reconstruct the universe" (Anderson, 1972:393–94). He asks us to consider the sciences arranged in roughly the hierarchy (adapted from Anderson, 1972) in the diagram.

social sciences
⇓
psychology
⇓
physiology
⇓

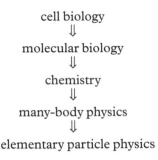

cell biology
⇓
molecular biology
⇓
chemistry
⇓
many-body physics
⇓
elementary particle physics

According to Anderson, a science higher up in the hierarchy obeys the laws of a science lower down. Many-body physics (solid state physics) obeys the laws of elementary particle physics. But it is not the case that many-body physics is "just applied" elementary particle physics. Rather "at each level of complexity entirely new properties appear," which require new research of as fundamental nature as any lower level: "At each stage entirely new laws, concepts, and generalizations are necessary, requiring inspiration and creativity to just as great a degree as in the previous one. Psychology is not applied biology, nor is biology applied chemistry" (Anderson, 1972:393).

What are these new complexities? Anderson notes that his own field of many-body physics, which is "closer to our fundamental, intensive underpinnings than in any other science in which non-trivial complexities occur," shows clearly how the "shift from quantitative to qualitative differentiation takes place"; viz., by means of "broken symmetry" (p. 393). As examples of broken symmetry phenomena from his area of study, Anderson cites superconductivity, antiferromagnets, ferroelectrics, and liquid crystals. The formation of a crystal lattice is the "most-studied and perhaps simplest example of what we call an 'emergent property': a property which is manifested only by a sufficiently large and complex system by virtue of that size and complexity." Anderson notes that "broken symmetry is actually the basic underlying concept of solid state physics" and that "many, if not most, of the interesting properties of condensed matter systems are emergent broken symmetry effects" (Anderson, 1994:587–88). The idea here is that, under certain conditions, a macroscopic system can exhibit properties like superconductivity and antiferromagnetism, which are "not only more than but very different from the sum of its parts." These properties are examples of "emergent" properties and broken symmetry is their source.

Chomsky has suggested that human language represents an important example of "emergence" in the mental domain:

There seems to be no substance to the view that human language is simply a more complex instance of something to be found elsewhere in the animal world. This poses a problem for the biologist, since, if true, it is an example of true "emergence" – the appearance of a qualitatively different phenomenon at a specific stage of complexity of organization . . . it seems to me today that there is no better or more promising way to explore the essential and distinctive properties of human intelligence than through the detailed investigation of the structure of this unique human possession. (Chomsky, 1968:70)

There are examples that suggest that the symmetry-breaking mechanism may also be quite important in areas of biological development.[17] We will suggest in chapter 5 that this mechanism may play a role in the development of the asymmetries found in human language, such as in word order. We are thus speculating that properties of language, such as syntactical asymmetries, are "emergent properties," the properties of which are not deducible from the lower levels of Anderson's hierarchy. What we would have then is a kind of "big bang" view of language development, in which a series of symmetry-breakings occur as the language faculty grows (develops) under the specific initial conditions of language input from the environment. The initial (genetic) state of the language faculty would represent the symmetrical state with respect to word-order possibilities. This is reflected empirically by the fact that each new-born child appears to be able to learn any possible word order in the world's languages, including the so-called free word order languages. The actual word order realized would result from an interplay of the underlying genetic system and the dynamics of growth, along with initial conditions provided by the language environment.

Weinberg considers the concept of "emergence" to be "well captured" by Anderson in the "More Is Different" essay (Weinberg, 1992:39). At the same time he declares himself to be a reductionist ("I consider myself a reductionist") in an illuminating essay in the same book, "Two Cheers for Reductionism." But as we have already seen, this is not a contradictory stance, in spite of some popular characterizations.[18] Both Anderson and

---

[17] See, for example, the discussion in chapter 5 of the Turing mechanism and that of the Fibonacci numbers in the sunflower. See also Goodwin, 1994. Anderson, 1972 leaves the question of the role of symmetry-breaking in life open: "Whether the development of life requires any further breaking of symmetry is by no means clear" (p. 395). He does add a few speculations on the role of such factors as "temporal regularity," and even specifically gives "spoken human language" as an example. See also Anderson for some (skeptical) comments on the role of broken symmetry and the concept of "dissipative structures" in self-organization of living systems (Anderson, 1981).

[18] See, e.g., Waldrop, who says of Anderson: "He had personally been fighting a guerilla war against reductionism for decades," citing the "More Is Different" article (Waldrop, 1992:81). As we noted above, in that essay Anderson declares that "we must all start with reductionism, which I fully accept."

Weinberg consider the higher level sciences in the hierarchy depicted above to obey the laws of the lower level sciences, and in this sense they consider themselves to be reductionists. Nevertheless, both believe in "emergent" phenomena; Weinberg uses temperature and entropy as examples of emergent concepts that "lose all meaning on the level of individual particles." For these reasons, neither the characterization of Anderson (by Waldrop) as fighting a guerrilla war against reductionism nor the characterization of Weinberg (by Ernst Mayr) as an "uncompromising reductionist" would appear to be fair. Weinberg prefers to reserve the word "fundamental" for the lowest level in the sense that what he calls the "arrows of explanation" all flow backward to that level, as depicted in the hierarchy above.

We must add an important caveat to our discussion of "reductionism." Chomsky notes that "To the extent that unification has been achieved, it has not been achieved through strict reductionism, except in rare cases. It's very commonly been the case that what we think of as more the fundamental science had to be radically revised" (Chomsky, 1994a:81). He notes that concepts such as the periodic table and the chemical bond could not be "reduced" to 19th-century physics, but nevertheless had great explanatory value. A fuller understanding of these chemical notions had to wait for the foundations of physics to be "expanded" to include quantum theory. For a more comprehensive discussion of how physics was expanded to incorporate chemistry and of the parallels with the mind/body issue, see Chomsky, 1995a. Nor is the situation described by Chomsky any different at the present. Glashow notes that, at the time that the quark was postulated, no particle with a fractional electric charge had ever been seen. Hence there were no such particles around to "reduce" the theory of hadrons to. Rather the theory of elementary particles would have to be "expanded" to accommodate such fractional charges. To give another example of "expanding" physics, in the late 1970s, Weinberg, and independently, Susskind, proposed a brand-new extra-strong force of nature, now called "technicolor" (still unconfirmed), to help account for the breaking of the electroweak symmetry (Weinberg, 1992:310).

BISHOP ON BIOLINGUISTICS

In a "News and Views" in *Nature* which reviews a study by Wright et al. on an auditory perceptual deficit in children (Wright et al., 1997), Bishop announces the demise of the idea that "language is genetically determined, developing according to a biological program"; see the abstract to Bishop, 1997. However, borrowing from W. C. Fields, we can say that the reports of its death have been greatly exaggerated.

It is claimed that "new studies of children with a 'specific language impairment' (SLI) indicate that, in fact, specialized language-learning systems do not exist, but that language develops through other, more general, perceptual or cognitive processes."

Bishop argues that one would not want to conclude from the fact that a gene can cause multiple dystrophy that there is a gene for walking. Similarly, one would not want to conclude from the fact that a gene is involved in grammatical impairment that there is a gene for talking (or grammar). But her argument doesn't go through either.

Suppose we identify an ill-defined heterogeneous group of people that all have problems in locomotion. The problems are more or less specific to walking, but a few might also have problems in other domains, like jumping, swimming, or dancing. Let's call the syndrome Specific Walking Impairment (SWI). Now suppose we discover a subset of people with SWI that have trouble with a particular performance test that involves timing. They can't walk with their legs in synch or stand still with their feet together. Do we now conclude that we have shown the incorrectness of the idea that walking is genetically determined, developing according to a biological program? Or that walking and other movements of the body must be due to nonspecific generalized timing procedures? A developmental biologist studying bodily functions would not leap to these conclusions. An interesting question is why so many researchers in psychology and the cognitive sciences are willing to embrace the analogous suspect argument when studying the mind.

Worse still, Bishop's own work shows that "auditory . . . mechanisms" are irrelevant to the question of whether language is genetically determined. In particular, she observes in her studies of the deaf, the well-established fact that even when the auditory perceptual system is completely blocked, language is still able to develop in a nonsequential manner through the visual use of sign language (Poizner, Klima, and Bellugi, 1987).

Most importantly, though, the proposal that language is genetically determined is based on a large number of converging lines of evidence, not just on one kind of impairment. The study of the biology of language is based on a wide range of converging evidence, as was discussed earlier – universal and comparative grammar, language acquisition and perception, sign-language, language-isolated children, creole language, family and twin studies of agrammatism, expressive and receptive aphasias, split brains, linguistic savants, and electrical activity of the brain. This is not to say that the study of language impairments, genetic or otherwise, is not of importance – quite the contrary. But such studies are still in their infancy. Careful studies, such as those being made by Gopnik, van der Lely (van der Lely, 1997; van der Lely and Stollwerck, 1996), their colleagues, and others (see chapter 4) are necessary in order to delineate the heterogeneous group of impairments, loosely called Specific Language Impairment, into various subclasses of deficits affecting grammar, articulation, perception, and other cognitive components, just as "mental retardation" has been broken down over the decades into various kinds of X-linked mental retardation, different kinds of fragile-X syndrome, and many others.

Recently, at a meeting of the British Association for the Advancement of Science, Bishop advanced a "radical new genetic explanation" for language disorders. She reports that the "the ability to learn to talk is genetic." The radical explanation is based on her studies of "family relationships," "identical twins," the rapidity of language learning, and poverty of the stimulus; i.e., the observation that "in Papua New Guinea, parents hold the belief they shouldn't talk to their children until they have something to say, but they still develop natural language." In short Bishop invokes many of the standard arguments developed over the last forty years in the biolinguistic program of Chomsky and others. Bishop even goes on to say that we need not be fatalistic about the fact that language is "tied to genes." We should someday be able to intervene "biochemically" in these "genetic disorders" and perhaps even come up with a "language drug" for the language-impaired.

USE OF LANGUAGE

Chomsky notes that the general question about language use "calls for the development of performance theories, among them, theories of production and interpretation" (Chomsky and Lasnik, 1993:509). Put in such general terms, the problem is beyond understanding: "It would be unreasonable to pose the problem of how Jones decides to say what he does, or how he interprets what he hears in particular circumstances."

However, aspects of the problem can be studied. In particular, it has been assumed that "one component of the mind/brain is a *parser*, which assigns a percept to a signal (abstracting from other circumstances relevant to interpretation)." The parser would have the (I-)language embedded in it and the parser itself would be embedded in other systems used for interpretation (Berwick, Abney, and Tenny, 1992).

Chomsky notes that it is well known that parsing illustrates one important way in which languages are "unusable:"

Parsing may be slow and difficult, or even impossible, and it may be "in error" in the sense that the percept assigned (if any) fails to match the SD [structural description] associated with the signal; many familiar cases have been studied. In general, it is not the case that language is readily usable or "designed for use." The subparts that are used are usable, trivially; biological considerations lead us to expect no more than that. (Chomsky and Lasnik, 1993:509)

Examples of parsing problems are "garden path sentences" and multiple embedding.

Similarly, one should not expect on a priori grounds that the languages specified by UG should be learnable. It could be that some languages are learnable and others are not and that the latter are or are not found among the world's languages. If the principles-and-parameters model is correct, then languages would be learnable, but, as Chomsky notes, this result would be empirically surprising.

4 Mechanisms of language

LANGUAGE AND GENETICS – MUTANTS OF THE MIND

The "great mutant hunt"

We have argued that principles of universal grammar (i.e., of syntax, morphology, semantics, and phonology) have, with respect to the nervous system, a status much like that of Mendelian laws of classical genetics (Jenkins, 1979). That is, they are an abstract characterization of physical mechanisms which, in this case, reflect genetically specified neural structures.

Moreover, we argued that it made no more (or less) sense to ask whether what we then called "Chomsky's laws" were "psychologically real" than it did to ask whether "Mendel's laws" were "physiologically real." If you were convinced by the evidence from the argument from poverty of the stimulus, or by other nonlinguistic evidence, that UG represented the genetic component or initial state of the language faculty, then it made sense to talk about the genes involved in the specification of the initial state. And one could ask the usual things that get asked about genes – what chromosomes are they on? Do they act in a dominant, recessive, polygenic,[1] or other fashion? What do they do – are they structural or regulatory genes? And so on.

Objections were raised that Mendel's laws were either outmoded or else, if they still were operative at all, they didn't have much to do with UG:

His [Mendel's] fundamental approach, using statistical methods and proposing abstract laws to describe the regularities, was a plausible one in the initial stages of the scientific study of heredity; but it would make no sense nowadays, with the knowledge we have acquired about the chemistry of the genetic program. (Coopmans, 1984:58)

---

[1] Polygenic inheritance is multiple-gene inheritance, where one trait can be affected by more than one gene.

His [Jenkins'] parallels cannot aid the integration of linguistic universals into the study of genetics because those universals simply do not "suppress" underlying structures in the way in which e.g. wrinkledness is "suppressed"; there is no sense in which the structures that violate Chomsky's laws are evident in one generation, "suppressed" in the next, and revealed anew in the one after. (Watt, 1979:133)

However, evidence is emerging that suggests at least some cases of agram-matism exhibit classical Mendelian inheritance patterns. Gopnik and her colleagues have argued that a dominantly inherited gene in a family they have studied (see below) affects morphological inflection: "Data are pre-sented that suggest that at least some cases of dysphasia are associated with an abnormality in a single dominant gene. The results of a series of tests on a large three-generation family, in which half of the members have dysphasia, are reported" (Gopnik and Crago, 1991:1).

As we have noted, the methods of classical genetics are vital in many areas of genetics where one still has little biochemical understanding or no handle on a given phenomenon (Jenkins, 1979). McClintock's work on maize, for which she was awarded the Nobel Prize in 1983, the year preceding Coopman's comments, relied on the same kinds of statistical counting methods originally used in classical genetics (even though she drew some non-Mendelian conclusions from her data). It was only later that her theory of transposable genetic elements received independent biochemical confirmation by the study of bacterial genetic elements called "transposons." Studies at the forefront of molecular biology today, such as work in developmental genetics on the fruit fly, still depend cru-cially on the use of the statistical methods of Mendel.

Let us return to Watt's objection that language universals don't get "suppressed" and reappear like pea color from one generation to the next. We did not mean to imply that each language universal corresponded in a point-by-point fashion to one specific language gene, which in turn segre-gated in Mendelian fashion, a view that Watt appears to be imputing to us. For, if language is polygenic; i.e., involves the interaction of many genes, as is the case for such traits as tallness (height) in humans, then there is no reason to expect to see particular language universals being suppressed and reappearing in successive generations in a simple dominant and reces-sive fashion. We will suggest below that there may be some genotypical variations in UG corresponding to observed linguistic phenotypes present in the human population (in Human). How these traits are inherited (dominant, recessive, polygenic, etc.) is a subject for empirical research.

In their study of song patterns in the cricket (*Teleogryllus*) Bentley and Hoy concluded that the gene systems underlying song were both poly-genic and multichromosomal (Bentley and Hoy, 1972). The study of such song parameters as the number of pulses per trill and the number of trills per phrase in *Teleogryllus* hybrids indicated polygenic inheritance: "no parameters are controlled by monofactorial inheritance involving a simple dominant–recessive situation . . . it appears that each song parameter is affected by a number of genes, resulting in a stable genetic arrangement well buffered against mutation" (Bentley and Hoy, 1972).

Moreover, the control of some characters is sex-linked while that of others is not, indicating that more than one chromosome is involved in the genetic system; i.e., it is multichromosomal. The study of the intertrill interval distribution indicated that this character is influenced by genes on the X-chromosome as well as by genes on other chromosomes. The authors conclude: "Consequently, even the more highly restricted set of genes regulating a single song parameter is distributed on more than one chromosome" (Bentley and Hoy, 1972). Hence, the "one gene–one parameter" hypothesis does not hold for certain animal communication systems such as these cases of cricket song. There is no more reason to expect or assume it must hold for the more complex system of human language.

This does not, however, exclude the possibility that some grammar variations might follow classical Mendelian laws. In addition, some speech disorders have been associated with simple autosomal or X-linked inheritance (developmental dysphasia, some cases of stuttering and dyslexia, X-linked mental retardation, etc.). Analogously, certain cases of stunted growth have also been noted to follow Mendelian patterns.

Chomsky has speculated that the initial state characterized by UG is "an element of the human biological endowment that appears to be subject to little variation apart from severe pathology" (Chomsky, 1991a:7). As a first approximation this seems true and the following kind of *Gedankenexperiment* is often carried out to support it: suppose John (from New York) is brought up in Rome and Gianni (from Rome) is brought up in New York. Since John learns Italian and Gianni English, this shows that John wasn't genetically wired to learn English nor was Gianni wired for Italian. We can carry this thought experiment out across all the languages of the world and it seems reasonable to conclude that UG (the initial state) is invariant. From a genetics point of view a lot of questions still need to be asked about John and Gianni. How do their intuitions about negative evidence for universal principles (*that*-trace violations, Subjacency, Binding, etc.) compare with their peers? If John or Gianni left an identical twin behind, how do their intuitions compare with those of their twins and the twins' peers? How do the intuitions of John, Gianni, and their identical twins compare with their real siblings? Or their adopted siblings? Or with their relatives? Is any familial patterning in judgments apparent?

Thus there could still be a considerable spectrum of variation in UG ranging from gross pathological conditions to more subtle UG variations not reported to the speech clinic. One source of genetic variation in UG might be at points of the system that are less central than the core principles. For example, consider the so-called "*that*-trace effect," seen in the following examples:

(1) Who do you think John saw t?
(2) Who do you think t saw Mary?
(3) Who do you think that John saw t?
(4) *Who do you think that t saw Mary?
(5) *Who do you think that t left?

Note that, in these examples, *who* can always be extracted from the object position of *saw*, whether or not the complementizer *that* is present, as in (1) and (3). However, *who* cannot be extracted from the subject position of *saw* unless *that* is absent; cf. (2) with (4) and (5). That is, the configuration excluded is when *that* is followed by the trace of the moved item *who*. Hence the term "*that*-trace effect."

There has been a lot work to try to subsume these effects under more general principles such as the Empty Category Principle (ECP). It has been found that these effects show a great deal of variation across languages and dialects. To account for this variation, the linguist will look for linguistic data that might act as a trigger to set a switch one way or the other in the relevant UG principle. One of the problems remaining to be explained is how *that*-trace violations are introduced without any positive linguistic evidence. Although one might appeal to spontaneous innovation, we wish to consider a different possibility here. Note that any time one proposes a principle of UG with a switch that can be set one or more ways, there are two ways that this neurogenetic switch can be reset – either (1) by being triggered by linguistic data or (2) it can be triggered directly in the genotype of a "founder" group and then propagated further by positive linguistic evidence. Although it may be difficult to tease out the effects of genetics from the effects of linguistic data, it is important to note that this hypothesis is testable in a variety of ways.

What kinds of tests might give evidence for this thesis? One could test siblings to see whether they have opposite judgments about the *that*-trace effect. If the *that*-trace effect is a UG variation, one would predict that such families should exist. The entire family could then be examined through multiple generations to look for a detectable genetic pattern of transmission (Mendelian or non-Mendelian).

Moreover, suppose we found a carrier of the genetic variation for the *that*-trace violation. If this carrier had an identical twin reared separately in a population that observed the *that*-trace filter, one might test the twin to see whether he or she had *that*-trace intuitions that diverged from the rest of the population. This would be predicted since the only evidence to the contrary is negative evidence.

Note that these kinds of language variations are not of the kind that would ever come to attention of speech therapists. Nor should they, since they appear to be perfectly harmless variations in syntax, found in many languages and dialects throughout the world. Reports of these variants would more likely be found on the pages of *Linguistic Inquiry* than in the *Journal of Speech and Hearing Research*. The kind of variation we are talking about here is like the polymorphic variation in the population for the perception of the color red or for tasting the chemical PTC.[2] Only here the variation involves the assignment of stars (*'s) in sentences like (4) and (5). If we wish, we can speak here of "language polymorphisms" or "UG polymorphisms," or simply language variants.

Although we have used the example of the "*that*-trace effect" for the sake of concreteness, the thesis we have outlined carries over to other areas of UG. Thus one might look for areas of idiolectal, dialectal, or cross-language variation (or "hot spots") with respect to other UG conditions – e.g., on binding, control, case, movement, etc.

Lightfoot has given an account of diachronic change in terms of parameter settings. He proposes specific linguistic mechanisms operative in historical change and suggests they be understood against the background of more general biological principles: "The picture of language change that emerges is one of 'punctuated equilibrium.' Languages are constantly changing gradually and in piecemeal fashion, but meanwhile grammars remain in equilibrium, unchanged in their structural properties. From time to time, however, they undergo more radical, catastrophic restructuring, corresponding to new parameter settings" (Lightfoot, 1991:173).

Lightfoot's proposals concern how new parameter settings might arise when the trigger is linguistic data. We are suggesting here that another possible source of innovations in historical change is genetic variations of the kind discussed in this chapter, which arise by garden-variety kinds of classical genetic mutation.[3]

The discussion of "subjacency mutants" with Chomsky in Huybregts

---

[2] PTC is phenylthiocarbamide, a chemical that tastes bitter to some people, but not others.
[3] E. J. Mange and A. P. Mange note that "mutations are the ultimate source of the variation on which evolution depends. Recombination of chromosome segments or migration of individuals can bring about reshuffling of alleles, yielding perhaps beneficial combinations, but all current genetically based differences between organisms derive from random mutations at some time in the recent or remote past" (Mange and Mange, 1994:430).

and Riemsdijk, which focuses on the problem of genetic variation, may understate the potential significance and relevance of language mutants to an understanding of the biological bases of language (Huybregts and Riemsdijk, 1982:24). There it is noted that such biologists as Luria have suggested looking for mutations in language; consider, for example: "A start on the biology of language can be made by observing the derangements produced by accidents or disease or genetic mutation or chemical poisoning onto linguistic functions on the one hand and on the brain network on the other hand" (Luria, 1975b:50).

But the discussion in Huybregts and Riemsdijk leaves the impression that these are primarily of interest for the study of genetic *variation*. It is true, as he notes, that the developmental biologist will often abstract away from genetic variation, unless he is specifically interested in the problem. Or as Goodenough has formulated the issue: "Whereas the molecular or chromosomal geneticist seeks to minimize variation by using *pure* lines, *stable* genetic markers, *uniform* enzyme assay systems, and so on, the population geneticist is primarily interested in variability, in the amount of variability within a population, and in the way genes change during evolution" (Goodenough, 1978:748).

The studies of Dobzhansky on variation are an example (Dobzhansky, 1962). The neurogeneticist will use isogenic lines of mice and genetic mosaics to reduce variation (Stent, 1981). Although the biolinguist cannot perform such controlled matings of humans, (s)he could, for example, study identical twins to achieve a similar effect, as in the agrammatism studies of Luchsinger.

However, the primary importance of mutant or aberrant gene structures to genetics is, perhaps somewhat paradoxically, for studying the *normal* unmutated form of the gene. This is because mutations can be used to do various kinds of gene mapping experiments to determine the physical location of the gene. Moreover, they can be used as probes to reveal underlying biochemical mechanisms; e.g., they can introduce blocks in metabolic pathways or, as overproducers, can serve as sources of gene products normally present only in minute quantities in the cell. Such an example is the work of Luria himself, who, e.g., used bacterial mutants lacking the enzyme adenosine triphosphatase to study the energetics of cell membranes (Luria, 1975a:35ff.). It has also historically been the case that geneticists have used the mutant primarily in an effort to understand the normal (wild-type) case rather than to study variation; a typical well-known example is Thomas Hunt Morgan's use of the white-eyed male mutant fly to demonstrate sex-linked inheritance (Jenkins, 1975:47–50). Of course, for ethical reasons, in the case of language we may not artificially induce mutations as Muller did in his studies of the fruit fly (Muller, 1977 [1946]). But this fact makes such rare mutations as do occur naturally even more valuable for the study of the biology of language. Mutants can, of course, be very profitably used as tools to study genetic variation as well, but just as many or more geneticists have engaged in what Brenner terms the "great mutant hunt" in order to probe normal gene structure and function (Brenner, 1979:2).

SOME CASE STUDIES[4]

Syntax in identical twins (Luchsinger)

In his study of speech disorders, Luchsinger pointed out the importance of identical (monozygotic) twins for the study of the development of grammar. His interest was in the study of cases of *agrammatism*; i.e., where some speech defect affecting grammar was present in the twins, as in the following example:[5]

A pair of nine year old identical twins were found to have exactly the same traits of character and language. They both had normal intelligence and both had quiet, withdrawn personalities. Their articulation appeared normal. However, at school their progress was hindered by exactly the same difficulties with sentence structure. For example, *both boys placed the sentence object at the end of the sentence or else deleted it completely.* This "language problem," which the father also suffered from until the age of ten, was an additional indication of hereditary origin in the sense of an inborn language defect. (Luchsinger and Arnold, 1965, emphasis ours)

Since identical twins (in general) have the same genes and hence the same genetic program, the presence here of a severe specific grammatical defect suggests the possibility of a common genetic defect in the twins. The fact that the father had a similar problem provides additional support for the view that a genetic defect is involved. Of additional interest is the fact that the twins were of otherwise normal intelligence. That is, we cannot ascribe the twins' severe language problem to a general mental retardation affecting all cognitive capacities.

In discussing syntactic speech disorders Luchsinger notes: "It seems particularly interesting to me that even disorders of the form and structure of speech exhibit genetic peculiarities" (Luchsinger, 1957:250).

---

[4] The case studies that follow vary greatly in the depth and thoroughness with respect to the linguistic analysis provided. Many questions can be raised with respect to the problems of properly characterizing the linguistic phenotype. It may be useful to read "The phenotype," in the next section, "Physical Mechanisms," for a discussion of some of these issues.

[5] The case of these two monozygotic twins, Seppli and Hans B., was first reported in Luchsinger, 1945.

More is involved here than recall of words; citing the German philosopher of language, Steinthal, Luchsinger notes that it is not the case that sentences are stored ready-made in memory (p. 250). In the terminology of modern linguistics, in addition to a (finite) lexicon of words, there must be (recursive) rule mechanisms for syntax. Along with word formation (*Wortbeugung*) rules there are rules of syntactic word order (*die Wortstellung im Satz* (*die Syntax*), p. 250). These are part of what Luchsinger calls the "inborn language endowment" (*anlagegemässe Sprachausstattung*, p. 251), which plays a much more important role in certain grammatical disorders than does experience, since even repeated correction of errors does no good. He notes that children often omit prepositions or misunderstand designations for place in expressions like *auf, über, unter dem Tisch* ("on, above, under the table"), even when their sense of orientation and perceptual abilities are preserved (p. 250).[6]

In the case studied by Luchsinger the twins both speak the same language (German) and hence make the same kind of error. However, identical twins with speech defects that are raised speaking different languages could in principle provide other kinds of tests of hypotheses about parameters in UG. The prediction from the theory of UG is that such twins raised speaking different languages (such as English, German, Italian, etc.) might show similar, *but not necessarily identical,* speech problems with movement or deletion of syntactic categories, reflecting the variation of parameters in UG chosen in various languages. If, as we have indicated, the development of grammar involves the selection of lexical or morphological parameters such as syntactic phrase categories to fix the domain of syntactic rules of movement (deletion, etc.) such as question inversion, verb placement (in German), gapping, etc., then there are a number of ways that the genetic program might go amiss in fixing such parameters. The wrong parameter for a given language might be fixed, too many parameters might be chosen, too few, none at all, etc. In these cases syntactic rules might have too wide or too narrow a range of application or otherwise not apply.

By testing intuitions in such identical twins, it becomes possible to provide additional confirmation (or refutation) of particular proposals about parameterized UG, and also to give a more precise meaning to the largely impressionistic term "agrammatism." It is now known from the

---

[6] Although Luchsinger places great weight on genetic mechanisms in syntax and grammar in general, he does explicitly note the importance of environment and social class; citing H. Hetzer he observes that although a child of well-educated parents may initially gain a temporary language advantage over the child of a worker, the latter will eventually catch up in ability. He also observes that one must not confuse pathological cases of grammatical errors with nonpathological efforts to be original or creative (*Originalitätssucht*, p. 250).

study of the auditory system that there are over one hundred distinct forms of hereditary deafness (McKusick, 1978: xxxiii–xxxv).[7] One must be prepared for the possibility that there may be as many kinds of agrammatic syndromes. One way to go about subclassifying such syndromes affecting grammar is by studying twin cases with specific grammatical defects like the problem with sentence-objects that Luchsinger discovered. Properties of UG can suggest what kinds of things are useful to test for. In the case of Luchsinger's twins, the theory of parameterized UG makes certain predictions about the appropriate domains for syntactic movement and deletion (in German) and one can try to test these predictions by constructing test examples for each of these domains. Although the example we have been discussing is a syntactic one, the study of semantic and phonological parameters in UG could, of course, similarly be made using identical twins with the appropriate speech disorder.

The study of such twin pairs would also have the attractive feature that one could more easily separate out the effect of genes from the environment because (1) the twins have identical genetic programs, (2) the twins are raised in two radically different speech environments, and (3) it cannot be objected that the twins picked up their speech defect by imitation of each other. One should also be on the lookout in such cases as these for any evidence of familial transmission of the speech disorder (as Luchsinger noted for his case) as supporting evidence for the genetic basis of the disorder.

The KE family

Hurst et al. did a genetic study of a British family with "developmental verbal apraxia" (Hurst et al., 1990). Inheritance of the speech disorder was found to be autosomal dominant and affected sixteen family members of thirty over three generations. They concluded that "its importance seems to be that there is a single gene coding for a pathway which is fundamental for developing intelligible language" (p. 354).

Gopnik and Crago did another study on members of the same family, focusing on specific problems with grammar and concluded that the affected children cannot construct general linguistic rules for grammatical features such as number, tense or aspect (Gopnik and Crago, 1991).

We will summarize these studies in the following sections.

---

[7] McKusick lists 124 forms based mainly on Konigsmark and Gorlin, 1976; in many of the syndromes there are defects other than just deafness; e.g., pleiotropisms (where more than one characteristic or function is determined by a single gene). In addition, in some cases the deafness may be a second-order side effect of something else.

Developmental verbal dyspraxia (Hurst et al., 1990)

Hurst et al. noted that their patients exhibited a number of problems in speech and language. As for the sound system, they reported articulation problems and moderate to severe dyspraxia resulting in unintelligibility. They observed simplification of consonant clusters (e.g., "boon" for spoon), and omission of initial and final consonants ("able" for table). Finally, syllables were sometimes dropped in polysyllabic words.

They also noted that all patients had "difficulty in constructing grammatical sentences." Moreover, they had delayed comprehension with respect to comparatives ("the knife is longer than the pencil"), passives ("the girl is chased by the horse"), and reduced relatives ("the boy chasing the horse is fat"). Finally they made naming errors ("glass" or "tea" for cup).

Developmental dysphasia and morphological inflection (Gopnik and Crago, 1991)

English syntax typically distinguishes singular nouns from plural nouns with a grammatical "number" marker:

book (singular) vs. books (plural)

This is a general rule which speakers of English can apply to new words they have never heard before; e.g., to nonsense words such as *wug*.

wug (singular) vs. wugs (plural)

In addition, there are well-known exceptions in English, which must be learned by rote; i.e., that are not rule-governed:

child (singular) vs. children (plural) [not childs]

Gopnik and Crago found that in syntactic contexts where you would expect a singular noun, a plural was often found:

a books [correct: a book]

Conversely, in plural syntactic contexts, a singular was found

three book [correct: three books]

Moreover, when given nonsense syllables, such as *wug*, they were unable to generalize to the correct plural form *wugs*.

However, it is not the case that these subjects were unable to learn the correct plural form above. It could be learned, but only with great effort. It was as if the form "books" were learned by rote, in much the same way as "children" is learned. In certain cases, even forty-year-olds continued to have problems with such forms. In effect, they had to learn "book" and "books" as separate forms.

However, it was clear that they had an intuitive grasp of the concept of "number." They were able to use plural numerical quantifiers with single nouns to get the idea of plurality across. One of the subjects was highly skilled with math and computers. The problem appeared to be with grammatical number, not with the concept of number itself in some other semantic or cognitive domain.[8]

Gopnik and Crago went on to show that they had analogous problems with past tense (walk vs. walked) and aspect (sing vs. singing). Again, though, they appeared to understand the conceptual and semantic notions involved and could use adverbs to force a past tense reading on the sentence when they needed to.

Vargha-Khadem and Passingham and their colleagues noted that, in addition to the problems Hurst et al. found (expressive speech, reversible passive, postmodified subjects and semantic naming errors), they also observed deficits in the areas of relative clauses and other embedded forms, receptive vocabulary, and repetition (Vargha-Khadem and Passingham, 1990). Vargha-Khadem et al. analyze this data further and conclude that: "This psychological profile indicates that the inherited disorder does not affect morphosyntax exclusively, or even primarily; rather, it affects intellectual, linguistic, and orofacial praxic functions generally. The evidence from the KE family thus provides no support for the proposed existence of grammar-specific genes" (Vargha-Khadem et al., 1995:930).

However, it is important to note that the evidence also provides no support against the existence of such genes nor any support for a general learning mechanism theory such as the connectionist framework (Elman et al., 1996). The reason for this can be seen by comparing the case of the KE family to a better understood case of Williams syndrome (see also

---

[8] There are languages, sometimes called "isolating" languages, like Chinese, which do not use morphological inflection to mark plurality, for example. It would be interesting to know whether a child with the deficit studied by Gopnik and Crago raised in a Chinese-speaking community would exhibit the same or different problems. It would also be of interest to look for any systematic variation in the gene responsible for the disorder in the KE family between populations of isolating languages and those with languages using morphological inflection, especially if, as we suggested earlier, slight genetic variation may possibly seed linguistic variation.

below), where cognitive defects are intermingled with vascular disease (Frangiskakis et al., 1996). Frangiskakis et al. discovered that at the molecular level there are actually (at a minimum) two genes involved in Williams syndrome, *elastin*, which is responsible for vascular disease and LIM-kinase 1, expressed in the brain, which may be partly responsible for some of the cognitive defects. Since the genes are contiguous, parts of each gene can be knocked out by a single deletion, giving rise to multiple phenotypic effects. However, the authors also describe cases with mutations in the *elastin* gene, which give rise to vascular problems, but do not produce cognitive abnormalities. Hence just looking at the heterogeneous phenotype does not tell you whether there are genes for discrete functions at the genomic level.

Similarly, in the cases studied by Gopnik and colleagues, there is no way of knowing how many genes are involved, what functions they have, or whether some genes are even multipurpose (see chapter 5). And, as Vargha-Khadem et al., concede:

> While they constitute only a part of the affected members' total syndrome, these speech and language difficulties are an important aspect of their phenotype. Knowledge of the neural and genetic correlates of this phenotype could thus provide important clues to some of the underpinnings of the primary human faculties of speech and language as well as of the many other functions in which the affected members are also impaired. (Vargha-Khadem et al., 1995:933)

Dyslexia

(Developmental) dyslexia, or specific language disability, is of great interest to the researcher of the biology of language, both because of the interesting linguistic peculiarities it presents, and because of the lines of evidence which suggest a genetic basis for certain cases of the disorder. Moreover, a number of cases of developmental dyslexia associated with abnormal brain structures, including language areas, have been identified (Galaburda, 1993). We will give a few examples of the linguistic disorders involved in dyslexia, briefly point out several kinds of evidence of its genetic origin, and then discuss the findings made in the dyslexic brain.

Dyslexia and linguistics

By way of illustration, a typical (though by no means the only) kind of error made by dyslexics is *reversal* – either of letters, parts of words, whole words, or sometimes even sentences. Typical letters to be reversed are *b* and *d*, *p* and *q*, etc. Typical pairs of words to be confused in reading by the dyslexic child are *saw* vs. *was, no* vs. *on,* etc.[9] Eileen Simpson, herself a dyslexic, gives us a vivid description of this problem

Miss Henderson and now Auntie: There seemed to be nothing I could do to please either of them. How, in the past, had it been so easy, so effortless to be a favorite? With a feeling of impending doom I would begin. I might get halfway through the first sentence before Auntie would say in a dry, controlled voice, "In the context the word cannot possibly be "saw." "The man saw going home." Does that make sense to you? It must be "was."

I'd repeat, "The man was going home." In the next sentence, or the one after, meeting the word again, I'd hesitate. Had I said "was" before and had Auntie corrected it to "saw," or vice versa? My brain ached.

"Don't tell me you don't recognize that word. *I just told it to you.* You're *not trying.*"

Both my teachers accused me of not trying. They had no idea what an effort I was making. Was, saw, was, saw. How were they so sure which it was? Rattled by Auntie's foot tapping, I decided for "saw."

"No, no, NO. How *can* you be so stupid? The word is 'was.' WASWASWAS. And for heaven's sake *stop sniveling.* If those nuns hadn't fallen for your tears, you'd be able to read by now and we wouldn't be going through this . . ." (Simpson, 1979:19–20)

In certain cases, the reversals may even affect the structure of entire sentences. E.g., Ingram reports the occurrence of errors comparable to the following where *the man saw a red dog* is read as *a red god was the man.* Here we have reversals of *saw* to *was, dog* to *god,* and superimposed on these, we observe switching of the subject noun phrase, *the man,* with the object noun phrase *a red dog,* a reversal at the level of syntactic structure (Ingram, 1960:256). Another kind of linguistic error of interest which persists in some dyslexic children is "mirror writing," often observed in left-handers, where letters, words, or more rarely, even entire sentences are written backwards so that what is written can only be read by holding it up to a mirror (Jordan, 1977:56–57).

We emphasize that there is considerable variation in the kinds and variety of linguistic errors made by the dyslexic, presumably reflecting a heterogeneity in causes (genetic and environmental). Dyslexic disorders range from the very mild to the very severe, as illustrated in the following text interpretation made by an adult dyslexic

(dyslexic's rendering): An the bee-what in the tel mother of the biothodoodoo to the majoram or that emidrate eni eni Krastrei, mestriet to Ketra lotombreidi to ra from treido as that.

---

[9] It is important to bear in mind that not all children who reverse letters and words are dyslexic. This is a stage which many normal children pass through.

(actual text): It shall be in the power of the college to examine or not every licentiate, previous to his admission to the fellowship, as they shall think fit. (Simpson, 1979:44–45)

Dyslexia and genetics

There have been two kinds of evidence that have traditionally provided arguments in favor of a genetic component in some (not all) cases of developmental dyslexia – these are (1) studies of *family pedigrees* (Borges-Osório and Salzano, 1985; Finucci and Childs, 1983) and (2) *twin studies* (DeFries, Fulker, and LaBuda, 1987). Stromswold provides a current survey and discussion of the literature on these topics (Stromswold, 1996).

In the case of *family pedigrees*, it has been noted that developmental dyslexia sometimes "runs in families," that is, may affect not only the patient under study but also several siblings in a given family, or their parents, grandparents, uncles, cousins, etc. (Eustis, 1947; Orton, 1937:127–30). Interestingly, sometimes, even when the reading disability itself appears only sporadically throughout several generations, one often observes other language disabilities in its stead – writing disability, delayed speech, stuttering, etc., as well as a family history of left-handedness and/or ambidexterity. This clustering of various kinds of language disabilities with left-handedness caused observers of this syndrome early on to hypothesize that what is sometimes called "incomplete lateralization" might underlie various kinds of abnormal speech development (Orton, 1937). Below we discuss the case of a patient with developmental dyslexia with a well-defined lesion in a speech area of the brain. It is worthwhile noting here that the patient's three brothers and his father (but not his mother or his sister) exhibited reading problems as well.

Twin studies provide the basis for a second argument for a genetic component in dyslexia, in that this genetic component should generally be evident more often in identical (monozygotic) twins, who have the same genetic program, than in fraternal (dizygotic) twins, who have no more genes in common with each other than they do with their other siblings.

The results of a series of studies of dyslexic twins by Hallgren (Hallgren, 1950:213–19), Norrie (Hermann, 1959), and Lamy (Lamy, Launay, and Soulé, 1952) were summed up by Brewer as follows: monozygotic – 22 concordant (both with dyslexia), 0 discordant (one twin with dyslexia); dizygotic – 14 concordant (both twins with dyslexia), 39 discordant (one twin with dyslexia) (Brewer, 1963:48). We note that some cases of dizygotic twins are concordant since it is possible (but not necessary) for each of the twins to inherit the genes underlying the reading disorder, just as any other brother or sister might.

Finally, we observe that both twin studies and family pedigree studies can complement and reinforce one another; e.g., when the monozygotic twins in question are not only both dyslexic, but also have a family history of the disorder. Lamy, Launay, and Soulé studied a pair of French monozygotic twins, Gilbert and Michel, who had above average intelligence on nonverbal tests, but who both still had quite specific deficits in reading and writing at age twelve and a half (Lamy, Launay, and Soulé, 1952). For example, on tests Gilbert wrote *il piroussait* for *il pourrissait*, *drenier* for *dernier*, *j'oubille* for *j'oublie*, and even misspelled his own name *Gilbert* as *Gilbret*, etc., to give a few illustrations (p. 1475).

In addition, there was a family history of reading and writing difficulty, and of left-handedness. For example, Gilbert and Michel had German cousins which included a pair of dizygotic twins, one with dyslexia, with a dyslexic brother (p. 1476). As we noted in the discussion of agrammatism in the twins studied by Luchsinger, it would be quite interesting to be able to study the linguistic errors made in the presumably rare cases of one identical twin raised in one country with reading problems in that language and the second identical twin raised in another country with reading problems in a different language. One could then better exclude environmental effects – imitation of one twin by the other, family influences, etc. In addition, though, one can in this way also study the unfolding of the same genetic program as it grapples with different linguistic structures in different languages.

Some conclusions on genetic studies of language

In the preceding section we have discussed some of the reasons that traditional genetic studies are important for elucidating the biological bases of language. From a theoretical point of view, we know that there are specific properties of language that appear to have a genetic basis, as was argued earlier. Hence it makes sense to screen the population for mutations that affect language. We have also suggested that tiny genetic variations may possibly seed linguistic variation, which is seen in the variety of the world's languages.

We have given examples for language of the kinds of studies that have been fruitful in elucidating the nature of other kinds of biological systems; e.g., familial studies and twin studies. In addition, chromosomal studies will be considered below (in the section, "The karyotype"). In particular, we would like to note that many of the studies suffer from a lack of in-depth linguistic analysis. In many cases this is attributable to the fact that these studies were done in a clinical setting in which no language professionals participated so that all that is available to us are some cursory observations of the "poorly developed speech" sort. This serves to highlight the importance of the kind of thorough and careful work of Gopnik, van der Lely, Stromswold, Rice, Wexler, their colleagues, and others, who have helped to set new standards for the kind of analysis necessary to obtain meaningful grammatical analyses in the study of developmental agrammatism.

In the next section we will go into these issues into greater detail (see the section "The phenotype") and place them in the context of a more systematic search for the physical gene mechanisms underlying language.

GENES INVOLVED IN LANGUAGE

Traditionally, genetic disorders have provided a window on physical mechanisms. In the subarea of biolinguistics dealing with genetic disorders some of the questions are:
What is the language phenotype?
What chromosome is the relevant gene located on?[10]
What is the function of the gene?
Where and when is the gene expressed?
But before we get into the particulars, we might speculate on how many genes there might be involved in language. The assumption that language is polygenic seems reasonable, even though the exact number of genes involved in specifying the neural pathways of language is unknown (as is the number of genes affecting tallness, or even the number of genes in the human genome, for that matter). A guess at the order of magnitude of the number of language genes is provided by Luria:[11] "At any rate, the genetic basis of human language is likely to involve not one or a few genes but thousands" (Luria, 1975b:50). Note that when we speak of genes involved in language, it is not logically necessary that these genes be *dedicated* to language.

To pinpoint a gene involved in language, or any gene for that matter, a number of steps may be taken, including some or all of the following:[12]
(1) characterize the phenotype
(2) examine the karyotype[13]

---

[10] For simplicity, we consider the case of a single gene here. In many cases the disorder may be of polygenic origin.

[11] Luria does not provide an estimate for the total number of genes in the human genome and such estimates have varied widely in the literature ranging from 100,000 to 200,000 and even a million genes. The most widely accepted current estimate is around 75,000–100,000.

[12] This sequence of steps has been termed "reverse genetics," but is now more commonly known as "positional cloning." Genes that have been successfully identified in this fashion include CFTR (cystic fibrosis), NF1 (neurofibromatosis), and DMD (Duchenne muscular dystrophy), to mention only a few.

[13] The karyotype is the entire set of chromosomes from a cell.

(3) perform linkage analysis[14]
(4) walk the chromosome
(5) clone the gene
(6) study the gene product
We will consider (1)–(6) in the following sections.

The phenotype

Characterizing the phenotype accurately (step 1) is crucial for linkage analysis (step 3) because whether or not a particular subject is scored as expressing the language phenotype will affect the lod score, or probability, of the gene locus being located on a particular chromosome.

Ideally, one would like to have grammatical disorders unaccompanied by general mental retardation or other kinds of cognitive problems. This may not always be possible in practice because of the complexity of genetic mechanisms – pleiotropy, polygenic interactions, etc. In reports of mental retardation, absence of language or developmental delay is often cited, since it is often the most obvious problem, but not necessarily the only one. One can try to rule out gross neurological damage or birth trauma, but this does not necessarily pick up more subtle kinds of damage. Imaging techniques like MRI can help here (Plante, 1991).

Similarly, it is important to keep in mind that "mental retardation" itself can be due to a wide range of causes, including the environment. At the beginning of the century, the mentally retarded included those with vitamin deficiency; e.g., the disease pellagra, which was brought about by a lack of the vitamin niacin, resulted in nervous system disorders which caused people to be committed to "insane asylums" (Kornberg, 1989). The retardation may even appear to run in families, if several generations are malnourished.

Moreover, not a few deaf people have been locked away as mentally retarded. For example, in a newspaper story entitled "Deaf Victim of Old South is Freed After 68 Years," we learn

Black and deaf, Junius Wilson was 28 when he was jailed, charged with assault with intent to rape. He was declared insane and sent to the state mental hospital for blacks. Then he was castrated. That was in 1925. Years later, the charge was dropped, but Wilson was left in a locked ward. On Friday Wilson, 96, was finally moved to his first real home in 68 years ... Wilson spent all those years [in Cherry Hospital], unable to communicate except by crude signs, grunts and gestures ... "In the segregated South, it was not unknown for black men to be charged with rape and dealt with in illegal and extralegal ways," said Daryl Scott, an assistant professor of American history at Columbia University. Wilson's situation came to light in 1991 when Wasson [Wilson's guardian] determined from reviewing

[14] Linkage analysis is the study of the coinheritance of a gene and a marker within a family.

records that Wilson was deaf, and not mentally ill. It took Wasson and a team of lawyers from Carolina Legal Assistance this long to get him out. (Thompson, 1994)

In addition, other mental patients "speaking gibberish" have turned out to be normal speakers of native American Indian languages.

When looking at a language disorder, it is particularly important to exclude not only deafness or muteness, but also more subtle hearing impairments or articulation problems. It may be crucial to the correct analysis of the disorder whether certain classes of sounds can or cannot be heard or pronounced.

To investigate whether the problem is a language deficit as opposed to some other kind of cognitive deficit, one can administer tests that show normal performance IQ with the exception of below normal verbal IQ. One can also check that one is not dealing with a more general cognitive syndrome, such as autism, or attention deficit disorder (ADD), often found in "LD" children with "learning disability."

Having established a language deficit (or variation), one can then proceed to narrow the problem down further. Is the problem (variation) syntactic, morphological, phonological, or semantic in nature, or some combination of these? Or is it due to some specific impairment (variation) in some other cognitive domain, possibly related to language? It is important to remember that just because one observes multiple effects of the mutation in several domains (e.g., phonology, syntax, some other cognitive domain), it does not follow that these effects are directly connected with each other, because of the existence of pleiotropy, as is pointed out in our discussion of the multipurpose gene *wingless* in chapter 5.

Finally, returning to the problem of characterizing the language phenotype, one also should rule out the possibility that the "impairment" is really just part of the dialect or vernacular speech of the speaker. Or, in the case of young children, one needs to rule out the possibility that the "errors" are just part of the normal errors made by children learning language.

Also, since we are interested here in genetic language disorders, it is important to examine whether the problem (variation) runs in the families under investigation, and if so, to collect family pedigrees.

The karyotype

In special cases, gross deletions, insertions, or translocations may be spotted visually by inspection of the chromosomes under a microscope (step 2). For example, translocations (and deletions) were important in the mapping and eventual cloning of the gene for Duchenne muscular dystrophy (DMD) (Watson, et al., 1992). Although this disease is transmitted as an X-linked recessive, and hence usually affects only males, a few rare female cases were discovered. These females had a balanced translocation between the X chromosome and a variety of different autosomes. However, the breakpoint on the X chromosome was always in band Xp21. This suggested that the gene was in that band and that its function had been mutated by the translocation there. This was confirmed by linkage analysis (see below) by finding a RFLP (marker) near Xp21 showing linkage to DMD.

Dyslexia

Froster et al. reported a family in which dyslexia cosegregates with a balanced translocation of chromosomes 1 and 2 (karyotype: 46, XY, t[1;2][1p22;2q31]) (Froster et al., 1993). The father and two sons, who had severely delayed speech development and writing and reading difficulties, carried the translocation, while the other members of the family without the impairment had normal chromosome analyses. No neurological abnormalities or dysmorphic features were found in the translocation carriers.[15]

Moreover, staining techniques can in theory yield markers linked to the gene of interest. Galaburda and Geschwind note an observation by Smith and colleagues (cf. Smith et al., 1983):

Recent work by Shelley Smith and co-workers has disclosed a strong linkage of the familial dyslexia phenotype to a highly fluorescent satellite on the 15th chromosome. The satellite is found in affected members and is absent in unaffected members of the same family in six of eight families. Since the neuropathology of clinical entities showing chromosomal alteration has not been worked out in detail, even for the common disorders, it is not known what possible effect on cortical organization a lesion in the 15th chromosome could have, although it is tempting to speculate about the possible effect of this chromosome on cerebral lateralization and malformations.[16] (Galaburda and Geschwind, 1981:285)

Incontinentia pigmenti (type 1) with X;5 translocation

Bitoun et al. report the case of a five-year-old girl with "total absence of speech" with type 1 Incontinentia pigmenti (IP), an X-linked dominant disorder, lethal in males (Bitoun et al., 1992). This particular patient also

---

[15] For additional commentary on this case, see (Rabin et al., 1993).
[16] A satellite is a "tiny knob of chromosomal material" sometimes found at the tips of the short arms of some chromosomes, including chromosome 15 (Mange and Mange, 1994:29).

exhibited dysmorphic features, pigmented skin lesions, alopecia, and an abnormal EEG as well as the speech delay. Moreover, this case is associated with an apparently balanced translocation (X;5) (p11.2;q35.2). As already mentioned in chapter 2, "Language investigation showed a language dysphasia with age appropriate development in all mental functions except for verbal language where a specific severe expressive language dysfunction (she only said two words) was noted with near normal language comprehension and normal cognitive functions" (Bitoun et al., 1992); And "The important point we wish to stress in this patient is the normality of all psychomotor tests including behavior, imitation, perception, fine and gross motor, eye–hand coordination as well as cognitive and mental functions except for this severe expressive language dysfunction."

The authors have made somatic cell hybrids (rodent x human) from Epstein-Barr virus immortalized peripheral lymphocytes in order to study DNA at the Xp11.2 breakpoint using Xp probes. They hope to find evidence for a deleted or disrupted Type 1 IP gene.

Other studies

In fragile X syndrome (discussed below) one can actually see a break in the chromosome at the approximate location of the defective gene (FMR-1). In the case of the family with the dominantly inherited speech order described above, Hurst et al. did a chromosome analysis on one of the affected members, but it was found to be normal (Hurst et al., 1990).

Linkage analysis

If no cytogenetic abnormality is found, the next step (linkage analysis – step 3), is to try to map the gene of interest on a particular chromosome by using DNA markers, including restriction fragment length polymorphisms (RFLPs),[17] variations in the number of tandem repeats (VNTRs),[18] sequence tagged sites (STSs),[19] and microsatellite repeats.[20] If enough markers are available, computer programs can produce a map of their order along a chromosome. If the marker is within 5 cM[21] of the gene of interest, it is considered to be linked.[22]

---

[17] RFLPs are short DNA sequences that differ between individuals and that can be used as genetic markers.   [18] Tandem repeats are repetitive DNA sequences that are adjacent.

[19] An STS is a unique DNA sequence used as a mapping location on a chromosome.

[20] A microsatellite repeat is a short repetitive DNA sequence.

[21] A centimorgan is a genetic measure that amounts to about a million base pairs.

[22] If the marker is within 5 cM of the gene of interest, it is considered to be linked closely enough to be used for some practical purposes; e.g., genetic counseling (Watson et al., 1992:29).

Dyslexia linkage studies

Smith et al. examined specific reading disability[23] with an apparent autosomal dominant pattern of inheritance in eighty-four individuals in nine families (Smith et al., 1983). The researchers performed a linkage analysis using twenty-one routine genotyping markers (such as blood type) as well as chromosomal heteromorphisms. The linkage analysis between reading disability and chromosome 15 heteromorphisms produced a significant lod score[24] of 3.241, indicating assignment of a gene for specific reading disability to chromosome 15. The authors conclude: "An opportunity to study the effects of one gene on information-processing has evolved from these studies" (p. 1347). A follow-up study was planned using recombinant DNA techniques to see if any polymorphisms associated with the specific reading disability might reflect variability in the $ß_2$-microglobulin gene, which is carried on chromosome 15 (Herbert, 1983).[25][26] However, another study was unable to confirm this linkage (Bisgaard et al., 1987).

In another familial study the complex segregation program, POINTER, was used to compare alternative genetic hypotheses on four samples of families used in earlier studies (Pennington et al., 1991). The results for three of the four families argued for major gene transmission, while the fourth sample supported multifactorial-polygenic transmission.

---

[23] What we are calling "specific reading disability" (or "dyslexia") is most likely a cover term for a heterogeneous collection of syndromes (as the authors explicitly recognize). A subset of these make up the hereditary dyslexias, which again undoubtedly form a heterogeneous class among themselves, as evidenced by the varying kinds of autosomal and sex-linked patterns of inheritance that are reported in the literature. Even a pure case of hereditary dyslexia might be polygenic in character so that differing phenotypes will be observed depending on the gene(s) involved. And finally, such factors as whether or not the mutation involves a structural or a regulatory gene, whether penetrance is complete or not, etc., could radically affect the observed phenotype.

[24] Housman, Kidd, and Gusella characterize the lod score as follows:

The "lod score" is the statistic used to evaluate significance of a linkage result. It is the logarithm of an odds ratio, the ratio being the probability of the observed data given a specific recombination frequency divided by the probability of those same data assuming independent segregation, i.e. a recombination frequency of 0.5. By convention, logarithms to the base 10 are used so that a lod score of + 3 or greater indicates that, as an explanation for the observed data, linkage at that particular value of recombination is at least 1000 times more likely than non-linkage (independent segregation). Conversely, by convention a lod score of less than − 2 is considered significant for excluding linkage at that recombination value. (Housman, Kidd, and Gusella, 1982:321)

[25] On the isolation and characterization of cDNA for human $ß_2$–microglobulin, see (Suggs et al., 1981).

[26] Tasset, Hartz, and Kao discuss methods for the isolation and characterization of DNA markers that are specific to human chromosome 15. In particular, they mention several markers that might be "very useful for establishing a linkage with chromosome 15 and one form of dyslexia" (Tasset, Hartz, and Kao, 1988).

The dominant gene affecting language in the British family (G6393)

There are currently two efforts underway to characterize and map the gene in the KE family. Pembrey summarizes the approach being used at the Hospitals for Sick Children and the Institute of Child Health (HSC/ICH) in the table:[27]

Finding the mutant gene *(from Pembrey, 1992:55)*

The general gene mapping approach	Finding the mutant gene in family G6393[28]
1. A clear-cut disorder (phenotype)	a. Characterize the speech/language disorder in family G6393
2. One or more large families where the disorder (or susceptibility to it) is inherited in a simple Mendelian fashion[29]	
3. Test for coinheritance with DNA sequences of known chromosomal location	b. Assign phenotypes and *then* map the mutation
4. Map disorder to a chromosomal region	
5. Build up a local physical map of overlapping fragments of DNA	
6. Search for DNA sequences characteristic of genes coding for proteins	c. Select 'neurogenes' mapping to the region as candidate genes
7. Test each candidate gene for appropriate expression	d. Test genes in the region for appropriate expression in fetal brain
8. Compare the DNA sequence of normal controls and subjects	e. When the mutant gene is characterized, look for minor variations in language-delayed children

Dunne et al. ran the simulation program SLINK (Ott, 1991) on this family pedigree to determine what kinds of LOD scores might be obtained (for purposes of gene linkage mapping), assuming certain boundary conditions are met (Dunne et al., 1993). They concluded that "there is reasonable probability that typing this family with microsatellite markers will yield significant LOD scores." They are currently searching other branches of the family for additional affected members.

---

[27] This is the standard approach that has been outlined in this chapter (Watson, et al., 1992).

[28] "Family G6393" is the designation for the family referred to earlier as the "KE family."

[29] A reader observed that in complex systems, like human language, similar phenotypes might result from many different gene mutations. In such systems, a small number of large families might be more informative for linkage analysis than a large number of small families, in certain circumstances. See Ott, 1991 (p. 105) for further discussion.

Fisher et al. reported the identification of a region on chromosome 7 which co-segregates with the "speech and language disorder" in the KE family, or, as it is now termed, the "Speech and Language Disorder with Orofacial Dyspraxia" (OMIM number 602081 in the Online Mendelian Inheritance in Man) (Fisher et al., 1998). Using microsatellite markers, they were able to map the locus (called SPCH1) to a 5.6–cM interval in 7q31. Preliminary (unpublished) brain-imaging studies indicated "functional abnormalities in motor-related areas of the frontal lobe," possibly due to "abnormal anatomical development of several brain areas, with a key site of pathology being located in the neostriatum."

Walking the chromosome

If a marker is found within 1 cM of the target gene, then "walking the chromosome" becomes feasible (step 4).[30] It is also highly useful if several flanking markers can be found that bracket the target gene from both sides. Walking the chromosome involves starting with a DNA probe near the marker and then finding a set of overlapping DNA segments that extend from the marker to the target gene, which can then be isolated and cloned.

The search for the Duchenne muscular dystrophy gene was helped by the discovery of a translocation in which the autosomal part of the translocated chromosome contained genes coding for ribosomal RNA. Since a DNA probe was already available for this segment, one could then walk from that point directly into the DMD gene.

In some cases, if some gene is already known to be located in the vicinity of the marker, that gene can be considered to be a "candidate gene."[31] This technique was used to isolate the fibrillin gene.

Cloning the gene

Cloning of FMR-1 gene (fragile X syndrome)

Much progress has been made toward a molecular characterization of the fragile X syndrome. The gene responsible for the fragile X syndrome,

---

[30] Even if a marker is not tightly linked, but is a reasonable distance away from the gene of interest, that marker may be useful for fetal testing.

[31] As a reader pointed out, the candidate gene approach, where available, is preferable to the more tedious technique of chromosome walking. It is also becoming increasingly the method of choice for several reasons. First, more and more genes are being identified as a result of the Human Genome Project, whose goal is to determine the entire nucleotide sequence of the human genome. Second, the functions of these genes can sometimes be determined through the study of animal models.

called FMR-1, has been cloned (Oberlé et al., 1991; Yu et al., 1991) and the findings reveal clues to the variability of the mental retardation, and hence possibly to that of the impaired speech development. An unstable mutation is associated with the FMR-1 gene. In particular, a "triplet repeat" of the bases CGG appears before the coding region at the 5' end of the gene. The normal size range of repeats appears to be on the order of 7–50. However, the sequence of CGGs appears to be expanded or amplified from generation to generation. The degree to which the repeat occurs appears to correlate with the degree of severity of the syndrome, as was found to be the case in Huntington's syndrome.

The amplification mechanism might also account for the peculiar genetics of the fragile X syndrome. In classical X-linked diseases, such as certain kinds of color-blindness, the condition usually shows up in males, but not in females. In fragile X syndrome, some of the males are asymptomatic, although the condition shows up again in their progeny, both males and females. Again, the number of CGG repeats present in a given person appears to correlate with the genetic pattern of transmission. Genomic imprinting is another explanation that has been offered for the variability and genetic transmission.

The normal gene expression patterns of FMR-1 in the brain and in other tissues has been studied as well (Hinds et al., 1993). The researchers note that "distinct irregularities of and developmental delays in speech, are associated with fragile X syndrome in young children. Such abnormalities may be connected with regional brain dysfunction, and parallels may be drawn between these regions and the expression patterns of the *fmr-1* transcript" (p. 41).

A knockout mouse[32] model for fragile X syndrome has been developed with behavioral deficits in water maze tests and with macro-orchidism (Comery et al., 1997). The knockout mice exhibit "altered dendritic spine morphology and density," which, the authors hypothesize, may affect "synaptic maturation and stabilization" (p. 5403). It has been found that the fragile X mental retardation protein is translated near neural synapses and may be of importance for the normal maturation and modification of synaptic connections (Weiler et al., 1997).

The gene product

Finally, if the gene can be successfully cloned (step 5), one can deduce the sequence of the protein product and in some cases one can isolate and study the protein product itself (step 6).

---

[32] A knockout mouse is a mouse that has a wild-type gene allele replaced by a mutant one.

If the linguistic phenotype shows variable expressivity within or across families, one can then attempt to correlate the severity of the phenotype with the kind of mutation present. One can determine the precise location of the gene mutation by DNA sequencing (Maxam and Gilbert, 1977; Sanger, Nicklen, and Coulson, 1977) and then try to correlate the position of the mutation with the phenotypic expression.

Williams syndrome

Bellugi et al. performed extensive neuropsychological tests on individuals with Williams syndrome (WS) and found linguistic abilities, e.g., lexical and grammatical abilities, to be relatively spared in comparison with Down syndrome individuals (Bellugi et al., 1990).[33] Some subjects are reported to show unusually rich vocabulary: "For example, when asked to generate animals, the WS subjects' word choices included such oddities as "unicorn," "tyrandon," "brontosaurus," "yak," "ibex," "water buffalo," "sea lion," "saber-toothed tiger," "vulture" (p. 116). In addition, these individuals show severe visuospatial defects. WS is associated with a number of developmental disorders, including cardiac defects, and disorders of connective tissue and the central nervous system. A particular cardiac defect, supravalvular aortic stenosis exists as a separate autosomal dominant trait. It has been determined that WS is a contiguous gene disorder, affecting multiple genes, in which the vascular and connective tissue abnormalities are caused by a deletion on the long arm of chromosome 7, including the elastin gene (Ewart et al., 1993). Cytoarchitectonic anomalies have been found in the brain of individuals with WS, particularly in area 17 (Galaburda et al., 1994).

MOLECULAR BASIS OF CRITICAL PERIOD AND ASYMMETRY

Molecular genetics may be making its first inroads into solving such classical biological puzzles as the triggering of critical period and asymmetry.

Critical period

There is reason to believe that language acquisition goes through a "critical period" during which the brain is thought to be particularly

---

[33] In this study Down syndrome individuals were used as controls. Because of the extensive testing done, the study also provides much useful information about the neuropsychological abilities present in Down syndrome. Down syndrome is usually caused by an extra chromosome 21, but can also be due to translocation heterozygosity.

"plastic."[34] Evidence adduced for this comes from studies of recovery from childhood versus adult aphasia, ease of second language acquisition in childhood and the study of children raised with limited exposure to language; see Corballis, 1991 for a review.

The visual cortex of the cat has been intensively studied as a model for the critical period, where well-documented changes in both anatomy and physiology take place during monocular deprivation (McCormack et al., 1992; Rosen et al., 1992). The "critical period" for this deprivation peaks in the cat visual system at 4–5 weeks. The authors compared cat visual cortex with frontal cortex and cerebellum and found distinctive developmental patterns of expression of "immediate early genes" (IEGs); in particular, of *egr*-1, *c-fos*, and *jun*-B.

Asymmetry

Another experimental path, a much more indirect path, which may ultimately shed some light on the developmental genetic foundations of language, is the investigation of the asymmetry of language in the brain. It is convenient to break down the problem of asymmetry into four areas – *functional, anatomical, architectonic*, and *biochemical* asymmetry.

In the late nineteenth century it was clearly established that there was a *functional* asymmetry in the representation of language in the brain, with language being localized in the left hemisphere in most people (Broca, 1861; Wernicke, 1874). Although for many years de Bonin (and others) denied anatomical asymmetry, Geschwind and Levitsky were able to establish an *anatomical* asymmetry between the left and right temporal planum areas (Geschwind and Levitsky, 1968).[35] Wada was the first to show that the planum asymmetry is present in the fetus and the newborn (Wada, 1969; Wada, Clarke, and Hamm, 1975). Chi, Dooling, and Gilles have shown that it can be observed as early as week 31 of gestation (Chi, Dooling, and Gilles, 1977:91).

Witelson and Pallie found the left-sided temporal planum to be statistically significantly larger in human brain specimens from a group of fourteen neonates (as well as in sixteen adults) (Witelson and Pallie, 1973). They conclude:

---

[34] It may be more correct to think of the term "critical period" as a cover term for multiple overlapping developmental windows.

[35] Gazzaniga has claimed that the measurements by Geschwind and Levitsky "do not reflect the real cortical area of this region," as ascertained by certain 3-D reconstructions of normal brains; see Gazzaniga, 1994:109, which contains further references to the literature.

It is suggested that this anatomical asymmetry is present before any environmental effects such as language learning and unimanual preference and may be an important factor in determining the typical pattern of left hemisphere speech lateralization found in most adults. Furthermore, it is suggested that this neonatal asymmetry indicates that the infant is born with a pre-programmed biological capacity to process speech sounds. (Witelson and Pallie, 1973:646)

Furthermore, Galaburda, Sanides, and Geschwind were able to show that the asymmetry holds at the *architectonic* level as well (Galaburda, Sanides, and Geschwind, 1978).[36]

Galaburda and Kemper examined the brain of a twenty-year-old accident victim who was diagnosed by psychological testing as suffering from a severe case of developmental dyslexia (Galaburda and Kemper, 1979). The key finding was the discovery of a structural abnormality in the tissue of an area of the brain normally involved in human language – the Tpt area on the temporal planum.[37][38]

Geschwind and Levitsky had demonstrated earlier that the temporal planum, an extension of Wernicke's area known to be involved in language comprehension, was larger on the left side of the brain in most cases (Geschwind and Levitsky, 1968). The basis for the gross left–right anatomical asymmetry in the temporal planum was ascertained to lie in the Tpt area (Galaburda et al., 1978): "Galaburda therefore measured the full extent of these regions in both halves of the brain. In the first brain

[36] Architectonics "refers to the study of the cellular arrangement in layers and columns in the cortex, and to general cell-packing density and cell size in cortical and subcortical structures." The advantage of studying architectonic areas over the study of gross anatomical landmarks is that such areas "probably correspond much more closely to regions of special functional differentiation of the brain and to regions with different connections" (Galaburda and Geschwind, 1981:280).

[37] Geschwind refers to the temporal planum as "an extension of Wernicke's area" (Geschwind, 1972:83). It was this area which Geschwind and Levitsky examined in their important paper (Geschwind and Levitsky, 1968) to establish conclusively a left–right anatomical asymmetry in the adult brain, a finding since confirmed both in adults and at earlier stages of development: "the posterior area of the planum temporale, which forms part of Wernicke's area, is generally larger on the left side" (Geschwind, 1979c:166).

The Tpt (temporoparietal; (Galaburda et al., 1978)) is a region with well-defined cellular architecture. Its location with respect to the temporal planum is as follows: "In the posterior temporal region an area known as Tpt . . . is found on the caudal most third of the superior temporal gyrus and on the posterior outer edge of the planum temporale (the part of the superior temporal plane lying posterior to Heschl's gyrus . . .)" (Galaburda and Geschwind, 1980:122). See below for a functional characterization of Tpt.

[38] In addition to the cortical abnormalities found in this case of developmental dyslexia, in a subsequent study Galaburda and Eidelberg reported bilateral lesions in the posterior thalamus of this subject in areas of probable relevance to language (Galaburda and Eidelberg, 1982). Moreover, Eidelberg and Galaburda found thalamic asymmetries in normal persons, the first demonstration of an anatomic asymmetry in a subcortical nuclear structure in man (Eidelberg and Galaburda, 1982).

studied, that of a highly verbal young lawyer, one of these regions, Tpt, was more than 7 times as large on the left side as on the right. Tpt is the major component of the posterior speech area of Wernicke" (Geschwind, 1979a:289).

The dyslexic brain studied by Galaburda and Kemper exhibited the following striking characteristics: (1) the Tpt area, normally larger on the left side of the brain, was the same size on both the left and the right. Although this in itself is not conclusive, Galaburda and Kemper discovered (2) there were polymicrogyria, abnormal pathological formations of brain tissue in the Tpt area on the left, (3) the normal columnar organization of this area was in disarray, (4) nerve-cell bodies were present in the topmost superficial area of the cortex, where they are normally not found, and (5) cortical tissue was found in the white matter, where it normally does not belong. None of these abnormalities was noted on the right side (or elsewhere in the brain).[39]

A lesion of the Tpt area is of linguistic interest, since "The location of this area corresponds to the center of the lesions resulting in Wernicke's aphasia . . . Furthermore the location of Tpt matches closely the central portion of the parieto-temporal speech region obtained by electrical stimulation" (Galaburda and Geschwind, 1980:122). The disorganization of brain tissue discovered by Galaburda and Kemper may be observed in the photomicrograph in Geschwind, 1979c (166).

It is of additional interest that in this particular case the patient's father and his three brothers were slow readers (but not his mother or his sister). The authors tentatively hypothesize that "a familial form of localized polymicrogyria may be responsible for the reading difficulties seen in this patient and in other male members of his family" (Galaburda and Kemper, 1979:99).

This case was the first architectonic study providing evidence for lesions in the brain associated with developmental dyslexia. There are now more such cases[40] of dyslexic individuals reported in the literature, all of which exhibit developmental anomalies of the cerebral cortex (such as dysplasias and ectopias)[41] and some of which have abnormalities in

---

[39] It should be pointed out that the brain tissue abnormality described here is characteristic of certain cases of epilepsy. And, in fact, the patient under discussion did begin having seizures at age sixteen (Galaburda and Kemper, 1979:94). However, these malformations are not usually seen in the speech area, so the fact that this one did and that the patient is dyslexic is at least suggestive, though not conclusive, that the abnormal tissue underlies the speech disorder (Geschwind, 1979b:69–70).

[40] About eight months of preparation are required by each brain (Langone, 1983).

[41] Dysplasias consist of "disordered cellular architecture" and ectopias consist of "the presence of neural elements in places from which they are normally absent" (Galaburda 1985:27).

subcortical structures (Galaburda, 1993:58; Geschwind and Galaburda, 1987:90). However, Livingstone et al. argue that some cases of developmental dyslexia may in part be due to defects in the visual system (the magnopyramidal system) (Livingstone et al., 1991).

It would be informative for follow-up linguistic testing to be done on the affected members of the families of the patients studied by Galaburda and Kemper to search for well-defined linguistic correlates of the observed brain lesions. The study of bilingual dyslexics or identical twins with dyslexia, speaking the same or different languages, with such lesions, insofar as available, would also, of course, be of the greatest linguistic interest. Such cases provide a mutually profitable sphere of cooperation for the linguist and the neuroanatomist. In addition, the identification of a specific lesion in a linguistic disability provides a handle as well as an impetus for the neuroanatomical comparison of other brain specimens with this case[42] (and the study of cases of other developmental language disorders – developmental aphasia, agrammatism, etc.).[43]

In recent years impetus has been given toward interdisciplinary collaboration between researchers in the area of learning disorders and immunologists by the development of the Geschwind hypothesis.[44] This hypothesis is put forth in Geschwind and Behan, 1982, and Geschwind and Behan, 1984, and further developed in Geschwind and Galaburda, 1987, to account for observed relationships between learning disorders like dyslexia, left-handedness, and various auto-immune diseases.[45] Geschwind and Behan found that left-handers had nearly three times as high a frequency of immune disorders as right-handers (Geschwind and Behan, 1982, 1984). In addition, they found that the relatives of the left-handers suffered from these same conditions at nearly twice the frequency

[42] The reason that anatomical studies of dyslexia have been so long in coming may lie in an observation made by Galaburda:

it does not seem that, until recently, a concerted effort had been made to secure for anatomical investigation those specimens of brains from dyslexic patients which might become available. The first such effort, to my knowledge, is being made by the Orton Society in the United States, which has set rolling a mechanism by which such specimens may be acquired and analyzed. It is only through the parallel advances of functional and anatomical models that we can hope to learn enough to begin to design potentially successful therapeutic approaches. (Galaburda and Geschwind, 1980:2)

[43] Bauman and Kemper have found abnormalities in the brain of a twenty-nine-year-old man with autism, using methods similar to those employed by Galaburda and Kemper on the dyslexic brain discussed earlier (Bauman and Kemper, 1985; Galaburda and Kemper, 1979). Problems with language acquisition have often been noted in studies of autistic children, although it is unclear to what extent autism is linked with specific linguistic deficits. In the case of the autistic brain, the abnormalities were located both in the limbic system and in the cerebellum.

[44] Sometimes referred to in the literature as the "testosterone hypothesis."

[45] In auto-immune disorders, the immune system attacks one's own tissues.

of the relatives of the right-handers. They also studied the frequency of childhood learning disabilities, such as dyslexia, stuttering, and autism in the two populations and in their relatives and found a higher frequency of these conditions in the strong left-handers as compared with the strong right-handers.

The basic idea of the Geschwind hypothesis is that elevated testosterone levels in males can often lead to a delay of neuronal migration in the left hemisphere, resulting in anomalous dominance[46] and anatomical disorders of the cerebral cortex (like the dysplasias and ectopias noted above), and hence a predisposition to learning disorders like dyslexia and stuttering. And simultaneously this excess can have a suppressive effect on the thymus, resulting in auto-immunity disorders later in life.

Shaywitz et al. performed functional magnetic resonance imaging on both dyslexic and nonimpaired subjects. They found that the dyslexic subjects exhibited "relative underactivation in posterior regions (Wernicke's area, the angular gyrus, and striate cortex)" as well as "relative overactivation in an anterior region (inferior frontal gyrus)." They concluded from their study that the dyslexics had a phonological impairment (Shaywitz et al., 1998:2636).

A natural question arises: do we find any *biochemical* asymmetries corresponding to the functional, anatomical, and architectonic asymmetries discussed immediately above? Several (naturally occurring) biochemical asymmetries have been reported in the human brain; viz., a neurotransmitter asymmetry in the thalamus (Oke et al., 1978). The researchers found that the pulvinar region on the left brain side of the thalamus was richer in norepinephrine than the region on the right side (p. 1412).[47] They also noted that patients undergoing thalamic surgery for dyskinesias or pain experienced postoperative difficulties in speech if the surgery was in left, but not right, pulvinar and ventrolateral regions (p. 1413). Although the authors do not know whether the norepinephrine asymmetry is related to the functional lateralization, they urge that the phenomenon be further investigated, concluding that, "the lateralization problem

---

[46] Geschwind and Galaburda distinguish standard dominance with "strong left hemisphere dominance for language and handedness, and strong right hemisphere dominance for other functions" from *anomalous dominance*, which refers to "those in whom the pattern differs from the standard form" (Geschwind and Galaburda, 1987). They estimate that "anomalous dominance will be found in approximately 30% to 35% of individuals, roughly the percentage in whom the planum temporale is not larger on the left side" (p. 70). They stress, however, that "most people with anomalous dominance do not suffer from the conditions mentioned and that what is being described are higher relative rates of certain conditions" (p. 83).

[47] They also found a further thalamic asymmetry in norephinephrine; viz. a higher concentration of the neurotransmitter on the right brain side of the thalamus in an area with connections to the somatosensory cortex.

impinges upon the entire spectrum of brain-behavioral research from the synapse to the sentence" (p. 1411).

Hansen, Perry, and Wada compared the left and the right temporal planums for asymmetries in amino acid content, but were unable to establish any (Hansen, Perry, and Wada, 1972). An asymmetry in choline acetyltransferase in the first temporal gyrus was reported (Amaducci et al., 1981; Sorbi et al., 1980) and the potential relevance of such studies to questions of asymmetry of language was noted with reference to Geschwind, 1979c[48]; see also Geschwind and Galaburda, 1984, 1987 for more examples and discussion. Much is becoming known about the molecular developmental pathways for both dorsal–ventral and left–right axes in mammals and birds; see Gilbert's discussion of the *situs inversus viscerum* (iv) gene and *sonic hedgehog* genes (and others) (Gilbert, 1997:647–50).

Asymmetries in nonhuman primates[49]

In this section we will discuss some asymmetries in nonhuman primates, that correspond to some of the classic language areas in humans. We will limit ourselves here primarily to the case of the planum temporale in the chimpanzee; additional cases may be found in the references cited.

LeMay noted that the study of asymmetries in the nonhuman primates goes back at least as far as 1892 with the work of Cunningham who "found the left sylvian fissure longer in the chimpanzee and macaque" (Cunningham, 1892; LeMay, 1985:235). Cunningham cites earlier work by Eberstaller on the Sylvian fissure in humans, who had concluded that it was "on an average, longer in the left hemisphere than in the right." Cunningham concludes on the basis of his experiments, "so there is also found in these higher apes and in man, going hand in hand with the development of the temporal lobe, several hidden gyri in the Sylvian fissure, which shorten the Sylvian fissure and increase the cortical district of that region in which we have to seek the *sensible Sprachcentrum*" (Cunningham, 1892:130). Thus by the late nineteenth century the comparison of the Sylvian fissure region of the temporal lobe in humans and nonhuman primates and the study of their left–right asymmetries had begun. Moreover, the importance of these anatomical regions for the study of language (*sensible Sprachcentrum)* was understood as well.

Yeni-Komshian and Benson cite a study by Fischer published in 1921

---

[48] Geschwind notes that Amaducci has also reported asymmetry of choline acetyltransferase in homologous structures in the rat (Geschwind, 1983a).

[49] We thank Marjorie LeMay and Grace Yeni-Komshian for helpful discussion of some of the issues and historical background of the work on brain asymmetries.

in which he examined the Sylvian fissure in 24 chimpanzee brains and reported that "50 percent of his specimens had longer left fissures (1 to 6 mm) and 17 percent had longer right fissures" (Yeni-Komshian and Benson, 1976:388–89). LeMay cites a later study by Beheim-Schwarzbach in 1975 that studied the "cytoarchitecture of the dorsal surface of the superior temporal gyri in the brains of two humans, a chimpanzee, and an orangutan. He reported similar asymmetries of the temporal regions in humans, the chimpanzee, and the orangutan" (Beheim-Schwarzbach, 1975, cited in LeMay, 1985:236).

LeMay and Geschwind studied asymmetries in the cerebral hemispheres of some great apes, lesser apes, New World monkeys, and Old World monkeys (LeMay and Geschwind, 1975). They measured the difference in height between the right and left Sylvian points. They found that "among 28 great apes, 17 showed asymmetries" while the asymmetry was "found uncommonly" in the other three groups of primates they examined. They conclude that "the results of this study suggest, however, the possibility that certain anatomical asymmetries seen in man may commonly be present in the orangutan and in some chimpanzees" (pp. 50–51).

Yeni-Komshian and Benson compared the length of the left and right Sylvian fissures of human, chimpanzee, and rhesus brains. Their measurements in humans confirmed other studies' findings that the "human Sylvian fissure is longer on the left than on the right." They also found that the "chimpanzee brains had a similar asymmetry but to a lesser degree than the human brains." No significant differences were found in rhesus brains. They observe that these length differences in humans have been "attributed to the greater length of the left planum temporale" (pp. 387–88), citing Geschwind. Thus, the "Sylvian fissure length may be considered an indirect measure of the homolog of the human planum temporale in the chimpanzee and rhesus brain." The reason that they did not measure the planum temporale directly was because "the sulcus of Heschl's gyrus, which is the anterior boundary of the planum temporale, is poorly developed in the chimpanzee and absent in the rhesus." Hence it was "difficult to identify the planum temporale in these species by macroscopic observation." They observe, however, that cytoarchitectonic studies had shown that the human planum temporale is "part of the auditory association areas TA and TB." These same areas have been identified in the chimpanzee and the rhesus and are "located, as in the human brain, on the superior surface of the temporal lobe" (p. 389). Thus, they conclude, as LeMay also notes ten years later, that "their sylvian fissure measurements included the homolog of the planum temporale in humans" (LeMay, 1985:236).

Shortly thereafter there were lively interdisciplinary discussions of the significance of the discoveries about the asymmetries in man and apes for language. Here is an exchange between Chomsky and Norman Geschwind at the conference on Maturational Factors in Cognitive Development and the Biology of Language held June 8–11, 1978:

CHOMSKY: What is known about cerebral asymmetries in the great apes?

GESCHWIND: LeMay and I looked for asymmetries in the brains of monkeys and did not find any. We did find that the great apes show an asymmetry in the Sylvian fissure similar to that in humans. The left Sylvian fissure tends to have a more horizontal course, while the right Sylvian fissure curves upward. In humans this is by far the most common pattern. In left-handers this pattern is still the most common one, but there is a higher percentage of cases without asymmetry of the Sylvian fissure.

CHOMSKY: What is the function of that area?

GESCHWIND: This is an asymmetry of a fissure, the indentation between parts of the brain. Obviously the asymmetry of the fissure implies that the brain areas around it must be different in some way. The major classical speech areas lie on the borders of the Sylvian fissure. In the course of primate evolution the Sylvian fissure appears to have shifted from a more vertical to a more horizontal configuration. This evolutionary trend appears to have progressed more on the left side than on the right.

CHOMSKY: Moving beyond phylogeny, can you say what the functions of the areas around that fissure may be?

GESCHWIND: In the human the areas around the Sylvian fissure on the left are particularly involved with language functions. It would be tempting to speculate that the regions around the Sylvian fissure in the great apes are subserving some function. I suspect that these areas are asymmetrical because there is some type of dominance, but no one has been able to ask the right question in order to determine what that dominance is.

CHOMSKY: Can you say anything about the functions of the asymmetries in apes?

GESCHWIND: Functional asymmetry of the hemispheres – differences in the performance of certain types of activity – are clearly well known in humans. Dewson has suggested that the left temporal lobe of the monkey is superior for certain types of auditory tasks. Denenberg and his co-workers at the University of Connecticut have brought evidence that there is an asymmetry for emotional behavior in the brain of the rat. Some recent work brings evidence that in Japanese monkeys the left hemisphere is better at recognizing species-specific cries. Unfortunately, in none of these species has anatomical asymmetry yet been demonstrated. There is also an asymmetry for bird song, in which the left side of the brain seems to be more important. Nottebohm has found male–female differences in the sizes of areas involved in bird song, but the issue of left–right asymmetry of these areas is still unclear. We do not yet know the function of the anatomical asymmetries in the brains of apes, but I suspect that these are related to functional dominance. (Caplan and Chomsky, 1980:310–11)

Gannon et al. recently provided more direct confirmation of the conclusions of Yeni-Komshian and Benson (Gannon et al., 1998). They examined 19 brains from chimpanzees (*Pan troglodytes*) and found that "the left planum temporale was significantly larger in 94 percent (17 of 18) of chimpanzee brains examined." They found the planum temporale (and Heschl's gyrus) landmarks to be "robustly represented" in their specimens and performed the measurements of the asymmetries using plastic templates. They also speculate about "several distinct evolutionary hypotheses," all of which are compatible with these findings, about the possible role of the anatomic substrate of the planum temporale in the evolution of human language and chimpanzee communication systems (pp. 220–21).

Although Gannon et al. present their findings in a balanced manner in the paper published in *Science*, the results are presented to the public in a misleading fashion. For example, in a press release from Columbia University, Gannon is cited as follows: "After 100 years of people doing comparative brain studies, you assume that the dogma is true. It came as quite a shock to discover that the chimpanzee brains did show the same asymmetry as humans" (Goodman, 1998). What "dogma" and what "shock?" As we have shown above, there is a rich tradition of studies of asymmetries in primate brains that goes back a hundred years that shows that the claim of a "dogma" in comparative brain studies is a myth. In fact, Gannon et al. even cite some of the relevant literature themselves in the scientific paper. Gannon is also reported in the press release as having "first theorized that the received wisdom [that chimpanzee brains did not show the same asymmetry as humans] might not be true" when he did some MRI studies of chimpanzee brains. Gannon may have first "theorized" it in the 1990s, but Cunningham had already presented empirical evidence against the "received wisdom" in 1892.

If anything, the opposite of what Gannon is claiming is true. The "received wisdom" for some years has been that symmetries, including that of the planum temporale exist in nonhuman primates. Compare our earlier discussion and also Geschwind: "These findings suggest that the asymmetry of the planum temporale is an important aspect of the anatomical lateralization of language to the left hemisphere. Yeni-Komshian and Benson [1976] have found a similar asymmetry in the chimpanzee" (Geschwind and Galaburda, 1984:13). Gannon et al. do cite two German studies from the 1930s, which "reported a lack of PT asymmetry in apes." These references were taken from a 1968 study by Geschwind and Levitsky (1968), but in light of all the evidence presented for asymmetry in primates since then, these two studies scarcely represent a "dogma" in 1998. In fact, the science section of the *New York Times* went so far as to cite the study of Gannon et al. as "challenging cherished notions of how language evolved in humans and why apes cannot talk," which goes far beyond any evidence presented in their paper (Blakeslee, 1998). And the reputable German weekly news magazine, *Der Spiegel*, reported that, until the study of Gannon et al. it had been believed that (1) no nonhuman primates had an asymmetry of the planum temporale and (2) the left and the right sides of the brains of nonhuman primates were absolutely equal (*absolut seitengleich*). Had the editors of *Der Spiegel* taken the trouble to check Medline on the Internet, they would have found that evidence had already been presented against thesis (2), and which at least questioned thesis (1), by the study of Beheim-Schwarzbach, which had been published in Germany more than twenty years previously.

5   Evolution of language[1]

INTRODUCTION

We now come to question (5) (from p. 1), "How did knowledge of language evolve?" Throughout contemporary work on biolinguistics, there has been great interest in questions of evolution of human language. To answer this question we need to come to understand two things: (1) how human language is designed; and (2) how these design features evolved in the brain of our species. The study of language design has been part of the subject of the earlier part of this book, where we have discussed the questions of "what constitutes knowledge of language?" and "how is this knowledge acquired?"

The study of properties of language design goes back to the earliest days of generative linguistics; e.g., the functional explanation for grammatical transformations based on certain assumptions about short- and long-term memory (Miller and Chomsky, 1963) and the functional motivation for syntactic output filters (Chomsky and Lasnik, 1977). With the emergence of more restrictive models of language in recent years as a result of work on the problems of structure (of language) and development, it has now become possible (tentatively) to take up the consideration of the question of language design. For example, the "minimalist program" focuses explicitly on questions of optimality of language design (Chomsky, 1995b, Chomsky, 1997b). Keep in mind that we are assuming that any research program that is investigating the evolution of language, is interested in language design in this sense and hence has a "minimalist program," even if it may be called something else. Hence our discussion in this chapter applies to the full spectrum of linguistic theories that have been proposed to characterize knowledge of language.

We have already discussed a number of its design features. These include its modular design; e.g., the division of labor between the language faculty and other performance modules. There also appears to be a

---

[1] A few sections in this chapter contain slightly modified material from parts of Jenkins, 1997.

number of submodules; e.g., the lexicon, the computational component, semantics, morphology, the phonological component, and phonetics.

Pursuing the minimalist line of argument, Chomsky notes that:

Recent work also suggests that languages may be optimal in a different sense. The language faculty is part of the overall architecture of the mind/brain, interacting with other components: the sensorimotor apparatus and the systems that enter into thought, imagination, and other mental processes, and their expression and interpretation. The language faculty *interfaces* with other components of the mind/brain. The interface properties, imposed by the systems among which language is embedded, set constraints on what this faculty must be if it is to function within the mind/brain. The articulatory and perceptual systems, for example, require that expressions of the language have a linear (temporal, "left-to-right") order at the interface; sensorimotor systems that operated in parallel would allow richer modes of expression of higher dimensionality. (Chomsky, 1996a:29)

Chomsky considers the specific example of the "displacement property":

In the computation of λ [i.e., a logical form representation – lj], there seems to be one dramatic imperfection in language design, at least an apparent one: the "displacement property" that is a pervasive and rather intricate aspect of language: phrases are interpreted as if they were in a different position in the structure, where similar items sometimes appear and can be interpreted in terms of conceptually natural relations. (Chomsky, 1996b:123)

Chomsky suggests that the reason for the "displacement property" might be found in terms of "interpretive requirements that are externally imposed." The idea here is to look at what appear to be imperfections in language design and, if possible, show that they are not really imperfections, but result from independently motivated constraints, in this case constraints imposed at the interface between language and interpretive systems external to language.

Let us mention a conceptually analogous argument from the physical sciences. A cusp formation is observable at the interface of certain kinds of crystals; for a photograph, see Peterson, 1988:69. Metallurgists had thought that this imperfection was due either to a dislocation in the crystal or to the fact that the crystal had formed under nonequilibrium conditions. Taylor and Cahn showed that neither need be the case (Taylor and Kahn, 1986). They demonstrated that this crystal "imperfection" was expected under equilibrium conditions given certain necessary assumptions about symmetry (anisotropy) and economy (minimization of energy). In particular, the cusp formation turned out to be one of twelve minimal surfaces predicted by their theory.

Lasnik presents a case study of how biolinguists go about studying the mechanisms of language and at the same time try to learn something about the question of language design (Lasnik, 1999). He reviews work on phrase movement over the past few decades based on a variety of languages, including English, Spanish, Irish, Japanese, Chinese, Palauan, Chamorro, Ewe, etc. An example from English is:

Who do [you think [that John believes [that Mary said [that Tom saw __]]]]?

Here, the question phrase *who* has moved to the front of the sentence from the object position after *saw*. The question is, does *who* move in one fell swoop to the beginning of the sentence or does it move step-wise ("successive-cyclically" is the technical term) to the front; i.e., through the position of *that* at the beginning of each clause. Chomsky originally presented evidence for the step-wise hypothesis, and supporting evidence was subsequently discovered in a number of other languages in favor of this idea (Lasnik provides extensive references). One might ask why language is designed with "short movement" rather than "long movement?"

Lasnik notes that it has been suggested that ease of processing might be part of the design motivation. Some of the evidence for this comes from languages where the position corresponding to *that* in the above example is morphologically marked (Irish) or syntactically distinguished (Spanish) at the beginning of each clause, so that one can, so to speak, follow a "trail" of markers from the moved item *who*, down to the position where it originated. However, Lasnik cites research on other languages where no such markers are found (English), or even where there is no visible phrase movement whatsoever, although the interpretation of the sentence is the same as if certain "movement" constraints had applied (Japanese, Chinese). He concludes that the design question for short movement is still open. However, at least one can see what kinds of evidence one can look for to investigate the question.[2]

Suppose, thirty years ago, when long movement was standardly assumed in linguistic work, we had asked why language is designed such that it has long movement. Consider now the following possible answers: long movement facilitates reproduction, winning friends and influencing people, communication, gossiping, ease of processing, or perhaps long movement was favored by natural selection. We can easily see why such answers are useless as explanations for language evolution. For, today, having learned that there is short movement, not long movement, we ask again why language was so designed. The nonanswers are the same: gossiping, winning friends, etc. However, by pinning down the syntactic mechanisms better, we at least begin to see how an argument could be made for processing in some of the cases and to understand what kind of evidence counts for or against such a hypothesis.

---

[2] The preceding is a condensed version of the much more thorough and interesting analysis given by Lasnik.

General design principles of language

Chomsky noted that when we begin to ask questions about language design, such as how optimal or perfect language is, considerations of economy arise, principles that are rooted in elegance rather than utility, "the kind of property that one seeks in core areas of the natural sciences, for example, searching for conservation principles, symmetry, and the like" (Chomsky, 1991b:49). Euler's view of economy was that "behind every phenomenon in our universe, we can find a maximum or minimum rule" (Hildebrandt and Tromba, 1996:34). Einstein captured the intimate connection between symmetry and design in the dictum "symmetry dictates design."

The reasons for our search for design principles, both general and specific, can be better understood if we briefly consider some of the intellectual antecedents and scientific traditions which bear on this question. In the Introduction, we noted Chomsky's discussion of the conceptual parallels between Goethe's idea of the *Urform*, Wilhelm von Humboldt's notion of the "organic form" of language, and the generative principles that "determine the class of possible languages": "innate organizing principles [of UG] determine the class of possible languages just as the *Urform* of Goethe's biological theories defines the class of possible plants and animals" (cited by Otero in Pinker and Bloom, 1990:750).

We noted that these ideas about language were further developed into what was termed the "principles-and-parameters" theory of the "mental organ" of language. As Chomsky has observed, the "Urform is a kind of generative principle that determines the class of physically possible organisms." But what are these generative principles?

Chomsky has emphasized the importance of the work of pioneers like D'Arcy Thompson for the study of this question. In addition, Alan Turing worked on a number of stimulating morphogenetic ideas with an eye on applying them to the study of the brain. Coveney and Highfield note that he wrote about these issues in a letter to the neurophysiologist J. Z. Young on February 8, 1951:

Stating that he was as yet very far from "asking any anatomical questions [about the brain]," he revealed that he was working on a mathematical theory of embryology that he believed gave "satisfactory explanations of (i) gastrulation (ii) polygonal symmetrical structures, e.g., starfish, flowers (iii) leaf arrangement, in particular the way the Fibonacci series (0,1,1,2,3,5,8,13 . . .) comes to be involved (iv) color patterns on animals, e.g., stripes, spots and dappling (v) patterns on nearly spherical structures such as some Radiolaria, but this is more difficult and doubtful." He said that he was doing this work because it was more tractable than directly attacking similar questions concerning the brain. But, he told Young, "The brain structure has to be one which can be achieved by the genetical embryological mechanism, and I hope that this theory that I am now working on may make clearer what restrictions this really implies." (Coveney and Highfield, 1995:388)

In fact, Turing's theory of reaction-diffusion mechanisms pointed the way to part of the answer to the question about generative principles; viz., to what are now called theories of dynamics. Turing was thus engaged in a program to lay a foundation for understanding Goethe's *Urform*, a journey which he hoped would lead him to the understanding of the brain. And like D'Arcy Thompson, Turing believed that some of the important principles might be revealed in the study of the occurrence of the Fibonacci sequence in plants.

Chomsky, in the tradition of D'Arcy Thompson and Turing, has also urged the study of properties of organisms that are rooted in the nature of the physical world, like symmetry, hence suggesting another line of investigation into the evolution of language:

It is in a way related to things like d'Arcy Thompson's attempt to show that many properties of organisms, like symmetry, for example, do not really have anything to do with a specific selection but just with the ways in which things can exist in the physical world. (Huybregts and Riemsdijk, 1982:23)

Guillen suggests in the following passage that this approach to the study of biology is in the spirit of Einstein ("symmetry dictates design"):

That conviction was reaffirmed most dramatically, when in September 1891, young Einstein came across a geometry book at the local bookstore. That "holy geometry book [made an] indescribable impression on me," Einstein would recall later, because it was perfectly and harmoniously logical, just like Nature.

Einstein's curiosity about the amity between mathematics and Nature increased even more when he learned about an intriguing sequence of numbers, called the *Fibonacci series*: 1, 1, 2, 3, 5, 8, 13, 21, 34, 55, 89, and so on. Even though it was not obvious, there was a pattern to these numbers: Each one was the sum of the two numbers before it (e.g., $13 = 8 + 5$).

First concocted in the thirteenth century by an Italian merchant named Leonardo "Fibonacci" da Pisa, the series had been widely regarded as little more than a numerical curiosity. But then, Einstein learned, botanists had discovered that there were surprising coincidences between the *numerical* pattern of the Fibonacci series and the *growth* pattern of many flowering plants.

As they developed, for example, the branches of a common sneezewort forked in exact accordance with the Fibonacci series. First the seedling's main stem forked (1), then one of its secondary stems forked (1), then simultaneously a secondary and tertiary stem forked (2), then simultaneously three lesser stems forked (3), and so forth.

Furthermore, Einstein learned, the numbers of petals of various flowers, too, recapitulated the numbers of the Fibonacci series: An iris almost always had three petals, a primrose five petals, a ragwort thirteen petals, a daisy thirty-four petals, and a michaelmas daisy either fifty-five or eighty-nine petals.

All these revelations had a single cumulative effect on the young Einstein: Since there was this wonderful parallel between Numbers and Nature, then why not use the laws of mathematics to articulate the laws of Nature? "It should be possible by means of pure deduction," he concluded, "to find the picture – that is, the theory – of every natural process, including those of living organisms." (Guillen, 1995:225–26)[3]

The young Einstein depicted by Guillen would not have been totally surprised to come across the following passage from a recent physics article:

In this Letter we study a physical system lying far away from botanics: an Abrikosov flux lattice in a layered superconductor. Surprisingly, it turns out that the dynamics of the lattice under variation of magnetic field gives rise to structures very similar to those known in botanics. In particular, pairs of consecutive Fibonacci numbers appear. (Levitov, 1991:224)

The author goes on to note that "besides opening a way to an alternative explanation of botanical phyllotaxis, this result suggests that phyllotaxis is a general phenomenon that must occur in all soft lattices subjected to strong deformation." We return below to some other proposals for phyllotaxis. Levitov explains the aim of this kind of research:

The ultimate goal of physics, of course, is to explain the tremendous variety of phenomena found in nature in terms of a few simple concepts. For instance, the arrangement of scales on a pineapple, magnetic flux lines in superconductors, and circulation cells in a convecting fluid can all be viewed as examples of phyllotaxis. This novel type of spatial ordering – which has challenged mathematicians and physicists for over a century – has recently been shown at MIT to evolve naturally from the deformation of a soft lattice. The resulting analytic results explain the occurrence of Fibonacci numbers in the periodicity of such structures. (Web page on Condensed Matter Physics, referencing Levitov's work: http://web.mit.edu/physics/www/research/Cond.html)

The further development of Turing's incipient "mathematical theory of embryology" has led to a flourishing research program of the role of dynamics in the development and evolution of morphological form, what Goodwin has called "generative biology"; see also Kauffman, 1993. Wolpert has also proposed what he calls the "generative programme," with some specific hypotheses for some developmental mechanisms, which might also be interpreted as a formulation of the generative principle of Goethe's Urform: "It [the embryo's developmental programme] is a programme that does not describe the final form, but a generative programme that contains the instructions for making the shapes" (p. 17). In his view there are constraints on what kinds of forms can be generated: "So, developmental mechanisms, together with their genetic control, put a severe constraint on the evolution of animal form . . . Therefore, not all

[3] It is unclear how much of this account is factual and how much is a re-creation of this period of Einstein's life, but we believe that this depiction captures that side of Einstein's thought that constantly sought unification in nature.

imaginable animals are possible" (p. 195). There are however, a number of interesting conceptual differences between the principles of Goodwin's "generative biology" and Wolpert's "generative programme"; consideration of these would take us too far afield, but see Webster and Goodwin, 1996 for more discussion.

Goethe's *Urpflanze* embodies the generative principles that determine the class of possible plants:

Die Urpflanze wird das wunderlichste Geschöpf von der Welt, um welches mich die Natur selbst beneiden soll. Mit diesem Modell und dem Schlüssel dazu kann man alsdann noch Pflanzen ins Unendliche erfinden, die konsequent sein müssen, das heisst, die, wenn sie auch nicht existieren, doch existieren könnten, und nicht etwa mahlerische oder dichterische Schatten und Scheine sind, sondern eine innerliche Wahrheit und Nothwendigkeit haben. Dasselbe Gesetz wird sich auf alles übrige Lebendige anwenden lassen. (Chomsky, 1966:24; quoted from Magnus, 1906)

The archetypal plant will be the strangest growth the world has ever seen, and Nature herself shall envy me for it. With such a model, and with the key to it in one's hands, one will be able to contrive an infinite variety of plants. They will be strictly logical plants – in other words, even though they may not actually exist, they could exist. They will not be mere picturesque and imaginative projections. They will be imbued with inner truth and necessity. And the same law will be applicable to all that lives. (Magnus, 1906 (1949):46)

In recent years transformations of the floral organs (sepal, petal, stamen, carpal) into one another by homeotic (*homeo* = similar) transformation has been demonstrated and intensively studied in such organisms as the weed *Arabidopsis thaliana*. These transformational effects have been shown to be possible by single-gene mutations. Three such genes have been found for *Arabidopsis*; if all three are mutated then leaves are produced as the default state; as Goodwin notes,

It has been known for a long time that the different organs of a flower are transformations of one another, and that all are transformations of leaves. This conclusion was based on the observation of intermediate states between organs that occur spontaneously in plants. Just over two hundred years ago, in 1790, Johann Wolfgang von Goethe proposed that all floral organs are derived from the basic leaf state by what he described as different qualities of sap. That was a stunningly accurate piece of deduction. (Goodwin, 1994:135–36)

Later on we will discuss another such case, the occurrence of the Fibonacci numbers (1 1 2 3 5 8 13 21 34 55 89 . . .) in plants. Goodwin shows that a conceptual unification of the case involving the Fibonacci numbers with the case of transformation of floral organs just discussed can be achieved. Thus we can begin to flesh out some of the details of the generative principles involved in Goethe's *Urpflanze* idea.

We will then go on to suggest that the occurrence of patterns such as word order in natural language might be interpreted in a way similar to the way Fibonacci numbers appear in the study of phyllotaxis; viz., as a result of symmetry-breaking. We do this by looking at symmetry properties in syntactical patterns and from these perhaps one might deduce the properties of the underlying form and, ultimately, "equations" of the mind. One could speculate that perhaps other differences between languages that have been observed by linguists are also a result of similar symmetry-breaking bifurcations. If so, we might then regard natural languages – English, Turkish, Japanese, etc. – as, in part, "cascades of symmetry-breaking bifurcations," to use a phrase of Goodwin (1994:111). Then there would be a physical basis for the resemblance Chomsky noted between the language organ and the generative principles implicit in the idea of Goethe's *Urpflanze* (or Humboldt's "organic form" of language).

SYMMETRY

> Neither the role of natural selection nor the laws of physics can be ignored; together they are responsible for development and evolution.
>
> John Tyler Bonner, Editor's Introduction, D'Arcy Thompson,
> On Growth and Form

Symmetry-breaking and the Turing system

Chomsky introduced the idea of economy principles ("least effort guidelines" in earlier work) into linguistics as part of what was later called the minimalist program (Chomsky, 1995b; see also Collins, 1997; Kitahara, 1997). These principles of linguistics eliminated "superfluous steps in derivations and superfluous elements in representations" (Chomsky, 1991b:49). He observed that the features one finds in "least effort" principles have a kind of generality, rooted in elegance rather than utility, "the kind of property that one seeks in core areas of the natural sciences, for example, searching for conservation principles, symmetry, and the like" (Chomsky, 1991b:49).

Thus Chomsky raises questions for linguistics and the science of the mind in general that are quite analogous to questions that have been raised in "core areas of the natural sciences"; e.g., physics, and that have their origins in antiquity. Is the universe parsimonious (Hildebrandt and Tromba, 1996)? If so, what principles dictate this parsimonious design? The answers given in classical physics were one form or another of a principle of "least action." (In earlier times, this principle was further derived from "God in his infinite wisdom"). We will investigate these topics in this section and offer some speculations on how syntactic phenomena such as word order (and perhaps other [a]symmetries of language) might have arisen as "emergent" phenomena through a symmetry-breaking mechanism.[4]

Chomsky has argued for a "naturalistic" stance toward the study of the biology of language; i.e., to treat "'mental' to be on a par with 'chemical,' 'optical,' or 'electrical'" (Chomsky, 1995a:1). We will continue to assume this approach as we turn to issues involving evolution. Because so little is known, we need to be willing to try out anything we have in our biolinguistic toolkit to attack the problem; as we will see, this can include everything from using zooblots to compare language genes with the genes of other species to using more indirect attacks on the problem with the aid of linguistic theory or nonlinear dynamics. Chomsky has emphasized the importance of physical constraints on possible pathways of evolution:

To move to more far reaching explanation [of evolution], you're going to have to find something about the space of physical possibility within which selection operates. That space might be extremely narrow. For example, it might be so narrow that under the particular conditions of human evolution, there's one possibility for something with 10^{11} neurons packed into something the size of a basketball: namely, a brain that has these computational properties. I don't propose that, but something like it could turn out to be true. There might be very narrow physical possibilities of the kind that, say D'Arcy Thompson and others talked about, that create a space within which reproductive success makes a difference. (Chomsky, 1994a:83–84)

To illustrate how the space of physical possibility can narrow down the choices for neural development, we note that Van Essen has proposed a "tension-based theory of morphogenesis" to account for the folding properties and compact wiring of various areas of the brain, such as the cortex. To support this hypothesis (clearly labeled as such), he examines data on wiring and folding in various areas of the brain and shows how many of these properties might by explained by a morphogenetic mechanism which involves mechanical tension acting along axons, dendrites, and glial processes. As he notes, the final shape of the brain would be determined by an interplay between genetics and physics (forces of tension), in which properties of symmetry are taken into account:

Morphogenesis entails an intricate choreographing of physical forces that cause differential tissue growth and displacement. Does this require an elaborate set of developmental instructions, transcending those needed to regulate the processes of neural proliferation, migration, axonal pathfinding, and synapse formation? If morphogenesis is driven largely by tension, the answer is no. Instead, the specificity of shape changes would largely be a by-product of factors that dictate

[4] See Fukui, 1996 for another line of investigation into these topics.

the connectivity and topology of the underlying neural circuitry. (Van Essen, 1997:318)

Van Essen observes that this hypothesis is in the D'Arcy Thompson tradition:

In a classic analysis of growth and form, D'Arcy Thompson discussed how tension and pressure can interact with structural anisotropies and asymmetries to determine the shape of biological structures. He applied this perspective to a variety of peripheral body parts, and even to plants, but not to the brain. The present theory of tension-based morphogenesis of the CNS can be viewed as a natural, albeit belated, extension of his pioneering ideas. (Van Essen, 1997:317)

We will provide further examples of proposals in the D'Arcy Thompson tradition that have been made for biological systems outside of language; viz., self-assembly in viruses, the evolution of the genetic code, and the origin of chirality in biological systems. In several of these cases, we will see how symmetry-breaking serves as the explanatory mechanism. But first let us say a few general words about the role of symmetry in science.

Ho-Kim, Kumar, and Lam note that in nature symmetry has both a restrictive and a predictive power (Ho-Kim, Kumar, and Lam, 1991:120). A simple example is that of the Platonic solids of which there are only five: the tetrahedron, the cube, the octahedron, the icosahedron, and the dodecahedron.[5] Symmetry forbids the occurrence of any other than these five. This is the restrictive aspect of symmetry. The predictive aspect comes in when we are able to predict that, say, a Martian, or the inhabitant of some other galaxy, will discover only these five solids and no more.[6] In a discussion of the occurrence of these "Platonic bodies" in the biological realm, D'Arcy Thompson specifically points out this restrictive property of symmetry on form (Thompson, 1992a:732–40). Thompson runs through some calculations using Euler's Law[7] for some possible and impossible configurations, commenting that "an apparently infinite variety of form is defined by mathematical laws and theorems, and limited by the properties of space and number."

---

[5] A Platonic solid is a regular convex polyhedron; i.e., a "volume bounded by plane faces which are identical regular polygons." Note that if you remove the symmetry restriction that the faces be "identical regular polygons," there are many more possibilities.

[6] Weinberg observes that when Kepler tried to explain the planetary orbits using the Platonic solids, the idea of applying symmetry considerations was the right idea, but he was applying it to the wrong problem. He notes the similarity to methods of the modern-day physicist who uses the symmetrical structures in (continuous) group theory to model the behavior of elementary particles (Weinberg, 1992:163–64).

[7] Euler's Law states that the number of vertices of a polyhedron, V, minus the number of edges, E, plus the number of faces, F, equals 2; i.e., $V - E + F = 2$. We will return to this law in the discussion of self-assembly in viruses.

The example just given concerns symmetries of physical objects, like tetrahedrons. The real restrictive power of symmetry principles comes in when we realize that they can restrict not only objects, but also physical laws.[8] For example, each of the space–time symmetries allows one to derive directly a law of conservation.[9] For example, the law of the conservation of energy is associated with the invariance of time.

Another important insight has been that symmetries may be spontaneously hidden or "broken." That is, even though the physical law itself may exhibit perfect symmetry, its realization in nature may be asymmetric. Gell-Mann characterizes spontaneous symmetry-breaking as follows: "The essence of spontaneous symmetry-breaking lies in this very circumstance: equations with a particular symmetry can have solutions that individually violate that symmetry, although the set of all solutions is symmetrical" (Gell-Mann, 1994:194).[10]

What Gell-Mann has in mind is here is electroweak theory. The equations (Yang-Mills field equations) possess perfect symmetry and predict massless particles. However, in nature the symmetric solution to these equations is unstable. The symmetry is broken by another field, the Higgs field. However, the set of all solutions is again symmetric.

Let us illustrate this idea with a simpler example, suggested by Weinberg (1992:308).[11] Suppose (contrary to fact) that there is an equation that relates the mass of the up quark to the mass of the down quark in the following way:

$$u/d + d/u = 2.5$$

Note that the equation is symmetric; for example, you can interchange u and d and the equation remains the same. Note that the up quark and the down quark cannot have the same mass; i.e., $u \neq d$ (or else $1 + 1 = 2.5$). However $u = 2d$ or $d = 2u$ are solutions to the equation. Either solution is asymmetric, but the set of all solutions, $\{ u = 2d, d = 2u \}$, is symmetric, as is the underlying equation.

Symmetry-breaking in a biological context goes back to work by Alan Turing. Turing is probably best known in computer science and in mathematical linguistics for his "Turing machine" theory. Work by Turing, Chomsky and many others has been integrated into what is sometimes

---

[8] As Weinberg puts it, "the symmetries that are really important in nature are not the symmetries of *things*, but the symmetries of *laws*" (Weinberg, 1992:137).
[9] "Noether's Theorem: symmetries imply conservation laws." (Weinberg, 1992:307).
[10] See Weinberg for additional general discussion of this point: "The symmetry of the equations is not necessarily reflected in each individual solution of these equations, but only in the pattern of *all* the solutions of these equations" (Weinberg, 1992:194).
[11] The equations for electroweak theory are obviously much more complicated than this illustration, but the principle is the same.

called the "Chomsky hierarchy" of grammars. What are probably less well-known, at least in the linguistics world, are his abstract mathematical studies on morphogenesis, in a paper written in 1952, one year before the discovery of DNA by Watson and Crick which marked the beginning of the revolution of molecular biology. This paper was titled "The Chemical Basis of Morphogenesis" and among the many intriguing ideas developed in it,[12] was his theory of reaction-diffusion mechanisms.[13] Implicit in this discussion was the idea of symmetry-breaking.

Turing proposed a set of chemical reactions involving autocatalysis[14] and diffusion and showed how such a mechanism might underlie certain kinds of pattern formation. His goal was to explain how certain "well-known physical laws" can account for the facts without any new hypotheses. For this reason, he did not actually perform the experiment, but suggested a hypothetical sequence of "imaginary reactions": "To specify actual substances, concentrations and temperatures giving rise to these functions would settle the matter finally, but would be difficult and somewhat out of the spirit of the present inquiry. Instead, it is proposed merely to mention imaginary reactions which give rise to the required functions" (Turing, 1952:43). And again: "It is thought, however, that the imaginary biological systems which have been treated, and the principles which have been discussed, should be of some help in interpreting real biological forms" (p. 72).

For a long time many people did not believe in the existence of Turing's "imaginary" systems (see Ball, 1994:311–14). However, in the early 1960s inorganic reactions were discovered with the properties postulated in Turing's theory; e.g. the Belousov–Zhabotinsky (B–Z) reaction.[15] Prigogine and Nicolis provided theoretical confirmation for the Turing mechanism within the framework of nonequilibrium thermodynamics (Prigogine and Nicolis, 1967).[16] And they argued that the importance of such mechanisms for biological processes go well beyond the morphogenetic systems discussed by Turing. In what *Nature* calls "the first clear example of Turing's reaction-diffusion wave in a biological system (p. v)," Kondo and Asai constructed a simulation program that

---

[12] Stewart and Golubitsky review Turing's ideas from the perspective of current views on symmetry (Stewart and Golubitsky, 1993: Chapter 7).

[13] Although we consider only the reaction-diffusion model here, numerous other mechanisms for pattern formation have been proposed; e.g., the ZPA model (for "zone of polarizing activity"). Gilbert presents a general overview of these models (Gilbert, 1997).

[14] Autocatalysis is the catalysis of a reaction by one of the reaction products.

[15] Actually such reactions were known as early as 1951, but were believed to be artifacts (Ball, 1994).

[16] They present calculations that they argue prove "the existence of a symmetry-breaking instability for the Turing mechanism, in situations sufficiently far from thermodynamic equilibrium" (p. 3550).

successfully predicted the pattern of stripes that appear on the skin of the angelfish (*Pomacanthus*) (Kondo and Asai, 1995). Meinhardt contrasts the dynamic regulation found in the angelfish with the "rigid coordinate system that operates in *Drosophila*" (Meinhardt, 1995). He notes that even in *Drosophila*, dynamic regulation can be observed in early developmental stages, so that the "rigid mechanism of stripe formation in *Drosophila* may be a late evolutionary modification of a genuine patterning process." See Kauffman, 1993 for an application of the Turing model to pattern formation in *Drosophila*.

It has also been proposed that the Turing reaction-diffusion mechanism might be able to explain the possible and impossible morphologies in vertebrate limb formation (Newman, Frisch, and Percus, 1988; Oster et al., 1988):

The identification of Mendelian "factors" was useful in the analysis of the transmission of traits before their chemical nature was understood even in principle. More recently, developmental and evolutionary roles continue to be ascribed to key genes, the majority of which are uncharacterized in terms of DNA sequence or specified product. We suggest that the identification of "Turingian factors," substances whose non-uniform stationary distributions depend on non-equilibrium biochemical processes which need not be fully characterized, can play a complementary role in the analysis of biological form. (Newman, Frisch, and Percus, 1988:190)

This story nicely illustrates the interweaving of genetics and epigenetics and the unification problem. Epigenetics is not an opposing view to genetics – they are complementary and interactive. Genes don't operate in a vacuum. As the genetic program unfolds, structures are built which in turn obey physical laws. What is important is to find the appropriate level of analysis at which something can be understood. Symmetry-breaking is best understood as an epigenetic process, not at the gene level. Put another way, there are no genes for symmetry-breaking.

Symmetry-breaking in the sunflower – the Fibonacci numbers

One of the problems that has fascinated scientists for centuries is the occurrence of the Fibonacci numbers in nature, particularly in plants:

$$1, 1, 2, 3, 5, 8, 13, 21, 34, 55, 89, 144 \ldots$$

In the sunflower, two interlaced families of spirals are seen in the head, one running clockwise and the other counterclockwise. For example, there might typically be 21 clockwise spirals and 34 counterclockwise spirals; 21 and 34 are two of the Fibonacci numbers. The study of the

Fibonacci numbers in plants makes up part of the field called *phyllotaxis*. According to D'Arcy Thompson, interest in the role of the Fibonacci numbers in the plant kingdom goes back at least as far as Kepler (Thompson, 1992a:923).

Douady and Couder have proposed a theory that would account for the occurrence of the Fibonacci numbers in the sunflower, along with some related facts.[17] It is important to note that the spatial arrangement of spirals that is visible to the human eye is actually of secondary importance. Of more importance is the temporal sequence; i.e., the fact that the primordia, the precursors of the leaves, petals, etc., appear during plant development along a spiral known as the *generative spiral*. If we measure the angle formed at the center of the spiral between successive primordia, called the *divergence angle*, it comes out to about 137.5°, a fact noted by one of the founders of modern crystallography, Auguste Bravais, and his brother, Louis.

There is an intimate connection between this angle and the Fibonacci numbers. If we take the ratio of successive Fibonacci numbers; e.g., $34:55$ ($\cong .61818$), this ratio approaches (the inverse of) a number known to the ancient Greeks as the golden number Φ:

$$\Phi = \frac{1+\sqrt{5}}{2}$$

If we multiply Φ by 360° we get 222.5°, which, when subtracted from 360°, yields 137.5°, the angle observed by the Bravais brothers.

The problem then is to account for the "golden angle" of 137.5°. Douady and Couder set up a physics experiment in which drops of silicone oil fell through a magnetic field into the center of a dish at regular intervals. The droplets became magnetic dipoles which then repelled each other radially at a fixed velocity. By adjusting the timing of the intervals at which the droplets fell, the spiral pattern that is seen in the sunflower head could be reproduced with the observed divergence angle of 137.5°. Not only did different timing patterns produce different Fibonacci numbers, but even the numbers from the so-called "anomalous" series (3, 4, 7, 11, 18 . . .) could be reproduced. "These are the characteristics of a direct symmetry-breaking bifurcation. Here it leads from an alternate pattern to a chiral spiral pattern" (Douady and Couder, 1992:2100).

They also showed that adjusting the divergence angle to rational fractions of 360° produced spiral patterns that were not tightly wound. In

---

[17] The technical details can be found in Douady and Couder, 1992, and 1993b. A more general presentation is given in Douady and Couder, 1993a, but this account is in French. An accessible interpretation of their results, which we draw on here, can be found in Stewart 1995a, 1995c.

terms of the sunflowers, this would mean inefficient seed-packing. In fact, as Stewart notes, the magic number Φ has the property of being the "most irrational" number.

Douady and Couder ran computer simulations and duplicated the above results.[18] Stewart speculates that the genes affect the timing of the appearance of the primordia (Stewart, 1995a). As he says, "it's a partnership of physics and genetics" (p. 99). We again have "an apparently infinite variety of form . . . limited by the properties of space and number," as noted earlier by D'Arcy Thompson (1992a:740).

Goodwin makes the following observation concerning the above example:

> Over 80 percent of the 250,000 or so species of higher plants have spiral phyllotaxis. This is also the dominant form generated in the model, which identifies it as the most probable form in the generative space of possible phyllotactic patterns. So we get an interesting conjecture: the frequency of the different phyllotactic patterns in nature may simply reflect the relative probabilities of the morphogenetic trajectories of the various forms and have little to do with natural selection. (Goodwin, 1994:132)

That is not to say that natural selection plays no role. Rather it is "in no sense a generator of biological form, but it may be involved in testing the stability of the form."

Self-assembly in viruses

There are several different ways that the outer shells of viruses can be made: one is called "morphogenetic pathway" and the other is referred to as "self-assembly" (Watson et al., 1987). The morphogenetic pathway is illustrated by the virus T4. There are three separate pathways for the head, tail, and tail fiber. There is a definite sequence of steps with different genes involved in each of the three pathways. After the head and tail are made, they are combined, and finally the tail fibers are added.

The second method of building shells, self-assembly, is illustrated by a wide variety of viruses, including poliovirus, which has an icosahedral shape. What happens here, however, is that the proteins needed to assemble the icosahedron are made by the genes, but not assembled under direct genetic control. Rather the proteins self-assemble spontaneously into an icosahedral shell, in accordance with the laws of thermodynamics (Berger et al., 1994).

---

[18] According to Stewart "M. Kunz of the University of Lausanne has proved the occurrence of the golden angle in Stéphane Douady and Yves Couder's dynamical model of plant growth using purely analytic methods – that is, without computer calculations. This work fills the final gap in the story leading from dynamics to Fibonacci spirals" (Stewart, 1995b:183).

What this example shows, among other things, is that conceptually similar design tasks can be solved in quite different ways. In the case of self-assembly, maximal advantage is being taken of physical principles that are not placed under direct genetic control, as they were, as we saw above, in the case of T4. In the latter case, numerous steps in viral shell assembly are guided by the specific expression of numerous genes. Of course physics is involved in the morphogenetic pathway case too, as always, but in a less autonomous fashion. And genes are involved in self-assembly; the appropriate protein subunits must be built. What these examples demonstrate is that it makes no sense to oppose natural selection to physical laws. Chomsky is correct to speak about the "space of physical possibility within which selection operates." The space here is restricted by such notions as symmetry, configurations of minimal energy, Euler's Law, etc.

Symmetry-breaking and the genetic code

Hornos and Hornos propose a theory for the evolution of the genetic code (Hornos and Hornos, 1993).[19] Each of the twenty amino acids is coded for by triplets of nucleic acid bases (codons). Since there are four bases – adenine (A), guanine (G), thymine (T) [or U in mRNA], and cytosine (C) – there are sixty-four available codons. Hence a given amino acid can be coded for by different triplets, a property of the code known as "degeneracy." However, a certain amount of symmetry is apparent, since it is often the case that the first two bases uniquely determine the amino acid; e.g. GUX, where X = U, C, A, G, codes for the amino acid valine. If this "quadruplet" symmetry held throughout the genetic code, then we would have sixteen quadruplets, each uniquely coding one amino acid, which would make the code symmetric under changes of the third base. But this would only give us sixteen amino acids. In order to code for all twenty amino acids, there must be degeneracy in the code. The genetic code has three sextuplets, five quadruplets, two triplets, nine doublets and two singlets.

Hornos and Hornos examined the classical and exceptional Lie groups[20] (SU(n), O(2n), Sp(n), and O(2n + 1), G_2, E_4, E_6, E_7, and E_8), which have played a fundamental role in studying the symmetries of the strong force (SU(3)), the weak force (SU(2)), and most recently, in superstring theory (E_8 X E_8). They looked for a group with an irreducible sixty-four–dimensional representation, corresponding to the sixty-four triplets; this restriction left them with SU(2), SU(3),

---

[19] This discussion closely follows the review of Stewart, 1994.

[20] Lie groups are mathematical structures used to describe continuous properties, such as the possible rotations of a sphere.

SU(4), Sp(4), Sp(6), SO(13), SO(14), and G_2. They then asked how the sixty-four–dimensional representation breaks up along a chain of subgroups in a way corresponding to the degeneracy of the genetic code: "The basic idea is to assume a fundamental group G and a chain of its subgroups. A dynamical process emerges assuming that the symmetry is successively broken throughout the chain" (Hornos and Hornos, 1993:4402).

As already discussed, symmetry-breaking is the process fundamental to physics (and other domains), whereby the symmetrical laws of nature yield asymmetrical solutions, such as the Higgs boson for electroweak theory; i.e., the unification theory for electromagnetism and the weak force. They propose that "the Sp(6) chain Sp(4) ⊗ SU(2) is the one that best reproduces the genetic code" and go on to compare the predictions of their theory for amino acid polarities with experimental results. Although this is work-in-progress – other properties of the amino acids must be studied and other groups will be investigated – a couple of general points can be made.

The point of all this is to do something analogous to what Chomsky calls narrowing "the space of physical possibility within which selection operates," as Hornos and Hornos explicitly note:

Starting with the 64 codons and arranging different ways of distributing them among the 20 a.a. [amino acids] and one termination code, Bertman and Jungck estimated that at least 10^{71} to 10^{84} different genetic codes like our contemporary one are possible. The central point in our analysis is that among this huge number of possible distributions of codons only a very limited number will correspond to Cartan symmetries and consequently generate an evolution pattern given by the group and its chains of subgroups. (Hornos and Hornos, 1993:4402)

The authors hope to study additional amino acid properties to discover the "property that guided the evolution of the code in this symmetry path." In a similar vein, Hornos and Hornos explicitly note that their approach to the study of the genetic code is not a substitute for microscopic analysis: "First it is not our intention to replace with our model a detailed microscopic biological, physical, and chemical analysis of the genetic code. Symmetry principles can and should be used only as a guide principle and a general framework in complement of a microscopic theory" (1993:4404).

In a review of Hornos and Hornos, Stewart makes the following observations:

They suggest that the first broken symmetry – where the 64 codons would code for just six amino acids – may represent a primordial version of the genetic code. The first step in its evolution. However, it is worth bearing in mind that symmetry-breaking is a mathematical technique for organising structure and need not correspond to temporal evolution. Hornos and Hornos's result may indicate potential patterns inherent in the molecular forms but not actually adopted by nature – clues to the "geography" of the space from which the genetic code was selected rather than relics of the actual selection process. (Stewart, 1994:16)

This point is also worth bearing in mind in connection with our discussion in the next section when we apply symmetry considerations to language. That is, these symmetries may be describing the "geography" of space, in Stewart's terms, or "the space of physical possibility within which selection operates," in Chomsky's words. The "relics" of the selection process, or the language symmetries that came into existence, may be partly determined by other kinds of factors, biological and otherwise.

Symmetry in linguistics

To clarify what is meant by symmetry, let us consider the simple example of a square. If we rotate a square about its center by 90 degrees, 180 degrees, 270 degrees, or 360 degrees (= 0 degrees), the square remains unchanged. These four rotations are known as the rotational symmetries of the square. Similarly, the square possesses four additional reflectional symmetries, two about its diagonals, and two more about its horizontal and vertical midpoints. These eight symmetry "transformations" form a mathematical structure known as a "group," in this case the group of symmetries of the square. Characterizing symmetries by means of a group has the advantage of providing us with a measure of the degree of symmetry of a geometric or physical object, or as we see directly below, of a mathematical or physical equation. In addition, we can also employ the methods of group theory to perform calculations and predict properties of a symmetrical structure.

As we just noted, not only objects, but also equations may possess symmetries. As we may recall from high school algebra, the graph of the equation for the parabola ($y = x^2$) has symmetry under reflection about the y-axis. Note that if we substitute $-x$ for x in the equation $y = x^2$, the form of the equation remains unchanged. Another way to say the same thing is that the equation is "invariant" under the following reflection transformation: $x \rightarrow -x$. In fact one of the key insights of Galois, the inventor of group theory, was that you can associate groups to polynomial equations in such a way that the symmetry properties of the group can be used to predict whether a given equation has solutions. This work was later extended by Sophus Lie, who extended group theory in order to be able to predict the solvability of differential equations as well. The result was that group theory now provided a powerful tool to study the symmetry properties of all kinds of equations from Newton's second law ($F = ma$), to Maxwell's equations for electromagnetism, to the equation(s) for the Theory of Everything.

As examples from biology where symmetry and economy principles interact in interesting ways, some of which we discussed earlier, we might include reaction-diffusion mechanisms (Turing structures), the double-helix, the structure of viruses, the structure of the genetic code, universal scaling laws, the occurrence of the Fibonacci numbers in phyllotaxis, and the bee honeycomb.

Recall the case of the genetic code from the previous section. As Stewart notes, symmetries of codes, like the genetic code, are not motions in space, like the example of the square just discussed. They are "operations that swap sequences of code symbols around":

Think about Morse code. Samuel Morse could have chosen to assign the same letter (S, say) to *every* sequence of dots and dashes. This system would have provided a highly symmetric code, but – of course – a totally useless one. Symmetric in what sense? For symmetries of codes, the relevant transformations are not motions in space; they are operations that swap sequences of code symbols around. A symbol sequence possesses such a symmetry if its *meaning* is unchanged by the swap. Now if all code sequences have the *same* meaning, then you can swap the symbols in any way you wish without changing that meaning. This is the sense in which my totally useless modification of Morse code is highly symmetric. (Stewart, 1998:57)

The way that the Morse code can become useful is through the device of symmetry-breaking, as Stewart observes:

My code could be made more useful by breaking the symmetry – for example, by assigning S to any sequence of dots (so that •, ••, •••,••••, and so on would all mean "S"), O to any sequence of dashes, and A to any sequence containing both dots and dashes. The resulting code would no longer be completely symmetric; for example, swapping all dots and dashes would turn the message SOS into OSO. The new code would retain some of the original symmetry, however; for instance, the message AAA would remain unchanged. We can imagine further losses of symmetry that would lead, step by step, to the code that is enshrined in cryptographic history, with ••• for S, - - - for O, and so on. (Stewart, 1998:57–58)

Similarly, the genetic code reveals some obvious (broken) symmetry:

Now think about the genetic code. We have already observed a key feature: The genetic code is redundant. That is, different triplets often code for the same amino acid. There is no great regularity to this lack of uniqueness, but a definite degree of symmetry – albeit imperfect – is clearly visible in the genetic code. Often, just the first two bases in a triplet determine the corresponding amino acid. For example GA? is always leucine, CG? always arginine. In short, the code for these amino acids is symmetric under changes of the third base. If this symmetry were perfect, then the 64 triplets would break up into 16 quartet triplets, such as GAC, GAG, GAA, GAT, with each triplet of the quartet coding for the same amino acid (but a different amino acid for each quartet). However, there are more than 16 amino acids, so sometimes the third base matters. Indeed sometimes the *second* base matters. Either way, the symmetry of the arrangement into quartets is broken. (Stewart, 1998:58)

Turning now to human language, note that the languages of the world permit a variety of different word orders. We restrict ourselves here to subject (S), verb (V), and object (O). For example, in English we have SVO as the principal word order in declarative clauses, as in *John saw Mary*. Other possible word orders attested in the languages of the world are: SOV, VSO, VOS, OSV, OVS. Some languages permit all of the possibilities, the so-called "free word order" languages. Other languages permit a subset of the six possible orders. However, not all sixty-three possible (ignoring the empty subset) subsets of orders are attested. For example, a language might have SVO and SOV orders. Sometimes one order appears to be more basic than the other, so that one speaks of a "basic" word order and a "derived" word order.

Again we find a spectrum of symmetry ranging from very symmetric (free word order) to less symmetric (fixed word order). As in the case of the genetic code, we might ask whether symmetry breaking may be playing a role. Several areas come to mind in which the symmetry-breaking hypothesis could be investigated: language development, language evolution, language change and language typology.[21] If so, it might be possible to study it abstractly; e.g., by studying how parametric variation determines the path which acquisition takes in the space of possible languages. From this point of view, the initial state (of the cognitive component) of the language faculty allows perfect symmetry with respect to word order. Then as we make transitions from one cognitive state to another: $S_0, S_1, S_2 \ldots S_n$, the perfect symmetry is broken, resulting in the word orders found in the language learned. One could also look for evidence of symmetry-breaking patterns in data from language typology, which, after all, reflects the final state of the acquisition process. One can also ask whether it is a mechanism that is operative in language change. Finally, one can ask whether symmetry-breaking played a role in the evolution of language analogous to the role that Hornos and Hornos have postulated for the evolution of the genetic code.

The task here would be to identify operations that leave some linguistic feature invariant when a linguistic operation is performed. For example, an operation might take a "basic" word order into a "derived" word order in a declarative clause, without changing the "meaning" (declarative) of

---

[21] For each of these cases, one can look at the specific areas of syntax, semantics, phonology, morphology, the lexicon, etc.

the sequence, much as the meaning of a genetic code triplet remains unchanged if we swap out the third base. For now, we only wish to point out that symmetry-breaking is a possible source in language of syntactic asymmetries such as word order. That is, it is not necessary to assume that all possible combinations of basic and derived word orders are hard-wired in the genes, with linguistic input determining the actually occurring word order. Instead another possibility is that UG for Human is maximally symmetric with respect to possible word orders, possibly apart from a preferred basic word order, which results from the necessity of linearizing spoken language. All other combinations of word order result from symmetry-breaking (linguistic input being the symmetry breaker). From a slightly different perspective, word order types would be the (asymmetric) stable solutions of the symmetric still-to-be-discovered "equations" governing word order distribution. Of course, we do not understand the neural basis of word order, as we do for the genetic code, so we cannot actually write down the relevant equations. Nevertheless, the tools of group theory may be able to aid in characterizing the symmetries of word order patterns. And, at the very least, we should bear in mind that properties of language, such as syntactic (a)symmetry, could in principle arise, like the Fibonacci numbers, by physical constraints, "limited by the properties of space and number," in D'Arcy Thompson's words.

Why are there asymmetries in Human?

Why doesn't language have maximal symmetry? Why don't we have free word order in Human? Why do we have the asymmetries observed for movement (conditions)? Why do we have movement (displacement) in Human at all? There may be multiple answers to these multiple questions. But symmetry-breaking provides us with some new tools to look at these problems. For if symmetry-breaking plays any role, then some of the ugly "imperfections" of the language faculty may be no more surprising than the "imperfections" seen in Turing stripe patterns, the (anomalous) Fibonacci patterns, the degeneracy of the genetic code (see below), or in the breakdown of gauge symmetry for that matter. Any symmetric system that dynamically evolves under varying conditions is subject to physical laws. Some of these laws concern the way that a symmetric system breaks down into systems with lower symmetry. The equations of the system under study can be perfectly symmetrical but, after symmetry-breaking, the particular state that the system ends up in is asymmetric. This is often because the symmetric state is unstable, whereas the asymmetric state turns out to be stable. Maynard Smith notes in his discussion of UG (see below) that "natural selection may not have picked on the simplest way" of doing things. From our perspective, if the laws governing a physical system present natural selection with a number of solutions, some of which are asymmetric and stable, and others which are symmetric, but unstable, it is quite possible that it will pick the asymmetric solutions, particularly if stabilizing and maintaining the symmetric solution is too costly.

In contrast to this approach, there are the views of evolutionary psychology which emphasize other factors in the origins of language: "Moreover, language is quite clearly adaptive, in the sense of inherently serving the goals of reproduction ... We rise to power, manipulate people, find mates, keep mates, win friends and influence people by language" (Pinker, 1995:233; see also Horgan, 1995; Pinker, 1994a). Although language can be used to find mates, this tells us nothing about the structural properties of language. For example, English SVO is not more "adaptive" than Japanese SOV for finding "mates." Similarly, eyes are also used to find mates, but this does not tell us anything about the chirality (handedness) of molecules in the eye. An account of the chirality of eye proteins in terms of "finding mates" would be promptly rejected. The fact that such adaptive accounts are so readily accepted about language and other areas in the cognitive realm provides yet another example of methodological dualism, as discussed in chapter 1 and below. In our view, the origins of (some) properties of language, such as (a)symmetries in syntax perhaps, would be more akin to the physical evolution of molecular chirality, as opposed to some implausible selectional account which claims such properties arose to "win friends and influence people."

Symmetry and beauty

Chomsky has suggested that "language is designed as a system that is 'beautiful,' but in general unusable ... (though with features that enable it to be used sufficiently for the purposes of normal life)" (Chomsky, 1991b:49). Weinberg has noted that it is *principles of symmetry* which give physical theories like general relativity and the standard model their beauty; i.e., "most of their sense of inevitability and simplicity" (Weinberg, 1992:136). By simplicity, Weinberg means simplicity of ideas (p. 134). He notes that Einstein's theory of gravitation with its fourteen equations is regarded as simpler than Newton's theory of gravitation with its three equations, because of the "simplicity of his [Einstein's] central idea about the equivalence of gravitation and inertia." To illustrate inevitability, Weinberg notes that Newton's theory of gravitation could be changed to have an inverse cube law rather than an inverse square law without abandoning its conceptual basis. But if you modified Einstein's theory in that way, the resulting theory "would be too ugly to bear" (p. 107). The properties of simplicity and inevitability combine to yield what Weinberg calls the "rigidity" of physical theories: [22] "The kind of beauty that we find in physical theories is of a very limited sort. It is, as far as I have been able to capture it in words, the beauty of simplicity and inevitability – the beauty of perfect structure, the beauty of everything fitting together, of nothing being changeable, of logical rigidity" (Weinberg, 1992:149). Weinberg cites quantum field theory as the kind of property that confers logical rigidity to a theory and gives "a really fundamental theory its beauty." He observes that quantum mechanics and special relativity are nearly incompatible without quantum field theory, which "imposes powerful restrictions on the ways that particles can interact with one another."

Kaku and Thompson elaborate on this same theme, noting that "Many possible universes that are compatible with relativity can be constructed. Likewise, many universes can be dreamed up that obey the laws of quantum mechanics. However, putting together these two yields so many divergences, anomalies, tachyons, and the like that only one iron-clad solution is probably possible" (Kaku and Thompson, 1995:194). They add that "a tremendous amount of symmetry is necessary to eliminate them [i.e., the divergences, etc.]" and that the superstring theory that solved these problems has the largest set of symmetries that physicists had ever seen. Hence in retrospect it appears that the physicists' search for beautiful physical laws led them to symmetrical equations which in turn yielded highly restrictive theories encompassing the world of the quantum and the world of relativity (quantum field theories):

Beauty $\Rightarrow$ Symmetry $\Rightarrow$ Restrictive theories of nature

How restrictive a theory can we get? According to Kaku and Thompson, a very restrictive theory:

For example, German physicists have compiled an encyclopedia, the *Handbuch der Physik*, an exhaustive work that summarized the world's knowledge of physics. The *Handbuch*, which physically occupies an entire bookshelf of a library, represented the pinnacle of scientific learning. If the superstring theory is correct, then

---

[22] Of course, in the final analysis, some beauty will always remain in the eye of the beholder. Crease and Mann note that Weinberg and Glashow, who incorporated spontaneous symmetry-breaking into their electroweak theory differed on the question of the beauty of the principle: "Some physicists, such as Glashow, think the hurlyburly of spontaneous symmetry breaking is so awkward and ugly that it is a gravy stain on the tie of physics. Others, such as Weinberg, regard symmetry breaking as a wonderful limiting device, for it means that nature and humanity are forced to work with local gauge invariance" (Crease and Mann, 1987:244).

all the information contained in this encyclopedia can be derived (in principle) from *a single equation*. (Kaku and Thompson, 1995:4)

Zee calls this writing down "the entire theory of the physical universe on a cocktail napkin." Note that the idea of deriving the physical theory of the universe from a "single equation" depends crucially on the formulation of physical laws in terms of the action principle ("principle of least action") the origins of which go back to classical physics (Zee, 1986:109). Otherwise, Newton's equations of motion alone would require more than a single equation on the back of a napkin. As Zee notes, under the action formulation, Newton's equations of motion, the eight electromagnetic equations of Maxwell (also see below), and the ten equations of Einstein, each reduce to a single action and the goal is to combine all of these into a still more comprehensive "action of the universe."

Kaku has noted that Maxwell's equations, as they are usually first taught, consist of "eight abstract equations, which are exceptionally ugly and very opaque" (Kaku, 1995:86). However, when time is treated as the fourth dimension, the equations can be written relativistically as a single equation using the Maxwell tensor and the simplicity and beauty become evident:

In one masterful stroke, the fourth dimension simplifies these equations in a beautiful, transparent fashion. Written in this way, the equations possess a higher *symmetry*; that is space and time can turn into each other. Like a beautiful snowflake that remains the same when we rotate it around its axis, Maxwell's field equations, written in relativistic form, remain the same when we rotate space into time. (Kaku, 1995:86)

Note that this restrictiveness induced by symmetry played a crucial role in Hornos and Hornos' proposal for the evolution of the genetic code discussed earlier. As Stewart observes, only eight groups qualified as having an irreducible sixty-four–dimensional representation and from these it turned out to be possible to construct only one sequence of broken symmetries that came close to reproducing the correct pattern (Stewart, 1994).[23]

We have suggested that the partial symmetries that are found in linguistics (in Human) may also be a reflection of hidden symmetries at another level, just as the partial symmetries (degeneracy) of the genetic code may obscure the "'geography' of the space from which the genetic code was selected," as Stewart put it. Hence it is totally appropriate to use beauty as

---

[23] Stewart notes that the fifth, and final, breakage of symmetry is not given by a subgroup and was partly determined on empirical grounds. What we may have then is "a 'frozen' version of one [a code] that ideally would have had 27 amino acids" (1994:16).

a guide to search for and try to reveal the underlying symmetry of linguistic principles, and ultimately, the linguistic equations of the mind.

A minimalist and internalist view of evolution of language

As we have seen, the minimalist program is in large part concerned with studying the question, "how did this knowledge [i.e., of language] evolve?" More specifically, it attempts to address questions about the design properties of language and to investigate how optimal these properties are. We have concluded that a possible (partial) answer to the questions about word order that we have been looking at would be that certain features of language evolved as a series of symmetry-breakings, which continue to be options in the epigenetic program, and which are in turn triggered by environmental input during ontogenesis. Central to this approach to the evolution of language, then, is the principles-and-parameters model of language acquisition. For the physical mechanisms that the principles-and-parameters model represents, when the dynamics are put back in, are what provide the internal developmental constraints to evolutionary change. How well does this view accord with current work in developmental biology? And what role would natural selection play in such an account?

Whatever the precise nature of the developmental mechanisms of the principles-and-parameters model turns out to be, it will in turn provide limits to what external factors, such as natural selection, can or cannot do. It is in this sense that we are calling this view of evolution of language an "internalist" view; for more discussion on the internalist approach to I-linguistics (biolinguistics) in other respects, see Chomsky, 1997c; see also Piattelli-Palmarini on "*neo*-neo-Darwinism" (Piattelli-Palmarini, 1989:9). Note that actual work in linguistics either implicitly or explicitly accepts the idea that a variety of factors (developmental, genetic, physical, selective) interact during the course of evolution. This truism is assumed in all fields of biology. The only reason for mentioning this fact here is that in recent years a vocal minority within the evolutionary psychology community has tried to elevate natural selection to an omnipotent design principle for evolution, with the result that a number of vacuous claims about language have been made. We consider these later.

The real question is *what* kinds of developmental, genetic, physical, and selective factors and constraints interact in evolution? Here a variety of interesting proposals have been put forth. For example, Raff is interested in the mechanisms that "connect development to evolution" that "may drive the internal part of evolution." Of these he goes on to say

This is a crucial topic because we are not merely interested in describing how developmental processes and patterns evolve. There is a much more profound issue in that existing developmental patterns and mechanisms influence or constrain what natural selection can elicit in the course of evolution. There are thus aspects of evolution that are controlled by the internal order of organisms, and potentially by evolutionary processes that operate internally on developmental features. (Raff, 1996:33)

Stephen Jay Gould points out that Francis Galton provided a useful metaphor for this "internal constitution" of an organism – the organism is like a polyhedral pool ball, while natural selection is like a pool cue:

Natural selection is like a pool cue. Natural selection hits the ball, and the ball goes wherever selection pushes it. It's an externalist, functionalist, adaptationist theory. In the nineteenth century, Francis Galton, Darwin's cousin, developed an interesting metaphor: he said an organism is a polyhedron; it rests on one of the facets, one of the surfaces of a polyhedron. You may still need the pool cue of natural selection to hit it – it doesn't move unless there is a pushing force – but it's a polyhedron, meaning that an internal constitution shapes its form and the pathways of change are limited. There are certain pathways that are more probable, and there are certain ones that aren't accessible, even though they might be adaptively advantageous. (Gould, 1995:53)

Chomsky notes that no one assumes that "every trait is specifically selected." Rather an organ might be developed for one purpose, and then be refined for a different purpose. He cites the standard case of the origin of insect wings as thermoregulators, but notes that "human mental capacities" may also have evolved as a by-product of something else. "In some cases it seems that organs develop to serve one purpose and, when they have reached a certain form in the evolutionary process, became available for different purposes, at which point the processes of natural selection may refine them further for these purposes . . . Possibly human mental capacities have in some cases evolved in a similar way" (Chomsky, 1988a:167).

Dennis Duboule has described the development of the vertebrate limb in similar terms:

Vertebrate limbs are an amazing example of successful adaptation to various environmental conditions. In higher vertebrates, forelimbs help to fly, swim, walk, dig, grasp, or play the Goldberg variations. Yet their basic structure (the sequence and spatial arrangement of bony elements) is always the same. This implies the existence of a unique developmental strategy for building a limb (a limb plan) that early on imposes a basic scheme, on top of which subsequent species-specific customizations occur. (Duboule, 1994:575)

Although, Duboule does not directly address the question of the role of natural selection here, from our vantage point, what he calls the "universal limb plan" is a result of the generative principles alluded to earlier, which specify part of the concept "possible organism" (Goethe's Urform) and which then interact in various ways with natural selection to yield "subsequent species-specific customizations."

A wide range of approaches to the problems of development and evolution are currently exploring various kinds of genetic, developmental, and physical constraints and their interactions with natural selection. These approaches include the critiques of the neo-Darwinian Synthesis by Eden and Schützenberger (Moorhead and Kaplan, 1967), the Resynthesis (Gilbert, Opitz, and Raff, 1996; Raff, 1996), the "pluralist" approach of Gould and Lewontin[24] (Gould, 1997b), "generative biology" in the sense of Webster and Goodwin (Webster and Goodwin, 1996), Kauffman's "order for free" (Kauffman, 1993), the investigations into "generic physical mechanisms" by Newman and others (Newman, 1992), the study of dynamic systems, in the sense of Turing, to give only a few examples. Also included is Jacob's study of the "possible and the actual" (Jacob, 1982). As he formulates it, "it is mainly through a net of developmental constraints that natural selection works by filtering actual phenotypes out of all possible genotypes." The minimalist–internalist view of evolution of (language)[25] is nothing more than the attempt to discover what works from these various approaches and to use that, to search for promising new avenues of research and to keep an eye on new developments coming down the road, in *Nature, Science, Cell, Development, Evolution* or wherever else they might come from.

EVOLUTION AND NATURAL SELECTION

Chomsky has noted that natural selection is only one of the factors operative in evolution: "Physical law provides narrow channels within which complex organisms may vary, and natural selection is doubtless a factor in determining the distribution of traits and properties within these constraints. *A* factor, not *the* factor, at least if we follow Darwin's sensible strictures" (Chomsky, 1995a:56).

---

[24] Gould and Lewontin also cite the work of D'Arcy Thompson (Gould and Lewontin, 1979). Moreover, Gould wrote an introduction to a reprint of D'Arcy Thompson and specifically mentions the example of the Fibonacci numbers in phyllotaxis as an example of Thompson's "theme" (Thompson, 1992b).

[25] There is a large literature on evolution of language. For additional perspectives, consult the following, which include additional references: Harnad, Steklis, and Lancaster, 1976; Lieberman, 1984; Bickerton, 1990; Pinker and Bloom, 1990; Corballis, 1991; Greenfield, 1991; Bradshaw and Rogers, 1993; Gajdusek, McKhann, and Bolis, 1994; Hurford, 1994a, 1994b; Wilkins and Wakefield, 1995.

He notes that Darwin denies ever claiming that natural selection is the exclusive source of evolutionary modification. In the last edition of *Origin of Species*, Darwin writes: "In the first edition of this work, and subsequently, I placed in a most conspicuous position – namely, at the close of the Introduction – the following words: 'I am convinced that natural selection has been the main but not the exclusive means of modification.' This has been of no avail. Great is the power of steady misrepresentation" (cited in Gould, 1980:49–50).

Darwin's view can be contrasted with another view that has recently surfaced in some quarters in cognitive psychology and evolutionary psychology. It was put forth in its strongest form by Pinker: "And here is the key point. Natural selection is not just a scientifically respectable alternative to divine creation. It is the *only* alternative that can explain the evolution of a complex organ like the eye" (Pinker, 1994a:360). The choice is "stark," Pinker continues – it is "God or natural selection" (p. 360). In what follows we will call this view the "God or natural selection" view. It is important to note at the outset that the current and standard view in biology is in agreement with Darwin, not Pinker; i.e., it is a truism that natural selection is only one factor among many other (physical) factors that interact in evolution. It is a logical fallacy to speak of natural selection in isolation as a design factor in evolution, as Pinker often does. As Darwin makes clear, natural selection is always selection of "something." That something is *variation* which is generated in and constrained by physical channels. The improper use of this terminology by Pinker has had a pernicious effect in linguistics discussions, but the use of the terminology is equally incoherent in any other area of cognitive science or evolutionary psychology, not to mention biology. We will return to some concrete examples later.

LANGUAGE AS A BY-PRODUCT

Chomsky has speculated that the language faculty may have arisen as a by-product of something else (Chomsky, 1988a:chapter 5). In addition, he has suggested that the number faculty may have arisen as a by-product of the language faculty. Let's run through the argument for the case of the number faculty here. He notes that:

Children have the capacity to acquire the number system. They can learn to count and somehow know that it is possible to continue to add one indefinitely. They can also readily acquire the technique of arithmetical calculation. If a child did not already know that it is possible to add one indefinitely, it could never learn this fact. Rather, taught the numerals 1, 2, 3, etc., up to some number *n*, it would assume that that is the end of the story. It seems that this capacity, like the capacity for language, lies beyond the intellectual range of otherwise intelligent apes." (p. 167–68)

Chomsky goes on to ask how the number faculty developed and concludes that "it is impossible to believe that it was specifically selected" (p. 168). The physical chemist P. W. Atkins argues the same point (for other kinds of mathematical capacities): "Mathematically capable human brains did not evolve because there were selective advantages in being able to solve quadratic equations or to write tensor field equations. There is no need to be able to solve Newton's equations, let alone Einstein's, when you are a monkey: it is better just to jump out of the way" (Atkins, 1994:119).

In fact there are cultures today that make no use of the number faculty, although they have the latent capacity to do so:

Cultures still exist today that have not made use of this faculty; their language does not contain a method for constructing indefinitely many number words, and the people of these cultures are not aware of the possibility of counting. But they certainly have the capacity. Adults can quickly learn to count and to do arithmetic if placed in the appropriate environment, and a child from such a tribe, raised in a technological society, could become an engineer or a physicist as readily as anyone else. The capacity is present but latent. (Chomsky, 1988a:168)

In fact, the capacity to use the number faculty was not used for most of human history. This suggests, as mentioned above, that this capacity was not specifically selected by natural selection:

In fact, the capacity was latent and unused throughout almost all of human history. It is only recently in evolutionary terms, at a time when human evolution had reached its current stage, that the number faculty was manifested. Plainly it is not the case that people who could count, or who could solve problems of arithmetic or number theory, were able to survive to produce more offspring, so that the capacity developed through natural selection. Rather, it developed as a by-product of something else, and was available for use when circumstances called it forth. (p. 168)

The "problem posed for biological theories," then, is "Why do we have the mathematical ability, since it was never a factor in evolution?" Chomsky concludes: "Now the answer to that must be that the mathematical ability is just a reflection of some other ability." What was this "other ability?": "At this point one can only speculate, but it is possible that the number faculty developed as a by-product of the language faculty" (p. 169).

The language faculty has the property of "discrete infinity": "To put it simply, each sentence has a fixed number of words: one, two, three, forty-seven, ninety-three, etc. And there is no limit in principle to how many words the sentence may contain" (p. 169).

Moreover, this property is extremely unusual, possibly unique, in the biological world:

Other systems known in the animal world are quite different. Thus the system of ape calls is finite; there are a fixed number, say, forty. The so-called bee language, on the other hand, is infinite, but it is not discrete. A bee signals the distance of a flower from the hive by some form of motion; the greater the distance, the more the motion. Between any two signals there is in principle another, signaling a distance in between the first two, and this continues down to the ability to discriminate. (p. 169)

Since the language faculty and the number faculty both have the property of discrete infinity, it may be that the latter developed as a by-product of the former: "In fact, we might think of the human number faculty as essentially an 'abstraction' from human language, preserving the mechanisms of discrete infinity and eliminating the other special features of language. If so, that would explain the fact that the human number faculty is available though unused in the course of human evolution" (p. 169).

Given the picture of development that is currently emerging in fly genetics, it is possible at least to speculate on possible scenarios of how this could happen. In discussing eye development in the fruit fly, Lawrence notes many genes might be important to eye development, but not necessarily specific to it:

Take the eye as an example: about 30% of all lethal mutations, when examined as clones in the eye, damage eye development. If about 90% of all genes can mutate to give a lethal [sic.], as is generally thought, this means that nearly one-third of all genes make some contribution to eye development. Of course, some of these are probably housekeeping genes, such as the universal proteins, actin and tubulin. However there is still room for genes that are important in eye design but are not specific to the eye. An example is *Notch* . . . The very long regulatory regions of genes, the conservation of many bits of these (when different species are compared) and the multiplicity of binding sites shown up by footprint experiments, all suggest that the majority of genetic information is engaged in regulation.[26] (Lawrence, 1992:195–96)

If this turns out to be true in general, then in some, perhaps many, cases it would not be appropriate to speak of a particular gene dedicated for language, even if that gene is crucial for development of the language faculty, but of a gene which is involved in language at development time t and position in space s (in the embryonic brain or wherever) and which may

---

[26] *Notch⁻* is a mutation named for its dominant phenotype – notches located in the wing edge of the fly (Lawrence, 1992:5).

be involved in some other function (say the number faculty) at time t' and position s'. A concrete example from fly genetics might be the "multipurpose gene" *wingless*: "The gene only encodes one protein but its purposes could be widely divergent, as may well be the case when it is activated as a segment polarity gene in the early embryo, in an inductive role in the visceral mesoderm of the gut later on or along the dorsoventral compartment boundary in the wing imaginal disc, even later" (Lawrence, 1992:74).

This does not, however, mean abandoning the notion of a "language organ" any more than it means giving up the idea that there is a physical organ called the eye. It just means that when talking about events at the gene level, we must keep our minds open to the possibility that genes involved in the design of the language organ might have multiple functions in development. If there is a multipurpose gene which is crucial for the property of discrete infinity in both the language faculty and the number faculty, is it a "language gene" or a "mathematics" gene? Both or neither, depending on your perspective. It subserves both faculties, but is not dedicated to either.

The ideas on multipurpose genes appear to carry over to behavior and learning (Greenspan, 1995). For example, it has been known for some time that the *period* gene in the fruit fly has an effect on circadian rhythms (e.g., waking and sleeping). It was discovered many years later that the same gene also has an affect on the rhythm of the courtship song of the male: "In a fascinating turn of events, Hall, Kyriacou and Michael Rosbash, also at Brandeis, have recently pinpointed the exact part of the gene that controls song rhythm. A small region in the middle is devoted to the song, and the balance of the gene controls other rhythms" (Greenspan, 1995:75).

It was even possible to cut out the middle of the gene controlling song rhythm and engineer another species of fruit fly to sing like the first:

That division of labor was deduced in part from the fact that a different species of fruit fly, D. simulans, has the same 24-hour cycle of activity and rest as is found in D. melanogaster but performs a song that differs in the intervals between pulses. The period gene in both species is similar, except for small differences in the middle region. What is more, genetically engineered flies that carry a hybrid period gene made by replacing the middle region of the D. melanogaster gene with the corresponding segment of D. simulans will "sing" just like D. simulans. (p. 75)

The author notes that "oddly, enough, no one has yet identified any gene involved in courtship that is dedicated solely to that behavior." Multiple genes are involved in male courtship (with more than a dozen discovered), but none appears to be dedicated to courtship alone, as we saw in the case of the *period* gene: "It may be that most genes underlying court-ship (and other behaviors) serve more than one function in the body. Identical genes may also be used for somewhat different purposes in males and females" (p. 75). The evidence may ultimately bear on the dis-cussion about whether human behavioral traits are controlled by single genes or multiple genes, views attributed, respectively, to Davenport and Galton (see article for some historical background): "There is every reason to believe that the genetic influences on behavior will be at least as complicated in people as they are in fruit flies. Hence, the notion of many, multipurpose genes making small contributions is likely to apply" (p. 78).

Tully has compiled some further examples from behavioral genetics of pleiotropic[27] effects, with no obvious biological connections to one other, found in single-mutants of *Drosophila*. For example, one mutant affects both courtship song and visual behavior, while another affects both phototaxis and olfaction (Tully, 1994). He observes:

These examples serve to emphasize the following generalization: the same muta-tion can cause defects in more than one biological process, but this observation by itself does not indicate that any two biological processes are causally related to each other. In the case of our earlier observations that some genetic lesions dis-rupted both learning/memory and neuroanatomy, therefore, we cannot conclude necessarily that the structural defects *cause* the functional ones. Another more general implication is that 'behavior-specific' genes may be rare, if not impossible. (Tully, 1994:62)

Tully goes on to note that one can sort out these pleiotropic effects in other more indirect ways; e.g., he cites some evidence that "'behavior-specific' [RNA] *transcripts* may exist in the absence of 'behavior-specific' *genes*" (p. 62). The above examples then make plausible the ideas that (1) genes involved in language need not be dedicated to solely one purpose, the point made earlier, and (2) it does not follow that the effect of a muta-tion in one cognitive domain is necessarily causally related to an effect in another cognitive domain.

One question that one might raise with respect to the proposal that the number faculty arose as a by-product of the language faculty is: given that there was no specific selectional pressure to preserve the number faculty, why didn't it disappear, like some superfluous trait? Supposing for a moment that the multipurpose gene picture is correct for lan-guage/number, one might speculate that, since one gene is subserving multiple purposes, there may be a point of no return in the evolutionary development of the gene, where it becomes extremely difficult to knock

---

[27] A gene is said to be *pleiotropic* if it affects more than one trait.

out the function for number without knocking out the function for language. But as Chomsky has noted: "That development [a mutation providing the capacity to deal with discrete infinity] would have been very useful for evolution. Biological success is defined in terms of the number of organisms. Now by that measure, humans are very successful . . . So the point is that the development of this system would have been of great biological utility" (Chomsky, 1988a:184). Presumably this would be even more the case, the more functions the gene assumes. Tully notes that the dunce gene in the fly, which is considered to be one of the prototypes for learning/memory genes, is known to encode for at least 10 RNA transcripts (Tully, 1994:63).

Note that, although one often loosely speaks of the "emergence of language," it is more precise to speak instead of particular "properties" of language. For no one is claiming that every subpart of the mechanisms of language was newly invented to subserve language. At the very least everyone would accept that the genes involved in the construction of the language areas use the same DNA as other cells and that the cells in the language areas have the same kind of housekeeping genes for cellular metabolism as other kinds of cells.

At the other end of the spectrum, we have argued that at higher levels, emergent properties apparently specific to language could appear in the unfolding dynamics of the system. And in between these two ends of the spectrum, there are many other possibilities. For example, we have just mentioned the example of multipurpose genes, which seem to be involved in different biological subsystems at different times during development:

The geneticists' and embryologists' approach to a gene has traditionally had one common feature – both are looking for a main function of the gene and have, by and large, disregarded the possibility that a gene could have several distinct roles. Molecular biology has suggested otherwise . . . The control elements are special, suggesting that evolution has tacked on extra jobs: of course, it is difficult to be sure which is the oldest and primary function. (Lawrence, 1992:74)

Molecular geneticist and science author, Robert Pollack speculates on the origin of the language faculty:

Even as we begin to understand the biology of thought and language, we must acknowledge how little we know about the genomic contribution to consciousness. The frontal regions of our brain, in which abstract notions are processed and which through their connections to the Broca region drive our language skills, develop from a segment laid down in early embryonic development by a member of a family of genes containing homeoboxes. But which homeobox genes are most closely associated with the assembly of the frontal regions of the brain in humans?

And did the duplication of a homeobox gene at the "head" of a family of genes, in an ancestral primate a few million years ago, set a primate line on the path to language, knowledge, and thought? Which genes are activated in the Broca region of the human brain, and the regions it feeds, as a two-year-old acquires grammatical language skills? We don't know the answers to any of these questions; it will be the task of a new generation of molecular neurobiologists, versed in the historical context of hominid evolution and the comparative anatomy and genetics of the primates, to search them out. (Pollack, 1994:165)

Although we may be some years from the answers to the questions Chomsky and Pollack raise, it must be realized at the same time that what the answers are is no longer solely a matter for philosophical discussion, but has already become part of a rapidly growing research area of biolinguistics. Although the preceding discussion, as it pertains to language, is largely speculation, it is testable speculation. Gedeon et al. provide an illustration of how to try to sort out these kinds of questions in their study of two unrelated boys with developmental disorders, both with submicroscopic deletions in Xq28 (a chromosomal locus), near FRAXE fragile site (see chapter 4):

The patient MK had only speech delay with otherwise normal development, while patient CB had global developmental delay that included speech delay. Detection of overlapping deletions in these two cases led to speculation that coding sequences of a gene(s) important in language development may be affected. (Gedeon et al., 1995:907)

The deletion in MK is wholly overlapped by the deletion in CB, suggesting that MK's smaller deletion is specific to speech delay, whereas CB's larger deletion accounts both for the speech delay and for more global developmental delay. Using zooblots,[28] the authors found sequence "homology with several other, more distant species, including dog, monkey, and chicken" (p. 913) and conclude that "this conservation during evolution suggested that this region contains sequences with functional significance in normal development" (p. 907).[29] This is precisely the kind of research that will be necessary to decide what genes and epigenetic processes are involved in "discrete infinity" in the language or the number faculty and to establish positively or negatively whether or not any of these genes have any sequence homology with other species. In chapter 4, we presented a systematic discussion of some of the ongoing research in this area.

---

[28] The zooblot is a procedure to study the degree of evolutionary conservation using genomic DNA from a number of different organisms.
[29] Homology means similar in structure (in this case DNA structure), reflecting a common evolutionary origin.

Ultra-Darwinism

Let us look more closely at what we can call the "ultra-Darwinist"[30] view on evolution of language, originally put forth by Pinker and Bloom (Pinker and Bloom, 1990). In contrast to the minimalist–internalist view, this view is externalist in nature, appealing to external exigencies such as reproductive success and winning friends and influencing people. Maynard Smith and Szathmáry discuss the ban on papers on the origin of language in France in 1866:

> We now turn to our second problem, the origin of human language. This is a topic that has a bad reputation among linguists. After the publication of Darwin's *Origin of Species*, many uncritical ideas about the evolution of language were proposed, to such an extent that, in 1866, the French Academy of Linguistics announced that its journal did not accept papers on the origin of language. Their reaction was probably justified, but the time has come to reopen the question. (Maynard Smith and Szathmáry, 1995a:71)

Maynard Smith and Szathmáry say it is time to "reopen the question," but then go on to embrace another dogmatic position, the ultra-Darwinist position of Pinker and Bloom, stated concisely with the slogan "God or natural selection," as we saw earlier. The example given was the eye, but the formulation was meant to apply to human language as well. This new ultra-Darwinist position tells us that there is *only one* scientifically respectable alternative – natural selection.

Maynard Smith and Szathmáry present an unusual argument for Pinker and Bloom's empty slogan; viz. that it "needed linguists to say it":

> How could this competence evolve? Pinker and Bloom (1990) have argued that linguistic competence is a complex adaptive organ, in this sense resembling the eye of a vertebrate or the wing of a bird, and must therefore have evolved by natural selection. Although, as the authors themselves emphasize, the statement is obvious, it needed linguists to say it. (Maynard Smith and Szathmáry, 1995a:71)

This statement is not obvious – it is senseless – and the fact that linguists proclaim it doesn't make it any less so. As we will see below, in Maynard Smith's own biological research, he has no use for the Pinker–Bloom pronouncements. His own work explores multiple factors in evolution such as developmental and physical, as well as selective, constraints. In actual work on the eye, Pinker–Bloom dogma is totally ignored. Cohen and Stewart discuss an example by Brian Goodwin concerning the evolution of the eye:

> Brian Goodwin sees development as a combination of natural "free-flow" dynamics and DNA-programmed intervention to stabilize a particular dynamic form.

[30] Or "ultraselectionist" view. See below.

Why should nature waste effort programming the shape of the organism into DNA if the laws of physics will produce it free of charge? It's like programming into DNA the fact that salt crystals must be cubical. For example, the eye – a shape that puzzled both Darwin *and* his detractors – is dynamically very natural. Rudimentary eyes can occur naturally without any special DNA coding. Natural selection can then refine the rudimentary eye into something more sophisticated, but it is the dynamics that gives selection a head start. (Cohen and Stewart, 1994:293)

In fact, the Pinker–Bloom slogan is not even an issue in actual work in biology, with journals and books vigorously debating the "resynthesis of developmental and evolutionary biology," "generative biology," "order for free" and the like. The common thread in all this work is that researchers are trying to *discover* the role of genes, developmental mechanisms, and natural selection in biological systems, not to embrace blindly a new dogma from cognitive linguists (Gilbert et al., 1996).

As is the case with any dogma, it has been greeted with almost religious fervor by some in the cognitive science community. As noted earlier, according to Dennett, Pinker saw "the light" of evolution, but after he led linguists out of the intellectual dark ages of the pre-1990s into it, they rubbed their eyes and found they had traded in standard science for dogma. One of the tenets of this dogma is that linguists had forsaken biology, in spite of the extensive biolinguistics literature to the contrary; cf. John Maynard Smith's admonition to "Chomsky and his students" that "linguistics cannot ignore biology"; see Maynard Smith, 1995. We will return to Maynard Smith's comments in a later section. Pinker, Bloom, and Dennett have a real problem on their hands when it comes to finding a place for Chomsky in the new mythology. Recall that their dogma has only two slots, God or natural selection. They can't put Chomsky into the slot for natural selection, because they have loudly proclaimed that he is "skeptical of Darwin," contrary to anything he has ever said or written about Darwin or natural selection (we have presented citations throughout). So that leaves them with only the God slot to put Chomsky in. At this point they get very inventive. According to Dennett, as we saw in chapter 1, Chomsky holds that language is a "God-given" organ.

Ultra-Darwinism contra creationism[31]

Pinker considers the ultra-Darwinist view of evolution to be an improvement over the creationist view of Reverend William Paley, which was

---

[31] Gould and Eldredge critique "Darwinian Fundamentalism" and "Ultra-Darwinism," respectively, from other angles (Eldredge, 1995; Gould, 1997a).

called "natural theology" at that time. However, natural theology had a long and distinguished tradition in science, extending back to Robert Boyle and Sir Isaac Newton, both practicing natural theologists. In fact, we argue that this strand of creationism, while irrational, presented a coherent scientific picture of the world, whereas the ultra-Darwinist view of Pinker, Bloom, Dennett, and Cziko (see below) is both irrational and incoherent.[32]

Pinker tells us that we have only two alternatives when studying language or any other complex organ: "God or natural selection." However, if these are our only two choices, then God wins out. For creationism, which the ultra-Darwinists reject, is irrational, but coherent. However, the ultra-Darwinist position is both irrational and incoherent.

Creationism is irrational in that it can "explain" whatever happens. Any property P (of language, etc.) as well as the property ~P can be "explained" in the same way; viz., by invoking divine intervention. However, it is coherent in that it accommodates the results of science; i.e., we have "anything discovered in biology + God." God enters into the picture by jump-starting the universe at the beginning (the Leibnizian position) or by continuously monitoring the universe (the Newtonian position).

If we go the route of the ultra-Darwinists and substitute "natural selection" for divine intervention, then we still have the problem of irrationality in that whatever happens has the same explanation. If we discover that languages are head-initial, following Kayne (Kayne, 1994), then we invoke natural selection (instead of divine intervention). If languages are head-final, we invoke natural selection again. But the ultra-Darwinists are also incoherent in that no account can be given of anything at all in terms of natural selection acting apart from the conditions imposed by physical law, biochemical law, and developmental genetics.

If we invoke evolution, with natural selection as only one factor, but adding in the laws of physics and development, we move to a picture that makes sense, but which still explains no more than creationism does. For, again, no matter whether languages turn out to be head-initial or head-final, the explanation is "evolution."

The fact is that we do not yet have an account for head-position in terms of the interaction of factors such as physics, developmental laws, and natural selection.[33] Our point here is simply that the framework for

[32] I am grateful to Noam Chomsky (p.c.) for pointing out the similarities and differences between ultra-Darwinism and classic creationist arguments such as Thomas Jefferson's "argument from design" presented in this section.

[33] A few speculations on the role of symmetry-breaking in word order phenomena were presented earlier.

understanding such problems needs to be based on the study of all these interacting factors, not on just one of them, and hence ultra-Darwinism represents a regression. The minimalist–internalist approach of biolinguistics provides us with such a framework; viz. that of standard (biological) science. The ultra-Darwinist approach, on the other hand, adds incoherence to the irrationality of the creationist approach.

Universal selection (ultraselectionism)

Cziko develops the Pinker–Bloom model with a slight twist in *Without Miracles: Universal Selection Theory and the Second Darwinian Revolution.* So as not to keep the reader in suspense, the twist is that Cziko believes he is able to derive from the "universal selection theory" that biolinguists (Chomsky, Piattelli-Palmarini, and Fodor are discussed) are "obliged to conclude that the genetic information for the human body, brain, and cognitive abilities was already contained in the very first organism that used DNA for its genes" (Cziko, 1995:302). So, in this scenario, Chomsky and colleagues are forced to conclude that the language genes were to be found in ancient bacteria (and presumably later in trees and elephants).

The argument goes like this: there are three major types of explanation for "origin and growth of knowledge" – providential, instructionist, and selectionist theories. Instructionist theories include discredited theories of Lamarckism and instructional immunological theories, so we can drop that option. That leaves us with either selectional or providential theories. Cziko uses the term "universal selection theory" as a cover term for all kinds of variants, including Darwin's natural selection, Edelman's "neural Darwinism," immunological selection, etc., most of which are also included in Dennett's discussion of selection. "Providential" refers to Bishop William Paley's "argument from design to divine providence." So we are essentially back to the familiar options

God or (universal) selection

That is, Cziko is carrying over the position of Pinker on evolution that natural selection is the only "scientifically respectable alternative to divine creation." In the last section, we have indicated why this is an irrational and incoherent move, and will document further reasons later. Cziko adds another twist in that he extends "selection" from the evolutionary domain to "universal selection," in order to include development of the immune system and acquisition of language, and other things, thus compounding the irrationality and incoherence, as we will see.

Keep in mind in what follows that, as before, selection is assumed to be the central factor in explanations of evolution. It is noted, with approval, that the "ultra-Darwinians" contemporary with Darwin "dared to explain all of evolution, including that of complex instinctive behaviors, solely through natural selection." Cziko notes that "ultraselectionists" is probably a more accurate term for "ultra-Darwinians" (after all, even Darwin, as Cziko notes elsewhere, was "convinced that natural selection has been the main but not the exclusive means of modification"):

And so it was left to the younger and more radical ultraselectionists, in particular August Weismann, to assert toward the end of the nineteenth century that natural selection was the sole process by which species grew in adapted complexity. And now more than 100 years later, this purely selectionist view of the emergence of design has so far withstood all challenges . . . and continues to be the foundation for modern biology. (Cziko, 1995:284)

The first step in the argument is to assert that Chomsky "rejects natural selection," despite an extensive literature that states Chomsky's real position: "Chomsky not only rejects natural selection as an explanation for the evolution of human language, but also rejects Darwinian explanations for certain well-understood biological phenomena." Some of Chomsky's statements on this matter can be found in the commentary to Pinker and Bloom's paper (Otero, 1990). But even though Cziko cites that paper in his bibliography and even though Paul Bloom reviewed Cziko's book for MIT Press and "offered his expertise for improving my [Cziko's] book," Chomsky's actual position is not presented, since the whole house of cards would collapse without this assumption.

So that leaves Chomsky (and colleagues) stuck in the "providential" category with Bishop Paley ("current providentialism"). Since they "deny" selection, and since selection is the only mechanism available for evolution and ontogenesis (learning), according to Cziko, they must be stuck. Because selection is the only way to learn, there is no way for them to get from DNA to the language faculty. They believe in "innatism," not selection, so all products of cognition, including language, must be in the DNA. More remarkably, since mouse genes and DNA sequences are similar to man's: "Now by Piattelli-Palmarini's (and Fodor's) reasoning, we would have to consider the mouse as having innate knowledge of human concepts and language (the genetic building blocks are all there; they just need to be rearranged a bit)" (p. 301).

Even more devastating, biolinguists have no way to get from the DNA to the language faculty. Here is where Bloom lends "his expertise" by providing a killer argument: Knowing the alphabet (a through z) does not provide knowledge about Macbeth. Nor is knowing the elements of DNA (A, T, C, G) the same as knowledge of language. "Unpredictable novelty emerges" from the DNA to yield language, but without selection, there is no way to get there, short of a providential miracle.[34] Hence an innate theory is "genetically providential."

Since language is innate; i.e., in the DNA, one is "obliged to conclude that the genetic information for the human body, brain, and cognitive abilities was already contained in the very first organism that used DNA for its genes" (p. 302).

The logic here is the same as Dennett used to get to Chomsky's "God-given language organ." There is only God or selection. Chomsky and colleagues deny selection. Therefore, they believe in God (or language floating around in DNA – genetic providentialism).

Cziko also quotes Niels Jerne extensively for his work on immunological selection. However, nothing in Jerne's work supports Cziko's bizarre misrepresentations of linguistic work. In fact, in Jerne's Nobel Prize address, we saw (in the Introduction) that he essentially repeats the position being criticized by Cziko. One can only wonder why Cziko does not attribute the same crackpot ideas to Jerne as he does to the linguists. In any case, once one tosses out the ultra-Darwinist strictures, and pursues the norms of scientific rationality, the entire issue evaporates. Their elaborate belief system forces the ultra-Darwinists into these contortions, because it doesn't occur to any of them that Chomsky and his colleagues might be, and are, positioned entirely outside the entire cult that has been constructed, in a domain called natural science. Like the space ship behind the Hale-Bopp comet, it all makes perfect sense to the ultra-Darwinists, as long as they ignore the fact that there is another world outside.

But once this is realized, the whole house of cards falls down, including Dennett's fervently held belief that Chomsky and his biolinguistic colleagues are threatened by "Darwin's Dangerous Idea"; i.e., natural selection, part of the central thesis of Dennett's 600–page book of that name.[35] The highlight of Dennett's discussion is the Chomsky contra Darwin debate, which has no basis in fact since both Darwin and Chomsky are on the written record as saying that selection as well as other factors play a role in evolution.

Pinker and Bloom have left Dennett what cynics might regard as the thankless task of "dislodging heroes from their pedestals," and Dennett notes that that is a task that "one does not lightly undertake." "Gould and Lewontin and Chomsky have so far all chosen to leave the counter-attack

---

[34] Note that nature, without the help of Darwinian natural selection, somehow got from the Big Bang to molecules that could replicate themselves. Following Cziko's logic, the mechanism must have been "a providential miracle."

[35] My comments here are restricted solely to Dennett's views on linguistics, not to the rest of his book.

to others, my criticisms being too far beneath their notice, one gathers, to merit any detailed public response".[36] The problem is, of course, that all Dennett has done so far is to ask Gould, Lewontin, and Chomsky to join him in uncritical acceptance of Pinker–Bloom's Central Dogma, in effect to extend them an invitation to join the scientific cult. But "biologists around the world" have rallied to Dennett's support: "It's been surprisingly easy to take, since my task has been far from thankless. Indeed, the thanks I have been receiving from biologists around the world has been most gratifying" (Dennett, 1996:36).

Comments of several biologists are prominently displayed on the book jacket of Dennett's *Darwin's Dangerous Idea* that could be construed as support for his views. It is important to note that none of these comments specifically mention the case of the evolution of human language. For example, E.O. Wilson lauds Dennett's "clear and rigorous testing of Darwinian theory". But there is no such clear and rigorous testing of Darwinian theory in the domain of language in Dennett's book. Dennett simply paraphrases Pinker and Bloom's position discussed earlier. Neither Pinker nor Bloom (nor anyone else) has advanced a theory of language which provides "clear and rigorous testing of Darwinian theory". Most biologists would regard human language as far too complex a system and too poorly understood to provide robust evidence for any theory of evolution. Finally, Dawkins speaks of Dennett's "devastating" critique that "American intellectuals have been powerfully misled on evolutionary matters". The "American intellectuals" are presumably Gould, Lewontin and Chomsky who, Dennett complains, have not publicly responded, as noted earlier.[37] However, once again, with respect to evolution of human language, there is no "devastating critique" offered by Dennett. There are only his misinterpretations of work in biolinguistics that we dealt with earlier.

Why did the study of evolution of language regress into ultra-Darwinism?

We have seen that ultra-Darwinism (ultraselectionism) represents a regression in the study of mind, including (bio)linguistics, where its nega-

---

[36] Gould has since provided a "detailed public response" to Dennett (Gould, 1997b). Since Dennett had raised no substantive issues, Gould confines himself to restating his "pluralist" position, minus Dennett's misrepresentations. The pluralist view, the Resynthesis view, the "minimalist–internalist" view under discussion here, and other formulations are all variations of the same general approach to the study of evolution. Gould argues that the pluralist position retains the insights of Darwin about the role of natural selection, but without the incoherent excesses of Dennett's position, which he terms "ultra-Darwinist fundamentalism."   [37] But see note 36.

tive influences have been most profoundly felt. We summarize here the reasons that ultra-Darwinism represents a regression. We have noted already that it is irrational in that it is able to explain both a property P and ~P by invoking the same principle; viz., "natural selection." It is incoherent in that no account can be given of anything in terms of natural selection, acting apart from physical and developmental laws. Hence ultra-Darwinist accounts rapidly deteriorate into "explanations" for anything at all.

For example, in *The Language Instinct*, Pinker "demonstrates" the power of natural selection to "explain" the design of language, including, as we noted, properties P and ~P. In *How the Mind Works*, he extends the ultra-Darwinist paradigm to virtually the entire mind. We find out that the same principle of natural selection that "explains" principles of UG, also provides an account of why Hugh Grant, "arguably the world's handsomest man, was arrested for having oral sex with a prostitute in the front seat of his car." Natural selection is truly a "universal acid," in Dennett's sense (Dennett, 1995). The problem is, of course, that, as we move to the "study of everything," natural selection has become vacuous as an explanatory principle. We can now account for P and ~P in any domain, with natural selection as the magic wand. Any time one has a principle – natural selection or any other – that explains limb bud formation, question formation, and Hugh Grant's sexual behavior in the front of a car, one should start getting worried that we have a vacuous picture of nature.

Our point here, of course, is not that natural selection does not play any role in the evolution of mind, but that it explains nothing without a detailed consideration of all the other factors. We could just as easily arbitrarily pick any physical principle, say the Pauli exclusion principle,[38] which accounts for the shell structure of atoms and their chemical properties, and say that it, not natural selection, is *the* design principle underlying rules of grammar and sexual promiscuity. For without it, the shell structure of atoms collapse and with it biochemistry and genetics, the basis of Darwin's variation. One could even join into the ultra-Darwinian hysteria and speak of the stark choice between "God or the Pauli exclusion principle" or "Pauli's Dangerous Principle" and of its "universal acid" character. This would, obviously, be just as wrong-headed as the ultra-Darwinian move. The real task in giving a scientific account of some evolutionary phenomenon is to tease out the relative contribution of all the factors involved – genetic, physical, developmental, or whatever, including natural selection.

---

[38] The Pauli exclusion principle dictates that not more than one electron can occupy the same quantum state at the same time. It explains how electron configurations in atoms are built up and accounts for the apparent solidity of matter (Glashow, 1994).

A final question that must be asked is the following: is there anything missing from the minimalist–internalist approach to evolution sketched above that the ultra-Darwinist account fills? That is, does the ultra-Darwinist account fill some explanatory gap in the standard approaches? We do not know of any. As far as we can see the ultra-Darwinist moves lead to irrationality, incoherence, and vacuity. As such, they represent a regression from a number of standard approaches from that in Darwin's *Origin of Species* up through current approaches in the Resynthesis. The question then becomes, why go backwards? And the answer is, "if it ain't broke, don't fix it."

As we have seen, the emergence of ultra-Darwinism (ultraselectionism) in linguistics represents a regression in the study of biology of language. We might inquire into the reasons that this step backwards took place. We can identify a number of possible reasons: (1) misunderstanding of the implications of the Darwinian theory of natural selection and variation, (2) "methodological dualism" – the insistence that the mind be studied differently from other bodily organs and other organisms, and (3) the appeal of a "modified tabula rasa" approach to the study of evolution.

As for (1), we think that it is arguable that some of linguistic ultra-Darwinism (ultraselectionism) is based on some misconceptions of Darwin's theory of variation and natural selection. For Darwin, natural selection acted upon variation, and the substrate of variation was just as important to him as natural selection was. He dealt with this important problem extensively in chapter 5, "Laws of Variation," in *Origin of the Species*, as well as in *Variation in Animals and Plants under Domestication*. Although the mechanisms were unknown to him, he understood that all variation selected upon was already generated prior to being presented to selection (we set aside here the fact that Darwin also entertained the possibility of inheritance of acquired characters). Now consider Cziko, who is discussing natural selection, which he calls "among-organism selection": "it [is] evident that . . . natural selection is therefore a creative process that constantly fashions innovative variations among which to select" (p. 302). But natural selection does not fashion variations, innovative or otherwise "among which to select." That is the whole point of Darwin's theory. Variation is presented for selection. That this is not just unfortunate choice of words is buttressed by Cziko's words a few pages earlier:

But for Piattelli-Palmarini (and also for Fodor . . .), all such products of human cognition must be innately specified before they can be selected, despite the fact that such a conclusion is inconsistent with what is now known of the immune system, that is, all antibodies are not innately specified in the genome but rather exist only as potentialities, the majority of which remain unrealized. It is also inconsistent with what is known about biological evolution. (Cziko, 1995:300)

However, it is not true that "all antibodies . . . exist only as potentialities, the majority of which remain unrealized." It is in fact, necessary that the antibodies be realized before exposure to antigen so that they may be selected. That is the way selection works in the immune system (and is consistent, not inconsistent, with "what is known about in biological evolution"). Alberts et al. write:

It is estimated that even in the absence of antigen stimulation a human makes at least 10^{15} different antibody molecules – its *preimmune antibody repertoire*. The antigen-binding sites of many antibodies can cross-react with a variety of related but different antigenic determinants, and the preimmune repertoire is apparently large enough to ensure that there will be an antigen-binding site to fit almost any potential antigenic determinant, albeit with low affinity. (Alberts et al. 1994: 1221)

Once the antibody has been selected there are additional mechanisms, such as somatic hypermutation, which can fine-tune the affinity of the antibody for the antigen. Hence it is quite correct for Piattelli-Palmarini to speak of "the innate repertoire of antibodies," which Cziko criticizes him for: "he [Piattelli-Palmarini] thus leads the reader to surmise that all possible antibodies are innately specified and therefore provided before any selection takes place" (Cziko, 1995:300). Piattelli-Palmarini does lead the reader to believe that because that is the way the immune system works, where "all possible" means up to the fine-tuning just mentioned.

The conclusion that Cziko fundamentally misunderstands the operation of selection is the only plausible explanation that helps us to explain the bizarre deductions discussed earlier that Cziko goes on to make; viz., that Piattelli-Palmarini (and Fodor) are forced to think the mouse has "innate knowledge of human concepts and language" (p. 301) and that biolinguists are "obliged to conclude that the genetic information for the human body, brain, and cognitive abilities was already contained in the very first organism that used DNA for its genes" (p. 302). Cziko also fails to keep in mind the important distinction between structure and function, development (or acquisition, in the case of language) and evolution. It is true that the word "selection" is used in all these contexts, but the underlying mechanisms need not be, and are not, identical across these domains. Ontogeny does not recapitulate phylogeny in the immune system or any other biological system. Selection in the day-to-day operation of the immune system has specific properties found only in that system. These properties need not carry over to proposals for learning, including language, although "selection" from a pre-existing repertoire of materials might be one of the properties of the system.

The whole discussion is beside the point anyway, since no one has proposed taking over the immune system lock, stock, and barrel in the literal sense as a model of language acquisition. In fact, most speculations in the literature on neural mechanisms for language acquisition have centered around synaptic formation as a selective mechanism (e.g., Changeux). At an abstract level, one can consider the principles-and-parameters model of language acquisition to be a proposal for a selective mechanism, where all the options for Human are present in the initial state (described by UG) and the selection is done by parameter-setting. But nothing in this model in any way depends on the details of the way that the immune system works.

Pinker and Bloom have criticized Gould and Chomsky for "nonselectionist" views of evolution, because the latter insist on the importance of physical and developmental constraints in addition to selective constraints in the theory of evolution: "Developmental constraints only rule out broad classes of options. They cannot, by themselves, force a functioning organ to come into being. An embryological constraint like 'Thou shalt grow wings' is an absurdity" (1990:104). But neither can selective constraints "force" a functioning organ to come into being. As we saw, natural selection can only act on already realized variation, a fact which Darwin emphasized. In fact, even staunch Darwinists like Maynard Smith are much closer to the position of Gould and Chomsky than to the position of Pinker and Bloom in their everyday work. For example, in a classic and much-cited paper from 1985, "Developmental Constraints and Evolution," Maynard Smith et al. insist that, in addition to selective constraints, there are "developmental constraints," and there are constraints that "are direct consequences of the laws of physics" (Maynard Smith et al., 1985:272). The task in studying development and evolution is to learn "in what ways development and selection interact to yield constraints." One must study examples that show "the interplay between developmental processes and selection operating simultaneously at various levels."

An illustration is given from work by Maynard Smith and Sondhi. They bred eleven generations of mutant *Drosophila* with a left ocellus, but lacking the right ocellus. The frequencies of left-handed and right-handed individuals remained the same; i.e., there was no heritable variance for handedness. However, the frequencies of flies with anterior and posterior ocelli could be altered. Considering this case and other cases of bilateral symmetry, the authors remark that "If, indeed, the requisite variation is not available, then many cases of bilateral symmetry may be consequences of a developmental constraint rather than selection" (Maynard

Smith et al., 1985:272). Many other cases like this can be taken from the same article (and from the literature), but we cite Maynard Smith and his colleagues, since even Pinker and Bloom would agree that Maynard Smith is no wild-eyed non-Darwinian developmentalist under the hypnotic spell of Gould and Chomsky. We think that Maynard Smith et al. have struck the proper balance here, as have Gould and Chomsky in their work, in noting that, as Chomsky put it, "selection is a factor, not the factor" in the theory of evolution. But, for some reason, when this approach is used in the study of mind, then Gould and Chomsky are branded as "nonselectionists" by Pinker and Bloom, and as "Darwin-hating academics," although the latter term is extended by Pinker to all of Pinker and Bloom's critics, at least insofar as they don't buy into the irrationality, incoherence, and vacuity of the ultra-Darwinist position (Pinker, 1997b). In ultra-Darwinism, deviation from the dogma earns one the title of "Darwin-hating academic."

Pinker has repeatedly rejected "physical law" as an explanation for processes of evolution. He goes out of his way to shoot down any suggestion that "physical" law could be a factor, except in a marginal way. For example, he criticizes Chomsky for introducing even so innocuous a trait as having a physical mass into discussions of evolution:

So the thesis is that natural selection is the only physical explanation of design that fulfills a function. Taken literally, that cannot be true. Take my physical design, including the property that I have positive mass. That fulfills some function – namely, it keeps me from drifting into outer space. Plainly, it has a physical explanation which has nothing to do with natural selection. (Pinker, 1997b:172, p. c. from Chomsky to Pinker, November 1989)

Pinker only grudgingly accepts gravity as a factor for "probable" conditions, acting on the "mass that keeps Chomsky from floating into outer space," but not as a factor for "improbable" conditions, like the property of having a vertebrate eye, which supposedly results from natural selection.[39] Elsewhere Pinker notes that "gravity alone may make a flying fish fall into the ocean, a nice big target, but gravity alone cannot make bits of a flying fish embryo fall into place to make a flying fish eye." For Pinker this would be like "the proverbial hurricane that blows through a junkyard and assembles a Boeing 747" (Pinker, 1994a:361).

Pinker has once again imposed his "either–or" view of evolution (cf. either "God or natural selection"). Here it is "either gravity or natural selection." He tells us that gravity alone can't make a flying fish eye. But

[39] Note that Pinker's comments about "probable" vs. "improbable" conditions remain vacuous until he has specified the physical space that natural selection is operating on in the case of the vertebrate eye.

the traditional view is that gravity and a host of other physical factors, along with genetic and developmental constraints interact with natural selection in the evolution of an organ or organism. Gravity (natural selection, etc.) is *a* factor, not *the* factor responsible. Neither the flying fish eye nor the language faculty arose full blown, analogous to a Boeing 747 being assembled from junk, by either natural selection or a hurricane. This is because neither natural selection nor other physical, genetic, and developmental constraints act apart from one another, but only through intricate mutual interactions, as played out in evolution.

Moreover, the dispute that Pinker is trying to pick with Chomsky over the role of physical constraints in biological form was already settled, at least as early as 1638, by Galileo, in his *Discorsi*, in favor of the traditional view:

> But it was Galileo who, wellnigh three hundred years ago, had first laid down this general principle of similitude; and he did so with the utmost possible clearness, and with a great wealth of illustration drawn from structures living and dead. He said that if we tried building ships, palaces or temples of enormous size, yards, beams and bolts would cease to hold together; nor can Nature grow a tree nor construct an animal beyond a certain size, while retaining the proportions and employing the materials which suffice in the case of a smaller structure. The thing will fall to pieces of its own weight unless we either change its relative proportions, which will at length cause it to become clumsy, monstrous and inefficient, or else we must find new material, harder and stronger than was used before. Both processes are familiar to us in Nature and in art, and practical applications, undreamed of by Galileo, meet us at every turn in this modern age of cement and steel. (Thompson, 1992a:27)

Galileo worked out quantitative laws and predictions for skeletal form and other phenomena, and made the prediction that trees could grow to a theoretical height of 300 feet. D'Arcy Thompson also mentions that Galileo realized that aquatic animals represented an exception to his growth constraints on skeletal form because the influence of gravity is diminished by the effects of buoyancy. And Herbert Spencer observed that the resulting ability to grow larger gave aquatic animals a "distinct advantage, in that the larger it grows the greater is its speed." By seeking to understand physical constraints, we are able to shed light on design features (the animal's "distinct advantage"). We come to understand how natural selection acts through physical channels. Such an approach is suspect to Pinker and the ultra-Darwinists, as the approach of "Darwin-hating academics." Better for them to say simply that, no matter what size the sequoia tree and the whale might be, natural selection designed them that way and drop the matter there. Thompson discusses many other interesting scaling phenomena and laws, in addition to the case of gravity.

Recently, citing work by D'Arcy Thompson and others, an elegant theory, involving a "universal scaling law," has been proposed to unify scaling laws from many domains (West, Brown, and Enquist, 1997).

Oddly enough, Maynard Smith, who has whole-heartedly endorsed Pinker and Bloom in their ultra-Darwinist attacks on "physical law," has himself been a major proponent of such "universal constraints":

Some constraints are direct consequences of the laws of physics, whereas others arise from invariant properties of certain materials or of complex systems. An example of the first sort [. . .] is a simple consequence of the law of the lever: any uncompensated change in the shape of a skeleton that increases the speed with which some member can be moved will reduce the force which that member can exert. Such examples do not depend on any distinctive features of organisms. Constraints of these sorts are universal in the sense that they apply, respectively, to all physical systems (and hence to all organisms), to all things built out of the materials in question (including organisms), and to all physical systems of the requisite complexity (including organisms). Accordingly, we call these "universal constraints." (Maynard Smith et al., 1985:267)

The authors go on to give examples of a variety of "local constraints" as well.

Pinker has attacked the idea that properties of symmetry in organisms derive from the physical world: "One cognitive scientist [Chomsky] has opined that 'many properties of organisms, like symmetry, for example, do not really have anything to do with specific selection but just with the ways in which things can exist in the physical world'" (Pinker, 1997b:168).

Pinker labels this proposal a "howler," which, according to the dictionary, means a "ridiculous, bad mistake." It is Pinker's view that

In fact, most things that exist in the physical world are *not* symmetrical, for obvious reasons of probability: among all the possible arrangements of a volume of matter, only a tiny fraction are symmetrical. Even in the living world, the molecules of life are asymmetrical, as are livers, hearts, stomachs, flounders, snails, lobsters, oak trees, and so on. (Pinker, 1997b:168)

Chomsky's approach to symmetry represents a radically different approach from Pinker's to the study of mind. When Pinker looks at the world he is struck by the fact that "most things that exist in the physical world" are not nice and symmetrical. Physical phenomena in both the inorganic world and the "living world" are messy and unsymmetrical. On the other hand, for Chomsky, and most scientists, the messy and asymmetrical surface phenomena are not of interest in themselves. What are of interest are the underlying mechanisms, whose symmetry is often masked by the asymmetrical surface phenomena. As we have seen, Chomsky's approach is in the tradition of Einstein, Weyl, Wigner, D'Arcy Thompson, and Turing; see also the contributions to the colloquium "Symmetries Throughout the Sciences" (Henley, 1996).

For Pinker, it is "obvious" why particles of matter exhibit the asymmetries that they do: "among all the possible arrangements of a volume of matter, only a tiny fraction are symmetrical." For several generations of physicists, such problems have been all but obvious. These physicists showed that you must look beyond the messy and asymmetrical phenomena to discover the underlying symmetries of the equations describing the universe. Then one can go on to determine the principles that break the symmetry of the system to give us the actual asymmetric situation that we observe in our world. As Weinberg put it: "The Universe is an enormous direct product of representations of symmetry groups. It's hard to say it any more strongly than that" (cited in Crease and Mann, 1987:187).

What we have found is another case of "methodological dualism," which says that when we are Maynard Smith or Pinker studying nonhuman organisms, or the nonmental aspects of humans, we are allowed to do rational science. But if we are studying things from the neck up, like language and mind, we have to toss out constraints which are "consequences of the laws of physics," and adopt an ultra-Darwinist position.

Methodological dualism

Although it is clear that physical factors (including here genetic and developmental factors) must be presupposed in any theory of evolution, Pinker and Bloom try to downplay the role that such constraints play in the explanation of the structure of human brains (Pinker and Bloom, 1990): "Of course, human brains *obey* [emphasis here and below – Pinker and Bloom] the laws of physics, and always did, but that does not mean that their specific structure can be *explained* by such laws."

Here Pinker and Bloom explicitly reveal their assumptions about the role that physics and developmental biology play in the study of language and mind (or anything else under the category of "human brains"). Human brains can only *obey* the laws of physics, but not be *explained* by them. What then does the explaining for human brains? The answer: natural selection. However, natural selection can explain absolutely nothing at all apart from physical factors. It is worth noting that the converse is not true, since variation in the physical world must exist prior to selection. Since variation precedes selection and since the range of variation is constrained by physical factors, these factors determine what is available or is not available to be selected. Furthermore, these selective forces can be strong or weak, and in the limit, zero. However, there can be no case where the contribution of physical factors is zero and the explanation lies with natural selection alone.

We could drop the matter here, on logical grounds. But there is a further problem with Pinker and Bloom's statement. Human brains are claimed to have some special status as compared with other biological systems with respect to whether or not physical laws can play an explanatory role. What we end up with is another of the many variants of what Chomsky has called "methodological dualism," where there is one set of ground rules for the study of the mind (and "human brains"), and another for everything else (Chomsky, 1994b).[40]

To see this let us replace the word "human brains" with the word "sunflowers":

Of course, sunflowers *obey* the laws of physics, and always did, but that does not mean that their specific structure can be *explained* by such laws.

As we have seen Douady and Couder were able to make quite specific predictions about the structure of the sunflower head involving such notions as Fibonacci numbers, golden mean, and golden angle by assuming that genetics interacts in a certain way with physical laws of growth dynamics. Under any reasonable interpretation of explanation, we can say both that the sunflower obeys the laws of physics and its specific structure can be explained by such laws.

Now let's try replacing "human brains" with "DNA":

Of course, DNA *obeys* the laws of physics, and always did, but that does not mean that its specific structure can be *explained* by such laws.

Fortunately, Watson and Crick did not set out to build their model of DNA with this methodological stricture in mind. Quite the opposite, their central focus was on physical principles: tautomeric shifts, stacking interactions, helical repeats, etc. Again just as the Fibonacci numbers were a clue to the spiral structures in the sunflower, so also were the diffraction patterns in the X-ray photograph of Franklin and Wilkins a crucial clue to the exact helical structure of DNA (Watson, 1969).

Let us turn briefly to Pinker and Bloom's account of constraints in universal grammar, in particular to the example of "Subjacency" that they give, which is operative in such contrasts as:
(1) What does he believe they claimed that I said?
(2) *What does he believe the claim that I said?

---

[40] More precisely, Chomsky characterizes methodological dualism as "the view that we must abandon scientific rationality when we study humans 'above the neck' (metaphorically speaking), becoming mystics in this unique domain, imposing arbitrary stipulations and a priori demands of a sort that would never be contemplated in the sciences, or in other ways departing from normal canons of inquiry" (Chomsky, 1994b:182).

They note that it has been proposed that such constraints might aid in the parsing, or processing, of sentences by listeners. So how did Subjacency come about? Pinker and Bloom conclude (Pinker and Bloom, 1990:718): "But by settling in on a particular subset of the range of possible compromises between the demands of expressiveness and parsability, the evolutionary process may have converged on a satisfactory set of solutions to one problem in language processing." Pinker and Bloom conclude that the "evolutionary process may have converged on" a solution to parsing problems involving the Subjacency constraint. This falls short of what they actually hoped to show; viz., that Subjacency was an adaptation and resulted from natural selection. For evolution is not the same as natural selection. It involves a host of other physical factors. Why did evolution "compromise" on Subjacency, as opposed to other conceivable constraints? The answer must be discovered by a consideration of the various genetic, developmental and physical factors that played a role in the "evolutionary process." These kinds of factors must account in large part, perhaps fully, for the properties of Subjacency, just as they play a central role in accounting for the spirals in sunflowers or the DNA double helix. But whether or not natural selection played any significant role in this particular case remains an open question and was left unanswered by Pinker and Bloom.

As already noted above, Pinker and Bloom's methodological dualism doesn't apply to John Maynard Smith when he studies the fruit fly. In that case, he is free, for example, to ascribe features of bilateral symmetry to the "consequences of a developmental constraint rather than selection." But when it comes to study of language and mind, talk of constraints other than natural selection is off limits. As Maynard Smith and Szathmáry reminded us earlier: "Pinker and Bloom [1990] have argued that linguistic competence . . . must therefore have evolved by natural selection. Although, as the authors themselves emphasize, the statement is obvious, it needed linguists to say it" (Maynard Smith and Szathmáry, 1995a). End of discussion. Pinker, Bloom, and Maynard Smith prescribe ultra-Darwinism for the study of biology of language, but reserve for themselves the right to invoke developmental constraints when needed. After reading Pinker and Bloom's harangues against the "Darwin-hating academics" who dare to speak of physical and developmental constraints, it will be somewhat a shock for the reader who comes across Maynard Smith et al.'s article, "Developmental Constraints and Evolution," where the same constraints are unabashedly advocated. One gets the same feeling as when Clinton advisor Dick Morris was found in bed with a high-priced call-girl, shortly after lecturing the rest of us on the importance of family values.

Modified tabula rasa approach to evolution

In many respects the attacks on the minimalist–internalist view of evolution remind of the behaviorist attacks forty years ago of the idea that language is to a considerable degree specified as part of the biological endowment of the individual. Galton's metaphor of natural selection as a pool cue acting on a billiard ball, representing the organism, is similar to the idea that the mind is a (modified) tabula rasa, malleable by the environment. Galton's second metaphor of natural selection acting on a polyhedron, constrained to move only in certain ways is similar to the idea that there are rich constraints on the directions that language can develop provided by our genetic constitution. Just as the internalist view of language development came under attack from behaviorists, so has the internalist view of Galton on evolution, as well as modern biolinguistic views on evolution of language, come under attack from ultra-Darwinists.

Gould, for example, presents the Galton metaphor of the polyhedron in a recent essay, noting that "I certainly think natural selection is an enormously powerful force" (Gould, 1995:63). In comments following this essay, Goodwin notes that "he [Gould] believes that natural selection is the final arbiter, the final cause in evolution" (p. 69). Yet on the same page, Pinker observes that Gould gives "short shrift to natural selection." And as already mentioned, Gould has been canonized along with Lewontin and Chomsky, and, by extension, any other critics of ultra-Darwinist dogma, as "a Darwin-hating academic." I think that we can fairly conclude that the idea of external constraints (the pool cue) dominating internal constitution (the pool ball) has a powerful hold on the ultra-Darwinist view of evolution of language. This is all the more peculiar, since as we have noted John Maynard Smith has no problem invoking internal constitution in the case of the fruit fly. Thus in many respects, the same issues that arose forty years ago in the arguments over internalist versus behaviorist views on knowledge and acquisition of language have re-emerged in the evolutionary context, where we find the minimalist–internalist view under attack again by extreme externalist (modified tabula rasa) views. It is interesting to note that this historical parallel has already been explicitly discussed in the literature dealing with the theory of development and evolution.

Amundson compares constraints in the theory of UG in "generative linguistics" with developmental constraints in embryology: "But, just as all languages generated by a universal grammar are governed by certain constraints, so are all of the possible outcomes of the embryological processes of a given phylum. The similarity here is not accidental – developmental theories are generative theories" (Amundson, 1994:570).

Amundson then compares the discussion between the Modern Synthesis adaptationists and "its developmentalist critics" to the "great black box debate" between behaviorists and "their opponents who favored cognitive and neurological theories." The behaviorists deny "the causal importance of internal states of the psychological organism, either cognitive or neurological states."[41] Similarly, the adaptationists "deny the causal importance of embryology to evolutionary theory" (p. 575). From the behaviorist viewpoint," the details of neurological or cognitive processes are seen as irrelevant to the explanation of behavior." Likewise, for the adaptationists, "the details of development are seen as irrelevant to evolution": "All that matters are the input–output characteristics of the black boxes. Genotypes determine phenotypes, and stimuli are connected to responses".

It is up to the developmental biologists, like the "cognitivists and neuropsychologists before them" to argue for "the causal relevance of the insides of a black box" (p. 576). Amundson notes that he presents the above analysis as an "explication, not a vindication, of developmentalist critiques of neo-Darwinism." For Amundson himself does not "share the common philosophical prejudice that behaviorism had obvious methodological flaws."

One could, of course, follow this line, but we already know the disastrous consequences that this course of action had in the case of studies of language in the Skinnerian behaviorist framework. Investigation of language was limited to the study of stimuli and responses, etc., while what was going on in the black box was simply ignored. As a result, the entire field had evaporated a few years later, because as soon as you began facing up to what mechanisms had to be inside the black box, the whole stimulus–response enterprise collapsed (Chomsky, 1959). The black box was also ignored by structural linguists, who, as we noted earlier, were more impressed by the diversity of language than by its universal properties. Again, once one looked a little into the black box and saw that language acquisition constraints were of central importance, that field also quickly disappeared. The ill-advised move to restrict yourself to certain kinds of evidence has been carried over into cognitive linguistics as well, where one arbitrarily stipulates that the study of linguistics must restrict itself to certain kinds of evidence, as in the example of Platonist linguistics (Chomsky, 1986:33–36). Analogously, one could make the irrational move to study evolution of language by saying, let's treat the language organ like a black box and ignore all the developmental constraints inside

---

[41] For discussion of current ideas on the nature of these "cognitive or neurological states" in the realm of animal cognition, see, e.g., Gallistel, 1993.

the box, and just study external factors, like communicative constraints. But this would be a totally arbitrary move, most likely with the same unpleasant results as before.

Similarly, Darwin could have said, "I am only going to look at whatever variation I find on the Galapagos islands. Don't talk to me about Mendelian factors, much less about DNA or eye or limb fields, or anything else you find in the black box." But as we know, Darwin was interested in evidence from wherever he could find it – domestication, embryology, the fossil record, etc., because he was interested in the further development and sharpening of his theory. Amundson lauds Darwin because he "wisely bracketed the mechanism of inheritance," his "huge" black box. However, Darwin had no choice, wise or unwise. The mechanism of inheritance was unknown to him. But had evidence from genetics been forthcoming a little sooner, we can assume that Darwin would have immediately seized on it, just as he did on all other kinds of evidence.

The same point can be made with the recent work on developmental pathways in the eye. Three animal phyla – vertebrates, arthropods, and mollusks – have developed complex eyes. As Gould notes, the "independent evolution of complex, image-forming eyes in all these groups has become our classic textbook illustration of the enormous power of natural selection to produce similar (and eminently useful) results from disparate starting points, a phenomenon called 'convergence'" (Gould, 1994:12). Such teachings (about natural selection) were "one of the linchpins of education in my [Gould's] graduate student days during the 1960s" (p. 14). But, Gould notes, this raises an important question: "Thus, eyes have become our standard illustration of natural selection's power and the organism's almost infinite malleability – like clay before a sculptor, to cite a metaphor often advanced at this point in the discussion. But are organisms so puttylike, and is natural selection so potent a builder?" (p. 12).

Gould notes that no "professional biologist" would argue that organisms are complete putty: "Of course no professional biologist would go so far in extolling selection and relegating preexisting structure to infinitely flexible raw material. Nonetheless, celebration of natural selection and de-emphasis of structural constraint has been the characteristic bias of evolutionary theory since the 1930s, when modern Darwinism began its deserved triumph" (pp. 12–14). The same can be said of various kinds of behaviorism (and present-day connectionism), where the de-emphasis of internal constraints and innate mechanisms has been the "characteristic bias." Of course, no one actually assumes a tabula rasa of the mind, or else one would not be able to get off the ground. Some innate internal mechanisms have to be assumed, so both behaviorists and connectionists always implicitly assume at least a "modified" tabula rasa; i.e., some internal structure, such as inductive or statistical procedures.

A line of inquiry to answer the question for the evolution of the eye would be to ask whether there are embryological constraints on eye formation, common developmental pathways or similarities in genetic regulation. One way to pursue this line of inquiry is to look for homologies in genes affecting eye development in different animal phyla.

Alternatively, one could say, "let's not look into the black box of embryology to see if there is anything that might affect my theory of convergence by natural selection. Instead, let's only seek out more examples of visual organs in nature that have been shaped by the wonderful powers of natural selection."

In fact, Ernst Mayr, the "dean of modern Darwinians," and an eloquent spokesperson for Modern Synthesis adaptationism, had argued that one needn't "even bother to look for genetic homology": "In the early days of Mendelism there was much search for homologous genes that would account for such similarities. Much that has been learned about gene physiology makes it evident that the search for homologous genes is quite futile except in very close relatives" (cited in Gould, 1997c:69).

But, if you are interested in evolution of the eye, it would clearly be an irrational move to ignore the embryology in the black box, as has been clearly shown by the discovery of homologous genes in the developmental pathways of the eye in different animal phyla (vertebrates, arthropods, and mollusks) (Tomarev et al., 1997). With these results in hand, let's return to Amundson's conclusion: "Developmentalists may or may not be able to demonstrate that a knowledge of the processes of ontogenetic development is essential for the explanation of evolutionary phenomena" (Amundson, 1994: 576). The work of Gehring and his colleagues shows that we can now replace Amundson's "may or may not be able to demonstrate that" with "have demonstrated that," certainly insofar as the development and evolution of the eye are concerned. Moreover, the conclusion generalizes in light of all the other results that have been coming out of developmental biology during the past ten years; e.g., the results on HOM-C and HOX genes, etc. As in the case of behaviorism, the Modern Synthesis risks irrelevance if it ignores what's inside the black box.

Chomsky Contra Darwin debate

Dennett's book "Darwin's Dangerous Idea" contains a section titled "Chomsky contra Darwin: four episodes" (Dennett, 1995:384). Here

Dennett is pushing the idea, initiated by Pinker, that Chomsky is "skeptical of Darwin" (see Pinker citation above). We present citations from Chomsky and Darwin, both making the same point – that natural selection is *a* factor in evolution, but not *the* factor. What we actually have is Pinker's and Dennett's misrepresentation of both Darwin and Chomsky being marketed to the public as a "Chomsky contra Darwin" debate – who, we've been told, want to have the third culture do the "serious thinking for everybody else."

The next claim by Dennett is that Chomsky has sought an "excuse for rejecting the obvious obligation to pursue an evolutionary explanation of the innate establishment of universal grammar." What is meant by "pursue an evolutionary explanation of X?" If X is the language faculty, then it means to pursue at least what we have called the five fundamental problems of biolinguistics: (1) structure, (2) acquisition, (3) use, (4) physical mechanisms, and (5) evolution. In our opinion, by pursuing these five questions in parallel, Chomsky and his colleagues in generative grammar have been studying exactly the questions that are necessary for any understanding of the evolution of language.

So what does Dennett think that Chomsky is rejecting? Pinker's slogan appears to be the crux of Dennett's otherwise puzzling crusade against Chomsky. It's either a "God-given language organ," in Dennett's words, or it's natural selection. But there is another alternative – rational science. All scientists from Darwin on, including the contemporary biologists that we have been discussing; e.g., Gould, Lewontin, Raff, Gilbert, Opitz, Webster, Goodwin, Kauffman, Newman, etc., base their work on the assumption that selection is subject to a variety of physical constraints, whether or not this truism is explicitly mentioned. The problem for them (and everybody else) is to sort out these factors and determine the constraints.

Finally, Dennett sees himself as doing the "dirty work" for Chomsky and Gould in that he has to go around and police not only applications of their work, but even *"likely misapplications"* (p. 393; emphasis is Dennett's) of their own work. Dennett assumes they are at least "embarrassed" to find themselves cited as the "sources of all this nonsense" – he lists ten "howlers" in his book, an example of which is: "Language is not designed for communication at all: it's not like a watch, it's like a Rube Goldberg device with a stick in the middle that you can use as a sundial" (p. 392). The ten howlers were supplied to Dennett by Pinker (p.c.). They consist of a list ("Pinker's list") of "the ten most amazing objections he and Bloom have fielded" (p. 392), presumably from comments at their talks. Another example: "Language can't be useful; it's led to war."

Dennett alleges, "if memory serves me," that "versions of most" of these howlers were expressed at the Cognitive Science Colloquium at MIT (December 1989) at which Pinker and Bloom spoke, although "no transcript of that meeting exists." Presumably Dennett is performing these mental somersaults to establish a link, no matter how tenuous, between unattributed comments about evolution made in a bar (or wherever) to Pinker and Bloom with Chomsky and Gould. Since the latter won't go out and police the public mind, Dennett is forced to do their "dirty work" for them. Moreover, Dennett can now add an eleventh "howler" to "Pinker's list;" viz., the fallacious idea of Pinker's and his that natural selection is able to act without physical constraints.

But then what is one to do about all the misapplications and misrepresentations of Chomsky in Dennett that we cited earlier? And what is one to do about potential misapplications in Dennett's work. How about this one, which might be called, "Dennett's Dangerous Idea": "The message is clear: those who will not accommodate, who will not temper, who insist on keeping only the purest and wildest strain of their heritage alive, we will be obliged, reluctantly, to cage or disarm, and we will do our best to disable the memes they fight for" (p. 516).

In the context, Dennett is referring to "religious memes" But who are the reluctant "we?" Is it Dennett's Judaeo-Christian colleagues? And who are in the cages? Is it the atheistic Viet Cong? Or does he mean the atheistic Viet Cong will be reluctantly obliged to cage Dennett and his colleagues and disable their memes. Probably not the latter. A reading of history shows that this particular meme has gotten a lot of wars and genocides going. But, in Dennett's view, the more important problem is that Chomsky and Gould haven't yet mounted a major campaign to enlighten the public on the "Rube Goldberg device." This "ignorance about evolution" was enough to shock Dennett into action: "In fact, it was reflecting on that meeting that persuaded me I could no longer put off writing this book" (p. 392).[42] The Rube Goldberg device has now been supplanted by Dennett's "Chomsky contra Darwin" debate.

Horgan, in a review of a meeting of evolutionary psychologists, interviews Pinker and Chomsky on the above issues (Horgan, 1995). An anonymous interviewee offers Horgan one last-ditch explanation for Chomsky's inability to see the light that Pinker and Dennett see so well. It's Chomsky's politics. What is not explained to us is why Pinker and Dennett's views on evolution aren't similarly due to their politics? Evidently it depends on who gets to police whose memes.

[42] The reference to "that meeting" is to the Cognitive Science Colloquium at MIT in 1989 mentioned above.

Maynard Smith on biolinguistics

In a review of Dennett's "Darwin's Dangerous Idea," John Maynard Smith makes the following remarks: "There is a lesson which Chomsky's students, if not the great man himself, will have to learn. Science is a unity. Biology cannot ignore chemistry, much as I wish it could; for the same reason, linguistics cannot ignore biology" (Maynard Smith, 1995 (November 30):48). This is fairly remarkable, since on the same page Maynard Smith notes that he is in agreement with many of the views of biolinguists. The only exception is the matter of evolution of language to which we return. For example he agrees that "there is indeed a special 'language organ' that enables children to learn to talk." This "special faculty" is "peculiar to humans"; in fact we find "an enormous gap between the best that apes, whales, or parrots can do and what almost all humans can do." This language faculty is "peculiar to language," which is part of the modularity thesis which says that "the mind contains specialized modules that evolved to perform particular tasks." Maynard Smith states that this modularity thesis is the "most interesting claim made by evolutionary psychologists," but this thesis predated the evolutionary psychologists by twenty-five years. There is an enormous literature about the modularity thesis in biolinguistics; see, e.g., Chomsky, 1975b. Finally, Maynard Smith also recognizes that the genetic analysis of language disorders may, as we argued earlier, help "reveal the nature and origin of the human language organ, just as it is already revealing how animal form appears during embryological development" (p. 48).

Up to this point, Maynard Smith is restating and approving versions of positions on biology and language that are standard in biolinguistics, as we have seen. We study (1), the language organ, (2), the development of the language organ, and (3), the evolution of the language organ. The understanding of (1) is essential to the understanding of (2), which in turn is essential to the understanding of (3). In the last step, we study physical and developmental constraints in conjunction with selective factors, exactly as Maynard Smith et al. argued in their important survey of this topic, or as others have argued, including Gould, Lewontin, or those working in the framework of the Resynthesis.

While it is true, as Maynard Smith notes, that "language is difficult because it leaves no fossils," one does not have to be out in the Olduvai Gorge to seek the fossils of the mind. Biolinguistics, through the kinds of studies touched on in this book – poverty of stimulus studies, comparative parametric studies, studies of pidgins and creoles, language disorders, and on and on – seeks to uncover the developmental constraints on the language organ. One hopes to supplement and extend this knowledge with more information from such domains as biochemistry, genetics, and physics. It is quite possible that in this search one may come across some informative fossils of the mind. We recall the earlier speculations of Pollack about the role of homeobox genes in brain development, our comments on the use of zooblots to look for homologs of genes involved in language development, and the interesting ongoing study of mechanisms of left–right asymmetry, which play a central role in the anatomy of the language areas of the brain. Far from ignoring biology, the very essence of biolinguistics is to focus on the biological nature of the language organ, its development, and its evolution.

Even though Maynard Smith has just sketched out the biolinguistic program which offers us the best chance to find some answers about the evolution of the language organ, he wonders: "Why does Chomsky not wish to think about evolution?" The question itself appears to be based on a citation from Chomsky, which was taken out of context: "In the case of such systems as language or wings, it is not easy even to imagine a course of selection that might have given rise to them" (Chomsky, 1988a:167). Let's take a look at the full context (the italics and capital letters are mine, not Chomsky's):

It surely cannot be assumed that every trait is specifically selected. *In the case of such systems as language or wings, it is not easy even to imagine a course of selection that might have given rise to them.* A rudimentary wing, for example, is not "useful" for motion but is more of an impediment. Why then should the organ develop in the early stages of its evolution?

In some cases it seems that organs develop to serve one purpose and, when they have reached a certain form in THE EVOLUTIONARY PROCESS, became available for different purposes, at which point the PROCESSES OF NATURAL SELECTION may refine them further for these purposes. It has been suggested that the development of insect wings follows this pattern. Insects have the problem of heat exchange, and rudimentary wings can serve this function. When they reach a certain size, they become less useful for this purpose but begin to be useful for flight, at which point they evolve into wings. Possibly human mental capacities have in some cases evolved in a similar way. (Chomsky, 1988a:167)

What we find is that, contrary to Maynard Smith's claim, not only has Chomsky thought about evolution, but considers specific lines of investigation. In the case of evolution of insect wings, he mentions the well-known work by Kingsolver and Koehl, which almost certainly was familiar to Maynard Smith (Kingsolver and Koehl, 1985). A great deal of evidence for this kind of evolutionary mechanism (a shift in function) has emerged in the decade since Chomsky made these remarks. In the case of evolution of mind, we see that he notes that "possibly human mental capacities have in some cases evolved in a similar way" as in the Kingsolver–Koehl scenario and goes on in the next several pages to sketch out how the number faculty might have "developed as a by-product of the language faculty." Compare also Chomsky's suggestion given below that the language faculty might have arisen through an integration of a "computational capacity" with a "conceptual capacity." Finally, he notes that we also need a deeper understanding of the "space of physical possibilities and specific contingencies" involved in evolution (of insect wings, language, etc.).

What Maynard Smith has done is lift out the sentence with the choice phrase "it is not even easy to imagine a course of selection," helping to perpetuate the myth that Chomsky (and "his students") are mystics that do not "wish to think about evolution." This myth has most recently become enshrined in the field of evolutionary psychology, the latest formulation being by Plotkin: "one of the oddities of recent human science is that Chomsky, the great proponent of the conception of language as an innate organ of mind, has long been of the view that language is not a product of evolution" (Plotkin, 1998:224). Plotkin, as opposed to Maynard Smith, doesn't even bother to supply us with so much as a misquotation. All references by Chomsky above (and in other writings) to "the evolutionary process" and to the "processes of natural selection" (in capital letters above), not to mention specific mechanisms, must and have been conveniently suppressed. At the same time, Plotkin approvingly cites work by Szathmáry and Maynard Smith, that places "language within the context of other major evolutionary events," unlike the work of the unenlightened hordes of (bio)linguists laboring under the delusion that "language is not a product of evolution," as documented (misquotation) by Maynard Smith. The unintended effect of this careless scholarship is that it makes it difficult to take the field of evolutionary psychology seriously concerning any area of cognition and the mind, when it so misunderstands and blatantly misrepresents ongoing work on the biology of language.

Maynard Smith is puzzled by Chomsky's views because he quotes him out of context. He then embraces an alternative misrepresentation suggested by Dennett: "Dennett, who is as puzzled as I am, has an interesting idea. Chomsky, he suggests, would readily accept an explanation of linguistic competence in terms of some general physical law, but not in terms of messy, ad hoc, contingent engineering design, which is the best that natural selection can do" (1995 (November 30):48). It is more puzzling that Maynard Smith would accept this caricature of evolutionary theory which pits evolution by "general physical law" against evolution by "natural selection," characterized "in terms of messy, ad hoc, contingent engineering design." Contrast Dennett's incoherent statement with the nuanced position of Maynard Smith himself where he argues for a careful investigation of constraints that are "direct consequences of the laws of physics" and the study of the "interacting mixture of developmental and selective factors," including a summary of the study discussed earlier where Maynard Smith and Sondhi argue that some cases of bilateral symmetry might be "consequences of a developmental constraint rather than selection." Given this, it is mysterious that he could so readily and uncritically accept the claims by Pinker, Bloom, and Dennett that biolinguistics is under the sway of "Darwin-hating academics," who are "skeptical of Darwin," and frightened by "Darwin's Dangerous Idea." We have argued at length against these misconceptions earlier in this chapter. As Chomsky observes: "The frantic efforts to "defend Darwin's dangerous idea" from evil forces that regard it as neither "dangerous" nor even particularly controversial, at this level of discussion, hardly merit comment" (Chomsky, 1996c:41).

Maynard Smith finds Chomsky's views on evolution "completely baffling"; e.g., the sentence about "language or wings" cited above, because he quotes it out of context, as we noted. To extricate himself from this "baffling" quandary, Maynard Smith proposes that organs "usually arise . . . as modifications of preexisting organs with different functions." But this is precisely the point that Chomsky made ten years earlier. When this is pointed out by Chomsky in a reply to Maynard Smith, he replies in turn as follows: "I am delighted that Professor Chomsky agrees that the origin of language, like that of other complex organs, must ultimately be explained in Darwinian terms, as the result of natural selection" (1996:41).

Maynard Smith still seems to miss the point. Chomsky nowhere makes a dogmatic statement of the form "X must be ultimately be explained by Y." Compare, in this regard, the statement "the atom must ultimately be explained by the laws of classical physics." Going back again to the context, he says "evolutionary theory . . . has little to say, as of now" about language and "progress may require better understanding" of the development of physical systems and "one direction of research is suggested," etc. In short, we are back to science as usual. We don't know what the answers will be. Will the answer be in Darwinian terms? This is meaningless. We will take whatever works from Darwin (natural selection, as one factor) and throw out what doesn't (pangenesis, gemmules, etc.).[43] We will also incorporate into our explanation of the evolution of the language faculty any physical, developmental, genetic, etc. constraints that we dis-

---

[43] Pangenesis is the incorrect idea of Darwin that acquired traits could be passed to the next generation by the mechanism of gemmules, which were thought to be the carriers of the acquired traits from throughout the body to the sex cells.

cover that work. There are no guarantees in science. We may have the hope or belief that we will come up with some naturalistic explanation, but that hope or belief does not substitute for the explanation. We have to come up with it by the canons of science rationality, not dogmatic assertion. When Chomsky says that "it is not easy even to imagine a course of selection that might have given rise to them [language or wings]," he is only saying that there remain considerable gaps in our understanding of underlying mechanisms and about the actual relative roles played by natural selection and many additional factors, such as physical factors and "specific contingencies." These "views on evolution" may still seem "baffling" to Maynard Smith, but they are widely shared throughout biology, and, in any case, the gaps in understanding will not go away by waving Pinker and Bloom's magic wand of natural selection over them.

Compare Statement A with Statement B:

Statement A (on evolution): I am delighted that Professor Chomsky agrees that the origin of language, like that of other complex organs, must ultimately be explained in Darwinian terms, as the result of natural selection.

Statement B (on development): I am delighted that Professor Chomsky agrees that development of language, like that of other complex organs, must ultimately be explained in Buffonian terms, as the result of (epi)genetics.

Statement B (on development) seems hardly newsworthy, for the reasons just discussed. Again apart from "must . . . be explained," all we are expressing is our hope (belief) that we can come up with some naturalistic explanation for the development of language, involving some complex interaction between genetics and epigenetic (and environmental) factors. Most would agree that this statement is a truism and that substantive proposals about the nature of this interaction are what are really of importance here. But then why does the analogous Statement A (on evolution) unleash the "frantic" desire to contain the "evil forces?" Put differently, why does the mention of Darwin mobilize furious defenses around "Darwin's dangerous idea," while the mention of Buffon elicits indifference.

A possible explanation for this (in addition to those we have discussed elsewhere in this chapter) is that the ultra-Darwinists have been hunkered down in the bunkers so long fighting the creationists that anyone that does not swear allegiance to Darwin and natural selection with sufficient vigor is considered suspect. Take Gould as an example. What are his views on natural selection? He writes "I certainly think natural selection is an enormously powerful force." His colleague Goodwin thinks Gould is too extreme in his advocacy of natural selection, writing that "he [Gould] believes that natural selection is the final arbiter, the final cause in evolution." Yet Gould is not rabid enough on the topic of natural selection for the ultra-Darwinists! Pinker writes, in a commentary to the very article where Gould says that "I certainly think natural selection is an enormously powerful force," that Gould gives "short shrift to natural selection." Maynard Smith writes that Gould "should not be publicly criticized because he is at least on our side against the creationists." The picture that emerges is that it doesn't really make any difference what role you think developmental (or physical, genetic, etc.) constraints do or don't play in evolution. If you are not sufficiently rabid on the topic of natural selection, you can avoid attacks in the scientific journals from the ultra-Darwinists by waging war against creationism.

Maynard Smith and Szathmáry raise an issue concerning "simplicity" of constraints in UG and natural selection (Maynard Smith and Szathmáry, 1995b). They note that linguists have postulated "null-elements" (indicated by the underscore) in such sentences as

> What did you see __?

In this particular case, the question word *what* has moved to the front of a sentence, leaving behind a null-element "__", which marks the place where *what* receives a thematic interpretation as patient.

They ask "why on earth should anyone believe this? Certainly speakers are not aware of leaving null-elements behind." They go on to point out correctly that part of the reason that linguists postulate these null-elements is that they can help to explain patterns of (un)grammatically. The example given by Maynard Smith and Szathmáry is

(1) How do you know who he saw?
(2) Who do you know how he saw?

where the first sentence is grammatical (as long as *how* is interpreted as "how do you know" and not "how do you see") and the second sentence is ungrammatical.

Maynard Smith and Szathmáry comment:

It is hard to for an outsider to decide how plausible this argument really is. We know that (1) is grammatical, but (2) is not. The linguists' argument is that the easiest way of explaining this grammatical insight (and, of course, others) is by postulating null-elements. As biologists know to their cost, there are dangers to this plausibility argument. There may be a simpler way we have not thought of, or natural selection may not have picked on the simplest way. For example, the simplest way of making segments is probably the one suggested by Turing, but it seems that animals do not do it that way. (1996:289)

But, as has often been noted with regard to constraints in UG, there is no reason to think that "natural selection" (i.e., evolution) did pick the simplest way.[44] There are a number of respects in which this solution is more complicated than easily imagined alternatives. In the first place, in Human, movement has the complication that words and phrases are heard in one place in the sentence and understood in another. Secondly, movement has the property of structure-dependence, discussed in chapter 3. Thirdly, movement obeys a set of constraints on where phrases can move to, of which Maynard Smith and Szathmáry give an illustration in (1), (2). Again, there would be no problem assigning the deviant structures a reasonable interpretation. It would appear then that "natural selection" (i.e. evolution) has picked out a complicated way to go. As for the notion that "there may be a simpler way we have not thought of" to describe the syntactic patterns above ("and, of course, others"), this is a commonplace of any empirical inquiry, not only linguistics. There is nothing that can be said further except that when Maynard Smith and Szathmáry have thought of a simpler way of analyzing these syntactic patterns (and others) and tested the consequences across a variety of languages, we will evaluate the proposal.

Maynard Smith and Szathmáry note that the simplest way of making segments is probably the Turing wave model, but that it is not clear that this model is the one that nature has actually favored.[45] One should not read too much into the particular null-element notation used by the linguist. We are abstracting away from concrete physical mechanisms, by necessity, since nothing is known here. This is different from the Turing wave model example, where at least model chemical reactions can and have been proposed.

The situation for biolinguistics is more parallel to historical developments in Mendelian genetics, where abstract factors were postulated, with no way to choose between physical mechanisms; e.g., is the genetic material DNA or protein? Linguists first observe that, in English, phrases are heard in one place and interpreted in another. Any theory of UG has to account for this fact in some way. One way is by means of movement and null-elements. They then try to make the theory compatible with a range of phenomena across a wide variety of languages. Linguists can go no further than this on the basis of internal linguistic evidence. The most that can be said is that any physical mechanism proposed for the language

[44] For the sake of argument, we assume here with Maynard Smith and Szathmáry, that these properties of UG were directly selected for by natural selection, contrary to the alternatives that we have been exploring. We also concede that there "may be a simpler way we have not thought of," but this is a truism of the scientific endeavor.

[45] But see more recent findings by Kondo and Asai (1995) and commentary by Meinhardt (1995), which we discussed earlier, where it is argued that the Turing system does operate in biological systems like the angelfish and may even be a evolutionary precursor to the rigid mechanism found in *Drosophila*.

faculty must be at least this complicated. As evidence becomes available from other domains, such as imaging, neurochemistry, etc., one can try to accommodate additional complicating factors as they come up.

However, understanding physical mechanisms can also clear up puzzles in the theory. As the geneticist Thomas Hunt Morgan noted in his Nobel Prize address:

The apparent exceptions to Mendel's laws, that came to light before long, might, in the absence of a known mechanism, have called forth purely fictitious modifications of Mendel's laws or even seemed to invalidate their generality. We now know that some of these "exceptions" are due to newly discovered and demonstrable properties of the chromosome mechanism, and others to recognizable irregularities in the machine. (Morgan, 1935:5)

HUMAN LANGUAGE AND APE COMMUNICATION

Ape communication – the ideological debate

When comparing human language with primate communication systems, it is necessary to distinguish (1) the ideological debate from (2) the scientific discussion. The ideological debate, often framed as "do apes have language?" is played out for the most part in the media and pop science literature. The "debate" is allegedly one between researchers on ape "language" and linguists, but is actually a one-sided debate, since most linguists (and most researchers on primate cognition) prefer to stick to the scientific questions and issues and to avoid the ideological fanaticism that has come to prevail in the field of ape communication. Savage-Rumbaugh, Bates, and a few others have promoted a bogus debate in the media for some years that goes like this: it has been shown that apes have "language," the only open question being, how much? e.g., that of a two and a half year old, or whatever. The proof: Kanzi, the bonobo (pygmy chimpanzee), featured in the cover stories of *Time* and *Newsweek*, and lauded for his "extraordinary facility for language" (Savage-Rumbaugh and Lewin, 1994: book jacket, hard-cover edition). The main question under discussion on this side of the debate is how much "language," Kanzi has: that of a two year old, a two and a half year old, a three year old, an adult, etc.

On the other side of the (concocted) "debate" are the linguists, "with the boundary between humans and nonhumans still being policed and maintained by the scientific community at large, with Chomsky as their guardian" (Savage-Rumbaugh and Lewin, 1994:25–26). But this "boundary wall between humans and apes has finally been breached" (p. 280). As Elizabeth Bates trumpets, "The Berlin Wall is down, and so is the wall that separates man from chimpanzee" (p. 178). The marketing blurb for a forthcoming book continues the earthshaking frenzy over Kanzi's exploits: a "scientific breakthrough of stunning proportions" and a "radical revision of the sciences of language and mind."

As Savage-Rumbaugh herself correctly notes, apart from "solicited comments in the popular press, linguists have been oddly silent in the scientific journals" (Savage-Rumbaugh and Lewin, 1994:166). This is, as we will see below, because the debate over whether chimpanzees have "language" is meaningless. We can easily see why if we compare the hysteria over Kanzi with another recent, but equally hotly contested, "debate" sponsored by the media, over whether Black English (Ebonics) is a "language." In some of the same prestigious publications that heralded the system of chimpanzee (or bonobo) communication as a "language," it was vociferously argued in editorials that Black English was not a "language" (Pullum, 1997). There was agreement by all sides of that debate that the language of, say, Chelsea Clinton, the President's daughter, was a "language." And, almost overwhelmingly, with a few lone voices in the wilderness disagreeing, Black English was declared not to be a "language." The only unresolved issue left to be debated on the intellectual scene was whether chimpanzees (or bonobos) had a "language," perhaps not equal to Chelsea Clinton's, but more like the language Chelsea had when she was two and a half years old. Both the chimp "debate" and the Ebonics "debate" are flawed in the same fundamental way.

There is a quite simple way out of this ideological morass which does not entail the counterfactual (and racist) conclusion that chimp "language" is a language whereas the "language" of the black child in the urban ghetto is not. And that is to recognize, as Chomsky argued years ago, and repeatedly since, that talk of "language" is meaningless. He formulated this important point as follows, in a conversation with David Premack, who did the pioneering work with the chimpanzee Sarah.

Imagine a theory of biology which was concerned in general with vision. Vision involves very different systems designed in different ways with different evolutionary histories. It doesn't make much sense to ask whether a camera is an eye. Similarly, it doesn't make much sense to ask whether some system of communication we make up is a language. The notion of vision and the notion of language are quite empty. There are no serious questions that can be asked about vision, or "language." There are questions that can be asked about specific systems such as insect vision or human language. (Weingarten, 1979:8)

That is, from the viewpoint of biology, the only meaningful approach to studying a biological system, whether that of a human, or that of a chimpanzee, is to study each one on its own terms and to determine the specific mechanisms that are operative in each system; see the next section for more comments about the particular mechanisms. Any kind of comparison across systems must then be based on a detailed comparison of these mechanisms. To study human language, we put aside the meaningless term "language," (except as a convenient shorthand) and seek to determine the mechanisms of I-language, or human language. In the case of the bonobo communication systems, we follow exactly the same procedure. We drop meaningless talk about "language,"[46] and focus in on specific systems, whether these be trail-marking systems, vocalizations used up in the trees, other systems used in the wild, or systems derivative thereof.

Applying the biological approach to the case of Black English, one can immediately conclude that Black English is an I-language in the same sense that "standard" English, French, or Japanese are. It exhibits exactly the same range of rich syntactic, phonological, and semantic mechanisms as the other languages. It also has the same unbounded capacity for expression of thought (see the discussion of "discrete infinity" below). We can now clearly see the ideological basis for the racist conclusion that Black English is not a language. At the level of biolinguistic mechanisms there is no property: "Black English will not help you to get a job in a white society." Similarly, if the results of the ape studies are looked at from the point of view of specific mechanisms, including the property of expressing unbounded thought using recursive mechanisms, then the clear conclusion is that English, Turkish, Russian, etc. must be grouped together with Black English, not ape language.

There is a further misconception about human language that drives the ideological debate. This misconception is that human languages are not a biological product of evolution, but are largely, or solely, the product of a "civilized culture" or of "Intelligence." No objections are raised when it is stated that the study of chimpanzee communication systems is a part of the study of animal biology. However, there has been enormous resistance, not only from the public, but also in academic circles, to the acceptance of the fundamental biological nature of human language, as we have documented in various places throughout this book. This contributes to the illusion that Kanzi's performance, no matter how flawed it may be, is considered to be a "breakthrough of stunning proportions," whereas the language performance of the black child in the ghetto is ridiculed, the mistake being that normal use of language is taken to be a mark

---

[46] The same problem arises when one asks whether Kanzi has the "language" of a two-and-a-half-year-old human child. It makes as much sense to ask whether my ability to find my way home at night is at the same level as that of a pigeon at the age of x weeks, for some x (Noam Chomsky, p.c.).

of "intelligence" rather than the product of biology. We now turn to (2), the scientific discussion about the similarities and the differences between human language and primate communication systems.

Primate communication systems – the scientific discussion

A great number of speculations about possible connections between human language and other systems have been offered, both in the modern biolinguistics era and before, including, e.g., gestural systems, animal communication systems (nonhuman primates, bird song), the visual system, etc.; see Hauser, 1996 for discussion and references. About twenty years ago, Chomsky suggested a fruitful way to look at and to investigate these kinds of questions. The particular question that Chomsky was considering was that of whether human language shared some properties with nonhuman primate systems; say, chimpanzees. At that time he concluded that "higher apes ... may ... be capable of elementary forms of symbolic function or symbolic communication" (Chomsky, 1980c:57). Chomsky goes on to note that the higher apes "may command" a "conceptual" system, including a system of "object-reference" and also "such relations as 'agent,' 'goal,' 'instrument,' and the like."[47] Such a conceptual system could permit an organism to "perceive, and categorize, and symbolize maybe even to reason in an elementary way," and also include other things "which may go beyond" basic elements such as "object identification" and "perceptual constancies," such as "planning and the attribution of intent to other organisms" (Huybregts and Riemsdijk, 1982:20). This is "one kind of system which may be shared in part with other primates."

Chomsky then turns to the question of what mechanisms might distinguish human language from other primate systems. He notes that a central design feature of human language is the "capacity to deal with discrete infinities through recursive rules," a property shared with the number faculty. He notes that when "that capacity links to the conceptual system, you get human language, which provides the capacity for thought, planning, evaluation and so on, over an unbounded range, and then you have a totally new organism" (Huybregts and Riemsdijk, 1982:21). This proposal still seems, some twenty years later, to be the most interesting area to investigate for answers about the differences between human language and other nonhuman primate communication

---

[47] Linguists sometimes refer to these as "thematic relations" in theories of semantics.

systems. And, in fact, linguistics work has shed, and continues to shed, a great deal of light on the specific design features and nature of these recursive mechanisms.

Another fruitful way to think of the study of biolinguistics from an evolutionary perspective is as the study of ape communication. This eliminates fruitless discussions along the lines of "do apes have language?"[48] The answer is now, yes, they do. They can talk English, Bulgarian, Mohawk, Turkish, and thousands of other (I-)languages. These apes evolved a number of specific design properties in their communication system (discrete infinity, structure-dependence, concatenation operations like Merge, etc.) and we would like to learn how this came about. The way that this can be learned has been the subject of this book. That is, we characterize the mechanisms of language, and of the development of language to learn what its design features are and then ask how these design features might have been implemented in evolution. In fact, there is some merit to the argument that the Department of Linguistics in many universities could just as easily be called the Department of Ape Communication. One of the reasons that there has been next to no funding for, say, theoretical syntax from biology sources, apart from applied areas, is the misconception mentioned above, that the subject is somehow "outside" biology, somewhere off in the so-called "humanities."

The same logic applies to the study of any other cognitive system in (human) primates, say, e.g., the conceptual system mentioned above. That is, we study the properties of the conceptual system; e.g., semantic properties like "Agent" and "Instrument," and we study how they develop in the infant, in order to determine their crucial design properties. Suppose now that we wish to test Chomsky's speculation that human primates share some of their design properties with other primates; e.g., bonobos. We would then repeat the same steps with the bonobos; i.e., study their conceptual system along with its development and identify the design features of these systems. We can then ask whether the human system is the same as or is (partly or wholly) different from the bonobo's. And here we would bring in any and all kinds of evidence. When Chomsky originally made this proposal about "shared" systems twenty years ago, he mentioned several lines of supporting evidence; studies of symbol systems in chimps, studies of humans with damage to their language (aphasia) that were able to use the kinds of symbol systems employed in chimpanzee studies; see references in Chomsky, 1980c:265.

---

[48] Here Savage-Rumbaugh is in agreement: "Humans are African apes, of an unusual kind" (Savage-Rumbaugh and Lewin, 1994:280).

And, of course, the list of potential evidence is open-ended: e.g., from imaging, studies of nerve circuits, studies of brain asymmetries in primates (see chapter 4), genetic experiments, etc. Of course, to make a direct evolutionary connection between these ape systems, there is still more work to do. One must find some property Z in the common ancestor such that one can make a plausible case that Z is the basis for the property in question shared between the two systems. Hence, (bio)linguistics provides an excellent and well-developed model for the study of any ape communication system, human or otherwise.

There is also a secondary question; viz., did apes develop the system found in humans only one time or did it happen more than once? Putting aside the possibility that the system may have arisen multiple times and then disappeared, we restrict ourselves to specific existing systems, such as the symbolic communication system used in the bonobo studies. It is important to pose this question carefully. As we saw, it is not enough to ask if the bonobo has "language." The question is meaningless, since we can define "language" anyway we like. So, for the moment, let's call the system described in bonobos, B-language (bonobo language). Now we ask: does B-language equal human language (I-language)? Even the most enthusiastic supporters of the symbolic abilities in nonhuman primates answer this question in the negative. Savage-Rumbaugh asks and answers this question as follows: "Do apes have language? The answer to this question, of course, is that they don't" (Savage-Rumbaugh and Lewin, 1994:157). In a recent interview, she also voices her doubt that Kanzi ever will: "They are asking Kanzi to do everything that humans do, which is specious. He'll never do that" (Dreifus, 1998:C4) She says the question needs to be framed in developmental terms, as: does Kanzi have the language of a one-year-old human infant, a two year old, a five year old, etc.? The answer favored by Savage-Rumbaugh is the language of a two-and-a-half year old human infant.

But the problem doesn't change, whether we ask if Kanzi has the I-language of an adult or that of a two and a half year old. Take the case of discrete infinity again. The question now becomes does the bonobo have the nerve circuits that in the two-and-a-half-year-old child go on to realize the property of discrete infinity and unbounded thought? Does he have some of these circuits? The rudiments of these circuits? Or none of these circuits, but some other circuits that specify his capacities? These are the central questions, but indirect evidence might be found by asking if the bonobo has (some of, none of) the complement of genes involved in the specification of these nerve circuits? This same array of questions must then be asked of all the other specific properties of language design; e.g., the particular constraints that the hierarchic concatenation operation

(Merge) obeys. These important questions about specific differences cannot be glossed over. It is necessary that we discover them, if we wish to address the question of how the mechanisms arose in evolution.

Savage-Rumbaugh rejects the "innatist view of language acquisition" outright: "It is true that the process of language acquisition through which most of us pass appears to be a near miracle, given the absence of what could be considered effective teaching. But that is an inadequate rationale for assuming the necessity of a unique, undetected brain structure" (Savage-Rumbaugh and Lewin, 1994:167–68). The rationale for assuming a brain structure underlying the process of language acquisition is not because it "appears to be a near miracle," but because of the huge mass of evidence from linguistics, neurology, and the cognitive sciences (discussed in this book and in the references) that leads us to this conclusion. Curiously, the evidence she is rejecting for the study of human language is the same kind of evidence she uses to study Kanzi: "ordering" in a "rule-based manner," "distinctions as agent and object," "productive" rule behavior; in short, evidence gathered over the "previous decade" by "linguists and psychologists" (p. 158–59). So if this kind of evidence can't be used to argue for "undetected brain structure" in humans, it can't be used for Kanzi's brain either.

Nor then can evidence from Kanzi be used to support Savage-Rumbaugh's "plausible alternative hypothesis" to explain human language acquisition; viz., that "comprehension drives language acquisition" (p. 168). She prefers this "alternative hypothesis" to the "innatist view of language acquisition" since, she alleges, the innatist hypothesis "effectively rests on a default premise: namely, that no other hypothesis offers an adequate explanation." But the shoe is on the other foot here. Savage-Rumbaugh can't claim that there is "no other hypothesis" than her hypothesis that "offers an adequate explanation." There are dozens of them, many of them within the principles-and-parameters approach, for example, but others as well. These alternatives are backed up by typological studies across hundreds of languages, as well as by child acquisition studies that investigate dozens of syntactic, semantic, phonological, and other properties.

On the other hand, the statement that "comprehension drives language acquisition" explains zero about language acquisition. In fact, it can't really be an alternative to the other theories of language acquisition, because all of these theories recognize the necessity to account for both production and comprehension, their interactions, and their developmental windows. Savage-Rumbaugh presents no evidence for her "alternative," other than her gut feeling that "comprehension" is the "essence of language," while "production, by contrast, is simple" (p. 174). We see no reason to give this intuition any more weight than the claim that the circuits for acoustic perception are the "essence of language," while the circuits for speech articulation are "simple."

As a side comment, we note that the use of the word "unique" appears to inflame the passions among some researchers on animal communication, for reasons that are unclear. Suppose that molecular biologists discovered a gene in fruit flies that was homologous to a gene involved in brain development in humans and that it turned out that, during evolution, a mutation occurred in that gene that, in conjunction with other factors, led to an important reorganization of nerve circuits that were critical to the development of human language. Such a finding would rightfully be recognized as a wonderful discovery. But would molecular biologists then descend into the ideological fanaticism of the discussions on ape communication, proclaiming that the "Berlin Wall" between the fruit fly and the human had been "breached," even arguing for "semi-human" status for the fruit fly. That is hard to imagine, so we put these ideological issues aside.

Chomsky is cited in Savage-Rumbaugh as saying that "if an animal had a capacity as biologically sophisticated as language but somehow hadn't used it until now, it would be an evolutionary miracle" (p. 165–66). Savage-Rumbaugh claims that Chomsky's point suggests "a lack of biological sophistication." His point is biologically sound. As he asks, if there is a language capacity in nonhuman apes, then "what was it doing there" until the ape experimenters found it, why wasn't it being used? Chomsky's conclusion is that "The answer to that must be that, again miracles aside, it is a concomitant of something else which was being used" (Huybregts and Riemsdijk, 1982:22). Hence the symbolic skills of the bonobo must at some level reflect innate capacities that are being used in the wild and that are being tapped into by the ape experimenters. In fact, Savage-Rumbaugh notes in a newspaper interview that: "I don't know what they do with their speech in the wild, but given that they learn it so easily in captivity there is a good chance that they are using it in the wild" (AP report, 1998). But, it is not enough to say that "there is a good chance that they are using it in the wild." To the degree that bonobo "speech" reflects a real biological system, honed by evolution, it is somehow being used or else "it is a concomitant of something else which [is] being used." She notes that the question cannot be settled at present because "it is impossible to study verbal communications between bonobos in the wild because they only vocalize when they are together in the trees," but that doesn't change the logic of the inquiry.

Terrence Deacon speaks of the "devastating challenge" the bonobo "Kanzi offers to the nativist, Chomskyan perspective," referring to

Kanzi's "sophisticated comprehension of normal spoken English, including the ability to analyze a variety of grammatical constructions" (Deacon, 1997:125). However, we will show that Kanzi presents a devastating challenge to Deacon's own views on language, not to "Chomskyans," or any biologist, for that matter. Deacon considers "two possible interpretations of Kanzi's success." One is that bonobos are "innately better [than other (sub) species] at language-type tasks," citing Savage-Rumbaugh's speculation that "bonobos in the wild might engage in spontaneous symbolic communication of a sort, though nothing quite so sophisticated and languagelike has yet been demonstrated." Thus the first interpretation is something along the lines that most biolinguists and biologists might entertain. But Deacon rejects the conventional biological approach in favor of the following hypothesis: "Kanzi learned better simply because he was so immature at the time" (Deacon, 1997:125).

From this point on, Deacon's "explanation" of Kanzi's ability descends into complete mysticism. We will trace out the path of Deacon's tortuous logic, but we want to give the reader a brief idea of where he is heading. Deacon wants to reject innate language mechanisms in humans also, in favor of the idea that children learn language because they have "immature" brains. For Deacon, language does not reside in the brain, as linguists, neurologists, and most biologists standardly assume; it is "outside the brain." Language exists in the form of viruses or parasitic organisms: "In some ways it is helpful to imagine language as an independent life form that colonizes and parasitizes human brains, using them to reproduce" (Deacon, 1997:111). In particular, Deacon's language viruses prefer to "colonize" the immature brains of young infants and young bonobos, like Kanzi. This is Deacon's "co-evolutionary theory of child language acquisition" (p. 139). He also claims that the language viruses can "genetically assimilate" over time into the brain by the mechanism of Baldwinian selection.[49]

Note that what Deacon has done in effect is to reject without argument most work on the biology of language, whether it be from linguistics, language acquisition, neurology, or any of a dozen other fields in favor of a literary metaphor, the idea of a language parasite co-evolving with the brain. He doesn't offer a clue as to how the many specific linguistic constraints and mechanisms in languages from Swedish to Tagalog follow from anything. As it stands, Deacon's system represents a complete regression in linguistics, with nothing put in its place. In the Preface to

---

[49] Baldwinian selection is a type of Darwinian selection in which behavior can influence the course of selectional forces. We will not discuss it further here, since we will argue below that Deacon's ideas on language evolution are based on language viruses, which seem to be literary metaphors that are immune to scientific study.

The Symbolic Species, Deacon states that: "I must admit that I have an attraction to heresies, and that my sympathies naturally tend to be with the cranks and doubters and against well-established doctrines" (Deacon, 1997:15). I would say that in his discussions of language, Deacon's sympathies lie firmly in the arena of the "cranks."

In the rest of this section, I will trace how Deacon gets himself into this dead end. Deacon's central assumption and the one that gets him into most trouble, is that for him "support" for language is not inside the brain, but "outside brains":

I think Chomsky and his followers have articulated a central conundrum about language learning, but they offer an answer that inverts cause and effect. They assert that the source of prior support for language acquisition must originate from *inside* the brain, on the unstated assumption that there is no other possible source. But there is another alternative: that the extra support for language learning is vested neither in the brain of the child nor in the brains of parents or teachers, but outside brains, in language itself. (Deacon, 1997:105)

The idea that "language acquisition must originate from *inside* the brain" is not an idea limited to "Chomsky and his followers." It is the standard view in the neurosciences and in the cognitive sciences and is backed up with all kinds of evidence from aphasia studies, imaging, electrical stimulation, and other kinds of evidence of the kind discussed in this book (and in Deacon's own book, for that matter). Nobody in the neurosciences or cognitive sciences holds "the unstated assumption that there is no other possible source" of support for language acquisition. It may be in the kidneys or even outside the brain in DNA viruses, for all anyone knows, but, on the basis of evidence presented thus far to the scientific community, it has been concluded by most that that support derives from "inside" the brain.

Actually, we will see later, Deacon himself waffles on this issue, smuggling innate support back into the brain in the form of what he calls an "innate bias for learning." This is no minor point because, once we start building in "innate biases for learning," why not have principles of UG too? The only conceivable reason for having one rather than the other (or both, if distinguishable) is that one or the other accounts better for the linguistic data from English to Swahili. But Deacon makes no effort to formulate the "innate biases" and hence has no account for specific linguistic mechanisms nor any alternative explanation for the voluminous evidence in the literature that supports theories of UG. As a result, his whole program comes crashing down at the start. He has an unlimited supply of unconstrained innate mechanisms (biases), but does not spell them out and present empirical support for them.

As for Kanzi, Deacon recognizes that he has a problem on his hands.

He starts with the question: "If the critical period effect is evidence of a language acquisition device, then why should an ape whose ancestors never spoke (and who himself can't speak) demonstrate a critical period for language learning?" (1997:126). We have already answered this earlier. If bonobos can manipulate symbols in a uniform fashion across the species and even do this in an effortless and spontaneous fashion, then it is natural to assume that this reflects some innate capacity that is somehow being used in the wild, or as a concomitant of something else used in the wild. As such, it would be no surprise to find that this capacity has some developmental window or other kind of "critical period." This would pose no mystery to ethologists. But the standard biological assumption is disturbing to Deacon, because a critical period and any associated innate developmental program for language is out for Deacon. Support for language must be somewhere "outside" the brain.

But then what can Deacon say about the fact that Kanzi's abilities seem to depend on an early developmental window, since the other infant chimpanzees studied did not learn as well, or as spontaneously, at a later age. Here is where Deacon simply stipulates that "Kanzi learned better simply because he was so immature at the time." This possibility is intriguing to Deacon, because of its "implications for human language development and evolution"; viz., "it forces us to turn our attention away from" the "contribution of something intrinsic to the species (i.e., an innate language competence or predisposition), and to pay attention to the relevance of maturational factors" (p. 126).

Here Deacon is treating "predispositions" and "maturational factors" as mutually exclusive alternatives. But in biology, including biolinguistics, these factors are inseparable. Any genetic predisposition is actualized in time (and space) according to a maturational schedule. But following Deacon's logic, innate predispositions and maturational factors are alternatives. Innate predispositions are out (language is outside the brain). So all we are left with are maturational factors. From this, it follows that Kanzi learned language simply because his brain was immature; i.e., he was exposed to early language (from outside the brain):

If early exposure to language is even part of the explanation for Kanzi's comparatively exceptional language acquisition, then it must be attributable to something about infancy in general, *irrespective of language*. And, if some nonspecific feature of immaturity accounts for Kanzi's remarkable success, then it must at least in part also account for human children's abilities as well. (Deacon, 1997:126–27)

So the initial state, as specified by UG, with its rich structure (and explanatory value) is out of the language acquisition device and, in its place, Deacon proposes "some nonspecific feature of immaturity" to bear the burden of explanation. He cites papers from Newport that he claims offer support for this proposal. But her point is quite different. She notes that one of the factors that might account for the different character of first and second language learning (and the nature of the critical period for first language learning) is that, when one is learning a first language, the learning process may be constrained by the maturation windows of non-language systems, such as memory (Newport, 1990, 1991).

But Newport is not tossing innate mechanisms and critical periods out the window. Nor is she claiming that innate dispositions and maturational factors form an absolute dichotomy. She is merely stating that not all maturational constraints in language learning need to be intrinsic to the language system. Other systems such as memory, perception, and attention may also impose maturational constraints on language learning. It is clear that, quite apart from language, the development of systems for memory, perception, and attention all must have their own innate programs and developmental windows under genetic control. Deacon notes that learning constraints such as "finding it difficult to hold more than a few words of an utterance in short-term memory at a time may all be advantages for language learning. This is the proposal that Elman and Newport each offers to counter the strong nativist alternative" (Deacon, 1997:135). This is not true. As Newport herself notes, there is no reason that a "strong nativist" theory cannot have these kinds of learning constraints and many do.

Then Deacon reverses course and tells us that "immaturity is not the whole explanation for the human language capacity." Here is where Deacon smuggles innate machinery back into the brain, postulating that we have an "innate *bias* for learning" (Deacon, 1997:141). Deacon is short on specifics, but, for example, states that "there may be the bias that favors the hierarchic phrase structure reflected in both acquisition and evolution of languages" (p. 140). We might ask Deacon why we don't just say that UG requires syntactic operations to be structure-dependent, or requires a Merge operation that concatenates hierarchically, or some other standard assumption?

Part of the answer may be that Deacon does not appear to be familiar with any of the linguistic theories that he is criticizing. He claims that the problem with all other approaches to language learning (his own excepted) is that they are based on

a misleading assumption that [language] learning is a one-dimensional process, in which a collection of individual memories is built up bit by bit, like adding items to a list, and in which general rules can only be derived by inductive generalizations from a finite set of instances. This blinkered view of learning has limited ... our analysis of how children acquire competence in producing a symbolic system that is structured like a hierarchic rule-governed logical system. (Deacon, 1997:140–41)

Here, as elsewhere, whenever he gets on the topic of linguistics, Deacon gets it wrong.

Generative linguistics originated with the rejection of the "blinkered view of learning"; i.e., the idea that learning proceeds by "inductive generalizations" of the sort Deacon mentions. In the early 1950s, in work on the first generative grammars, Chomsky had become convinced of the "failure of inductive, data-processing procedures" (p. 30) that had been developed in structural linguistics. Nelson Goodman's work further suggested to him "the inadequacy in principle of inductive approaches" (p. 33). In fact, the "blinkered view of learning" had been influential only in structural linguistics, behaviorism, in areas of the philosophy of language, etc., but never in generative linguistics, where it had been concluded early on that progress in understanding language could only be made by "abandoning all inductive methods, in a strict sense" (p. 32). As Chomsky noted, in taxonomic and empiricist views, we find "nothing that even faintly suggests a way of overcoming the intrinsic limitations of the methods of [inductive operations] ..." (Chomsky, 1965:57). Although the literature on this topic is too extensive to survey here, there is a good discussion of the failure of induction in Piattelli-Palmarini, 1980. Deacon's apparent unfamiliarity with the basic assumptions of work on generative grammar may help explain his puzzling admonishment that "rather than a language organ or some instinctual grammatical knowledge, what sets human beings apart is an innate *bias* for learning." By now it is obvious that Deacon is playing word games. He has banished innate principles from the brain, relabeled them as innate biases, and re-imported them into the brain.

Deacon has an opportunity here to rescue himself from mysticism. Since he recognizes that he needs "innate biases" such as the one cited for "hierarchic phrase structure," he might pause here and take a look at English, Bulgarian, Japanese, etc., and ask what kinds of hierarchic principles (biases) need to be spelled-out. This would lead him very rapidly down the empirical road of having to account for the very heavy constraints placed on his innate "bias" in order to satisfy simultaneously the properties that are universal and those that vary in those languages. He would quickly see that, to derive the specific "hierarchic" properties of human language requires more than vague references to "biases," and he would be back in the business of standard science. But instead of making this, to our mind, rational decision, Deacon, with his "attraction to heresies," remains wedded to the preconception that language is "outside" the brain, and to fulfill this preconception, comes up with the literary metaphor of language as an organism outside the brain, either a virus or other parasitic organism, that co-evolves with the brain. We turn to this subject in the next section.

Deacon's view of language as a parasite or virus

Deacon has embraced the view that language is some kind of "parasitic organism," or perhaps a "virus" that infects the immature brains of young children in order to reproduce itself. Deacon, who is "against well-established doctrines," explicitly rejects the standard picture of biology of language which says that the development of language proceeds like any other biological system, whether the eye, the chick hind limb, or the heart. Language develops by passing through a series of developmental states, the course of which is affected by experience and maturation. In this standard picture of language acquisition, the crucial events affecting language development – gene regulation, the development of neural circuits, synaptic communication, etc. – are taking place *inside* the brain, not outside.

As far as we can tell, the move to language viruses solves no outstanding problems in the biology of language, but does create a whole host of problems for Deacon. According to Deacon, language does not evolve in the brain, but "evolves" outside the brain. Hence the subtitle of his book, *The Co-Evolution of Language and the Brain*. It is important here not to forget that we are dealing with a metaphor. It is true that one informally speaks of the "evolution of language," but this is just a way of saying that the language faculty (language mechanisms, language circuits of the brain, etc.) evolve. Co-evolution is used in biology to refer to live organisms. Languages, like English, change (historically, diachronically), but they do not "evolve." By what mechanisms does Deacon's language "virus" evolve and how does it work? For ordinary biological viruses, these mechanisms are well understood. At this point it is fair for the biologist to ask: "well, how does your virus 'grow' and how does it 'evolve?'" Here Deacon invokes the "parasite" theory of Christiansen: "my own view is probably closest to that proposed in a recent paper by Morton Christiansen" (p. 112).[50] So let us turn to that paper.

Christiansen interprets language as "an organism": "Following Darwin, I propose to view natural language as a kind of a beneficial parasite – i.e., a nonobligate symbiont – that confers some selective advantage onto its human host without whom it cannot survive" (Christiansen, forthcoming). The reference to Darwin is to some remarks that he made about the "struggle for existence" among "the words and grammatical forms in each language": "A language, like a species, when once extinct,

[50] Deacon means Morten, not Morton, Christiansen.

never ... reappears ... A struggle for life is constantly going on among the words and grammatical forms in each language. The better, the shorter, the easier forms are constantly gaining the upper hand ... The survival and preservation of certain favored words in the struggle for existence is natural selection" (Christiansen, forthcoming:9).

The move to parasites on the basis of this metaphoric description by Darwin is dubious. We must not forget that Darwin did not have the knowledge of genes, DNA, neurogenetics of behavior, etc., that we have today. To fill this gap he postulated gemmules in his theory of pangenesis and described language as "organic beings." If Darwin, the scientist, knew what we do today, it seems reasonable to think he would drop pangenesis and the theory of language as "organic beings" and would be trying to describe the body and the mind within the framework of developmental biology that we have today.

Christiansen (and Deacon) are in the position of Darwin in the 1800s. They have locked themselves into a metaphoric description of language[51] with no known account of the "beneficial parasite" or language "virus" in terms of standard developmental biology. As Christiansen puts it, "the fact that children are so successful at language learning is therefore more appropriately explained as a product of natural selection of linguistic structures, rather than natural selection of biological structures, such as UG." It is up to Christiansen to come up with a rational proposal that has testable empirical consequences. As it now stands, the reader is being asked to embrace a metaphor in some domain outside biology, in fact, outside the natural sciences, apparently in some Platonic heaven.

So let us examine the central argument against "principles of UG": "At this point it is furthermore illuminating to recall that the putative principles of UG are *not* established, scientific facts ... The Government and Binding framework ... underlying UG is merely one amongst many linguistic theories – albeit perhaps the most dominant one" (p. 11). He lists some other alternatives, including Categorial Grammar, Dependency Grammar, Lexical Functional Grammar, and Generalized Phrase Structure Grammar.[52] This is true, but doesn't help out the "parasite" theory any. Christiansen is assuming that the theories of UG that he is criticizing represent an "alternative" to (or are incompatible with) "learning and processing constraints." This is false. As noted earlier, these kinds

[51] The move to parasites and viruses is purely voluntary in this case. Darwin postulated gemmules, since there was no better theory around.
[52] He asserts that these alternative theories do not necessarily have transformations in the sense of the Government and Binding framework. But this is irrelevant, since the alternatives all have an equivalent way of expressing the dependency between a moved phrase and its gap.

of considerations have played a role in UG for the last forty years (Miller and Chomsky, 1963); see Berwick et al., 1992; Lasnik, 1999, for more recent discussion.

All of the above theories have something that the parasite theory doesn't; viz., each of them is a real, not metaphoric, theory of language. Each talks about specific antecedent–anaphor relations, phrase dislocation, word order, Case, etc. in a variety of languages – English, Turkish, Mohawk, etc. Moreover, each of them can be interpreted in various ways as theories of language acquisition with an initial state and parametric variation. They can be also used to interpret standard data from specific language disorder, aphasia, etc., consistent with current understanding. They can all be instantiated in parsing or processing theories, using the kind of functional arguments reviewed by Lasnik (Lasnik, 1997). The "parasite" theory on the other hand is immune from such empirical verification, as Christiansen himself notes: "This does, of course, not relieve the present theory from the burden of providing explanations of language universals – predominately couched in terms of learning and processing constraints. Indeed, its future success as a theory of the evolution of language depends in part on whether such explanations will be forthcoming" (forthcoming:12). Christiansen cites recent work on "processing constraints" that hold hope for the parasite project, but as we have seen, processing constraints and language design in general are an integral part of all the other alternative UG theories, so the parasite theory, if and when it is forthcoming, will still have to be evaluated against the others on a case-by-case basis. The remaining arguments of Christiansen are simply that language learning *might* proceed not by language-specific mechanisms, but by general mechanisms of "hierarchically organized sequential structure" (p. 35) and that these general mechanisms could have been the products of adaptation by evolution. However, it is idle to speculate further, since we lack even rudimentary predictions from the parasite model to compare with a wide range of linguistic constructions across many languages that have been studied often in great depth in standard biolinguistic models of UG. Christiansen says that it is "important to note that the explanandum [for the parasite model] is the behavioral data, not the theory-laden constructs that these empirical observations have given rise to (albeit linguistic theories do provide useful guidelines and descriptive frameworks)" (p. 12). At the same time, it is also important to note that once the "theory-laden constructs" with the wealth of explanatory insights that they provide into varied constructions across many languages have been tossed out, one is left, for the time being, holding nothing more than a parasite metaphor in some Platonic heaven. To the degree that Deacon's program depends on Christiansen's parasite analysis, it would appear that, for the moment at least, Deacon's entire program collapses, for the reasons given above, since he has no characterization at all for the central notion of biolinguistics; viz., language. At one point Deacon makes the following curious observation: "The adaptation of the parasite to its hosts, particularly children, provides the basis for a theory of prescient language learning. Though this is a caricature, it is no less so than the nativist and empiricist alternatives, and it captures much more accurately the dynamic push and pull of biases that have shaped both languages and the human brain" (Deacon, 1997:113). It seems odd that Deacon would characterize the central concept of his theory as a "caricature." It is either a serious empirical proposal or not. If it is, then the term "metaphor" seems more appropriate than "caricature" for the language parasite. The "nativist" alternative, on the other hand, as noted, has fully characterized the technical term "(I-) language" and provided a wealth of evidence for particular views about the role that the concept plays in biolinguistics.

Deacon's "argument from incredulity"

We noted earlier that Deacon misunderstood biolinguistic theories of language acquisition as theories about mechanisms based on "inductive generalizations." This may be part of the reason he was led down the garden path of "language viruses." An additional reason may derive from the fact that he has completely misunderstood positions in the linguistics literature on evolution of language. In particular, he makes reference to the "hopeful monster" theory of human language evolution: "The single most influential "hopeful monster" theory of human language evolution was offered by the linguist Noam Chomsky, and has since been echoed by numerous linguists, philosophers, anthropologists, and psychologists" (Deacon, 1997:35). Deacon appears to equate all standard theories of linguistics based on the notion of UG with the "hopeful monster" theory. Proponents are alleged to believe that language must have arisen by a "miraculous accident," or "divine intervention," or some "freak mutation" (p. 35). Deacon (1992:50) says, language competence would have to have appeared "as a result of a single evolutionary accident that yielded a brain so radically changed as to contain all the innate prefigurements of modern language structure." The single "evolutionary accident" would have to have been "some neurological mutation" (p. 51). He calls this the "argument from incredulity," and a "cure that is more drastic than the disease" (p. 104) and compares it with the "search for phlogiston" (p. 38).

Deacon's source for his discussion of the single neurological mutation is Bates, Thal, and Marchman, 1991. From the three assumptions that (1) there are universal principles across languages, (2) they are not "learned" by environmental input (poverty of the stimulus), and (3) they appear to be specific to language, they make the curious deduction that there are only two possible explanations for the universal principles: "Either universal grammar was endowed to us directly by the Creator, or else our species has undergone a mutation of unprecedented magnitude, a cognitive equivalent of the Big Bang" (Bates, Thal, and Marchman, 1991:30). How do the authors derive one mutation from assumptions (1)–(3)? How do they calculate their mutation rate? It sounds like the number was picked out of the air. Why not pick 6 or 1,039 mutations out of the air instead? They then find themselves in a "dilemma." To get out of the quandary they put themselves in, they make another dubious move. They propose throwing out the principles-and-parameters model along with thirty years worth of strong evidence gathered from thousands of languages and dialects through comparative studies of syntax, semantics, phonology, acquisition studies, etc.

In its place, they suggest substituting a vaguely specified connectionist model, whose main virtue is that it can mimic the process of forming past tenses (walk → walked) with partial success. Bates, Thal, and Marchman have thrown out the baby out with the bathwater. Of course, as we saw in chapter 3, the hope of Bates and some connectionists is that the connectionist model will someday exhibit even greater abilities, perhaps including many other cognitive domains. That newer "probabilistic systems" are "far more powerful" than "simple nets of old" is not in doubt. Unconstrained probabilistic systems are even capable of uncovering predictions of President Kennedy's assassination from the Torah, as we recently learned. The real problem is, as always, in restricting the power of one's acquisition model to pick out exactly those properties found in the universal language *Bauplan*. In fact, it is revealing that a study found that the performance of some neural networks (e.g., "Elman networks") was improved by providing the system with information from UG; i.e., "part-of-speech tagging" and "subcategorization" information. In addition, the network received information normally not given to the child; viz., grammaticality status (Lawrence, Giles, and Fong, 1997:4).[53]

Returning to Deacon, I think his term "argument from incredulity" better describes the proposal of Bates, Thal, and Marchman. Given the choice between an unconstrained connectionist net and the Creator, Deacon might be better off with the latter. Deacon adds a second argument of his own against the idea of a universal *Bauplan* of language. He

---

[53] Although the authors claim that "the goal of the experiment is to train a model from scratch," without the "bifurcation into learned vs. innate components assumed by Chomsky," they have in effect given their network access to information from UG.

claims that arguments that attribute properties of language to "unana-lyzed brain structures" pass the buck to neurologists. However, this is simply science as usual. The idea of a universal *Bauplan* for animals and plants goes back centuries, yet it is only in the last ten years that develop-mental biologists have been able to work out the physical details in terms of homeobox genes and the like. Similarly, it took nearly a hundred years to discover the physical basis for Mendel's factors. The understanding of genetic inheritance in terms of computations with factors was years ahead of a comparable understanding in terms of biochemistry and quantum chemistry (3–D structure and bonding). It wouldn't be in the least sur-prising to find that we are in the same situation with the language *Bauplan* and the mental computations of language. As for Deacon's charge (1992:51) that (bio)linguists "stifle serious attempts to explain these phe-nomena in functional and semiotic terms," Deacon should feel free to pick up a copy of *Linguistic Inquiry* or any other journal with specific pro-posals about the principles of UG and try explaining them in functional and semiotic constraints as an exercise. If he succeeds in doing that, we can then judge whether that helps us to analyze his constraints in terms of "brain structures," without passing the buck on to others. Deacon's studies of the neural circuits of primates with various tracer techniques are a valuable window on the brain and may well someday help lead to the answers about the mechanisms of human language. But these studies will quite likely have to be supplemented by many other advances in neurol-ogy, neurogenetics, and developmental neurobiology before we will be able to pose and answer the questions about the language *Bauplan* that we are most interested in. Flippant charges about "creationist explanation" (Bates, Thal, and Marchman) and "some neurological mutation" do not help us move towards that goal.

Deacon juxtaposes "the hopeful monster" theory with the idea that lan-guage must have been selected for: "If symbolic communication did not arise due to a "hopeful monster" mutation of the brain, it must have been selected for" (Deacon, 1997:376). Why this bizarre dichotomy, and not some other? In Deacon's mind, standard theories of UG necessarily entail "hopeful monster" mutations. By fiat, Deacon declares that "no innate rules, no innate general principles, no innate symbolic categories can be built in by evolution." Grammars are shielded "from the reach of natural selection" (p. 339). Needless to say, Deacon's own innate learning biases are within the reach of natural selection. Again, we are playing more word games with the word "innate," which we can dispense with along with the language viruses. Once we do so, we can get on with the standard scientific problem of determining the design features of language and considering the contribution of genetics, development, and other physical and selective factors in the evolution of the language faculty. As we noted earlier, Chomsky has proposed that certain design features of human language could have arisen through "shift of function"[54] and subsequently come under selectional pressure. Thus it appears that only Deacon and some of the connectionists are left in a meaningless and muddled debate about "hopeful monsters."

[54] Jeremy Ahouse has noted (p.c.) that "shift of function" is more perspicuous and less misleading than more traditional terminology such as "preadaptation," and I adopt this terminology throughout.

6   Conclusion

In this book we have investigated aspects of the "five fundamental problems of biolinguistics":
(1) What constitutes knowledge of language?
(2) How is this knowledge acquired?
(3) How is this knowledge put to use?
(4) What are the relevant brain mechanisms?
(5) How does this knowledge evolve (in the species)?
As we have seen these comprise the classical questions asked about any biological system: (1) structure of the system, its function, and its use, (2) its development, and (3) its evolution. Our system of interest is language, so the areas pertinent to biolinguistics are (1) language, (2) development of language, and (3) evolution of language.

We have asked how the answers to these questions might be at least partially unified with each other and integrated into the natural sciences. We have argued that the evidence points toward a picture of unification in which there are a variety of cognitive systems, including language, each having its own specific properties and mechanisms. The available evidence appears to argue against the idea of a homogeneous and general purpose cognitive system designed to learn language, American history, and basket-weaving, or, as some would argue, even pigeon behavior.

We have also argued that the evidence for biolinguistics should include any and all relevant evidence. This is dictated by the constraint that scientific theories typically are radically underdetermined by evidence so we seek evidence wherever it is available. So, for example, in order to choose between particular formulations of a theory of English syntax, we can, and typically do, consider evidence from Japanese, Mohawk, Turkish, or any of the numerous other languages that have been investigated over the last forty years from the biolinguistic perspective. Evidence has been drawn from studies of: universal and comparative grammar (syntax, semantics, morphology, lexicon, phonetics, phonology), acquisition in children, psycholinguistic tests, perceptual studies, articulatory and acoustic phonetics, brain injuries and diseases (aphasias, aprosodias, etc.), split-brains, language-isolated children (Genie)[1], developmental disorders (Laura, etc.), electrical activity (e.g., ERPs), imaging (PET, MRI, etc.),[2] genetic disorders (sporadic and familial), twin studies, language in the deaf (sign-language), language in the blind, linguistic savants, pidgin and creole languages. Note that all of these categories of evidence cross-cut. For example, included among twin studies are studies of both normal and disordered speech. Or, the study of sign-language can include sign-language in aphasics, sign-language in the language-isolated (e.g., the case of Chelsea), and sign-language in linguistic savants. The list of sources of evidence is essentially open-ended, new evidence perhaps appearing in this week's issue of *Nature, Science, Cell, Evolution, Linguistic Inquiry*, etc.

Note also that our discussion here is not limited to any one specific linguistic approach to the analysis of language. There are a variety of linguistic models under investigation for different domains of language: syntax, semantics, morphology, lexicon, phonetics, phonology. For example, in addition to the many alternatives that explicitly assume a principles-and-parameters approach to the study of UG and/or a minimalist program in the discussion of language design, there are a number of models under investigation that implicitly assume these ideas; e.g., in the area of syntax, we have, among others, Lexical Functional Grammar (LFG), Generalized Phrase Structure Grammar (CPSG), and Categorial Grammar. These models, regarded as biological theories of the language faculty, also attempt to account for (1) the universality versus the diversity of human language and (2) language design. Each of these theories can be interpreted as a theory of language acquisition with an initial state and parametric variation. They can all be instantiated in parsing and processing theories. They also can all be used to interpret data from specific language disorders, aphasia, etc. In fact, each one has ways to describe specific antecedent–anaphor relations, phrase dislocation, word order, Case, etc. across a variety of languages, from English to Mohawk to Turkish. Of course, a fair question is to what degree all these various approaches might fall together at some level, another aspect of the unification problem for language that is on the research agenda.

In order to answer question (1) "What constitutes knowledge of language?," it was first necessary to say what is meant by "language." We found that it made sense to regard the mind/brain as a set of interacting modules, including the language faculty, the number faculty, the visual

---

[1] A language-isolated child who was discovered at age thirteen and who was unable to develop more than a rudimentary syntax (Curtiss, 1977).

[2] ERP = event-related potential, PET = positron emission tomography, MRI = magnetic resonance imaging.

system, etc. (*modularity*). The evidence for distinguishing a language faculty comes in part from studies of the dissociation of language abilities from other abilities, but perhaps primarily from the demonstration of properties intrinsic to the language faculty (the principles-and-parameters model). We also set aside the study of such issues as free will and causation of behavior (Descartes' problem).

We next identified a cognitive system in the language faculty, abstracting away from performance systems; viz., C–I, the conceptual–intentional component, and A–P, the articulatory–perceptual component. The cognitive system passes through a series of intermediate states $(S_0 \ldots S_i \ldots S_n)$. We can distinguish an initial state, S_0, from a final state, S_n, by using all the kinds of evidence discussed above. We can identify the intermediate states, S_i, by acquisition studies in children, using similar kinds of evidence. Abstracting away from gross pathology as well as individual variation, the theory of the initial state is represented by the principles-and-parameters model of UG. During acquisition the parameters in UG are set, resulting in a system called I-language, or simply language, in the final state of the adult. I-language is not identical to the final state, S_n, but abstracts away from factors such as heterogeneity (multiple dialects, speech registers, etc.) as well as historical factors.

Once we have identified a genetic component of language, given by the theory of UG, we can then turn to ask about genetic mechanisms. Here we noted that one must take into account the interplay of genetic and "epigenetic" factors. That is, we must consider not only what genes are involved in language, but how the genetic program unfolds in the physical world, which may include a whole host of factors, such as genetic background, laws of physics, social environment, etc. We gave as examples symmetry-breaking in the evolution of the genetic code and Turing's notion of a morphogenetic field.

We suggested that to study the genes involved in language, one should look at (1) the principles of UG; e.g., the operation of hierarchical concatenation (Merge), conditions on pronominal reference (c-command), etc. and (2) the areas where UG permits parametric variation. Evidence has been put forth that the source for this variation is in the lexicon, in particular in the functional part of the lexicon, involving such morphological categories, as inflection. Hence it would be predicted that some harmless genetic variation might be permitted in this area, much as we find variation in color perception, the tasting of PTC, etc. We also noted that genetic methodology has reached a point where one can seriously contemplate studying the genes involved in language, and hence indirectly, the developmental genetics of language.

Finally, the question of language evolution was considered. The first step was to identify features of language design. For example, the computational model has a number of design properties such as the operation of Merge, with associated properties (recursion, cyclicity). Development of language, as we saw, also exhibits a kind of division of labor between general principles that account for the universality of language and some parameterization, perhaps in the inflectional system of the lexicon, which accounts for the diversity of language.

The question of how such design features evolved is more difficult to answer. There are no early fossils of the language faculty and the course of evolution depends on many different kinds of factors, including historical accidents that we cannot always reconstruct. Some of these factors include genetic mutation, genetic regulation, developmental constraints, physical factors, natural selection, historical contingencies, etc. Hence, the answers to some questions may remain speculative and other areas of inquiry might remain mysteries.

But there are a number of directions that one might investigate. For example, we suggested that one might explore the role of symmetry-breaking in the development and evolution of language. And, as we noted earlier, Chomsky suggested that "shift of function" might have played a role in the evolution of language. In recent years many other examples of such shift of function have been documented in biological systems. Under one scenario, Chomsky suggested that human language might have resulted from the integration of a "conceptual capacity" with a "computational capacity," that could deal "with discrete infinities through recursive rules" (Huybregts and Riemsdijk, 1982). The conceptual capacity that we share(d) with other primates "permits us to perceive, and categorize, and symbolize maybe even to reason in an elementary way, but it is only when linked to the computational capacity that the system really becomes powerful" (p. 20).

In current theories, the central recursive rule of the computational system is Merge. Merge takes (sub)lexical items and computes larger structures (words, phrases, and sentences) from them. These structures are subsequently mapped onto sound and meaning. In these terms, Chomsky's account of the emergence of human language might have as one central element the following:

conceptual capacity + Merge/Move operations → human language

The "shift of function" in this case would be to "the capacity for thought, planning, evaluation, and so on, over an unbounded range, and then you have a totally new organism" (Huybregts and Riemsdijk, 1982:21).

When might we hope to have some understanding of problems such as what Marshall has termed the "anatomy of WH-movement" (Marshall,

1980)? David Hubel, a pioneer in the study of the brain's visual system, has reflected on the future prospects for the study of the neurobiology of the brain:

How long it will be before one is able to say that the brain – or the mind – is in broad outline understood . . . is anyone's guess . . . A revolution of truly Copernican or Darwinian proportions may never come in neurobiology, at least not in a single stroke. If there is one, it may be gradual, having its effect over many decades. Every stage will surely bring human beings closer to an understanding of themselves. (Hubel, 1979:46)

Not to end on too pessimistic a note let us remember that science also occasionally moves in unpredictable spurts forward, as we are reminded by the story concerning the "anatomy" of the chemical syntax of DNA. As recently as 1968, Chargaff, whose important work on the chemical composition of DNA helped to guide Crick and Watson to deduce the structure of DNA, commented in a review assessing the current state of the field of DNA research, with some pessimism (quoted in Maxam, 1983:133):

A detailed determination of the nucleotide sequence of a DNA molecule is beyond our present means, nor is it likely to occur in the near future . . . Even the smallest functional DNA varieties seen, those occurring in certain small phages, must contain something like 5000 nucleotides in a row. We may, therefore, leave the task of reading the complete nucleotide sequence of a DNA to the 21st Century which will, however, have other worries. (Chargaff, 1968:310)

However, not many years later Maxam was able to report that

Ten years of effort to find a thoroughgoing method for sequencing DNA culminated in 1975–1977 with the introduction of three in succession . . . we have discovered a regulatory syntax in one dialect, prokaryotic, but not in the other, eukaryotic . . . it was mainly this wish to learn DNA syntax, how it programs its own transcription, replication, and recombination, that sustained the search for easy ways to sequence DNA and RNA. (Maxam, 1980)

In essence the problem confronting the biolinguist is quite similar to that of the molecular biologist seeking to understand the dialects of prokaryotes and eukaryotes; viz., to reveal the "regulatory syntax" of UG, the yet unknown developmental nervous pathways, which are set into motion by cellular and linguistic parameters. And, ultimately, to understand better human language, we can also be helped along by a better understanding of the language of the cell. For the key to a complete unraveling of the physical mechanisms underlying language and other cognitive abilities in the nervous system will depend in part on our ability to use molecular grammar to isolate, study, and characterize those stretches of DNA in our genome which contain the genetic program underlying language.

We may then try to begin to answer the question – to rephrase Brenner – of how a fertilized egg with 10^9 nucleotide pairs of DNA can learn a language.[3]

Twenty years ago, in a book of essays in honor of Eric Lenneberg, Chomsky spoke of the prospects for the field of biolinguistics. His words have proven true, as we hope to have shown, but also remain valid for the current generation of biolinguists:

The study of the biological basis for human language capacities may prove to be one of the most exciting frontiers of science in coming years. (Chomsky, 1976, 1980a:216)

---

[3] The relevant portion of the original citation reads "how a fertilized egg with 10^9 nucleotide pairs of DNA can make a human being" (Brenner, 1979:3).

References

Alberts, B., Bray, D., Lewis, J., Raff, M., Roberts, K., and Watson, J. D. (1994) *Molecular Biology of the Cell*. New York: Garland.

Amaducci, L., Sorbi, S., Albanese, A., and Gainotti, G. (1981) Choline Acetyltransferase (CAT) Activity Differs in Right and Left Human Temporal Lobes. *Neurology* **31**, 799–805.

Amundson, R. (1994) Two Concepts of Constraint: Adaptationism and the Challenge from Developmental Biology. *Philosophy of Science* **61**(4), 556–78.

Anderson, P. W. (1972) More Is Different. *Science* **177**(4047), 393–96.

   (1981) Some General Thoughts About Broken Symmetry. In N. Boccara (ed.), *Symmetries and Broken Symmetries in Condensed Matter Physics*, pp. 11–20. Paris: IDSET.

   (1994) Theoretical Paradigms for the Sciences of Complexity. In *A Career in Theoretical Physics*, pp. 584–93. Singapore: World Scientific.

AP Report (1998) Bonobos Use Symbols to Mark Jungle Trails. http://forests.org/gopher/africa/apesmark.txt

Atkins, P. W. (1994) *Creation Revisited*. London: Penguin.

Ball, P. (1994) *Designing the Molecular World: Chemistry at the Frontier*. Princeton: Princeton University Press.

Bates, E., and Elman, J. (1996) Learning Rediscovered. *Science* **274**(5294), 1849–50.

Bates, E., Thal, D., and Marchman, V. (1991) Symbols and Syntax: a Darwinian Approach to Language Development. In N. A. Krasnegor, D. M. Rumbaugh, R. L. Schiefelbusch, and M. Studdert-Kennedy (eds.), *Biological and Behavioral Determinants of Language Development*, pp. 29–65. Hillsdale, NJ: Lawrence Erlbaum Associates.

Bauman, M., and Kemper, T. L. (1985) Histoanatomic Observations of the Brain in Early Infantile Autism. *Neurology* **35**(6), 866–74.

Beadle, G., and Beadle, M. (1979) *The Language of Life*. New York: Anchor.

Beheim-Schwarzbach, D. (1975) Further Studies of the Cytoarchitectonic Division in the Dorsal Surface of the 1st Temporal Gyrus of a Linguistic Genius and 2 Anthropoids. *Zeitschrift für Mikroskopisch-Anatomische Forschung* **89**(5), 759–76.

Bellugi, U., Bihrle, A., Jernigan, T., Trauner, D., and Doherty, S. (1990) Neuropsychological, Neurological, and Neuroanatomical Profile of Williams Syndrome. *American Journal of Medical Genetics Supplement* **6**, 115–25.

Bentley, D. R., and Hoy, R. R. (1972) Genetic Control of the Neuronal Network

Generating Cricket (*Teleogryllus gryllus*) Song Patterns. *Animal Behavior* **20**, 478–92.

Berger, B., Shor, P. W., Tucker-Kellogg, L., and King, J. (1994) Local Rule-Based Theory of Virus Shell Assembly. *Proceedings of the National Academy of Sciences USA* **91**(16), 7732–6.

Berwick, R. C. (1982) Locality Principles and the Acquisition of Syntactic Knowledge. Doctoral dissertation, MIT, Cambridge, MA.

Berwick, R. C., Abney, S. P., and Tenny, C. (eds.) (1992) *Principle-Based Parsing: Computation and Psycholinguistics*. Dordrecht: Kluwer Academic.

Berwick, R. C., and Weinberg, A. S. (1983) The Role of Grammars in Models of Language Use. *Cognition* **13**(1), 1–61.

(1984) *The Grammatical Basis of Linguistic Performance: Language Use and Acquisition*. Cambridge, MA: MIT Press.

Bickerton, D. (1984) The Language Biogram Hypothesis. *Behavioral and Brain Sciences* **7**(2), 173–221.

(1990) *Language and Species*. Chicago: University of Chicago Press.

Bisgaard, M. L., Eiberg, H., Moller, N., Niebahr, E., and Mohr, J. (1987) Dyslexia and Chromosome 15 Heteromorphism: Negative Lod Score in a Danish Study. *Clinical Genetics* **32**, 118–19.

Bishop, D. V. M. (1997) Listening Out for Subtle Deficits. *Nature* **387**(6629), 129–30.

Bitoun, P., Philippe, C., Cherif, M., Mulcahy, M.-T., and Gilgenkrantz, S. (1992) *Incontinentia pigmenti* (type 1) and X;5 translocation. *Annales de Génétique* **35**(1), 51–54.

Blakeslee, S. (1998) Brain of Chimpanzee Sheds Light on Mystery of Language. *New York Times*, January 13, p. C3.

Bloom, P. (ed.) (1994) *Language Acquisition: Core Readings*. Cambridge, MA: MIT Press.

Bobaljik, J. D. (1995) Morphosyntax: the Syntax of Verbal Inflection. Doctoral dissertation, MIT, Cambridge, MA.

Boller, F., and Green, E. (1972) Comprehension in Severe Aphasics. *Cortex* **8**(4), 382–94.

Borges-Osório, M. R. L., and Salzano, F. M. (1985) Language Disabilities in Three Twin Pairs and their Relatives. *Acta Geneticae Medicae et Gemellologiae* **34**, 95–100.

Boxer, S. (1985) Food for Thought: Does the Brain Have a Produce Section? *Discover*, October, p. 10.

Bradshaw, J. L., and Rogers, L. J. (1993) *The Evolution of Lateral Asymmetries, Language, Tool Use, and Intellect*. San Diego: Academic Press.

Brenner, S. (1979) Introduction. In R. Porter and M. O'Connor (eds.), *Human Genetics: Possibilities and Realities*, pp. 1–3. Amsterdam: Excerpta Medica.

Brewer, W. F., Jr. (1963) Specific Language Disability: Review of the Literature and Family Study. Honors Thesis, Harvard College.

Broca, P. (1861) Remarques sur le siège de la faculté du langage articulé; suivies d'une observation d'aphémie (perte de la parole). *Bulletins de la Société Anatomique de Paris, 2ème série* **6**, 330–57.

Brockman, J. (1995) *The Third Culture: Beyond the Scientific Revolution*. New York: Simon and Schuster.

Butterworth, B. (1983) Biological Twists to Grammar. *New Scientist* **100**(1380), 187.

Calvin, W. H., and Ojemann, G. A. (1994) *Conversations with Neil's Brain.* Reading, MA: Addison-Wesley.

Caplan, D., and Chomsky, N. (1980) Linguistic Perspectives on Language Development. In D. Caplan (ed.), *Biological Studies of Mental Processes,* pp. 97–105. Cambridge, MA: MIT Press.

Caramazza, A. (1996) The Brain's Dictionary. *Nature* **380**(6574), 485–86.

Chargaff, E. (1968) What Really is DNA? In J. N. Davidson and W. E. Cohn (eds.), *Progress in Nucleic Acid Research and Molecular Biology,* pp. 297–333. New York: Academic Press.

Chi, J. G., Dooling, E. C., and Gilles, F. H. (1977) Gyral Development of the Human Brain. *Annals of Neurology* **1**(1), 86–93.

Chomsky, N. (1957) *Syntactic Structures.* The Hague: Mouton.

  (1959) A Review of B. F. Skinner's *Verbal Behavior. Language* **35**(1), 26–58.

  (1964) A Review of B. F. Skinner's *Verbal Behavior.* In J. A. Fodor and J. J. Katz (eds.), *The Structure of Language: Readings in the Philosophy of Language,* pp. 547–78. Englewood Cliffs, NJ: Prentice-Hall.

  (1965) *Aspects of the Theory of Syntax.* Cambridge, MA: MIT Press.

  (1966) *Cartesian Linguistics.* New York: Harper and Row.

  (1968) *Language and Mind.* New York: Harcourt, Brace and World.

  (1975a) *The Logical Structure of Linguistic Theory.* Chicago: University of Chicago Press.

  (1975b) *Reflections on Language.* New York: Pantheon.

  (1976) On the Biological Basis of Language Capacities. In R. W. Rieber (ed.), *The Neuropsychology of Language: Essays in Honor of Eric Lenneberg,* pp. 1–24. New York: Plenum.

  (1978) An Interview with Noam Chomsky. *Linguistic Analysis* **4**(4), 301–19.

  (1979) *Language and Responsibility: Conversations with Mitsou Ronat.* New York: Pantheon.

  (1980a) On the Biological Basis of Language Capacities. In *Rules and Representations,* pp. 185–216. New York: Columbia University Press.

  (1980b) Rules and Representations. *The Behavioral and Brain Sciences* **3**(1), 1–61.

  (1980c) *Rules and Representations.* New York: Columbia University Press.

  (1981) *Lectures on Government and Binding.* Dordrecht: Foris.

  (1983) Things No Amount of Learning Can Teach. In C. P. Otero (ed.), *Noam Chomsky: Language and Politics,* pp. 407–19. Montreal: Black Rose.

  (1986) *Knowledge of Language: its Nature, Origins, and Use.* New York: Praeger.

  (1988a) *Language and Problems of Knowledge: The Managua Lectures.* Cambridge, MA: MIT Press.

  (1988b) Language and the Human Mind. In C. P. Otero (ed.), *Language and Politics,* pp. 253–75. Montreal: Black Rose.

  (1990) On Formalization and Formal Linguistics. *Natural Language and Linguistic Theory* **8**(1), 143–47.

  (1991a) Linguistics and Adjacent Fields: a Personal View. In A. Kasher (ed.), *The Chomskyan Turn,* pp. 3–25. Cambridge, MA: Basil Blackwell.

  (1991b) Linguistics and Cognitive Science: Problems and Mysteries. In A.

Kasher (ed.), *The Chomskyan Turn*, pp. 26–53. Cambridge, MA: Basil Blackwell.

(1992) Language and Interpretation: Philosophical Reflections and Empirical Inquiry. In J. Earman (ed.), *Inference, Explanation, and Other Frustrations*, pp. 99–128. Berkeley: University of California Press.

(1993) A Minimalist Program for Linguistic Theory. In K. Hale and S. J. Keyser (eds.), *The View from Building 20*, Cambridge, MA: MIT Press.

(1994a) *Language and Thought*. Wakefield, Rhode Island, and London: Moyer Bell.

(1994b) Naturalism and Dualism in the Study of Language and Mind. *International Journal of Philosophical Studies* 2(2), 181–209.

(1995a) Language and Nature. *Mind* 104(413), 1–61.

(1995b) *The Minimalist Program*. Cambridge, MA: MIT Press.

(1996a) Language and Thought: some Reflections on Venerable Themes. In *Powers and Prospects: Reflections on Human Nature and the Social Order*, Boston: South End Press.

(1996b) Some Observations on Economy in Generative Grammar. Published in P. Barbosa, D. Fox, P. Hagstrm, M. McGinnis, and D. Pesetsky (eds.) (1998), *Is the Best Good Enough?: Optimality and Competition in Syntax*, pp. 115–27. Cambridge, MA: MIT Press and MIT Working Papers in Linguistics.

(1996c) Language and Evolution (Reply to Maynard Smith). *New York Review of Books*, February 1, p. 41.

(1997a) Language and Cognition. In D. M. Johnson and C. E. Erneling (eds.), *The Future of the Cognitive Revolution*, pp. 15–31. New York: Oxford University Press.

(1997b) Language and Mind: Current Thoughts on Ancient Problems. *Pesquisa Linguistica* 3(4).

(1997c) Language from an Internalist Perspective. In D. M. Johnson and C. E. Erneling (eds.), *The Future of the Cognitive Revolution*, pp. 118 35. New York: Oxford University Press.

Chomsky, N., and Halle, M. (1964) *The Sound Pattern of English*. Cambridge, MA: MIT Press.

Chomsky, N., and Lasnik, H. (1977) Filters and Control. *Linguistic Inquiry* 8(3), 425–504.

(1993) The Theory of Principles and Parameters. In J. Jacobs, A. von Stechow, W. Sternefeld, and T. Vennemann (eds.), *Syntax: an International Handbook of Contemporary Research*, pp. 506–69. Berlin: de Gruyter. (Reprinted in Chomsky, 1995b).

Chomsky, N., and Miller, G. A. (1963) Introduction to the Formal Analysis of Natural Languages. In R. D. Luce, R. Bush, and E. Galanter (eds.), *Handbook of Mathematical Psychology*, pp. 269–322. New York: John Wiley.

Christiansen, M. H. (forthcoming) *Language. as an Organism: Implications for the Evolution and Acquisition of Language*. http://www-rcf.usc.edu/~mortenc/lang-org.html.

Cohen, J., and Stewart, I. (1994) *The Collapse of Chaos*. New York: Viking.

Collado-Vides, J., Magasanik, B., and Smith, T. F. (eds.) (1996) *Integrative Approaches to Molecular Biology*. Cambridge, MA: MIT Press.

Collins, C. (1997) *Local Economy*. Cambridge, MA: MIT Press.

Comery, T. A., Harris, J. B., Willems, P. J., Oostra, B. A., Irwin, S. A., Weiler, I. J., and Greenough, W. T. (1997) Abnormal Dendritic Spines in Fragile X Knockout Mice: Maturation and Pruning Deficits. *Proceedings of the National Academy of Sciences USA* **94**(10), 5401–04.

Coopmans, P. (1984) Surface Word-Order Typology and Universal Grammar. *Language* **60**(1), 55–69.

Corballis, M. C. (1991) *The Lopsided Ape, Evolution of the Generative Mind*. New York: Oxford University Press.

Coveney, P., and Highfield, R. (1995) *Frontiers of Complexity*. New York: Random House.

Crease, R. P., and Mann, C. C. (1987) *The Second Creation*. New York: MacMillan.

Crick, F. (1995) *The Astonishing Hypothesis: the Scientific Search for the Soul*. New York: Simon and Schuster.

Cunningham, D. J. (1892) *Contribution to the Surface Anatomy of the Cerebral Hemispheres, Cunningham Memoirs*. Dublin: Royal Irish Academy of Science.

Curtiss, S. (1977) *Genie: a Psycholinguistic Study of a Modern Day "Wild Child."* New York: Academic Press.

(1981) Dissociations between Language and Cognition. *Journal of Autism and Developmental Disorders* **11**, 15–30.

Cziko, G. (1995) *Without Miracles: Universal Selection Theory and the Second Darwinian Revolution*. Cambridge, MA: MIT Press.

Damasio, A., and Damasio, H. (1992) Brain and Language. *Scientific American* **267**(3), 89–95.

Damasio, H., Grabowski, T. J., Tranel, D., Hichwa, R. D., and Damasio, A. R. (1996) A Neural Basis for Lexical Retrieval. *Nature* **380**(6574), 499–505.

Däniken, E. v. (1970) *Chariots of the Gods?: Unsolved Mysteries of the Past*. New York: G. P. Putnam's Sons.

Davidoff, J. (1991) *Cognition and Color*. Cambridge, MA: MIT Press.

Davis, P. J., and Hersh, R. (1981) *The Mathematical Experience*. Boston: Houghton Mifflin.

Deacon, T. W. (1992) Brain–Language Coevolution. In J. A. Hawkins and M. Gell-Mann (eds.), *The Evolution of Human Languages*, pp. 49–83. Redwood City, CA: Addison-Wesley.

(1997) *The Symbolic Species: the Co-Evolution of Language and the Brain*. New York: W. W. Norton.

DeFries, J. C., Fulker, D. W., and LaBuda, M. C. (1987) Evidence for a Genetic Aetiology in Reading Disability of Twins. *Nature* **329**(6139), 537–39.

Dennett, D. C. (1995) *Darwin's Dangerous Idea*. New York: Simon and Schuster.

(1996) The Scope of Natural Selection. *Boston Review*, October/November, pp. 34–36.

Dennis, M., and Whitaker, H. (1976) Language Acquisition Following Hemidecortication: Linguistic Superiority of the Left Over the Right Hemisphere. *Brain and Language* **3**, 404–33.

Devlin, K. (1996a) Are Mathematicians Turning Soft. *Focus*, April 1. http://www.maa.org/devlin.devlinangle.april.html.

(1996b) Soft Mathematics: the Mathematics of People. Resources for Math and Decision Making: Original Articles, Mathematics Awareness Week 1996. http://forum.swarthmore.edu/social/articles/softmath.short.html.

(1997) *Goodbye, Descartes.* New York: John Wiley.

Dobzhansky, T. (1962) *Mankind Evolving: the Evolution of the Human Species.* New Haven: Yale University Press.

Donald, M. (1991) *Origins of the Modern Mind.* Cambridge, MA: Harvard University Press.

Douady, S., and Couder, Y. (1992) Phyllotaxis as a Physical Self-Organized Growth Process. *Physical Review Letters* **68**, 2098–101.

(1993a) La Physique des Spirales Végétales. *La Recherche* **24**(250), 26–35.

(1993b) Phyllotaxis as a Physical Self-Organized Growth Process. In J. M. Garcia-Ruiz (ed.), *Growth Patterns in Physical Sciences and Biology,* pp. 341–52. New York: Plenum.

Dreifus, C. (1998) She Talks to Apes and, According to Her, They Talk Back. *New York Times,* April 14, p. C4.

Duboule, D. (1994) How to Make a Limb? *Science* **266**(5182), 575–76.

Dunne, P. W., Doody, R., Gopnik, M., and Ashizawa, T. (1993) Simulation Analysis of a Large British Pedigree Segregating a Newly Characterized Autosomal Dominant Language Disorder: Familial Developmental Dysphasia. *American Journal of Human Genetics* **53**(3), 1692.

Dyson, F. J. (1964) Mathematics in the Physical Sciences. *Scientific American* **211**(3), 128–46.

Eddington, A. (1935) *New Pathways in Science.* Cambridge: Cambridge University Press.

Eibl-Eibesfeldt, I. (1970) *Ethology: the Biology of Behavior.* New York: Holt, Rinehart and Winston.

Eidelberg, D., and Galaburda, A. M. (1982) Symmetry and Asymmetry in the Human Posterior Thalamus, I. Cytoarchitectonic Analysis in Normal Persons. *Archives of Neurology* **39**, 325–32.

Eigen, M., and Winkler, R. (1983) *Laws of the Game: how the Principles of Nature Govern Change.* New York: Harper and Row.

Einstein, A. (1996) The Fundamentals of Theoretical Physics. In *The Theory of Relativity and Other Essays,* pp. 53–65. New York: Citadel.

Eldredge, N. (1995) *Reinventing Darwin: the Great Debate at the High Table of Evolutionary Theory.* New York: John Wiley and Sons.

Elman, J. L., Bates, E. A., Johnson, M. H., Karmiloff-Smith, A., Parisi, D., and Plunkett, K. (1996) *Rethinking Innateness.* Cambridge, MA: MIT Press.

Eustis, R. S. (1947) The Primary Etiology of the Specific Language Disabilities. *The Journal of Pediatrics* **31**(4), 448–55.

Ewart, A. K., Morris, C. A., Atkinson, D., Jin, W., Sternes, K., Spallone, P., Stock, A. D., Leppert, M., and Keating, M. T. (1993) Hemizygosity at the Elastin Locus in a Developmental Disorder, Williams Syndrome. *Nature Genetics* **5**(1), 11–16.

Finucci, J. M., and Childs, B. (1983) Dyslexia: Family Studies. In C. Ludlow and J. A. Cooper (eds.), *Genetic Aspects of Speech and Language Disorders,* pp. 157–67. New York: Academic Press.

Fisher, S. E.,Vargha-Khadem, F.,Watkins, K. E., Monaco,A. P., and Pembrey, M. E. (1998) Localisation of a Gene Implicated in a Severe Speech and Language Disorder. *Nature Genetics* **18**, 168–70.

Frangiskakis, J. M., Ewart, A. K., Morris, C. A., Mervis, C. B., Bertrand, J., Robinson, B. F., Klein, B. P., Ensing, G. J., Everett, L. A., Green, E. D., Pröschel, C., Gutowski, N. J., Noble, M., Atkinson, D. L., Odelberg, S. J., and Keating, M. T. (1996) LIM-kinase1 Hemizygosity Implicated in ImpairedVisuospatial Constructive Cognition. *Cell* **86**(1), 59–69.

Fritzsch, H. (1983) *Quarks: the Stuff of Matter.* NewYork: Basic.

Froster, U., Schulte-Körne, G., Hebebrand, J., and Remschmidt, H. (1993) Cosegregation of Balanced Translocation (1;2) with Retarded Speech Development and Dyslexia. *Lancet* **342**(8864), 178–79.

Fukui, N. (1996) On the Nature of Economy in Language. *Cognitive Studies* **3**(1), 51–71.

Gajdusek, D. C., McKhann, G. M., and Bolis, L. C. (eds.) (1994) *Evolution and Neurology of Language.* Amsterdam: Elsevier.

Galaburda, A. M. (ed.) (1993) *Dyslexia and Development, Neurobiological Aspects of Extra-Ordinary Brains.* Cambridge, MA: Harvard University Press.

Galaburda, A. M., and Eidelberg, D. (1982) Symmetry and Asymmetry in the Human Posterior Thalamus, II. Thalamic Lesions in a Case of Developmental Dyslexia. *Archives of Neurology* **39**, 333–36.

Galaburda, A. M., and Geschwind, N. (1980) The Human Language Areas and Cerebral Asymmetries. *Revue Médicale de la Suisse Romande* **100**(2), 119–28.

(1981) Anatomical Asymmetries in the Adult and Developing Brain and their Implications for Function. In L. A. Barness (ed.), *Advances in Pediatrics,* pp. 271–92. Chicago:Year Book Medical.

Galaburda, A. M., and Kemper,T. L. (1979) Cytoarchitectonic Abnormalities in Developmental Dyslexia: a Case Study. *Annals of Neurology* **6**(2), 94–100.

Galaburda, A. M., Sanides, F., and Geschwind, N. (1978) Human Brain: Cytoarchitectonic Left–Right Asymmetries in the Temporal Speech Region. *Archives of Neurology* **35**(12), 812–17.

Galaburda, A. M., Wang, P. P., Bellugi, U., and Rossen, M. (1994) Cytoarchitectonic Anomalies in a Genetically Based Disorder: Williams Syndrome. *Neuroreport* **5**(7), 753–57.

Gallistel, C. R. (1993) *The Organization of Learning.* Cambridge, MA: MIT Press.

(1997) Neurons and Memory. In M. S. Gazzaniga (ed.), *Conversations in the Cognitive Neurosciences,* pp. 71–89. Cambridge, MA: MIT Press.

Gannon, P. J., Holloway, R. L., Broadfield, D. C., and Braun, A. R. (1998) Asymmetry of Chimpanzee PlanumTemporale: Humanlike Brain Pattern of Wernicke's Language Area Homolog. *Science* **279**(5348), 220–22.

Gazzaniga, M. S. (1994) Language and the Cerebral Hemispheres. In D. C. Gajdusek, G. M. McKhann, and L. C. Bolis (eds.), *Evolution and Neurology of Language,* pp. 106–9. Amsterdam: Elsevier.

(1998) *The Mind's Past.* Berkeley: University of California Press.

Gedeon, A. K., Keinänen, M., Adès, L. C., Kääriäinen, H., Gécz, J., Baker, E., Sutherland, G. R., and Mulley, J. C. (1995) Overlapping Submicroscopic

Deletions in Xq28 in Two Unrelated Boys with Developmental Disorders: Identification of a Gene Near FRAXE. *American Journal of Human Genetics* **56**(4), 907–14.

Gell-Mann, M. (1994) *The Quark and the Jaguar*. New York: W. H. Freeman.

Geschwind, N. (1972) Language and the Brain. *Scientific American* **226**(4), 76–83.

(1974) *Selected Papers on Language and the Brain*. Dordrecht: D. Reidel.

(1975) The Apraxias: Neural Mechanisms of Disorders of Learned Movement. *American Scientist* **63**, 188–95.

(1979a) Anatomical and Functional Specialization of the Cerebral Hemispheres in the Human. *Bulletin et Mémoires de l'Académie Royale de Médecine de Belgique* **134**(6), 286–97.

(1979b) Asymmetries of the Brain – New Developments. *Bulletin of the Orton Society* **29**, 67–73.

(1979c) Specializations of the Human Brain. *Scientific American* **241**(3), 180–99.

(1983a) Biological Foundations of Cerebral Dominance. *Trends in Neurosciences* **6**(9), 354–56.

(1983b) The Organisation of the Living Brain. In J. Miller (ed.), *States of Mind*, pp. 116–34. New York: Pantheon.

Geschwind, N., and Behan, P. O. (1982) Left-handedness: Association with Immune Disease, Migraine, and Developmental Learning Disorder. *Proceedings of the National Academy of Sciences USA* **79**(16), 5097–100.

(1984) Laterality, Hormones, and Immunity. In N. Geschwind and A. M. Galaburda (eds.), *Cerebral Dominance: the Biological Foundations*, pp. 211–24. Cambridge, MA: Harvard University Press.

Geschwind, N., and Galaburda, A. M. (eds.) (1984) *Cerebral Dominance: the Biological Foundations*. Cambridge, MA: Harvard University Press.

(1987) *Cerebral Lateralization*. Cambridge, MA: MIT Press.

Geschwind, N., and Levitsky, W. (1968) Human Brain: Left–Right Asymmetries in Temporal Speech Region. *Science* **161**(3837), 186–87.

Gilbert, S. F. (1997) *Developmental Biology* (5th ed.). Sunderland, MA: Sinauer Associates.

Gilbert, S. F., Opitz, J. M., and Raff, R. A. (1996) Resynthesizing Evolutionary and Developmental Biology. *Developmental Biology* **173**(2), 357–72.

Glashow, S. L. (1994) *From Alchemy to Quarks*. Pacific Grove, CA: Brooks/Cole.

Glashow, S. L., with B. Bova (1988) *Interactions*. New York: Warner.

Gliedman, J. (1983) Interview: Noam Chomsky. *Omni*, November, p. 113–14, 116, 118, and 171–74.

Goldsmith, J. A. (ed.) (1995) *The Handbook of Phonological Theory*. Cambridge, MA: Blackwell.

Goodenough, U. (1978) *Genetics* (2nd ed.). New York: Holt, Rinehart and Winston.

Goodman, D. (1998) Similarities Found in Human, Chimp Brains. Unpublished manuscript. *http://www.columbia.edu/cu/pr*.

Goodwin, B. (1994) *How the Leopard Changed its Spots*. New York: Charles Scribner's Sons.

Gopnik, M. (1990) Feature Blindness: a Case Study. *Language Acquisition* **1**(2), 139–64.

Gopnik, M., and Crago, M. B. (1991) Familial Aggregation of a Developmental Language Disorder. *Cognition* **39**(1), 1–50.

Gould, J. L., and Marler, P. (1987) Learning by Instinct. *Scientific American* **256**(1), 74–85.

Gould, S. J. (1980) Natural Selection and the Human Brain: Darwin vs. Wallace. In *The Panda's Thumb*. New York: W.W. Norton.

(1994) Common Pathways of Illumination. *Natural History*, **103**(12), 10–20.

(1995) The Pattern of Life's History. In J. Brockman (ed.), *The Third Culture*, pp. 51–73. New York: Simon and Schuster.

(1997a) Darwinian Fundamentalism. *The New York Review of Books*, June 12, pp. 34–37.

(1997b) Evolution: the Pleasures of Pluralism. *The New York Review of Books*, June 26, pp. 47–52.

(1997c) As the Worm Turns. *Natural History* **106**(1), 24–27, 68–73.

Gould, S. J., and Lewontin, R. C. (1979) The Spandrels of San Marco and the Panglossian Paradigm: a Critique of the Adaptationist Programme. *Proceedings of the Royal Society* **B205**, 581–98.

Green, E., and Boller, F. (1974) Features of Auditory Comprehension in Severely Impaired Aphasics. *Cortex* **10**(2), 133–45.

Greenfield, P. M. (1991) Language, Tools and Brain: the Ontogeny and Phylogeny of Hierarchically Organized Sequential Behavior. *Behavioral and Brain Sciences* **14**(4), 531–95.

Greenspan, R. J. (1995) Understanding the Genetic Construction of Behavior. *Scientific American* **272**(4), 72–78.

Griffiths, A. J. F., Miller, J. H., Suzuki, D. T., Lewontin, R. C., and Gelbart, W. M. (1993) *An Introduction to Genetic Analysis* (5th ed.). New York: W. H. Freeman.

Guillen, M. (1995) *Five Equations that Changed the World*. New York: Hyperion.

Hackl, M. (1995) Verb-Zweit bei Agrammatismus – Zwei Fallstudien. MA Thesis, University of Vienna.

Haider, H. (1985a) The Case of German. In J. Toman (ed.), *Studies in German Grammar*, pp. 65–101. Dordrecht: Foris.

(1985b) A Unified Account of Case- and θ-Marking: the Case of German. *Papiere zur Linguistik* **321**, 3–36.

(1985c) Chance and Necessity in Diachronic Syntax – Word Order Typologies and the Position of Modern Persian Relative Clauses. In J. Fisiak (ed.), *Papers from the 6th International Conference on Historical Linguistics*, pp. 199–216. Amsterdam: Benjamins.

Håkansson, G. (1989) The Acquisition of Negative Placement in Swedish. *Studia Linguistica* **43**(1), 47–58.

Hallgren, B. (1950) Specific Dyslexia ("Congenital Word-Blindness"): a Clinical and Genetic Study. *Acta Psychiatrica et Neurologica (Scandinavica)*, supplement 65.

Hansen, S., Perry, T. L., and Wada, J. A. (1972) Amino Acid Analysis of Speech Areas in Human Brain: Absence of Left–Right Asymmetry. *Brain Research* **45**, 318–20.

Harnad, S. R., Steklis, H. S., and Lancaster, J. (eds.) (1976) *Origin and Evolution of Language and Speech*. New York: Annals of the New York Academy of Sciences.

Harris, Z. S. (1955) From Phoneme to Morpheme. *Language* 31(2), 190–222.

Hart, J., Jr., Berndt, R. S., and Caramazza, A. (1985) Category-Specific Naming Deficit Following Cerebral Infarction. *Nature* 316(6027), 439–40.

Hauser, M. D. (1996) *The Evolution of Communication*. Cambridge, MA: MIT Press.

Hayes, J. R., and Clark, H. H. (1970) Experiments on the Segmentation of an Artificial Speech Analogue. In J. R. Hayes (ed.), *Cognition and the Development of Language*, pp. 221–33. New York: John Wiley and Sons.

Heilman, K., Scholes, R., and Watson, R. (1975) Auditory affective agnosia. Disturbed Comprehension of Affective Speech. *Journal of Neurology, Neurosurgery and Psychiatry* 38(1), 69–72.

Heilman, K. M., and Satz, P. (eds.) (1983) *Neuropsychology of Human Emotion*. New York: Guilford Press.

Henley, E. M. (1996) Symmetries Throughout the Sciences. (Colloquium papers) USA 93, 14215–301.

Herbert, W. (1983) Scientists Find Hereditary Form of Dyslexia. *Science News* 123(12), 180.

Hermann, K. (1959) *Reading Disability: a Medical Study of Word-blindness and Related Handicaps*. Springfield, IL: Charles C. Thomas.

Hildebrandt, S., and Tromba, A. (1996) *The Parsimonious Universe*. New York: Springer–Verlag.

Hinds, H. L., Ashley, C. T., Sutcliffe, J. S., Nelson, D. L., Warren, S. T., Housman, D. E., and Schalling, M. (1993) Tissue Specific Expression of FMR-1 Provides Evidence for a Functional Role in Fragile X Syndrome. *Nature Genetics* 3(1), 36–43.

Ho-Kim, Q., Kumar, N., and Lam, C. S. (1991) *Invitation to Contemporary Physics*. Singapore: World Scientific.

Horgan, J. (1994) Gruff Guru of Condensed-Matter Physics. *Scientific American* 271(5), 34–35.

(1995) The New Social Darwinists. *Scientific American* 273(4), 174–81.

Hornos, J. E. M., and Hornos, Y. M. M. (1993) Algebraic Model for the Evolution of the Genetic Code. *Physical Review Letters* 71(26), 4401–404.

Housman, D., Kidd, K., and Gusella, J. F. (1982) Recombinant DNA Approach to Neurogenetic Disorders. *Trends in Neurosciences* 5(9), 320–23.

Hubel, D. (1996) A Big Step Along the Visual Pathway. *Nature* 380(6571), 197–98.

(1979) The Brain. *Scientific American* 241(3), 38–46.

(1988) *Eye, Brain, and Vision*. New York: W. H. Freeman.

Huber, W. (1978) A Neurolinguistic Look at Language Universals. In H. Seiler (ed.), *Language Universals,* pp. 185–206. Tübingen: Gunter Narr Verlag.

Hughes, C. P., Chan, J. L., and Su, M. S. (1983) Aprosodia in Chinese Patients With Right Cerebral Hemisphere Lesions. *Archives of Neurology* 40(12), 732–36.

Hurford, J. R. (1994a) Evolutionary Modelling of Language (Appendix) In D. C.

Gajdusek, G. M. McKhann, and L. C. Bolis (eds.), *Evolution and Neurology of Language*, pp. 149–57. Amsterdam: Elsevier.

(1994b) Linguistics and Evolution: a Background Briefing for Non-Linguists. In D. C. Gajdusek, G. M. McKhann, and L. C. Bolis (eds.), *Evolution and Neurology of Language*, pp. 158–68. Amsterdam: Elsevier.

Hurst, J. A., Baraitser, M., Auger, E., Graham, F., and Norell, S. (1990) An Extended Family with a Dominantly Inherited Speech Disorder. *Developmental Medicine and Child Neurology* 32(1), 352–55.

Huybregts, R., and Riemsdijk, H. C. van (eds.) (1982) *Noam Chomsky on the Generative Enterprise: a Discussion with Riny Huybregts and Henk van Riemsdijk*. Dordrecht: Foris.

Ingram, T. T. S. (1960) Paediatric Aspects of Specific Developmental Dysphasia, Dyslexia and Dysgraphia. *Cerebral Palsy Bulletin* 2(4), 254–77.

Jackendoff, R. (1994) *Patterns in the Mind*. New York: Basic HarperCollins.

Jacob, F. (1976) *The Logic of Life: a History of Heredity*. New York: Vintage.

(1977) Evolution and Tinkering. *Science* 196(4295), 1161–66.

(1978) Darwinism Reconsidered. *Atlas,* January (Translated from *Le Monde*, September 6–8, 1977).

(1982) *The Possible and the Actual*. Seattle: University of Washington Press.

Jenkins, J. B. (1975) *Genetics*. Boston: Houghton Mifflin.

Jenkins, L. (1972) Modality in English Syntax. Doctoral dissertation, MIT, Cambridge, MA.

(1979) The Genetics of Language. *Linguistics and Philosophy* 3, 105–19.

(1997) Biolinguistics – Structure, Development and Evolution of Language. In V. Solovyev (ed.), *The 40th Anniversary of Generativism*, Web Journal of Formal, Computational and Cognitive Linguistics 1.2. Department of Computer Science, Kazan State University.

Jenkins, L., and Maxam, A. (1997) Acquiring Language (Letter). *Science* 276(5316), 1178–79.

Jerne, N. K. (1967) Antibodies and Learning: Selection versus Instruction. In G. C. Quarton, T. Melnechuk, and F. O. Schmitt (eds.), *The Neurosciences: a Study Program,* pp. 200–05. New York: Rockefeller University Press.

(1985) The Generative Grammar of the Immune System. *Science* 229(4718), 1057–59.

Joos, M. (ed.) (1957) *Readings in Linguistics*. Washington: American Council of Learned Societies.

Jordan, D. R. (1977) *Dyslexia in the Classroom* (2nd ed.). Columbus, OH: Charles E. Merrill.

Jusczyk, P. W. (1997) *The Discovery of Spoken Language*. Cambridge, MA: MIT Press.

Kaku, M. (1995) *Hyperspace*. New York: Doubleday.

Kaku, M., and Thompson, J. (1995) *Beyond Einstein*. New York: Doubleday.

Kauffman, S. A. (1993) *The Origins of Order*. Oxford: Oxford University Press.

Kayne, R. S. (1984) *Connectedness and Binary Branching*. Dordrecht: Foris.

(1994) *The Antisymmetry of Syntax*. Cambridge, MA: MIT Press.

Kean, M.-L. (1974) The Theory of Markedness in Generative Grammar. Doctoral dissertation, MIT, Cambridge, MA.

Kingsolver, J. G., and Koehl, M. A. R. (1985) Aerodynamics, Thermoregulation, and the Evolution of Insect Wings: Differential Scaling and Evolutionary Change. *Evolution* **39**, 488–504.

Kitahara, H. (1997) *Elementary Operations and Optimal Derivations*. Cambridge, MA: MIT Press.

Kolb, B., and Whishaw, I. Q. (1980) *Fundamentals of Human Neuropsychology*. San Francisco: W. H. Freeman.

Kondo, S., and Asai, R. (1995) A Reaction-Diffusion Wave on the Skin of the Marine Angelfish *Pomacanthus*. *Nature* **376**(6543), 765–68.

Konigsmark, B. W., and Gorlin, R. J. (1976) *Genetic and Metabolic Deafness*. Philadelphia: W. B. Saunders.

Kornberg, A. (1989) *For the Love of Enzymes*. Cambridge, MA: Harvard University Press.

Lamy, M., Launay, C., and Soulé, M. (1952) Dyslexie spécifique chez deux jumeaux identiques. *La Semaine Des Hôpitaux de Paris* **28**(35), 1475–77.

Langer, R. E. (1947). Fourier's Series: the Genesis and Evolution of a Theory. *American Mathematical Monthly*, Supplement, **54**(7), 1–86.

Langone, J. (1983) Deciphering Dyslexia. *Discover*, pp. 34–42.

Larsen, B., Skinhøj, E., and Lassen, N. A. (1978) Variations in Regional Cortical Blood Flow in the Right and Left Hemispheres During Automatic Speech. *Brain* **101** (Part II), 193–209.

Lasnik, H. (1999) On the Locality of Movement: Formalist Syntax Position Paper. In M. Darnell, E. Moravscik, M. Noonan, F. Newmeyer, and K. Wheatly (eds.), *Functionalism and Formalism in Linguistics* vol. I, pp. 33–54. Amsterdam: Benjamins.

Lavenda, B. H. (1985) Brownian Motion. *Scientific American* **252**(2), 70–85.

Lawrence, P. A. (1992) *The Making of a Fly*. Oxford: Blackwell Scientific.

Lawrence, S., Giles, C. L., and Fong, S. (1997) *On the Applicability of Neural Network and Machine Learning Methodologies to Natural Language Processing*, Technical Report UMIACS-TR-95–64 and CS-TR-3479. NEC Research Institute, Princeton, and Institute for Advanced Computer Studies, University of Maryland.

LeMay, M. (1985) Asymmetries of the Brains and Skulls of Nonhuman Primates. In S. D. Glick (ed.), *Cerebral Lateralization in Nonhuman Species*, pp. 233–45. Orlando, FL: Academic Press.

LeMay, M., and Geschwind, N. (1975) Hemispheric Differences in the Brains of Great Apes. *Brain, Behavior and Evolution* **11**, 48–52.

Lenneberg, E. H. (1967) *Biological Foundations of Language*. New York: John Wiley and Sons.

Levitov, L. S. (1991) Phyllotaxis of Flux Lattices in Layered Superconductors. *Physical Review Letters* **66**(2), 224–27.

Lieberman, P. (1984) *The Biology and Evolution of Language*. Cambridge, MA: Harvard University Press.

Lightfoot, D. (1982) *The Language Lottery: Toward a Biology of Grammars*. Cambridge, MA: MIT Press.

(1991) *How to Set Parameters: Arguments from Language Change*. Cambridge, MA: MIT Press.

Lines, M. E. (1994) *On the Shoulders of Giants*. Bristol and Philadelphia: Institute of Physics.

Livingstone, M. S., Rosen, G. D., Drislane, F. W., and Galaburda, A. M. (1991) Physiological and Anatomical Evidence for a Magnocellular Defect in Developmental Dyslexia. *Proceedings of the National Academy of Sciences USA* **88**(18), 7943–47.

Locke, J. L. (1993) *The Child's Path to Spoken Language*. Cambridge, MA: Harvard University Press.

Lorenz, K. Z. (1981) *The Foundations of Ethology*. New York: Simon and Schuster.

Luchsinger, R. (1945) Agrammatismus und syntaktische Redestörungen. *Schweizerische Lehrerzeitung (Pro Infirmis)* **90**(17), 273–75.

(1957) Agrammatismus und Dyslalie bei eineiigen Zwillingen. *Acta Geneticae Medicae et Gemellologiae* **6**(2), 247–54.

Luchsinger, R., and Arnold, G. E. (1965) *Voice–Speech–Language, Clinical Communicology: its Physiology and Pathology*. Belmont, CA: Wadsworth.

Luria, A. R. (1972) *The Man with a Shattered World*. New York: Basic.

Luria, S. E. (1973) *Life, the Unfinished Experiment*. New York: Charles Scribner's Sons.

(1975a) Colicins and the Energetics of Cell Membranes. *Scientific American* **233**(6), 30–37.

(1975b) What Can Biologists Solve? In A. Montagu (ed.), *Race and IQ*, pp. 42–51. New York: Oxford University Press.

Magnus, R. (1906) *Goethe als Naturforscher*. Leipzig: Barth (Trans., H. Norden, Abelard-Schuman Ltd New York, 1949).

Mange, E. J., and Mange, A. P. (1994) *Basic Human Genetics*. Sunderland, MA: Sinauer.

Marshall, J. C. (1980) The New Organology. *The Behavioral and Brain Sciences* **3**(1), 23–25.

(1985) A Fruit By Any Other Name. *Nature* **316**(6027), 388.

Marslen-Wilson, W. D., and Tyler, L. K. (1997) Dissociating Types of Mental Computation. *Nature* **387**(6633), 592–94.

Maxam, A. M. (1980) Nucleotide Sequencing of DNA. Doctoral dissertation, Harvard University.

(1983) Nucleotide Sequence of DNA. In S. M. Weissman (ed.), *Methods of DNA and RNA Sequencing*, pp. 113–67. New York: Praeger.

Maxam, A. M., and Gilbert, W. (1977) A New Method for Sequencing DNA. *Proceedings of the National Academy of Sciences USA* **74**(2), 560–64.

Maynard Smith, J. (1995) Genes, Memes, and Minds: Review of Daniel Dennett's *Darwin's Dangerous Idea*. *New York Review of Books*, November 30, pp. 46–48.

(1996) Language and Evolution (Reply to Noam Chomsky). *New York Review of Books*, February 1, p. 41.

Maynard Smith, J., Burian, R., Kauffman, S., Alberch, P., Campbell, J., Goodwin, B., Lande, R., Raup, D., and Wolpert, L. (1985) Developmental Constraints and Evolution. *The Quarterly Review of Biology* **60**(3), 265–87.

Maynard Smith, J., and Szathmáry, E. (1995a) Language and Life. In M. P. Murphy and L. A. J. O'Neill (eds.), *What is Life? The Next Fifty Years*, pp. 67–77. Cambridge: Cambridge University Press.

(1995b) *The Major Transitions in Evolution.* W. H. Freeman.

McCarthy, R. A., and Warrington, E. K. (1990) *Cognitive Neuropsychology: a Clinical Introduction.* New York: Academic.

McCormack, M. A., Rosen, K. M., Villa-Komaroff, L., and Mower, G. D. (1992) Changes in Immediate Early Gene Expression During Postnatal Development of Cat Cortex and Cerebellum. *Molecular Brain Research* **12**, 215–23.

McGinn, C. (1981) Review of Noam Chomsky, *Rules and Representations. Journal of Philosophy* **78**(5), 288–98.

McKusick, V. A. (1978) *Mendelian Inheritance in Man: Catalogs of Autosomal Dominant, Autosomal Recessive, and X-Linked Phenotypes* (5th ed.). Baltimore: Johns Hopkins University Press.

Medawar, P. B., and Medawar, J. S. (1978) *The Life Science.* London: Paladin Granada.

Mehler, J., and Dupoux, E. (1994) *What Infants Know.* Cambridge, MA: Blackwell.

Meinhardt, H. (1995) Dynamics of Stripe Formation. *Nature* **376**(6543), 722–23.

Mermin, N. D. (1990) *Boojums All the Way Through.* Cambridge: Cambridge University Press.

Miller, G. A. (1991) *The Science of Words.* W. H. Freeman.

Miller, G. A., and Chomsky, N. (1963) Finitary Models of Language Users. In R. D. Luce, R. Bush, and E. Galanter (eds.), *Handbook of Mathematical Psychology,* pp. 419–92. New York: John Wiley.

Monod, J. (1974) *Chance and Necessity: an Essay on the Natural Philosophy of Modern Biology.* New York: Collins/Fontana.

Moorhead, P. S., and Kaplan, M. M. (eds.) (1967) *Mathematical Challenges to the Neo-Darwinian Interpretation of Evolution.* Philadelphia: Wistar Institute Press.

Morgan, T. H. (1935) The Relation of Genetics to Physiology and Medicine. *Scientific Monthly* **41**, 5–18.

Motz, L., and Weaver, J. H. (1989) *The Story of Physics.* New York: Avon.

Mukerjee, M. (1996) Explaining Everything. *Scientific American* **274**(1), 88–94.

Muller, H. J. (1977 [1946]) The Production of Mutations. In *Nobel Lectures in Molecular Biology 1933–1975,* pp. 25–42. New York: Elsevier.

Newman, S. A. (1992) Generic Physical Mechanisms of Morphogenesis and Pattern Formation as Determinants in the Evolution of Multicellular Organization. In J. Mittenthal and A. Baskin (eds.), *Principles of Organization in Organisms,* pp. 241–67. Reading, MA: Addison–Wesley.

Newman, S. A., Frisch, H. L., and Percus, J. K. (1988) On the Stationary State Analysis of Reaction-Diffusion Mechanisms for Biological Pattern Formation. *Journal of Theoretical Biology* **134**, 183–97.

Newport, E. L. (1990) Maturational Constraints on Language Learning. *Cognitive Science* **14**(1), 11–28.

(1991) Contrasting Conceptions of the Critical Period for Language. In S. Carey and R. Gelman (eds.), *The Epigenesis of Mind: Essays on Biology and Cognition,* pp. 111–30. Hillsdale, NJ: Lawrence Erlbaum.

O'Grady, W. (1997) *Syntactic Development.* Chicago: University of Chicago Press.

Oberlé, I., Rousseau, F., Heitz, D., Kretz, C., Devys, D., Hanauer, A., Boué, J.,

Bertheas, M. F., and Mandel, J. L. (1991) Instability of a 550–Base Pair DNA Segment and Abnormal Methylation in Fragile X Syndrome. *Science* **252**(5010), 1097–102.

Ojemann, G. A. (1983) Brain Organization for Language from the Perspective of Electrical Stimulation Mapping. *Behavioral and Brain Sciences* **6**(2), 189–230.

Oke, A., Keller, R., Mefford, I., and Adams, R. N. (1978) Lateralization of Norepinephrine in Human Thalamus. *Science* **200**(4348), 1411–13.

Orton, S. T. (1937) *Reading, Writing and Speech Problems in Children.* New York: W. W. Norton.

Oster, G. F., Shubin, N., Murray, J. D., and Alberch, P. (1988) Evolution and Morphogenetic Rules: the Shape of the Vertebrate Limb in Ontogeny and Phylogeny. *Evolution* **42**(5), 862–84.

Otero, C. P. (1988) *Noam Chomsky: Language and Politics.* Montreal: Black Rose.
  (1990) The Emergence of *Homo Loquens* and the Laws of Physics (Reply to Pinker and Bloom). *Behavioral and Brain Sciences* **13**(4), 747–50.

Ott, J. (1991) *Analysis of Human Genetic Linkage.* Baltimore: Johns Hopkins University Press.

Pais, A. (1986) *Inward Bound: of Matter and Forces in the Physical World.* Oxford: Clarendon.

Pembrey, M. (1992) Genetics and Language Disorder. In P. Fletcher and D. Hall (eds.), *Specific Speech and Language Disorders in Children: Correlates, Characteristics, and Outcomes,* pp. 51–62. San Diego: Singular.

Pennington, B. F., Gilger, J. W., Pauls, D., Smith, S. A., Smith, S. D., and DeFries, J. C. (1991) Evidence for Major Gene Transmission of Developmental Dyslexia. *Journal of the American Medical Association* **266**(11), 1527–34.

Peterson, I. (1988) *The Mathematical Tourist.* New York: W. H. Freeman.

Piattelli-Palmarini, M. (1974) *Program Activities in 1974.* Paris: Centre Royaumont Pour une Science de l'Homme.
  (1980) (ed.) *Language and Learning: the Debate Between Jean Piaget and Noam Chomsky.* Cambridge, MA: Harvard University Press.
  (1989) Evolution, Selection and Cognition: from "Learning" to Parameter Setting in Biology and in the Study of Language. *Cognition* **31**(1), 1–44.
  (1994) Ever Since Language and Learning: Afterthoughts on the Piaget–Chomsky Debate. *Cognition* **50**, 315–46.

Pinker, S. (1994a) *The Language Instinct.* New York: William Morrow.
  (1994b) On Language (interview). *Journal of Cognitive Neuroscience* **6**(1), 92–97.
  (1995) Language is a Human Instinct. In J. Brockman (ed.), *The Third Culture,* pp. 223–38. New York: Simon and Schuster.
  (1997a) Evolutionary Perspectives. In M. S. Gazzaniga (ed.), *Conversations in the Cognitive Neurosciences,* pp. 111–29. Cambridge, MA: MIT Press.
  (1997b) *How the Mind Works.* New York: W.W. Norton.

Pinker, S., and Bloom, P. (1990) Natural Language and Natural Selection. *Behavioral and Brain Sciences* **13**(4), 707–84.

Planck, M. (1993) The Unity of the Physical Universe. In *A Survey of Physical Theory,* pp. 1–26. New York: Dover.

Plante, E. (1991) MRI Findings in the Parents and Siblings of Specifically Language-Impaired Boys. *Brain and Language* **41**(1), 67–80.

Plotkin, H. (1998) *Evolution in Mind*. Cambridge, MA: Harvard University Press.

Poizner, H., Klima, E. S., and Bellugi, U. (1987) *What the Hands Reveal about the Brain*. Cambridge, MA: MIT Press.

Pollack, R. (1994) *Signs of Life*. Boston: Houghton Mifflin.

Prigogine, I., and Nicolis, G. (1967) Symmetry-Breaking Instabilities in Dissipative Systems. *J. Chem. Phys.* **46**, 3542–50.

Pullum, G. K. (1989) Formal Linguistics Meets the Boojum. *Natural Language and Linguistic Theory* **7**(1), 137–43.

(1991) *The Great Eskimo Vocabulary Hoax*. Chicago: University of Chicago Press.

(1997) Language that Dare not Speak its Name. *Nature* **386**(6623), 321–22.

Rabin, M., Wen, X. L., Hepburn, M., Lubs, H. A., Feldman, E., and Duara, R. (1993) Suggestive Linkage of Developmental Dyslexia to Chromosome 1p34–p36. *Lancet* **342**(8864), 178.

Radford, A. (1990) *Syntactic Theory and the Acquisition of English Syntax: the Nature of Early Child Grammars of English*. Oxford: Blackwell.

Raff, R. A. (1996) *The Shape of Life*. Chicago: University of Chicago Press.

Riemsdijk, H. C. van (1978) *A Case Study in Syntactic Markedness: the Binding Nature of Prepositional Phrases*. Lisse: Peter de Ridder.

Rizzi, L. (1982) *Issues in Italian Syntax*. Dordrecht: Foris.

Roberts, I. (1996) *Comparative Syntax*. Oxford: Oxford University Press.

Roberts, L. (1989) Are Neural Nets Like the Human Brain. *Science* **243**(4890), 481–82.

Roeper, T., and Williams, E. (1987) *Parameter Setting*. Dordrecht: D. Reidel.

Rosen, K. M., McCormack, M. A., Villa-Komaroff, L., and Mower, G. D. (1992) Brief Visual Experience Induces Immediate Early Gene Expression in the Cat Visual Cortex. *Proceedings of the National Academy of Sciences USA* **89**(12), 5437–41.

Ross, E. D. (1981) The Aprosodias: Functional–Anatomic Organization of the Affective Components of Language in the Right Hemisphere. *Archives of Neurology* **38**(9), 561–69.

(1993) Nonverbal Aspects of Language. *Neurologic Clinics* **11**(1), 9–23.

Ross, E. D., and Mesulam, M.-M. (1979) Dominant Language Functions of the Right Hemisphere? Prosody and Emotional Gesturing. *Archives of Neurology* **36**(3), 144–48.

Rothi, L. J., McFarling, D., and Heilman, K. M. (1982) Conduction Aphasia, Syntactic Alexia, and the Anatomy of Syntactic Comprehension. *Archives of Neurology* **39**(5), 272–75.

Roush, W. (1996) Fly Sex Drive Traced to *fru* Gene. *Science* **274**(5294), 1836.

Ruelle, D. (1991) *Chance and Chaos*. Princeton, NJ: Princeton University Press.

Saffran, J. R., Aslin, R. N., and Newport, E. L. (1996) Statistical Learning by 8–Month-Old Infants. *Science* **274**(5294), 1926–28.

Sanger, F., Nicklen, S., and Coulson, A. R. (1977) DNA Sequencing with Chain-Terminating Inhibitors. *Proceedings of the National Academy of Sciences USA* **74**, 5463–67.

Savage-Rumbaugh, E. S., and Lewin, R. (1994) *Kanzi: the Ape at the Brink of the Human Mind*. New York: John Wiley and Sons.

Seidenberg, M. S. (1997) Language Acquisition and Use: Learning and Applying Probabilistic Constraints. *Science* 275(5306), 1599–603.

Shaywitz, S. E., Shaywitz, B. A., Pugh, K. R., Fulbright, R. K., Constable, R. T., Mencl, W. E., Shankweiler, D. P., Liberman, A. M., Skudlarski, P., Fletcher, J. M., Katz, L., Marchione, K. E., Lacadie, C., Gatenby, C., and Gore, J. C. (1998) Functional disruption in the organization of the brain for reading in dyslexia. *Proceedings of the National Academy of Sciences USA* 95(5), 2636–41.

Short, N. (1994) Rolling Back the Frontiers in the Brain. *Nature* 368(6472), 583.

Simpson, E. B. (1979) *Reversals: a Personal Account of Victory over Dyslexia*. Boston: Houghton Mifflin.

Sklar, R. (1968) Chomsky's Revolution in Linguistics. *The Nation*, September 9, pp. 213–17.

Smith, N., and Tsimpli, I.-M. (1995) *The Mind of a Savant: Language Learning and Modularity*. Oxford: Blackwell.

Smith, S. D., Kimberling, W. J., Pennington, B. F., and Lubs, H. A. (1983) Specific Reading Disability: Identification of an Inherited Form through Linkage Analysis. *Science* 219(4590), 1345–47.

Sorbi, S., Amaducci, L., Albanese, A., and Gainotti, G. (1980) Biochemical Differences Between the Left and Right Hemispheres? Preliminary Observations on Choline Acetyltransferase (CAT) Activity. *Bollettino Società Italiana Biologia Sperimentale* 56(21), 2266–70.

Sorensen, R. (1991) Thought Experiments. *American Scientist*, May–June, pp. 250–63.

Stachowiak, F.-J., Huber, W., Kerschensteiner, M., Poeck, K., and Weniger, D. (1977) Die globale Aphasie: Klinisches Bild und Überlegungen zur neurolinguistischen Struktur. *Journal of Neurology* 214(2), 75–87.

Stent, G. S. (1981) Strength and Weakness of the Genetic Approach to the Development of the Nervous System. In W. M. Cowan (ed.), *Studies in Developmental Neurobiology: Essays in Honor of Viktor Hamburger*, pp. 288–321. New York: Oxford University Press.

Stewart, I. (1994) Broken Symmetry in the Genetic Code. *New Scientist* 141(1915), 16.

(1995a) Daisy, Daisy, Give Me Your Answer, Do. *Scientific American* 272(1), 96–99.

(1995b) Mathematical Recreations, Feedback. *Scientific American* 273(4), 182–83.

(1995c) *Nature's Numbers*. New York: Basic.

(1998) *Life's Other Secret*. New York: John Wiley and Sons.

Stewart, I., and Golubitsky, M. (1993) *Fearful Symmetry*. London: Penguin.

Stromswold, K. (1996) The Genetic Basis of Language Acquisition. In A. Stringfellow, D. Cahana-Amitay, E. Hughes, and A. Zukowski (eds.), *Proceedings of the 20th Annual Boston University Conference on Language Development*, vol. II, pp. 736–47. Somerville, MA: Cascadilla.

Suggs, S. V., Wallace, R. B., Hirose, T., Kawashima, E. H., and Itakura, K. (1981) Use of Synthetic Oligonucleotides as Hybridization Probes: Isolation of

Cloned cDNA Sequences For Human ß₂-microglobulin. *Proceedings of the National Academy of Sciences USA* **78**(11), 6613–17.

Sutherland, S. (1993) Evolution Between the Ears. Review of Michael Gazzaniga, *Nature's Mind New York Times,* 7 March.

Szathmáry, E., and Maynard Smith, J. (1995) The Major Evolutionary Transitions. *Nature* **374**(6519), 227–32.

Tasset, D. M., Hartz, J. A., and Kao, F.-T. (1988) Isolation and Analysis of DNA Markers Specific to Human Chromosome 15. *American Journal of Human Genetics* **42**, 854–66.

Taylor, J. E., and Kahn, J. W. (1986) Catalog of Saddle Shaped Surfaces in Crystals. *Acta Metallurgica* **34**(1), 1–12.

Teuber, H.-L. (1967) Lacunae and Research Approaches to Them, 1. In C. H. Millikan and F. L. Darley (eds.), *Brain Mechanisms Underlying Speech and Language,* pp. 204–16. New York: Grune and Stratton.

Thompson, D. A. W. (1992a) *On Growth and Form.* New York: Dover.
   (1992b) *On Growth and Form, an Abridged Edition,* edited by J. T. Bonner (Canto ed.). New York: Cambridge University Press.

Thompson, E. (1994) Deaf Victim of Old South is Freed After 68 Years. *Boston Globe,* February 6, p. 2.

Tomarev, S. I., Callaerts, P., Kos, L., Zinovieva, R., Halder, G., Gehring, W., and Piatigorsky, J. (1997) Squid Pax-6 and Eye Development. *Proceedings of the National Academy of Sciences USA* **94**(6), 2421–26.

Tucker, D. M., Watson, R. T., and Heilman, K. M. (1977) Discrimination and Evocation of Affectively Intoned Speech in Patients with Right Parietal Disease. *Neurology* **27**(10), 947–50.

Tully, T. (1994) Gene Disruption of Learning and Memory: a Structure-Function Conundrum. *Seminars in the Neurosciences* **6**(1), 59–66.

Turing, A. M. (1952) The Chemical Basis of Morphogenesis, *Philosophical Transactions of the Royal Society of London B,* vol. 237, pp. 37–72.

Van der Lely, H. K. J. (1997) Narrative Discourse in Grammatical Specific Language Impaired Children: a Modular Language Deficit. *Journal of Child Language* **24**, 1–36.

Van der Lely, H. K. J., and Stollwerck, L. (1996) A grammatical specific language impairment in children: an Autosomal Dominant Inheritance? *Brain and Language* **52**, 484–504.

Van Essen, D. C. (1997) A Tension-Based Theory of Morphogenesis and Compact Wiring in the Central Nervous System. *Nature* **385**(6614), 313–18.

Vargha-Khadem, F., and Passingham, R. E. (1990) Speech and Language Defects, Scientific Correspondence. *Nature* **346**(6281), 226.

Vargha-Khadem, F., Watkins, K., Alcock, K., Fletcher, P., and Passingham, R. (1995) Praxic and Nonverbal Cognitive Deficits in a Large Family with a Genetically Transmitted Speech and Language Disorder. *Proceedings of the National Academy of Sciences USA* **92**(3), 930–33.

Wada, J. A. (1969) Interhemispheric Sharing and Shift of Cerebral Speech Function. *Excerpta Medica,* Int. Congress Series, **193**, 296–97.

Wada, J. A., Clarke, R., and Hamm, A. (1975) Cerebral Hemispheric Asymmetry in Humans: Cortical Speech Zones in 100 Adult and 100 Infant Brains. *Archives of Neurology* **32**(4), 239–46.

Waldrop, M. M. (1992) *Complexity*. New York: Simon and Schuster.

Walker, E. (1978) (ed.) *Explorations in the Biology of Language*. Montgomery, VT: Bradford.

Watson, J. D. (1969) *The Double Helix*. New York: New American Library.

Watson, J. D., Gilman, M., Witkowski, J., and Zoller, M. (1992) *Recombinant DNA* (2nd ed.). New York: W. H. Freeman.

Watson, J. D., Hopkins, N. H., Roberts, J. W., Steitz, J. A., and Weiner, A. M. (1987) *Molecular Biology of the Gene*. Menlo Park, CA: Benjamin/Cummings.

Watt, W. C. (1979) Against Evolution (an Addendum to Sampson and Jenkins). *Linguistics and Philosophy* 3, 121–37.

Webster, G., and Goodwin, B. (1996) *Form and Transformation: Generative and Relational Principles in Biology*. Cambridge: Cambridge University Press.

Weiler, I. J., Irwin, S. A., Klintsova, A. Y., Spencer, C. M., Brazelton, A. D., Miyashiro, K., Comery, T. A., Patel, B., Eberwine, J., and Greenough, W. T. (1997) Fragile X Mental Retardation Protein is Translated Near Synapses in Response to Neurotransmitter Activation. *Proceedings of the National Academy of Sciences USA* 94(10), 5395–400.

Weinberg, S. (1974) Unified Theories of Elementary-Particle Interaction. *Scientific American* 231(1), 50–59.

(1992) *Dreams of a Final Theory*. New York: Vintage.

Weingarten, S. (1979) Encounter: Species of Intelligence. *The Sciences*, November, pp. 6–11, 23.

Wernicke, C. (1874) *Der aphasische Symptomencomplex. Eine psychologische Studie auf anatomischer Basis*. Breslau: Cohn and Weigert.

West, G. B., Brown, J. H., and Enquist, B. J. (1997) A General Model for the Origin of Allometric Scaling Laws in Biology. *Science* 276(5309), 122–26.

Wexler, K., and Manzini, M. R. (1987) Parameters and Learnability in Binding Theory. In T. Roeper and E. Williams (eds.), *Parameter Setting*, pp. 41–76. Dordrecht: D. Reidel.

Wigner, E. P. (1979) The Unreasonable Effectiveness of Mathematics in the Natural Sciences. In W. J. Moore and M. Scriven (eds.), *Symmetries and Reflections*, pp. 211–37. Woodbridge, CT: Ox Bow Press.

(1987) Physics and the Explanation of Life. In J. H. Weaver (ed.), *The World of Physics*, pp. 679–88. New York: Simon and Schuster.

Wilkins, W. K., and Wakefield, J. (1995) Brain Evolution and Neurolinguistic Preconditions. *Behavioral and Brain Sciences* 18(1), 161–226.

Witelson, S. F., and Pallie, W. (1973) Left Hemisphere Specialization for Language in the Newborn: Neuroanatomical Evidence of Asymmetry. *Brain* 96, 641–46.

Witten, E. (1996) Reflections on the Fate of Spacetime. *Physics Today* 49(4), 24–30.

Wright, B. A., Lombardino, L. J., King, W. M., Puranik, C. S., Leonard, C. M., and Merzenich, M. M. (1997) Deficits in Auditory Temporal and Spectral Resolution in Language-impaired Children. *Nature* 387(6629), 176–78.

Yamada, J. E. (1990) *Laura, a Case for the Modularity of Language*. Cambridge, MA: MIT Press.

Yeni-Komshian, G. H., and Benson, D. A. (1976) Anatomical Study of Cerebral

Asymmetry in the Temporal Lobe of Humans, Chimpanzees, and Rhesus Monkeys. *Science* **192**, 387–89.

Yu, S., Pritchard, M., Kremer, E., Lynch, M., Nancarrow, J., Baker, E., Holman, K., Mulley, J. C., Warren, S. T., Schlessinger, D., Sutherland, G. R., and Richards, R. I. (1991) Fragile X Genotype Characterized by an Unstable Region of DNA. *Science* **252**(5010), 1179–81.

Zaidel, E. (1980) Clues from Hemispheric Specialization. In U. Bellugi and M. Studdert-Kennedy (eds.), *Signed and Spoken Language: Biological Constraints on Linguistic Form*, pp. 291–340. Deerfield Beach, FL: Verlag Chemie.

Zee, A. (1986) *Fearful Symmetry*. New York: MacMillan.

Zweig, G. (1980) (ed.) *Proceedings of the Fourth International Conference on Baryon Resonances*. Toronto: University of Toronto Press.

Index

Abney, 12, 36, 71, 107
acquisition of language, 2, 3, 5, 6, 7, 8, 13, 26, 27, 28, 35, 48, 57, 70, 75, 76, 77, 80, 81, 82, 83, 86, 91, 92, 95, 96, 98, 99, 100, 101, 106, 133, 144, 163, 168, 181, 187, 188, 195, 196, 199, 214, 216, 218, 221, 228
adaptation, 85, 86, 169, 194, 196, 198, 223, 224, 227
adaptationists, 196
agrammatism, 91, 106, 110, 114, 115, 116, 123, 124, 137
Ahouse, 227
AI, 11
Alberts, 187
Allen, 100
Amaducci, 139
American Sign Language, 67
Amundson, 195, 196, 197, 198
Anderson, 102, 103, 104, 105
animal communication, 8, 10, 111, 211, 215
anomia, 59, 61
ape communication, 208, 212, 213, 215
aphasia, 3, 10, 26, 27, 31, 59, 62, 63, 75, 91, 106, 134, 136, 137, 212, 217, 223, 229
aprosodia, 62, 63, 228
Arabidopsis thaliana, 150
architectonic, 134, 135, 136, 138
argument from incredulity, 224, 225
Aristotle, 49, 51
Arnold, 115
articulatory-perceptual component, 69, 230
Asai, 155, 156, 207
Aslin, 90, 91, 92, 93, 101
asymmetry, 24, 104, 133, 134, 135, 138, 139, 140, 141, 142, 143, 152, 153, 164, 165, 192, 202, 213
Atkins, 172
autism, 126, 137, 138
autocatalysis, 155

auto-immune diseases, 137
auto-immunity, 138

Baldwinian selection, 216
Ball, 155
Bar-Hillel, 1
Bates, 85, 89, 90, 91, 92, 98, 99, 208, 224, 225, 226
Bauman, 137
Bauplan, 76, 78, 225, 226
Beadle, G., 4
Beadle, M., 4
beauty, 165, 166, 167
Behan, 137
Beheim-Schwarzbach, 140, 143
Bell, 23, 34
Bellugi, 30, 67, 106, 133
Belousov-Zhabotinsky (B-Z) reaction, 155
Benson, 139, 140, 141, 142
Bentley, 110, 111
Berger, 158
Berndt, 61
Berwick, 12, 36, 71, 75, 81, 107, 223
Bickerton, 81, 170
biolinguistics, 1, 2, 3, 4, 8, 9, 10, 11, 12, 13, 15, 19, 20, 25, 26, 27, 28, 29, 32, 38, 48, 49, 51, 54, 56, 68, 86, 87, 90, 92, 94, 95, 99, 100, 101, 102, 105, 124, 144, 168, 177, 179, 180, 181, 184, 199, 201, 202, 204, 207, 211, 212, 213, 218, 224, 228, 233
bioprogram hypothesis, 81
bird song, 5, 88, 93, 141, 211
Bisgaard, 129
Bishop, 80, 105, 106, 107
Bitoun, 63, 64, 127, 128
Black English, 209, 210
Blakeslee, 143
B-language, 213
Bloom, 54, 81, 86, 147, 170, 178, 179, 180, 181, 182, 183, 184, 188, 189, 191, 192, 193, 194, 199, 200, 204, 205